BOY'S OWN HANDBOOK

BY

CECIL H. BULLIVANT

AUTHOR OF "HOME FUN"

" now!"

MAGNA BOOKS

ISBN 1 85422 705 X

This edition published 1994 by
Magna Books, Magna Road
Leicester LE18 4ZH
Produced by
The Promotional Reprint Company

Printed in Finland

CONTENTS

PART I

THE WORKSHOP AT HOME

PART II

INDOOR HOBBIES

PART III

COLLECTING

PART IV

OUTDOOR HOBBIES

CONTENTS

PART V

THE KEEPING OF PETS

PART VI

PREFATORY NOTE

THE wide field of Hobbies now open to every boy is so vast that it would be manifestly impossible to exhaust the subject in the limited space at my disposal. My intention in writing the following pages has been to give a boy information which will enable him to embark at once upon any hobby that may appeal to his individual taste, and with this in view I have tried to make this book a guide to some of the less-known paths of hobby lore.

Too much stress cannot be laid upon the important part that a boy's hobby plays in the formation of his character. A man or a boy without a hobby is like a vessel without a keel—he lacks just that which will keep his mind well balanced. The more interests one has, the greater is the field of pleasure in life that stretches before one. Kept within proper limits a hobby is a sure preventive against narrow-mindedness: not only that, it forms a delightful companion for spare time—a companion as close and dear as any human friend.

If the perusal of my book serves to introduce but one of my readers to a hobby that will become a life-long solace and amusement, my endeavours will have proved successful—my labours will not have been in vain.

CECIL HENRY BULLIVANT.

EVERY BOY'S BOOK OF HOBBIES

PART I.—THE WORKSHOP AT HOME

CHAPTER I

CARPENTRY AND JOINERY

A PLAIN TALK FROM BENCH TO READER

THERE is little exaggeration in saying that a knowledge of Carpentry is indispensable to every boy. Putting aside for a moment the fact that the desire to "make something" is inherent in human nature, there is scarcely a hobby under the sun which does not demand a certain amount of practical skill and constructive ability. No matter what his hobby, the ardent devotee likes to do everything for himself, and without a knowledge of the rudiments of Carpentry, how can he hope to accomplish this? There is, moreover, a very practical side to the question. The great majority of schoolboys have had to realise the fact that pocket-money is not inexhaustible, and that the purchase of cabinets, bookshelves and so forth makes sad havoc with the weekly or monthly allowance. Now all this can be remedied with a little practical knowledge of sawing and planing. A few pence will purchase the wood, a certain amount of care will ensure its being properly worked, and with an outlay of perhaps two or three shillings, the hobbyist will find himself in possession of a cabinet or similar article for which he would possibly have had to pay perhaps as many pounds.

A great deal of misunderstanding has arisen concerning the terms carpentry and joinery. So general is the confusion between the two words that what is generally termed carpentry is in reality nothing but joinery. It may therefore be explained at once that carpentry, technically known as "Carcase Work," is the art of fixing together large pieces of timber for making roofs, sheds, and similar parts of general building work.

Joinery, as its name implies, refers to the making of joints, and fitting smaller pieces of wood together in the construction of boxes, tables, drawers, shelves, and the interior fittings of houses, &c.

3

The Outfit

An old proverb says that a bad workman complains of his tools. But there is something more than the proper manipulation of tools required to make a good workman. Care and precision are essential qualities in a carpenter, for without them the best tools in the world are useless.

As the cost of the outfit is no inconsiderable item in the equipment of a carpenter's shop, it must be clearly understood from the beginning that a certain amount of expense will be involved in connection with the hobby.

The prices hereafter quoted are for new tools, but practically any implement can be purchased at a very low price from a second-hand shop, where such things as chisels and gouges in all sizes and shapes may often be procured for a few pence.

Saws

(1) Carpenter's hand-saw, with teeth varying in number from 5 to 6½ to the inch. These saws are generally made from about 20 in. to 28 in. in length, and have wooden handles to suit the conformity of the hand; a medium size, say 26 in., is recommended. Price from 4s. 6d.

(2) Tenon saw, with a 14-in. blade and a brass or iron back to render the blade stiff. This saw is used for cross-cutting and making neat joints. Price from 3s. 6d.

(3) Dovetail saw. This is a miniature tenon saw with a blade 7 in. or 8 in. long and an open handle. Price from 2s. 6d.

(4) Pad or keyhole saw. This tool is used for cutting keyholes and making all small turned cuts in woodwork. The handle, which is hollow, has a brass ferule with two screws which hold the taper blade at any length required. Price from 10d.

(5) Bow saw or turning web. This is used for cutting curves, round outlines, &c. Price from 4s.

Planes

(1) Jack plane, used for knocking off rough surfaces and preparing coarse work for the trying plane. Price from 4s.

(2) Trying plane, for use after the jack plane. It smooths the roughly-worked surface. Price from 5s. 6d.

(3) Smoothing plane. This is employed for finishing and giving the final touches to all prepared work. Price from 2s. 6d.

CHISELS

Chisels can be purchased in sizes ranging from $\frac{1}{8}$ in. to $1\frac{1}{2}$ in. The larger sizes should be bevelled if possible, as such work as dove-tailing is greatly facilitated thereby. Prices from 7d.

FIG. 1.—How to hold a Chisel.

The sash mortice chisel is a strong, handy tool, useful for working the lighter portions of morticing.

An example of how to hold a chisel is shown in Fig. 1.

GOUGES

Gouges, made in similar sizes and at similar prices to chisels, are ground, or, as carpenters say, cannelled, inside and outside.

Scribing gouges are sold in different curves, Fig. 2, and are used

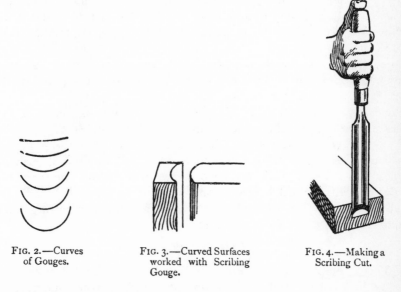

FIG. 2.—Curves of Gouges.

FIG. 3.—Curved Surfaces worked with Scribing Gouge.

FIG. 4.—Making a Scribing Cut.

for preparing one curved surface to butt against another, Figs. 3 and 4.

Firmer gouges are made stiffer than the above, and those with an outside cannel are used for scalloping out depressions beneath the surface of any work.

DRAW-KNIFE

This instrument is used, as shown in Fig. 5, for roughing out curves and rounded surfaces, and also for making chamfers.   Price from 1s. 6d.

SPOKESHAVE

The spokeshave is employed for finishing the work after the draw-knife has been used.   Price from 1s. 6d.

METAL RATCHET BRACE

This implement, which is used for boring holes of any size, is

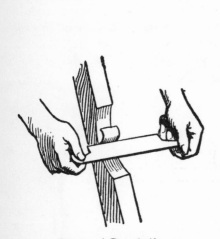

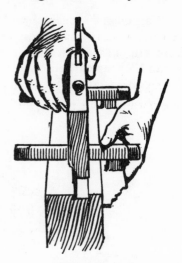

FIG. 5.—A Draw-knife.   FIG. 6.—Using the Plough Plane.

especially handy for working in awkward positions.   Price from 4s. 6d. Sets of bits for use with the brace will cost a few shillings.

PLOUGH PLANE

This is employed, as shown in Fig. 6, for cutting grooves or, as this process is technically called, rebating.   Price from 12s. 6d.

GIMLETS AND BRADAWLS

These tools are used for boring small holes, and can be purchased for a few pence.

SCREWDRIVERS

For ordinary use cabinet-makers' screwdrivers are the best to obtain, and are sold in large and small sizes. Price 9d.

HAMMER

A hammer of the London or Exeter pattern can be obtained from any ironmonger. Price from 1s.

MALLET

A good beech-wood mallet is the most serviceable. Price from 1s. 4d

SET-SQUARES AND BEVELS

Carpenters' squares, with good ebony or rosewood stocks, and bevels similarly made, can be obtained from any toolmaker. Prices from 1s.

GAUGES

These are sold in two patterns: The simple gauge, for marking a line parallel to a planed surface, price from 6d.; the morticing gauge,

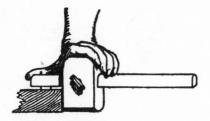

FIG. 7.—Morticing Gauge.

for marking off tenons and mortices as shown in Fig. 7, price from 1s. 9d.

SUNDRIES

A two-foot rule, spirit-level, pair of spring-nut American combination compasses, pair of carpenters' pincers, and a glue-pot, all of which can be obtained for about 1s. each, will be necessary to complete the outfit of the workshop.

Mitre blocks and shooting blocks can also be bought at 1s. and 2s. 6d. respectively.

SOME HINTS ON SAWING

When sawing, the utmost care must be exercised to avoid the use of any wilful force in driving the saw. The action should be even and regular, with an easy, steady motion. Any violence or undue exertion will either cause the saw to snap, or will buckle it up and render it useless for further work.

When using the tenon saw mark the wood with a sharp knife, instead of with a pencil. This is known as making a "striking line," and, as it produces a narrower and more exact line than a pencil, a neater cut is ensured.

As a general rule, it may be remarked that in all sawn joints, such

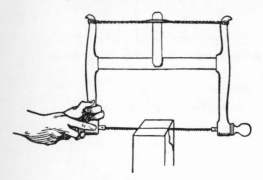

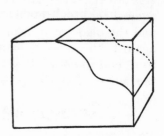

FIG. 8.—Using the Bow Saw.   FIG. 8A.—Marking for Bow Saw.

as the housing joint, the saw is worked inside the striking line on the one piece of wood, and outside it on the other.

For using the bow saw, Fig. 8, both sides of the wood should be marked with the desired curve, as seen in Fig. 8A, as this prevents any uneven sawing on either side.

PLANES AND PLANING

There is a certain knack required in holding a plane which has much to do with success in turning out good work. Fig. 9 illustrates

FIG. 9.—Correct position in which to hold Jack Plane.   FIG. 10.—Holding the Smoothing Plane.

the correct method of holding either the jack or trying plane. As the smoothing plane is somewhat differently shaped, a glance at Fig. 10 will demonstrate how it should be held.

To ascertain whether the surface of a small piece of wood has been planed evenly, the wood should be held level with the eye, the iron of the set-square placed across it and passed from end to end. If any light appears between the metal and the wood, it proves an uneven surface.

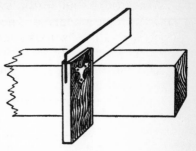

In Fig. 11 is seen the method of ascertaining if an adjacent side is at right angles to a level surface. The stock of the set-square must be placed against the side already proved level, and the blade or iron pressed closely against the freshly-worked surface

FIG. 11.—Using the Set-square.

from end to end. If it fits tightly against both surfaces of the wood, the angle of the edge is certainly true.

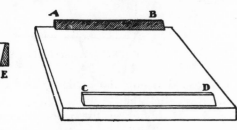

FIG. 12.—The "Trueing Sticks."

To discover if a large surface, such as the top of a table, is evenly planed, two pieces of wood known as "trueing sticks" are placed as shown in Fig. 12, and the eye is run along to notice if the top lines AB and CD exactly coincide. These "trueing sticks" can be made by sawing through the length of a squared-up piece of wood, E, Fig. 12, shown in section.

When planes are purchased new from the tool-maker, the iron, or blade, is ground back at an acute angle to allow of several whettings on

FIG. 13.—Sharpening a Plane Iron.

FIG. 14.—Sharpening a Plane Iron.

the oilstone. The method of sharpening a plane iron is shown in Figs. 13 and 14. The blade must be held rigid and drawn backwards and forwards with an easy motion, great care being taken to prevent any " wobbling."

To remove a plane iron, tap the fore part of the plane smartly with the mallet ; the wedge that keeps the blade in position can then be extracted, and the iron taken out.

Practice alone will teach the exact amount that the blade should project beneath the under surface of the plane, but it must not be allowed to protrude too far, as this will ruin the edge of the iron when any attempt is made to plane.

SHARPENING CHISELS AND GOUGES

Chisels are sharpened with the bevelled side against the oilstone. When sufficient edge has been obtained, the tool should be turned and passed over the stone once on the flat side, this serving to remove the

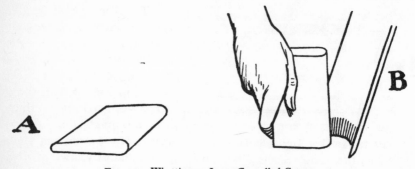

FIG. 15.—Whetting an Inner Cannelled Gouge.

very minute turned edge that will have been produced by rubbing one side of the metal.

Outer cannelled gouges are sharpened on the oilstone in the same manner as chisels. Inner cannelled gouges are whetted on a slip stone A, as shown at B, Fig. 15.

THE OILSTONE

The best oilstone to purchase is Lily White Washita, costing, un-cased, about 2s. 6d. Care should be taken in its selection, and it must be noticed especially that there are no flaws in the surface, which should be of a silvery-grey colour.

The whetting capacity may be tested by running the thumb-nail from end to end. If it be a good stone it will give the nail a per-ceptible edge.

Sweet oil or neat's-foot oil is the best to use with the oilstone, and a few drops only should be applied to the surface.

MATERIAL

Yellow deal should always be employed for outside work, as, the turpentine not having been extracted, this wood is less subject to the effects of weather.

White deal, which contains no turpentine, is suitable for all inside work. The prices of both these woods are very moderate, and spare pieces for small work can always be obtained very cheaply from any carpenter if he is told for what purpose they are required.

Quartering, *i.e.* squared lengths of wood, is sold at prices varying from 4s. per 100 feet.

Match-boarding can be bought at 8s. per square of 100 feet superficial.

NAILS

Carpenters usually employ cut clasp nails, costing about 2d. per lb. These should be driven into the wood with the grain. French nails, which are round, are also largely used, and may be purchased at the same price.

GLUE

Glue costs sixpence a pound, and is sold in cakes. Several pieces should be broken off with the pincers or hammer and left to soak in cold water for twelve hours. They may then be placed in the well of the glue-pot, the outer receptacle of which must be three parts filled with water, and the whole allowed to simmer slowly over the fire.

Glue should be used quickly, and applied liberally, but not with undue profusion.

" KNOTTING "

Before painting wood it is essential that the knots be covered with "knotting." If this is neglected, when the paint has dried, the knots in the material will show up aggressively through the colour.

JOINTS

THE GLUE JOINT

When two lengths of wood are to be glued side by side, as, for example, in making the surface of a table, the following method should be employed :—

With a jack plane smooth the edges to be glued, finish with the trying plane, and test them with the set-square. When this has been done lay the two pieces in the position they will eventually occupy, and hold them against the light to ascertain if any unevenness is

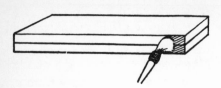

FIG. 16.—The Glue Joint.

FIG. 17.—Clamp for Glue Joint.

apparent. If there should be any, it must be rectified before proceeding further.

Place the boards one upon the other, as in Fig. 16, and sweep the glue-brush over both edges at once.

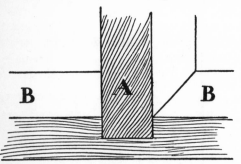

FIG. 18.—The Housing Joint.

Now place the glued edges together, rub the two boards several times against one another, up and down, finishing in position. Lay them on a level surface, and temporarily fasten them together with small clamps, as in Fig. 17.

The glue should be allowed twenty-four hours to harden, and when dry the surface may be cleaned with the plane, and any unevenness removed with sand-paper.

THE HOUSING JOINT

The housing joint depicted in Fig. 18 is made in the following manner:—For the sake of example, let it be supposed that the two pieces of wood A and BB measure $\frac{3}{4}$ in. square, and that A is to be fitted into B.

Two parallel lines, CD and EF, Fig. 19, must be marked

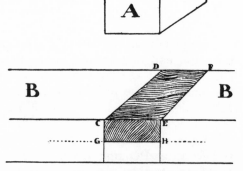

FIG. 19.—How to make the Housing Joint.

with a striking knife across BB at a distance of $\frac{3}{4}$ in. from each other. Set the gauge to $\frac{1}{4}$ in. and mark a line at GH on both sides of the wood, and also mark the perpendicular lines CG and EH with the set-square.

Placing the tenon saw against the inside of the line CD, cut down to G and repeat the process at EF, sawing down to H. Holding a ⅜ in. chisel as in Fig. 1, cut away the portion between the saw-cuts, shaded in Fig. 19.

The end of A can now be inserted in this joint, and secured with a nail from the other side of BB.

THE MORTICE JOINT

This joint is shown complete in Fig. 20. In this case the tenon C, cut in the piece of wood B, exactly fits the mortice or hole in A.

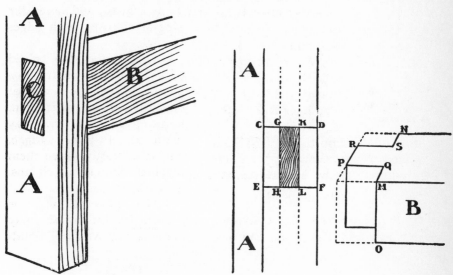

FIG. 20.—The Mortice Joint.   FIG. 21.—Marking the Mortice Joint.

Supposing A and B to be 1 in. quartering, at the distance of 1 in. from the end of B, mark the straight line MN, Fig. 21, and carry it round all four sides of the wood as partly seen at MO. Then, setting the mortice gauge to ⅓ in., mark the lines PQ and RS from the end to MN. Continue these lines down the end of the wood B, and again on the opposite side of the quartering.

Make two parallel cuts with the tenon saw along and through the wood at PQ and RS as far as the line MN. Then, turning the wood on its side, saw down the line MO as far as Q, and similarly from N to S, which will detach the pieces on each side, shown by dotted lines in the figure, and leave the tenon QPRS to fit into the mortice in A.

To cut this mortice, mark off CD and EF at 1 in. from each other in the other piece of quartering A, and continue the lines all round the wood with the morticing gauge still set at ⅓ in. ; then mark the lines GH and KL, making similar lines on the opposite sides.

Working each side alternately, chisel out the shaded portion with a mortice chisel as shown in Fig. 22, until the mortice is complete and ready to receive the tenon previously cut in B.

MITRE JOINTS

The joint A shown in Fig. 23 is very simply made, each piece of wood being sawn in turn upon the mitre block. The ends are then placed in position and glued or nailed.

When an angle other than a right angle is required, as seen in B, Fig. 23, a full-sized working drawing should be made showing the angle GFH. The lines KE and CL are then drawn parallel to GF

FIG. 22.—Making a Mortice.

and FH respectively, and a line FD marked from the point of intersection to F. The stock of the bevelling iron must then be placed against GF and the blade put into position against FD. The required angle is thus obtained, and when marked out upon

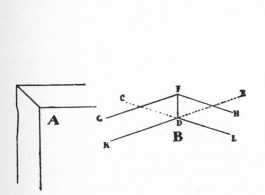

FIG. 23.—Mitre Joints.

FIG. 24.—Planing against Shooting-board.

the wood, and sawn, the pieces can be placed against the shooting-board as seen in Fig. 24, and smoothed off with a trying plane.

THE DOVETAIL JOINT

The object of dovetailing, shown in Fig. 25, is to make a lock joint that shall prevent two pieces of wood, A and B, straining away from each other.

Supposing that A and B are each ½ in. thickness, start work on the piece B by marking a line AC, Fig. 26, with a marking gauge, the point of which is sufficiently sharp to cut the line in the wood.

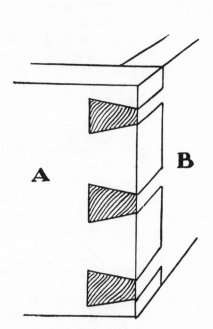

FIG. 25.—The Dovetail Joint.

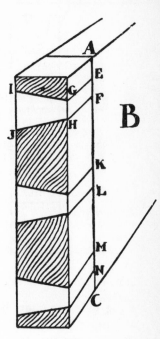

FIG. 26.—Pins for Dovetail.

The line AC must be ½ in. from the end of B, and must be carried round on all four sides of the wood.

At a distance of ¼ in. from A mark the point E on the line AC, and from E measure ⅛ in. to F. Mark K ¾ in. from F, and the points L, M, N, at alternate distances of ⅛ in. and ¾ in., as seen in Fig. 26. By means of the set-square carry lines similar to EG and FH from all these points to the edge of the wood.

Fig. 27 shows the same piece of wood viewed from the other side. On the line AC mark E ³⁄₁₆ in. from A, F ¼ in. from E, G ⅝ in. from F, and so with the other points as shown in the diagram. Carry lines from these points to the edge as before, and join them across the end of the wood to those already marked on the other side and illustrated in Fig. 26.

Cut down through the thickness of the wood with the dovetail saw at IG and JH, Fig. 26, as far as the line AC, repeating this with all the other points. When this has been done remove the portions shown in shading, Fig. 26, with a chisel, thus leaving three dovetail pins.

Upon the other piece of wood the reverse process is carried

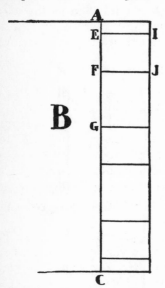

FIG. 27.—Markings for the Pins.

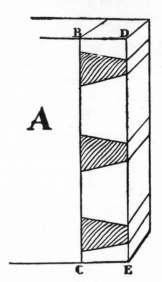

FIG. 28.—Sockets for Dovetail.

out on the side, as may be seen from Fig. 28. The gauge is run down at ½ in. as before, but on the line BC points are marked to correspond with those made in Fig. 27, whilst against DE they are made to correspond with those shown on AC, Fig. 26. The shaded parts in Fig. 28 are sawn and chiselled out, and when completed make three sockets to hold the pins already described.

The two pieces of wood can then be fitted together and glued.

FIG. 29.—The Templet.

THE TEMPLET

By using the templet shown in Fig. 29 this laborious method of marking out the wood is simplified. This templet, which can be purchased from any carpenter for a few pence, is made of some hard wood and has a flange on either side. For marking off the dovetails the templet is placed on its side, the flange against the edge of the wood, as shown in Fig. 30, and the lines struck in against the side.

All complicated work is adapted from one or other of the joints above described. The greatest care and precision should be exercised in

FIG. 30.—Using the Templet.

making them neat and true, as the whole success of joinery depends upon the accurate construction of the joint employed.

CHAMFERS AND BEVELS

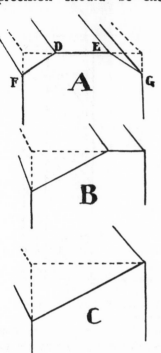

FIG. 31.—Chamfers and Bevel.

The equal chamfer shown at A, Fig. 31, is made by dividing the end of the wood into three equal parts by lines at D and E. On the side of the wood are marked off F and G according to the angle required. The portions included in the dotted lines on either side are then roughed off with the draw-knife and finished with the trying plane.

The unequal chamfer seen at B, Fig. 31, is made by dividing the end of the wood into two unequal portions, and then working in the same manner as above described.

To make the bevel C, Fig. 31, draw a line on the side of the wood as in the case of the chamfer, and then pare down until this line is reached and the required angle has been obtained.

HOW TO MAKE A CARPENTER'S BENCH

All joinery and carpenter's work is done upon a proper bench, which can be made according to the following instructions. A glance at Fig. 32 will show the appearance of the bench when completed.

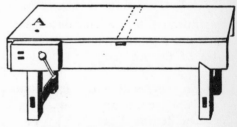

FIG. 32.—The Carpenter's Bench.

Cut three 9 in. boards of 1¼ in. stuff, each 7 ft. in length, and, after planing and smoothing, glue them together with a glue joint, and leave to dry for twenty-four hours.

Now set to work upon the four legs, which must be cut of 3 in. by 3 in. quartering in pieces 2 ft. 6 in. long. Square off both ends of each leg.

For the rails cut four lengths of 3 in. by 2 in. wood, each length

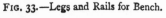

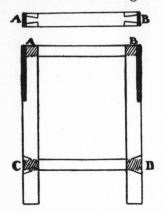

FIG. 33.—Legs and Rails for Bench.

FIG. 34.—Legs prepared for Side-board.

measuring 2 ft. Make a dovetail pin at both ends of two of these pieces to fit into sockets in the legs at the top as seen at AB, Fig. 33.

The two lower rails must be morticed and wedged into the legs as seen at CD, Fig. 33.

The two flaps shown at the sides of the bench, Fig. 32, are cut of

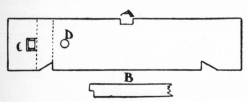

FIG. 35.—Flaps for Front Side of Bench.

1 in. stuff, 7 ft. long and 9 in. wide, and are let into the legs in the following manner: Cut portions from the outside of each leg as shown in black, Fig. 34, sufficiently deep to contain the flap seen in Fig. 35, and to allow it to come flush with the outside of each leg.

Before fastening them, however, in each flap cut a notch A in the centre of the top edge, to contain the centre beam B seen in the diagram and in the dotted lines in Fig. 32, which is made of 2½ in. quartering, and will extend from one side to the other beneath the top.

A bench chop and screw, Fig. 36, must now be purchased from any carpenter for about 3s. 6d. Two holes, one square, C, and the other round, D, Fig. 35, should be cut in the left-hand front of one of the flaps to receive the rod and screw of the chop, to come each side of the leg. At the same time a wooden channel or box must be fixed to the inside of the adjacent leg to contain this rod and allow it to slide backwards and forwards with ease.

Fasten the screw nut of the chop to the inside of the round hole D, insert the chop screw, and the whole contrivance will be complete.

FIG. 36.—Bench Chop and Screw.

The cross beam can now be fastened in the slots already made to receive it, and placed in position as indicated by the dotted lines. The top of the bench may then be screwed in its place.

At one end of the bench, A, Fig. 32, a stop will have to be made for planing against. A large screw proves the best for this purpose, as it can be adjusted to whatever height is required.

THE BENCH HOOK

The bench hook shown in Fig. 37 is cut of 3 in. by 3 in. quartering in an 18 in. length, and is sawn as shown in the diagram, leaving a projection at either end.

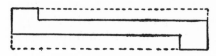

FIG. 37.—The Bench Hook.

This is used for holding wood in position whilst sawing, one end gripping the bench, the other serving as a stop for the timber, Fig. 38. Before the stop is ready for

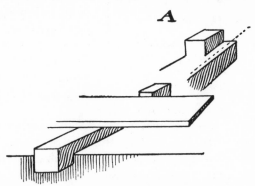

A

FIG. 38.—The Bench Hook in Use.

use, however, the end should be sawn as shown at A. This serves to prevent the saw cutting the surface of the bench.

To Conceal a Nail

Raise a strip of wood with the chisel as shown in Fig. 38A, and,

FIG. 38A.—Concealing a Nail.

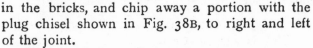

FIG. 38B.—The Plug Chisel.

driving the nail in the portion thus uncovered, glue down the strip over the nail-head, and sand-paper the wood.

Plugging a Wall with a Wooden Wedge

With the point of a bradawl find the spot where there is a joint in the bricks, and chip away a portion with the plug chisel shown in Fig. 38B, to right and left of the joint.

Then take a piece of wood and pare it away as shown in Fig. 38C. Drive this plug into the wall, and then saw off the projecting end flush with the wall.

FIG. 38C.—A Wooden Plug.

Driving Wooden Stakes into the Earth

Wood that is to be driven into the earth should be tarred, and then charred in a fire, to preserve it from rotting. Slovenly workmen use pitch only, but it is apt to rot away. Charring is the only method to be relied upon.

A Home-made Bracket

The simple bracket shown in Fig. 39, measuring 12 in. by 6 in.,

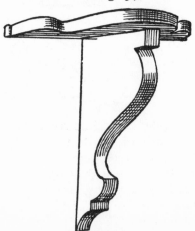

FIG. 39.—A Simple Bracket.

can be made from two ends of $\frac{3}{4}$ in. material. The outline must be marked on the wood, Fig. 40, and cut round with the bow-saw.

The support can be fitted into the top, either by a simple housing joint, or by means of a dovetailed groove made in the following manner :—

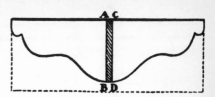

FIG. 40.—Outline of Bracket.

Saw two lines AB and CD, Fig. 40, at a dovetail slant, Fig. 41, C, and chisel out the socket thus made. Then cut a similar dovetail end right along the edge of the support, Fig. 41, A and B, thus making it possible to slide the latter into the shelf, where it may be glued or nailed.

How to Make a Dovetailed Drawer

This is simply the dovetail joint put to practical use, as may be seen in Fig. 42.

Having ascertained the width, depth, and length of the drawer to be made, the sides are socketed to receive the pins in the front and

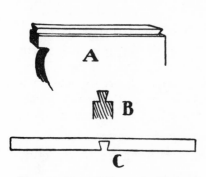

FIG. 41.—Dovetail Groove for Bracket.   FIG. 42.—End Elevation of Dovetailed Drawer.

back of the drawer, and grooved, as seen in dotted line, to receive the bevel-edged bottom piece, at a depth of $\frac{1}{2}$ in.

Having fastened the front, one side, and the back in place, slide the bottom into position and then fit in the remaining side and fasten with glue.

How to Make a Recess Cupboard

In describing the cupboard illustrated in Fig. 43, it is assumed that the back and sides will be formed by the walls of the recess. The following instructions are based upon the recess measuring 3 ft. 6 in., the cupboard being of an equal height.

With the exception of the wood for the door panels, the material used throughout is $1\frac{1}{4}$ in. deal.

The two stiles A and B are cut 3 ft. 6 in. long and 3 in. wide.   The top C and the bottom D, which are of the same length, but 2 in. and 1½ in. wide respectively, are morticed into the stiles.

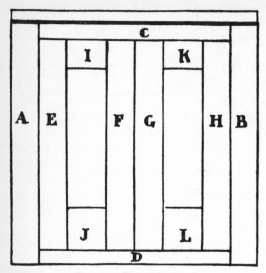

FIG. 43.—Recess Cupboard.

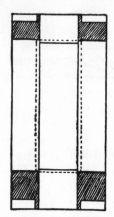

FIG. 44.—Mortice of the Rails in Cupboard.

The stiles of the doors, E, F, G, H, must now be cut 3 ft. 2½ in. long and 3 in. wide.   The top rails I and K will be each 1 ft. 6 in. in length

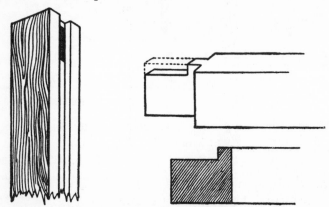

FIG. 45.—Tenon for Rail Mortice Joint.   FIG. 46.—Morticing Stile.

and 3 in. wide.   The bottom rails J and L, whilst of the same length, will be 3¾ in. wide.

Mortice the rails of both doors into the stiles, as seen in shading, Fig. 44.   The tenons, made as in Fig. 45, are fitted into the morticed stiles as seen in Fig. 46; but before fastening them, rebate a groove along the inner edges to receive the panels, which are made of ½ in. planed wood, and bevelled to allow of their being fitted into the grooves, as shown at A and B, Fig. 47. They should be slid into place before the morticed joints are finally secured.

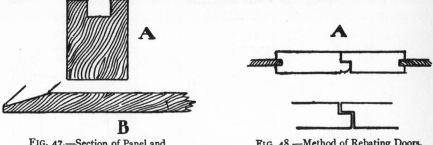

FIG. 47.—Section of Panel and grooved Stile.

FIG. 48.—Method of Rebating Doors.

The framework is fastened into the recess against four strips of wood nailed to the wall, whilst the top of the cupboard is screwed to the top strips and thus held in place.

A simple brass or iron bolt upon one of the doors, and sliding into a socket inside the lower rail D, Fig. 43, will serve to keep it in position, and, when a lock is adjusted to the other door, the whole cupboard can be securely closed. Fig. 48 shows the method of

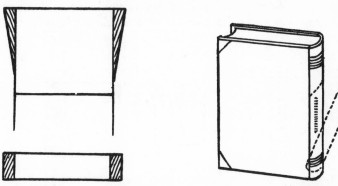

FIG. 49.—Wedging a Mortice Joint.

FIG. 50.—The Secret Money-box.

rebating the doors to make them shut flush, A depicting the front side with an ornamental bead. To strengthen a morticed joint, they should be wedged as indicated by the shaded portions of the diagrams, Fig. 49.

HOW TO MAKE A SECRET MONEY-BOX

The secret money-box shown in Fig. 50 can, with a little care, be made from a cigar-box or piece of thin mahogany.

Cut two pieces measuring 7½ in. by 4¼ in. from the wood of a cigar-box, and glue them to two deal blocks, A and B, Fig. 51, the lower block, B, being slightly wider than A. These blocks should come within ¼ in. of the edges, so that a strip of wood, ⅛ in. thick, can be mitred and glued between the cedar boards, as shown by the thin line at C. When glued, the front slip can be slightly curved, as seen

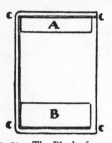

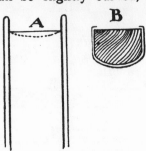

FIG. 51.—The Blocks fastened
to the Covers.

FIG. 52.—Curving the Edges
with Sand-paper.

at A, Fig. 52, to resemble the leaves of a book, by means of a sand-paper block. This sand-paper block, illustrated at B, Fig. 52, consists simply of a piece of sand-paper bent round a wooden block curved to the required outline.

The back of the book has now to be constructed, and very nice

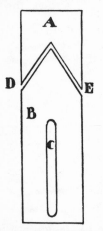

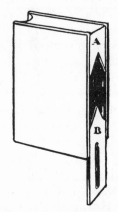

FIG. 53.—Panel with Slot at
the Back of the Box.

FIG. 54.—The Sliding Panel.

work will be required if the money-box is to prove a success.

A piece of wood, Fig. 53, must be cut, and a large slot C made in the position indicated in the figure. This strip of wood is then divided with a dovetail saw into two pieces, A and B, by the inverted V-shaped cut DE, and the top piece fitted and glued to the top of the back as seen in Fig. 54.

The edges of the lower part of this strip of wood B should now be bevelled off like the lid of an ordinary pencil-box, whilst the projecting

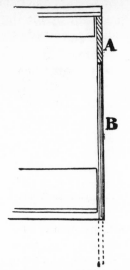

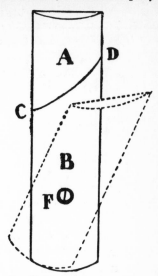

FIG. 55.—Section of Sliding Panels.   FIG. 56.—Back of the Secret Money-box.

sides of the covers can be bevelled inwards correspondingly, so that B can slide up and down as seen in Fig. 54, shown in section, Fig. 55.

Now cut a piece of wood similar to that already described in Fig. 53, and round the surface as shown in Fig. 56. Saw this piece diagonally across at CD in such a way that the upper end D corresponds with the point E in Fig. 53. Glue the top piece A, Fig. 56, over the upper end of the box so that it comes flush with the side.

All that now remains to be done is to fasten the remaining portion B, Fig. 56. This is effected by boring a hole at F so that a screw, passing through this hole and the slot, can be fastened in the block of wood in the box, whilst B will revolve upon it fairly easily, as seen in Fig. 56.

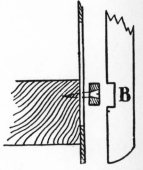

FIG. 57.—Method of fixing Screw.

The screw head can be concealed with putty, the book painted to resemble a real volume, and a title—The Secret of Wealth, or the like —painted on the back.

This screw can also be concealed by cutting a piece out of B, Fig. 56, in the manner shown in Fig. 57, and passing the screw through a piece of wood of the same size, then gluing it back into B as seen in the same illustration.

HOW TO MAKE A BICYCLE SHED

A lean-to shed as seen in Fig. 58, costing 18s. 6d., can be easily constructed for a bicycle, the measurements being roughly 4 ft. 9 in. high,

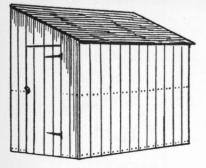

6 ft. 6 in. long, 3 ft. 6 in. wide, and 4 ft. at the drop end. The instructions here given are, of course, equally applicable to any similar erection.

The framework, the pieces of which must be entirely completed before the shed is erected, will be made of 2 in. by 2 in. quartering, of which approximately 140 ft. will be required. A square of match-boarding, ⅝ in. size, will be necessary for the outside.

The joints throughout are housed,

FIG. 58.—A lean-to Bicycle Shed.

each joint being secured by two nails.

A study of the various diagrams will show the dimensions of the lengths of wood required for the construction of the framework.

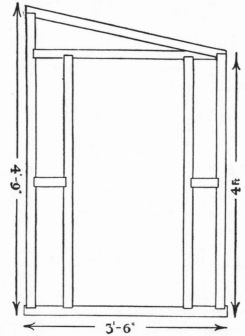

FIG. 59.—Framework of Doorway of the Shed.

The side containing the door is depicted in Fig. 59, from which the method of fastening the framework can be observed.

The other side, of more simple construction, is shown in Fig. 60. Fig. 61 depicts the elevation of the framework for the front.

FIG. 60.—Framework of End of the Shed.

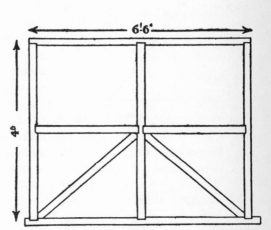

FIG. 61.—Framework of Front of the Shed.

The framework of the front and two sides having been completed, these can now be put together against the wall. The front is "butted" or fitted in between the two sides and screwed to them, through the thickness of the wood as shown in Fig. 62, where A and B represent the two pieces of framework.

The wall must now be plugged at the top and bottom to enable the sides to be screwed thereto through the framework.

Having secured the front and two sides, the rafters of the roof may now be cut as shown in Fig. 63. They are fastened by nailing

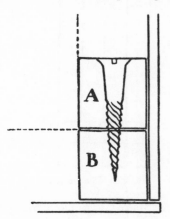

FIG. 62.—Method of Screwing the Front.

FIG. 63.—Rafter for the Roof.

them to a beam plugged in the wall at the required height from the top ends of the rafters, whilst the lower ends are nailed to the top rail of the front.

The frame must be carefully squared after the manner shown in Fig. 64, the straight rod being placed from corner to corner, so that

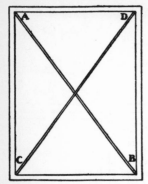

it can be proved that the length from A to B is equal to that from C to D, whilst the other corners are treated similarly.

The next thing to do is to nail the matchboarding along the sides and front, naturally leaving the space for the doorway clear. The beading must be left outside, and the boarding should overlap the beams by 1 in. at the top and $\frac{3}{4}$ in. at the bottom, the latter being embedded in earth or cement.

The overlapping ends at the top, A, must now be levelled with a saw to the height of

FIG. 64.—Squaring the Framework.

the top rail, as seen at C, Fig. 65.

The match-board of the roof can now be nailed on with the beading inside, and trimmed down at D, to overlap the front rail by 2 in., to serve as eaves.   B, Fig. 65.

Nothing now remains but to make the door, which is very simply constructed after the manner shown in Fig. 66.   Two pieces of deal

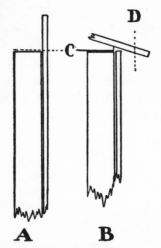

FIG. 65.—Trimming the Match-board.

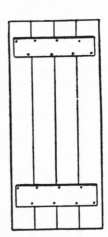

FIG. 66.—The Door.

are laid flat, and match-boarding nailed over them, two nails being used for each board, the lower nail being nearest the side that will eventually be hinged.   This serves to lessen the strain on the nails, and renders the door more durable.

The door can now be fastened in place, with a couple of cross garnets (or large hinges) and fitted with a hasp and padlock.

To preserve the roof against the ravages of the weather, it may be covered with felt or tar.

How to Make a Plate-rack

The familiar plate-rack of modern homes seen in Fig. 67 is an article of utility which may be easily constructed.

The materials required are a number of curtain-rods, which

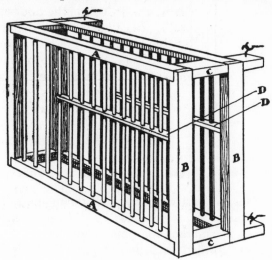

Fig. 67.—The Plate-rack.

are divided out to 28 sticks, each 22 in. long, and also some lengths of planed hard wood—elm, oak, or teak—1½ in. by ¾ in. section from which are cut—

4 lengths A	. . . . .	31½ in. long.
4 ,, B	. . . . .	22 in. long.
4 ,, C	. . . . .	10 in. long.
2 ,, D	. . . . .	24 in. long.

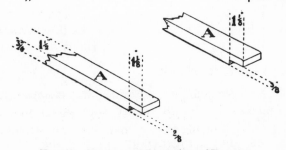

Fig. 68.—Mortices and Dimensions of Top Rails.

A, Fig. 68; B, Fig. 69; and C, Fig. 70, are morticed and screwed together as shown in Fig. 71—the chisel and tenon saw being used carefully throughout so as not to exceed the depths required— and then each of the pieces A, reckoning the lengths as that lying between the pieces C, is divided into 15 equal parts. At each of

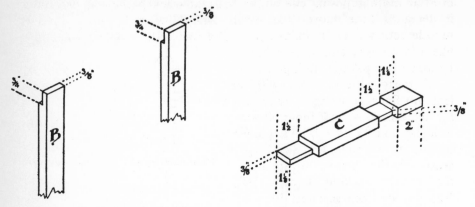

FIG. 69.—The Uprights showing Mortice.   FIG. 70.—Morticed Crosspiece.

the 14 division lines, holes are drilled right through just large enough to receive the curtain-rods, which may be slid into place temporarily, whilst the D pieces are marked for similar holes.

When these are drilled and the D pieces strung on the rods, they butt right against the B

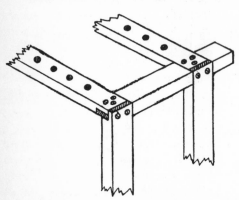

FIG. 71.—Crosspiece and Uprights joined.

pieces at one end, whilst at the other—where they do not reach—three spaces between the rods are left undivided in order to accommodate large dishes. Small brads, driven through the A and D pieces into the rods, hold the latter in position, and the D pieces are held so that the upper divisions are shorter than the lower, in order to suit small and large plates respectively.

The rack may be suspended by screwing hooks into the projecting ends of the C pieces, which will engage with similar hooks or staples driven into the wall.

Articles of this kind are generally left unvarnished as the water drains off rapidly, and therefore affords the wood no opportunity to rot.

How to Make a Folding Dining-table

Another article of furniture may now be considered. Although of a far more imposing effect than the plate-rack previously described, it demands little more than plain straightforward work, whereby muscle action may be cultivated. The materials may cost something like a sovereign, and the object to be made is a folding dining-table.

A fairly empty room with at least no floor covering is necessary for its erection, and the first step is to lay four 3 ft. by 1 in. planed boards, 11 in. wide, and the longer seasoned the better, together on the floor. Packing boards BB, Fig. 72, are then screwed down at

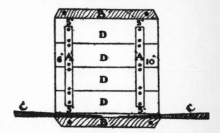

Fig. 72.—Making the Table-top.

each end, and the edges of the planed boards, DDDD, having been glued, wedges, CC, are driven in so as to close the planks up tightly together.

Whilst drying, battens of ¾ in. hard wood, 10 in. shorter than the table's width, are screwed across as at AA, Fig. 72, and when matters are thus made secure another set of boards is similarly treated. The two are now placed end to end on the floor with battened sides uppermost and bars of 2 in. by ⅝ in. deal, one foot long, are screwed to I, Fig. 73, in the positions EEE, so that half their lengths project. On the latter, 6-in. slips of wood, FFFF, 1¼ in. wide by ⅝ in. thick, are screwed down at either side on each of the pieces, E, and over all are then fixed rectangles of thin wood, 6 in. by 4½ in. by screws which pass right through the F pieces to the table boards, so that a slot is formed for the 6 in. of each E bar which projects over the side No. 2. Black-lead lubrication is used to make them slide easily, and a ¼ in. hole, G, is drilled right through each outside slot and bar, so that short iron rods, H, can be introduced to prevent the halves parting, Figs. 73 and 74.

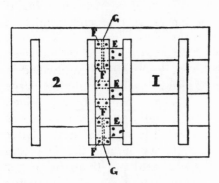

Fig. 73.—The Two Sides placed together.

Four table legs, turned from 4 in. by 4 in. timber, must be

next procured at a wood merchant's, and the square ends cut downwards on two adjacent sides to a depth of 5 in., Fig. 75.

Designating the sides as A, B, C, D, two of the legs are cut downwards along the D sides for 3 in. and bored to a depth of 3 in. on the

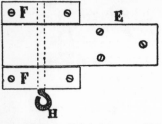

FIG. 74.—Method of joining the two Halves.

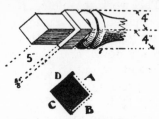

FIG. 75.—Top of the Leg.

A sides with a $\frac{5}{8}$ in. hole, which is continued, $\frac{3}{8}$ in. diameter, to a total
depth of 3 in., whilst the other two legs are similarly cut and drilled on
the C and B sides, Fig. 76. One of the former pair is then joined

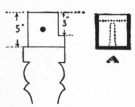

FIG. 76.—Elevation of the Top of the Leg.

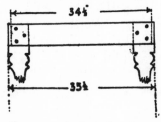

FIG. 77.—The End of the Table.

with one of the latter by screwing the ends of a board of $\frac{1}{2}$ in. planed
hardwood, $35\frac{1}{2}$ in. long and 5 in. deep, to the B and A sides respectively, and a similar board, $34\frac{1}{4}$ in. long and 3 in. deep, to the D and C

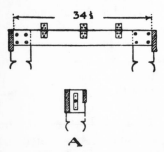

FIG. 78.—The Hinges placed on the Legs.

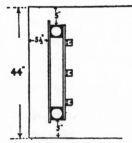

FIG. 79.—Position of Legs on the Table.

sides, see Figs. 77 and 78. The pairs of legs are fixed to the under
surface of the table by means of three hinges apiece, Fig. 78, screwed to
the 3-in. hardwood braces, facing and being distant $5\frac{1}{2}$ in. from the end

edges of the table, whilst their ends are equidistant from the side edges. The necessary measurements and arrangements are depicted in Fig. 79.

FINISHING THE TABLE

This work completed, the table's halves are brought together so that the projecting bars engage with their slots, and the two iron rods, Figs. 73 and 74, are pushed through in order to secure matters. The table is upside down, and, the legs being held upright, lengths of 5 in. wide hardwood are cut so as to fit up against the A and B faces of the legs, whilst pressing against the projecting ends of the 5-in. braces, thus tending to force the legs apart. They are therefore maintained in a correct position to support the table's weight. The only essential work remaining is to bore holes in the long 5-in. stretchers' corresponding sockets, so as to preclude the possibility of the stretchers being displaced.

A finishing touch is given to the table's appearance by covering it with red baize, which may be glued on and tacked under tape round the edges. However, this embellishment is best postponed until the table is thoroughly seasoned, because otherwise the boards, in warping and straining against the battens beneath, may curl at their corners and need smoothing with a jack plane in order to level the surface.

CHAPTER II

THE "BOY'S OWN DEN"

AND HOW TO MAKE IT

FIG. 1 depicts the appearance a room should present when finished according to the instructions laid down in this chapter. Apart from the pictures, mirror, coal-scuttle, table, and chairs, with which any

FIG. 1.—The Boy's Own Den.

parents who take a pride in their boy's own room should be willing to supply him—the total cost of making the cosy "Den" should not exceed thirty-five shillings.

A plan of an ordinary room is shown in Fig. 2, the walls of which, for the sake of reference, are numbered from 1 to 4.

Wall No. 1, of course, does not appear in the finished picture, but will be accounted for later. Against wall No. 2—in which is the door —will be seen a very useful and ingenious combination unit system bookcase, bed or lounge, and clothes cupboard; in the picture it appears merely as a curtained-off, outstanding cupboard, surmounted by a few rows of tastefully arranged books on shelves.

Beneath the window, wall No. 3, is an article of furniture that should be dear to the heart of every home-loving boy—a combination

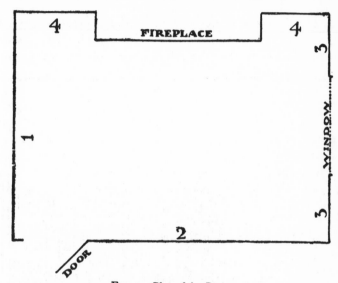

FIG. 2.—Plan of the Room.

desk, writing-table, drawing-board, and "hold-all," which should appeal alike to the business boy, the artist, and the student.

The only other necessary adjunct to guarantee the tidiness of the "Boy's Own Den" is the extremely useful and easily constructed cupboard to the left of the fireplace.

To finish a preliminary survey of the apartment, notice should be taken of Fig. 3, which provides a representation of a rack stand, suitable for holding such impedimenta as cricket bats, walking-canes, hockey sticks, golf clubs, and so forth.

Thus it will be seen that each article provided ensures comfort, utility, and tidiness combined, and these, together with the general atmosphere of cosiness engendered by the big armchair, warm-coloured table-cloth, and tastefully decorated walls, should make the home-made "den" a place to be proud of.

Before embarking on a detailed description of the methods for constructing the various articles that have been mentioned, it must be

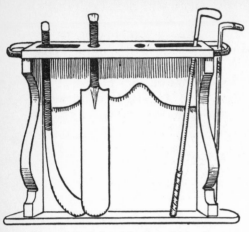

FIG. 3.—Rack Stand for Bats, Sticks, &c.

assumed that the boy who is anxious to provide himself with a practical apartment where he may reign supreme, is willing to expend upon it a share both of his spare time and spare cash. The extent of the latter will be regulated by his natural aptitude for carpentry and general utility jobs ; and although the finished product, with care and forethought, should rank with the best plain articles purchasable, the total outlay made by the amateur carpenter upon them should not exceed, if the instructions given are carefully carried out, the modest estimate given.

This chapter has been purposely designed to follow the one on Carpentry, in which full information is given relating to the more technical parts of the work, such as dovetailing, grooving, gouging, planing, sawing, &c.

A start may very well be made on

THE COMBINATION WRITING-TABLE, READING-DESK, DRAWING-BOARD, AND "HOLD-ALL,"

the finished appearance of which is shown in Figs. 4 and 5 respectively. The former depicts the completed drawing - board and "hold-all," which, with the addition of a covering slab, gives the writing-table, Fig. 5.

The following will be found convenient dimensions upon which to commence operations for constructing the

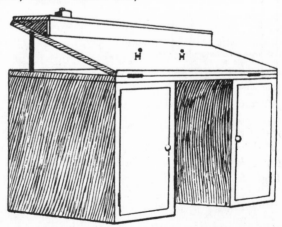

FIG. 4.—Complete Drawing-board and Hold-all.

body of the desk and the drawing-board top: length 3¾ ft., height 28 in., width 22 in.

First dovetail and glue together, out of ¾-in. deal, two box-like cup-boards 14 in. wide, 26 in. high, and 22 in. deep, leaving, in each, one side for the addition of a door, which may be easily fixed by means of 1½-in. brass or iron butts and closed with an ordinary catch turning on a screw handle into a grooved slot.

FIG. 5.—The Writing-table.

As secrecy forms no inconsequential item in the programme of every boy, the very natural desire to have things under lock and key may be met by the substitution of an ordinary iron or brass lock in place of the simple catch.

To reap full benefit from the cupboards, each should be provided with two or three shelves, regulated, as to distances apart, by grooves similar to those at BB, Fig. 7. These cupboards can be utilised for the storage of foot-balls, dumb-bells, cricket balls, pads, bails, and other paraphernalia.

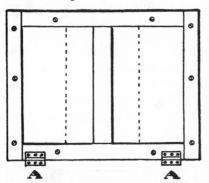

FIG. 6.—Framework of Drawing-board.

The next essential is a frame made of 1¼-in. deal, measuring 3¾ ft. by 22 in. It should be dovetailed and glued with a centre stay for support as shown in Fig. 6. The purpose of this frame, which should be screwed firmly down on to the two cupboards, placed 17 in. apart for knee-room, is to form a base for a drawing-board hinged on two 2-in. butts, AA, Figs. 6 and 7.

The drawing-board next claims attention.

Drawing in its many branches plays so prominent a part both in school and life work of so many boys and young men, that proper materials for its execution are an absolute necessity, and doubtless many hundreds of readers will appreciate the benefits to be derived from following out the instructions given below.

Glue together sufficient well-seasoned ¾-in. pine boarding to form a slab of the same size as the frame.

Fig. 8 shows the front, and Fig. 8A the back of the board when

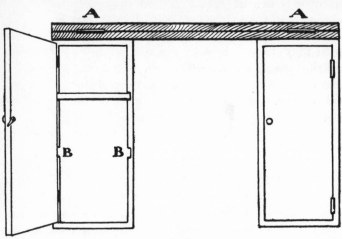

FIG. 7.—Front View of Drawing-board and Hold-all.

completed, the stays, BB, in the latter, being necessary to prevent the warping or other changes produced by varying temperatures. A little more than ordinary care in fixing these stays (best made from oak ¾ in. by 4 in.) should be exercised, as much dampness, or extremes of heat

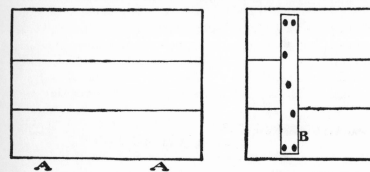

FIG. 8.—Front of the Board.   FIG. 8A.—The Back of the Board.

or cold will cause the board to lose its perfect flatness. To this end, the screw holes must be gouged out at the top and also made a little larger than the diameter of the smooth body of the screw. Such a precaution allows the screw some little freedom in case of contraction or expansion of the wood. Fig. 9 makes this quite clear.

Before hinging the board to the frame, screw along one side a length of flat beading, to form a ledge for holding pencils and to prevent loose materials slipping to the floor. To maintain a comfortable angle for working purposes, fix an iron prop, having a hole drilled at one end, by means of a piece of metal cut to the shape shown in Figs. 10, 11, and 11A. This prop, swinging freely at F, drops its other end into a slot in the frame at C, Fig. 10. Should any difficulties be experienced in getting the piece of metal cut to the

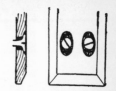

FIG. 9.—Screw Holes to allow Expansion.

desired shape, simply attach the prop loosely at one end with a strong screw, and when it is desired to shut down the drawing-board to form the base of the writing-table, run a screw eye through the other hole into the side of the frame, Figs. 10 and 11A.

The larger groove E, Fig. 10, is to take the projection of the metal plate when the drawing-board lies flat, as in Fig. 12.

The movable ledge depicted in Fig. 4, and in section, Fig. 13, is for holding pens, ink, and miscellaneous drawing materials, and can be quite easily constructed on the lines indicated by the diagrams. Particular care must be taken to fix the hinges as shown. The dotted lines indicate the position which the ledge occupies when not in use.

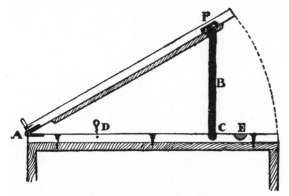

FIG. 10.—Section of Drawing-board in Position.

A further useful addition is a book-rest, of strong iron wire bent

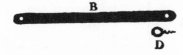

FIG. 11.—Metal Support.   FIG. 11A.—Metal Prop.

to the shape shown in Fig. 14, and attached by means of two holes bored in the drawing-board at HH, Fig. 4.

The making from ½-in. deal boarding of a table-top of the required size completes the combination, save for the addition, for ornamental purposes, of a flat oak beading 2½ in. wide and grooved to fit close to the deal base, as illustrated in Fig. 15. The long brass screws II,

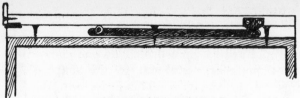

FIG. 12.—Section of Drawing-board closed.

Fig. 16, keep the table-top firmly in position for writing purposes, and permit of its being removed when the drawing-board is required. The

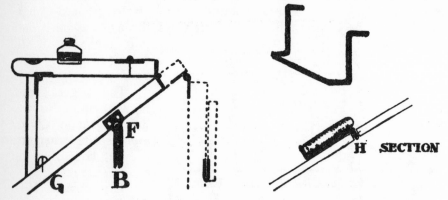

FIG. 13.—Section of Movable Ledge for Pens.

FIG. 14.—Iron Wire Book-rest.

general effect is considerably enhanced by gluing over the bare deal surface a rectangular strip of stamped imitation leather or American

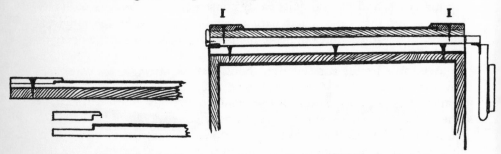

FIG. 15.—Section of Top of Writing-table.

FIG. 16.—Section of Combination Desk closed.

cloth. Figs. 5 and 16 give the pictorial and sectional views of the desk complete.

COMBINATION BOOK-CASE, BED OR LOUNGE, AND CLOTHES CUPBOARD

There is little point in a boy possessing a "den" of his own unless it serves some real, practical purpose, and helps to minimise the worry to which a mother is often put in her endeavours to accommodate her son with a room for his work and his belongings. To this end the ingenious article, a brief description of which heads this paragraph, has been designed, and not the least of its many useful functions is that of providing a comfortable sleeping-place for any chum who may

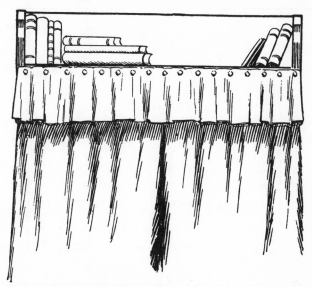

FIG. 17.—Combination Bed, Lounge, Book-case and Cupboard.

be asked to stay the night. Fig. 17 conveys some idea of the appearance the affair should present when the "shut-up bed" is locked against the wall (No. 2) and a few books are in position on the shelf. The fact that curtains and a little drapery conceal the presence of the "let-down" bedstead should prove an added advantage, particularly as the recess may be made to serve the purpose of a wardrobe when the bed or lounge is not in use.

Commence by constructing from lengths of 1-in. deal a framework (*i.e.* the sides and top) similar to that illustrated in Fig. 18. Useful dimensions are: length 5½ ft., height 5 ft., depth 10 in. In the inner side of each upright cut a square groove 3 ft. 8 in. from the ground, and let into these grooves a length of strong, square 1½-in.

battening, A, Fig. 18. This is termed "housing." (See chapter on Carpentry.) A length of ¾-in. boarding, 5 in. wide, should next be let into grooves cut into the uprights as previously explained, but at a height of 20 in., B, Fig. 18. As this boarding is to support a considerable part of the weight of the bed and sleeper, it should further be strengthened by an extra and narrower piece similarly fixed in the uprights and firmly screwed at C, Fig. 18. A glance at B and C, Figs. 18 and 19, makes this clear. The gluing and screwing on of the top piece completes the framework, which should then be clamped against the wall by means of iron angle brackets. The wall of brick behind

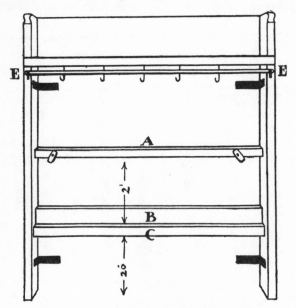

FIG. 18.—Framework for Combination Bed, &c.

the lateral strips should be plugged with wood (see "Plugging" in chapter on Carpentry), and the whole thing tightened up with screws and nails.

Those boys whose parents are blessed with ample sleeping accommodation will not need to go to the trouble of providing a homemade bedstead, but will simply use the cupboard as a receptacle for clothes, &c.

We next come to the constructing of the framework of the bed, best made from lengths of strong battening 2 in. wide, 1½ in. deep, carefully dovetailed and screwed in the form of a rectangle. Stout webbing nailed cross-wise provides a support for a thin mattress, which can be purchased at small expense. Before attaching the bed by long iron hinges to the stay B, the side away from the wall must be provided with a movable oak leg at each end, Fig. 20.

Each leg should swing freely on a stout screw, and to enable it to

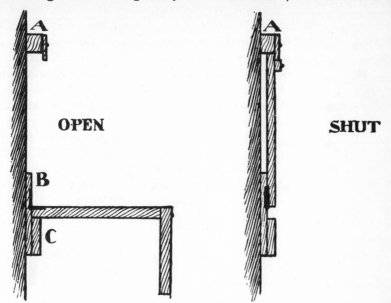

FIG. 19.—The Bed let down.   FIG. 19A.—Bed closed.

support a considerable weight, a thick hinge, the corner of which has been filed off, can be added at the point shown in Fig. 21, the shaded portion, A, of the hinge being the part to be removed. It should be

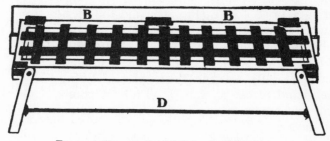

FIG. 20.—Framework of Bed showing Webbing.

borne in mind that only the upper side, B, of the hinge is to be screwed, the portion C being left free, so that when the leg is drawn up from the ground the lower half of the hinge may fold back as indicated in the section, Fig. 21. Still further to keep the legs in position when the bed is let down, hook on an iron or wooden bar as shown at D, Fig. 20.

All that now remains to be done is to supply some simple means whereby the bed may be kept conveniently in position when not in use. When the mattress has been removed and the legs brought parallel with the sides, the bed frame folds back against the wall, and can be held fast with wooden buttons, A, Figs. 18, 19, and 19A. Figs. 19 and 19A give in section the bed let down and closed. Screw hooks in the top cross-piece will serve for hanging clothes.

FIG. 21.—Arrangement for strengthening leg-supports.

To those who have gone so far, the adding of bookshelves will present no difficulty. They may be constructed from thinner wood on the plan indicated in Figs. 22 and 22A, which also show how, when the first row becomes filled, a second shelf with side supports can be fixed. A finished effect will be given if the sides of the top shelf are cut away as in Fig. 22A.

Having thus far progressed, it may be as well to invoke the aid of

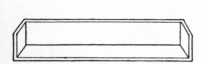

FIG. 22.—Front View of additional Shelf.

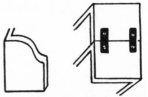

FIG. 22A.—Method of joining additional Shelves.

your mother or sister in securing those finishing touches suggested by the double curtain, opening and closing on rings sliding along a brass rod E, Fig. 18, and the inexpensive, tacked-on valance appearing in Fig. 17. To ensure tidiness, the bedclothes, cushions, and rugs (should the let-down bed-frame be used as a lounge) can be stowed neatly away in the cupboard fitting into the left-hand recess of wall 4. (Full directions for making this cupboard appear in the chapter on Carpentry, page 21.)

The last item of home-made furniture to go against wall No. 1 is the

RACK STAND FOR CRICKET BATS, GOLF CLUBS, HOCKEY STICKS, &c.

Three-quarter-inch deal will serve throughout.

Cut out top, bottom, and side pieces on the plan shown in Figs. 23, 24, 25, and 25A; add a half-circle

SIDE PIECE

FIG. 23.—Side of Rack Stand.

of hoop iron to each end of the top, screw the several parts into position, stain and varnish, and the result should be as depicted in Fig. 3.

Meting out similar treatment to the other articles of furniture previously described should put the owner of the " Home-made Den " into possession of a comfortable, ornamental, and useful apartment.

TOP PIECE

FIG. 24.—Top of Rack Stand.

Little more remains to be done. Most boys are enthusiasts in one or other branch of sport, and he who is an exponent of the art of fencing might give the finishing touches to his "den" by hanging

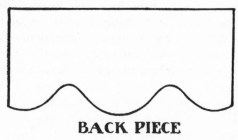

BACK PIECE

FIG. 25.—Back of Rack Stand.

upon the wall over the fireplace a pair of fencing-foils and a mask, as shown in Fig. 1. Crossed single-sticks, together with boxing-gloves, with which at some time in their youthful days most lads have more than a passing acquaintance, could be made admirably to fill the space over the bat, hockey, and golf-club stand.

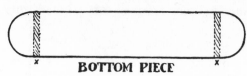

BOTTOM PIECE

FIG. 25A.—Bottom of Rack Stand.

In " Home Fun," a companion volume to " Every Boy's Book of Hobbies," published at 6s., will be found, on pages 404–409, full and explicit instructions on " How to make a Telephone " at a cost of 6s. 6d. The telephone described can be fitted from the ground floor to the rooms above, or from your friend's house to your own. It is impossible to overestimate the convenience of such a simple but useful piece of apparatus, and every boy who wishes his "den" to be thoroughly well equipped should instal for himself a " Home-made Telephone."

CHAPTER III

HOW TO MAKE A SCHOOL BOX WITH SECRET COMPARTMENTS

THERE are always certain things, whether they be letters, or "tuck," copies of a favourite paper, or photos of those at home, that a schoolboy wishes to keep under lock and key. Moreover, there is seldom enough room in the best of schools for all the particularly and especially private belongings which accumulate as the term drags on its weary course. In the present chapter will be explained the method of making a strong and handy box, in which all manner of personal belongings may be securely hidden from prying eyes.

The box about to be described is not large, and is in nowise intended to replace the chest for clothes and linen which usually accompanies a boy to school. It is rather a private box, little larger than a fair-sized writing-desk, the outside measurements being, 2 ft. long, 1 ft. 4 in. wide, and 14 in. high.

The material may be chosen according to individual taste and pocket-money, but there is really no need to use oak or more expensive woods, as a very neat and serviceable box can be made of $\frac{3}{4}$-in. planed yellow deal, short pieces of which may be bought for a few pence from any carpenter. When stained or painted this presents a very nice appearance.

Square and plane two pieces of wood measuring 2 ft. by 14 in., and into these dovetail two other pieces, 1 ft. 4 in. by 14 in., according to the instructions given in Chapter I.

Before attaching the bottom to the box, ten grooves should be made inside the framework, as shown at the places marked A, B, and C, in Fig. 1, the black portions in that figure being explained at a later stage. These grooves can be very simply made by sawing to the depth of $\frac{1}{4}$ in. and chiselling out cleanly.

The bottom should now be made and screwed securely in place, whilst the lid, which may be a flat piece of wood hinged with $2\frac{1}{2}$ in. butts, should be rendered dust-proof by nailing half round beading as shown in section, Fig. 2. Naturally this beading can be fixed on three sides only of the lid, for the back, to which the hinges are attached, must be left free.

With a little extra trouble, however, a deep lid can be made to allow of articles being strapped inside. In this case lengths as used for making the box, but only 2½ in. deep, should be dovetailed to-

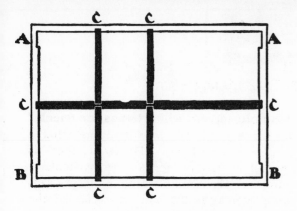

FIG. 1.—The Grooves inside the Box.

FIG. 2.—The Beading on the Lid.

gether, have a top screwed on, and be hinged to the box as shown in Fig. 3.

Angle plates screwed to the corners will serve to strengthen the box, and can either be purchased or made from thin sheet iron.

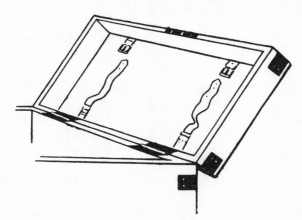

FIG. 3.—A Box-lid with Straps.

Twelve angle plates in all will be required, three at each corner, although, when a box lid has been made, an extra four will be needed.

These angle plates are easy to make. Cut the required number of pieces, measuring 4 in. by 2 in., and pierce them with screw-holes as seen in Fig 4, then bend them in the middle, to the right angle shown in section at A in the same diagram. These plates can be

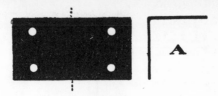

FIG. 4.—The Angle Plates.

painted black when the chest is finished, and will prove as ornamental as they are serviceable.

THE INTERIOR OF THE BOX

A SECRET COMPARTMENT

For the purpose of providing a secret compartment no better device could be employed than that of a false bottom. Cut two lengths of ¾-in. deal, 3 in. wide and 21 in. long, and two pieces of the same material

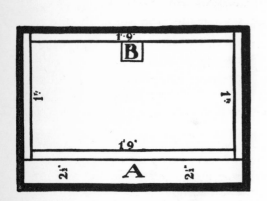

FIG. 5.—Supports for the False Bottom.

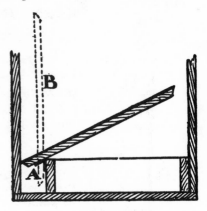

FIG. 6.—The False Bottom.

equally wide but 12 in. long, and glue these four lengths inside the box as shown in Fig. 5, thus leaving a space at A in which the false bottom can work.

Now plane down a piece of wood measuring 1 ft. 10 in. by 1 ft. 2½ in., and sand-paper this to fit exactly into the box, bevelling the edges as seen in section in Fig. 6.

Upon the real bottom of the box at the spot marked B, Fig. 5, glue the square of wood, measuring 2⅜ in., shown at A, Fig. 7.

In Fig. 8 is shown the top of the false bottom, to which the two long strips of wood, A, made of $\frac{1}{2}$ in. material and measuring 2 in. in depth, must be glued. These pieces should be placed each at a distance of $2\frac{1}{2}$ in. from the sides of the box. Now make three cross-pieces B, and glue them to the

FIG. 7.—The Block for the Secret Spring.

false bottom in the positions shown in the diagram, care being taken to see that they do not catch against the sides of the box.

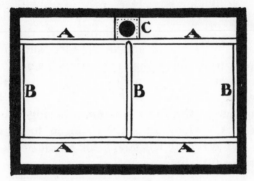

FIG. 8.—The Top of the False Bottom.

A small box C, the top of which should contain a circular hole, must then be placed in position, the top coming flush with the tops of the compartments. A safety ink-pot can be kept in this well, whilst the compartments on either side will serve for pens, pencils, or the like.

The false bottom can now be hinged to the partitions in the manner shown in Fig. 6. It can then be made to rise into a perpendicular position, as indicated by the dotted lines at B.

The next thing to make is the secret spring, with its catch. Obtain a piece of spring steel about 4 in. in length, and fasten to this a piece of lead shaped in the form of a catch as seen at B, Fig. 9, the whole spring A being fastened to the block C by the rivets shown in section at D.

FIG. 9.—The Secret Catch.

A small slot, A, Fig. 10, will have to be cut in the false bottom, and into this the catch must fit in such a way that when it is closed down, the head of the spring catch in the box C will secure the bottom in place, whilst, by passing the finger through D and pressing back the catch, the false bottom can be lifted. It is therefore obvious that the head of the lead catch must allow for the thickness of the false bottom.

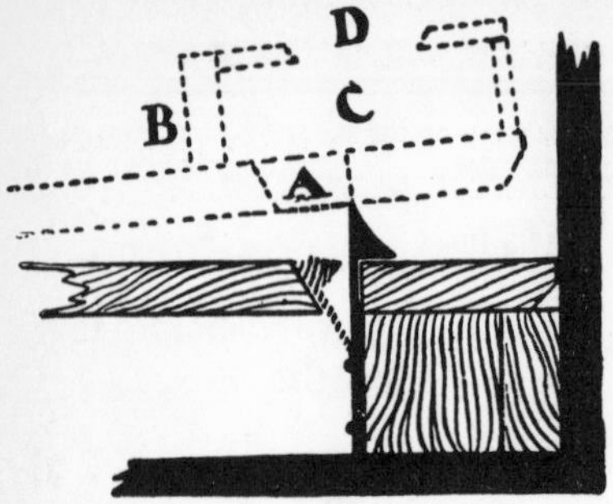

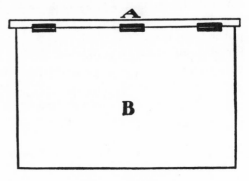

FIG. 10.—The Secret Catch in place.

THE TRAYS

As it now stands, the chest contains the secret compartments beneath the false bottom, and the series of partitions glued above the false bottom. The next thing to make is a tray to lie upon these partitions, and this tray must be cut in the form shown in Fig. 11.

Returning for a moment to Fig. 1, a strip of wood must be made long enough and of sufficient width to fit into the grooves AA. This piece of wood is depicted at A, Fig. 11. Make the tray B of the same dimensions as the false bottom, allowing of course for the width of the piece A. The tray is then hinged to A, and, when the latter has been slid down the grooves, the whole tray should lift up and down freely on the hinges.

Returning yet again to Fig. 1, the partitions shown in black must be cut, 7 in. deep, and made to slide easily up and down in the grooves already made at C to receive them.

There will now be a space of 8 in. left between the top of these partitions and the lid, and this may be occupied by a similar tray, the strip of wood in this case being placed on the other side to fit into the corresponding grooves at B in Fig. 1. This second tray will thus rest upon the partitions in the lower tray.

FIG. 11.—The Tray.

A sectional view of the box will now appear as in Fig. 12, which may be thus explained :—

The shaded portion at the bottom represents the secret receptacle beneath the false bottom. The false bottom with its small divisions C conceals the secret cavity, and in its turn is covered by the lower tray B, which slides down the groove to the depth indicated by the arrow on the right-hand side of the figure. The further partitions CC serve to support the top tray A, which slides in grooves shown by the other arrow.

It will thus be seen that to reach the compartments on the lower tray it will only be necessary to raise the upper tray on its hinges. To get at the compartments beneath the lower tray, the partitions must be slid out and the lower tray raised on its hinges. To obtain access to the secret compartment, both trays should be entirely removed, the secret catch pressed back, and the false bottom lifted, thus revealing a chamber, the existence of which would never be suspected by the casual observer.

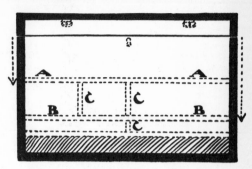

FIG. 12.—A Sectional View of the Box.

As for the uses to which this box may be put, there is but little need to enlarge on the subject. Larger objects will naturally be placed on the upper tray, where there is the most space, but all smaller things can be packed away below in compartments suited to their size and shape. Indeed the uses to which this box may be put are so numerous that it must be left to the reader to find out for himself what an invaluable treasure he has acquired in its possession.

CHAPTER IV

HOW TO MAKE A PUZZLE BOX

A Mystery for Your Friends

THE article about to be described calls for considerable care, inasmuch as exact measurements and working are required. There is always some inexplicable charm about a puzzle, appreciable alike to the mystified and the initiated, for it amuses the former, and, rightly or wrongly, evokes in the latter a sense of superiority which is, after all, quite natural. The puzzle box would serve to keep knick-knacks, e.g. stamps, studs, nibs, money, &c.

For that part of the box which is to serve as a receptacle, a block of hard wood, planed smooth and squared to the size of 4 in. by 2 in. by ¾ in., with the grain running lengthways, is required, and must be hollowed out until the bottom and sides remain as thin as practicable, although the ends are left ¼ in. thick.

At one end, A, two slots, C, are cut to the depth and position shown in Fig. 1,

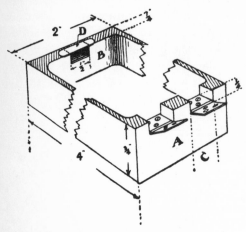

FIG. 1.—Prepared Body of the Box.

whilst at the other end, B, another slot is cut, which, however, does not extend through to the outer wall. In the former slots two brass hinges are fitted, whilst over that at B, a thin brass plate, D, is screwed, being recessed to lie flush with the upper surface of the wood.

The lid, with which we have now to deal, is made of a piece of hard wood similar to that previously used, planed and sand-papered down to $\frac{3}{16}$ in. thickness, and cut, with square corners to size, 4 in. by 2 in., the grain running lengthways as before.

To the underside and towards one end, A, is glued a batten of the

shape C, Fig. 2, which is cut from ⅛ in. wood.   Its essential features
are:—

a. That the length shall be slightly less than the width inside the
box.

b. That the two projecting pieces, when the lid is closed down,
shall lie snugly in the hinge slots shown at A, Fig. 1.

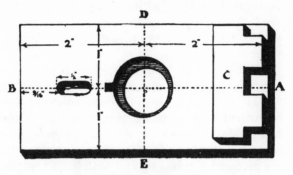

FIG. 2.—Lid of the Puzzle Box.

A 1-in. circular hole is next drilled in the centre of the lid, *i.e.*
where the axes B A, and D E, Fig. 2, cross, to a depth of ⅛ in.
(reckoning from the batten side), and finished right through with a ¾ in.
hole.   In addition to this a slot $\frac{3}{16}$ in. wide, and ½ in. long is cut along
the axis B A, commencing $\frac{9}{16}$ in. from B, and another slot ⅛ in. by

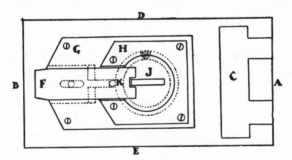

FIG. 3.—Locking Arrangement in the Lid.

⅛ in. cut only to the depth of the larger circular hole, and extending
from it towards the former slot.

THE LOCKING ARRANGEMENT

Now from Figs. 3, 4, and 5, which show the locking arrangement in
several aspects, it will be seen that five distinct parts, F, G, H, J and K.

are comprised therein, the last named being simply a $\frac{1}{16}$ in. ball of steel as used in bicycle bearings. The dimensions of the four former parts are best shown in their separate sketches, Figs. 6, 7, 8, 9 respectively, and the ensuing brief particulars will make them comprehensible.

F is cut with a sharp penknife and warding file out of hard fretwood $\frac{1}{8}$ in. thick, sand-papered down; if they cannot be obtained separately, this and the knob will be best cut in two pieces and glued in a hole in the correct position.

G is cut with similar implements, and, possibly, fret-sawn from $\frac{1}{16}$ in. wood, the level edges being blackleaded.

H is cut from $\frac{1}{16}$ in. hard fretwood.

FIG. 4.—Section of Lid.

J should be turned from a piece of hard wood to the dimensions shown, but if this is not possible, it may be carefully cut from a piece of $\frac{1}{4}$ in. wood and the embossed disc, M, glued on afterwards. Another idea is to

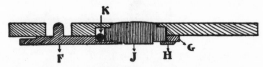

FIG. 5.—Another View of Lid in Section.

screw on a disc of metal—*e.g.* a new farthing, with three short screws. The projecting piece, N, can be glued and pinned in place. L is a $\frac{1}{8}$ in. hole cut to a depth of $\frac{1}{8}$ in. on the upper edge of the I in. disc. The edge of this piece must be blackleaded, as must the circular hole in the part G.

PIECING THE LID TOGETHER

Following the plan of previous explanations, the method of piecing the lid parts together is best seen from Figs. 3, 4 and 5. The

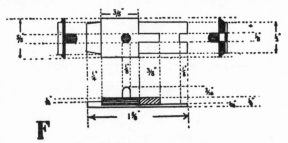

FIG. 6.—The Dimensions of F.

wood disc, J, is first placed in position (with the embossed portion, M, Fig. 9, towards the outside of the lid), and then the steel ball dropped into place, followed by the piece, F. Lastly, G and H are screwed down—accurately with respect to F and J—two screws passing through G alone, and four through both H and G. The lid is fitted to the top of the box by screwing the hinges to the projecting parts of the batten, C, Fig. 2.

The actual locking piece is F, which slides backwards and forwards,

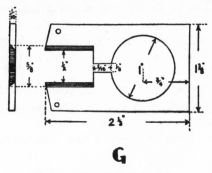

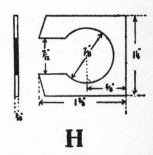

FIG. 7.—The Dimensions of G.   FIG. 8.—The Dimensions of H.

thus engaging with the brass strip over the slot at B, Fig. 1. In the position of the mechanism, shown by Fig. 3, the bolt, F, cannot be pushed back to allow of the lid opening, because the steel ball falls

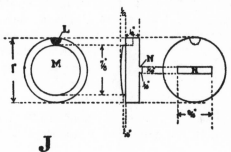

FIG. 9.—The Dimensions of J.

into the hole cut therein, whilst M is locking that also. If, however, F is first pushed back towards B, Fig. 3, so that J may be revolved until the steel ball falls into the hole (to accomplish which the box must be inverted), then M can be pushed right back and the lid released.

CHAPTER V

HOW TO MAKE A WILY WIZARD'S TABLE

WITH WHICH MARVELLOUS MAGICAL MYSTERIES ARE EASILY PERFORMED

WHILE an account of scientific conjuring or expert legerdemain plays no part in the instructions conveyed in this book, the following few hints on the construction of a most mystifying but easily-made conjuror's portable table, will be found of intense interest to every boy who wishes to shine in the eyes of his fellows as a most remarkable exponent of wizardry.

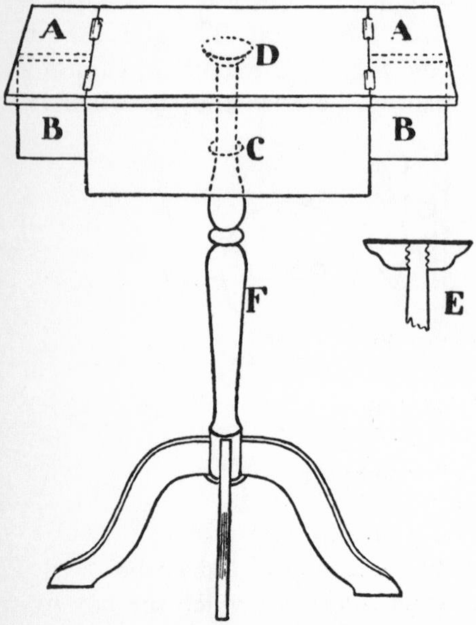

Now the conjuror's most constant and safest companion is, of course, his table. The table to a conjuror is what the brush is to the painter or the instrument to a musician. Without it he is at a loss to entertain, unless he has at his fingers' ends the skill engendered by years of ceaseless practice in the art of making those bewildering sleights and passes which teach us the somewhat disconcerting truth that the quickness of the hand deceives the eye.

For the purpose of amateur entertaining, or even for home purposes, the conjuring table is of but little use unless it can be packed in a handy portable form. The one described below is similar in every detail to that used by a leading travelling magician to whom the writer is indebted for the many little ingenious devices explained. First procure a wooden box about 2 ft. long by 18 in. wide and 10 in. deep, and, as a preliminary measure, remove one of the long sides. Next, securely nail down a smooth lid in one piece, which

FIG. 1.—The Construction of the Table.

should project ¾ in. at either end of the short sides. The removed side has then to be fixed to the bottom of the box by means of hinges, and, when it is dropped outwards, held in a horizontal position by strong tapes attached to each end.

To return to the box which forms the top of the table. Hinge to the short sides two flaps, AA, Fig. 1, 10 in. wide—*i.e.* of the same depth as the box, so that when these are dropped down the whole may be packed in compact form. The flaps are hinged from beneath and supported by the projections BB, which in turn are hinged to the centres of the short sides of the box in such a manner that, when pulled out, they support the flaps AA, thus forming an extended table, as illustrated by Fig. 1.

In the centre of the bottom of the box cut a hole, C, Fig. 1, and to the underside of the top at D, fix a circular wooden block, with a thread to receive the main support F, which passes through C and screws into position as shown by E. Any cabinet-maker possessing a lathe will turn such a support with accompanying legs for a shilling or so.

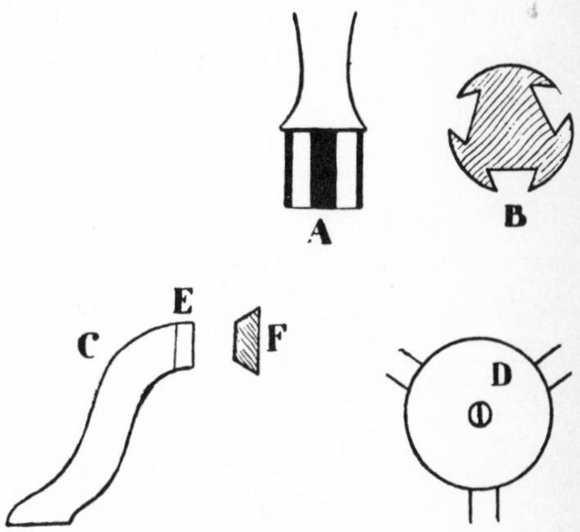

FIG. 2.—Construction of the Legs.

MAKING THE LEGS

The construction of the legs which fit into the base of the main support is clearly indicated by Fig. 2. A is the bottom of the support with three grooves cut and shaped as at B. Into each of these, slides a curved leg, C. At the point marked E, the curved leg should be splayed out to the shape of F, in section, to fit tightly into the main support. The legs are then held in position by a circular metal plate screwed underneath the main support, as shown by D.

By far the most important part of the conjuror's table is the arrangement at the back. The back flap, A, in Fig. 3, already referred to, should be beaded along three sides (indicated by thick black lines) to prevent any article placed thereon falling to the floor. The padding of the flap with thick felt or cloth ensures the noiseless reception of anything the conjuror might wish secretly to drop upon it.

The two mysterious-looking pieces of apparatus (marked respectively B and C, Fig. 3) which appear at either side of the flap A are known as "hanging servantes." By a servante is understood any receptacle for holding or catching discarded, vanished, or surreptitiously acquired articles. The servantes depicted consist of

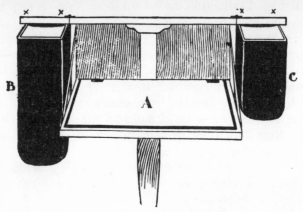

FIG. 3.—Back of the Table with Servantes.

any black material made into the form of bags or stockings, and are kept open by means of stout wire frames fixed to the flaps at XXXX.

A closer reference to Fig. 4 gives a more detailed idea of how a servante is made and the method of fixing it to the table flaps.

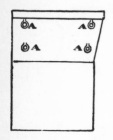

AAAA are four eyelets screwed into the underside of the flaps. Through these eyelets are pushed the wire ends, BB, supporting the open black bag C, Fig. 4.

The portable table is now complete. When taken to pieces, the box-like part will permit of the introduction of the conjuring apparatus necessary for an entire performance. Thus the young magician has, in a handy carrying form, all that he can possibly require for an entertainment.

However, it may be that his ambitions will lead him to desire the very useful article known as

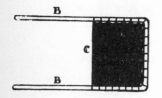

FIG. 4.—The Servante.

THE BLACK ART TABLE,

which, by reason of its possessing "traps," lends itself to the performance of more ambitious tricks. Primarily, the purpose of the Black Art table is to vanish things, and as this forms a great part of the work of every conjuror, needless to say such a table is of immense utility. From the point of view of the audience, the table presents a weird and fantastically designed appearance. However, the purpose of the extraordinary design with which the top is decorated becomes more apparent on glancing at Fig. 6, which shows a sectional view of the somewhat wily affair.

On a square wooden top are cut three circular holes of different sizes, ranging in diameter from 4 in. to 8 in., AAA, Fig. 6. These holes act as "traps" for the disappearance of any article of which the conjuror desires to rid himself. The curious part about these traps is that they have no top coverings. In fact, they remain always open, with the black cloth bags attached beneath, as shown in the diagram. But how does it happen that the holes are invisible to the

FIG. 5.—The Table-top.

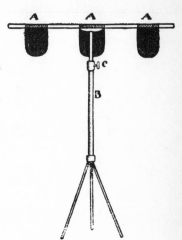

FIG. 6.—The Traps.

audience? This is where the geometric design of white lines drawn on the dead black surface of the table-top comes in. Three of the nine circles—which, the young conjuror must decide for himself—are cut clean away. In Fig. 5 they are indicated by the dots. Now, as the bags attached are also dead black, the "traps" easily escape the notice of the spectator, who sees an apparently solid table-top.

The tripod support B, Fig. 6, takes the form of an ordinary portable brass stand, such as is used by a musician, screwing at the top into the thread of a metal block which any ironmonger can procure. The sliding rod which adjusts the height of the table can be raised or lowered by means of the screw at C. To hide the bags from the view of the audience, tack a long fringe round the table-top.

CHAPTER VI

A NOVEL PHOTO-FRAME

EASILY MADE IN SPARE TIME

How often do boys, happy possessors of photos of relatives, school chums, favourite pets, &c., take great delight in showing these pictures to their admiring friends, and yet how often do they sigh for some adequate method of displaying them to advantage?

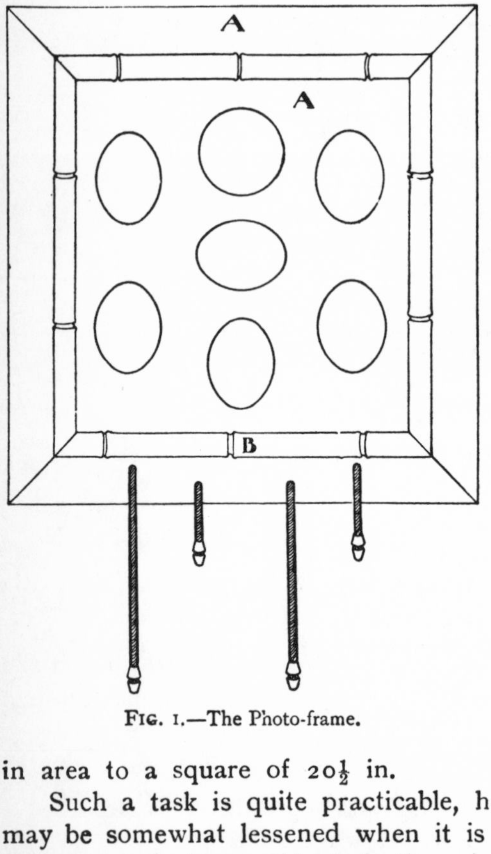

FIG. I.—The Photo-frame.

They complain either that, if in separate frames these treasures take up too much room, or, if not in frames, they get poked away in some forgotten or inaccessible place.

In other words, they are sadly in need of a frame which, while capable of displaying several photos, yet is not so inconveniently large as those usually adopted for the purpose.

It cannot be wondered at, therefore, that they will doubt the possibility of constructing a frame which, although capable of displaying no less than nineteen photos, may be restricted in area to a square of 20½ in.

Such a task is quite practicable, however, and their amazement may be somewhat lessened when it is explained that to accomplish this seemingly impossible task, they simply resort to the method of constructing a frame containing two discs, each of which may be

60

made to revolve slowly behind an aperture made in the face of the frame.

Such a frame will be found in itself quite an ornament, for, covered with plush, AA, Figs. 1 and 2, and decorated with bamboo, B, it proves very attractive to the eye.

FIG. 2.—Section of Frame.

To the casual observer it appears simply as a wall ornament, showing half-a-dozen photos, but upon closer inspection its greater utility is revealed, for, by pulling a cord, a disc is slowly revolved, showing, as it passes an opening to the front mount, the seven photos it contains. When this disc has completed one revolution, it is brought to a standstill, and a second disc may be set in motion, thus displaying six more photos, in this way bringing the number exhibited up to nineteen.

Before explaining in detail the construction of this novel frame, the reader would do well to become acquainted with the materials required, and the very small expenses to be incurred by their purchase. The accompanying list is therefore drawn up to furnish this information, and to satisfy him that the total outlay need not exceed the modest sum of four shillings.

MATERIALS REQUIRED	ESTIMATED COST	
	s.	d.
8 feet of moulding	1	0
1 yard of plush 18 in. wide	1	6
2 round perforated chair seats (14 in. diameter) . .	0	8
Glass, 14¾ in. by 14¾ in.	0	3
1 6-foot bamboo rod, ¾ in. diameter . . .	0	3
Sheet of stout cardboard, 14½ in. by 14½ in. . . .	0	0
Blind roller end, 2 in. diameter (to serve as band wheel) .	0	0½
Total	3	8½

In purchasing the moulding, which may be obtained from any timber yard, make sure that it is of the right dimensions, or you will put yourself to extra labour in the way of planing, &c. A glance at Fig. 3, which shows a section of the required moulding, with its dimensions, will greatly assist in its selection. Should you be unable to get moulding quite to these dimensions, you must at least insist on its being 3 in. wide and 2 in. deep, as it may then be planed to the required shape. No difficulty will be experienced, of course,

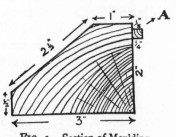

FIG. 3.—Section of Moulding.

in purchasing the glass, but, as the inside of the frame is a square with sides 14½ in., the square of glass should have sides of only 14⅜ in., thus allowing sufficient room for fitting. In Fig. 3, A is the beading to support the glass.

Obtaining the bamboo and the cardboard should present no difficulties, the former being purchasable from any oil-shop, or draper's, whilst the latter may be cut from the lid of a large hat-box; or, failing this, may be bought from the stationer's for a penny.

Nothing now remains to be provided but a few small fittings, such as washers, cord, &c., the cost of which is trifling. These will be referred to from time to time as the construction is explained, and, with all the materials at hand, the reader should now attempt the practical work.

THE PRACTICAL WORK

Your first task must be the construction of a frame, and this raises no insuperable difficulties if the following instructions be carried out, especially should your moulding be of the required pattern.

The frame is to consist of four pieces of moulding, each end of which is cut, as shown in Fig. 4, to an angle of 45°. To

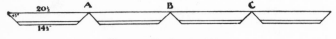

FIG. 4.—Cutting the Sides.

obtain these pieces, take the 8-foot length of moulding and cut one end to a mitre of 45°, after which cut a similar mitre 20½ in. away at the point A, as shown in Fig. 4. This will provide you with one side of the frame; the edges of this side being 20½ in. and 14½ in.

FIG. 5.—Method of fixing Joints.

respectively. By repeating this process three times, the other three sides are accounted for in a very easy manner, although it must here be impressed upon the reader that the cutting of the mitres must be very carefully and accurately undertaken, or considerable difficulty will be experienced in obtaining a perfectly square frame.

Your next care must be to fix these four sides together to form the frame. To do this, place two of them together as shown in Fig. 5, ascertain that they form a true right angle, and then, through the side of one, bore two holes with a small bradawl. Now, opening the joint well, fill in with plenty of hot glue, and then close it quickly, taking care that the arms are in their proper positions.

To keep the joints quite true, carefully drive brads into the holes made for that purpose.

In this way half of your frame is accounted for, and, by treating each of the other corners in the same manner, you will be furnished with a good strong frame capable of withstanding considerable strain.

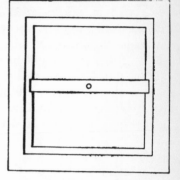

FIG. 6.—Cross-bar for Frame.

Now it must be remembered that the frame is to contain two discs, each of which, of course, must revolve on a spindle firmly placed in the centre. You will readily understand, therefore, that your next step must be to arrange for the fixing of this spindle, and this necessitates the placing of a wooden bar right across the front of the frame, Fig. 6. For this purpose prepare a wooden bar 15½ in. long, 1½ in. broad, and ¼ in. thick.

Now, when this bar is in position, it will be covered by the sheet

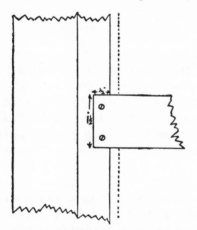
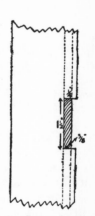

FIG. 7.—Method of fixing Cross-bar. FIG. 8.—Groove for Cross-bar.

of glass forming the face of the frame, and for this reason it becomes necessary to sink it into the frame. You will thus be obliged to cut a groove in each side, having a length of 1½ in., a width of ½ in., and a depth of ⅜ in., Figs. 7 and 8. These will allow the cross-bar, when placed in position, to be set back ⅛ in. from the extreme front of the frame, so that the thickness of the glass will be accounted for. The cross-bar may then be permanently fixed by means of glue and a few brads.

Your next duty must be to arrange for a ledge on which to rest the glass, and for this you must purchase or cut lengths of beading $\frac{1}{4}$ in. by $\frac{1}{4}$ in. This must be glued round the inside of the frame, and, as in the case of the cross-bar, set back $\frac{1}{8}$ in. from the front of the frame to allow for the thickness of the glass, Figs. 7 and 8. It might here be mentioned that this beading may be easily obtained by cutting off $\frac{1}{4}$ in. strips from the lid of a Hudson's Soap box, the thickness of which will be found to measure about $\frac{1}{4}$ in.

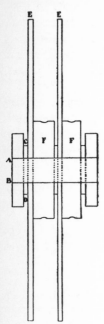

FIG. 9.—Section of Revolving Disc.

It would be useless, of course, to fix the glass in position at this stage, for that is one of the very last operations to be performed. Attention instead must be turned to the cutting and fixing of the spindle on which the two discs are to revolve.

As regards the cutting, that is quite an easy matter, for it simply consists of severing a piece of wood $1\frac{7}{8}$ in. long from a curtain-rod of $\frac{1}{2}$ in. diameter. This will constitute an admirable spindle, which may be accurately fixed in position.

FIXING THE SPINDLE

Unless the spindle be quite perpendicular with the front of the frame, the discs will not revolve truly. The spindle is to be fixed in the cross-bar, and, to ensure its being absolutely in the centre of the frame, two diagonals of the square should be drawn. It will then be found that their point of intersection falls on the cross-bar, and at this spot a hole just capable of taking the spindle should be bored. This done, glue in the spindle, AB, Fig. 9, flush with the outer surface of the cross-bar.

You are now in a position to prepare the discs, to each of which is to be attached a band wheel. It will be recalled that these discs are in reality circular chair seats with diameters not exceeding 14 in., and, as such, have one of their sides concave.

The band wheels also require a few explanatory words. As near as possible they should be 2 in. wide, $\frac{7}{16}$ in. thick, with a central hole of $\frac{1}{2}$ in. diameter.

On the concave side of each disc, EE, fix, by means of glue and a few brads, one of the band wheels FF in a perfectly central position. It is next necessary to continue the hole of the band wheel through the disc, thus allowing the whole to fit quite easily over the spindle.

All is now ready for fixing these discs on the spindle, provided, however, you have obtained a few washers not exceeding $\frac{1}{12}$ in. in thickness.

Start by placing one of these washers over the spindle, gluing it to the cross-bar as shown at CD in Fig. 9. Then, having glued a washer to each of the band wheels, place a disc on the spindle in such a manner that its convex side touches the washer CD. In precisely the same way, slip the remaining disc over the spindle, and all is ready for fixing the back cross-bar. This, both in dimensions and position, resembles that across the front of the frame, and rests in two grooves each $\frac{1}{4}$ in. deep.

It will then be noticed that, since the discs and this back cross-bar fit quite easily over the spindle, they may be removed whenever occasion requires. As it will frequently become necessary to remove them for various reasons, the cross-bar should only be temporarily fixed by a couple of screws.

THE REVOLVING DISCS

Attention must again be directed to the discs, which have each to be covered on one side with stout cartridge-paper, divided into sections, and provided with a small piece of brass to act as a stop-point.

The covering of the face side of the disc with paper needs no explanation, but for the divisions, which number seven on each disc, it is necessary to divide the circumference into seven equal parts, and join the points of division to the centre. You will remember that the first disc is to be provided with an opening, this enabling the back disc, when in revolution, to display its seven photos one by one.

This opening is in the form of an oval, having diameters of 4 in. and 3 in. respectively. It should first be drawn on the disc, and then cut out by means of a key-hole saw.

The bottom of the opening must be at least $\frac{3}{4}$ in. from the outer edge of the disc, the reason for this becoming apparent later.

Having cut the opening to your satisfaction, edge it with plush. This is done by covering the face side of the section with hot glue, and then placing a piece of plush over it. When quite dry, turn the disc AA over, and cut out a piece of plush smaller than the size of the opening. Now make side cuts nearly to the wood of the disc, pull the plush back, and glue down the edges as shown in Fig. 10.

Each of the discs must be supplied with a stop-point, which will later be used to keep the discs in position.

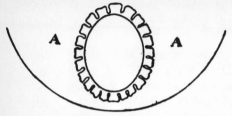

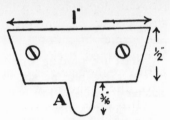

FIG. 10.—Edging the Opening with Plush.

FIG. 11.—Brass Stop-point.

These stop-points are cut out of a brass plate $\frac{1}{16}$ in. thick, 1 in.

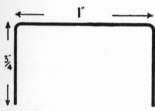

FIG. 12.—Wire Stop.

long, and $\frac{3}{4}$ in. wide, the shape resembling that shown in Fig. 11, care being taken, however, that when fixed as shown in Fig. 13, the overlapping point depicted at A, Fig. 11, does not exceed $\frac{3}{16}$ in. in length.

Naturally these stop-points must be provided with an object against which to act, and this object consists of a piece of hard wire, bent as shown in Fig. 12. The arms of this hoop should be 1 in. apart and each $\frac{3}{4}$ in. long.

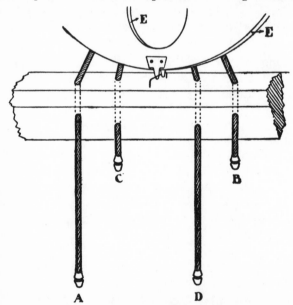

FIG. 13.—The fixing of Stops and Cords.

Then, carefully finding the middle of the bottom side of the frame, drive in the hoop perpendicular to the front of the frame, until but $\frac{1}{8}$ in. projects above the surface.

The stop-points on the discs, coming in contact with the wire stop thus placed, prevent the discs from completing another revolution in the same direction, although they are capable of being turned back through the same space until they arrive at the same side of the stop, Fig. 13, where the back disc is shown at EE.

It is quite understood, of course, that the discs are revolved by means of cords, so that your next task must be to arrange holes for these cords, and to fix them in position. For the first disc, therefore, on each side of the stop, and 5 in. away from it, a hole must be bored which is $\frac{7}{8}$ in. from the extreme front of the frame.

FIG. 14.—The Bamboo Knob.

The holes for the back disc are provided in like manner, being, however, $1\frac{1}{2}$ in. from the extreme front of the frame, and only $2\frac{1}{2}$ in. from the wire stop. Next cut two cords, each long enough to take one complete turn round the band wheel, and at the same time have the two ends 9 in. and 11 in. respectively.

A finishing touch is given to these cords by the attachment of bamboo knobs at the ends. To accomplish this, take a bamboo rod of $\frac{3}{4}$ in. diameter and cut off four joints in such a manner that there is $\frac{1}{2}$ in. of wood above the joint and $\frac{3}{4}$ in. below it, Fig. 14. Then, after tapering each end of the knobs with a penknife, bore through the joint a hole just large enough to take the cord, which should then be knotted, the knot remaining hidden within the knob, Fig. 15.

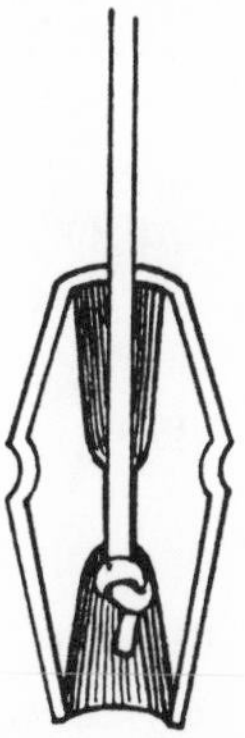

The arrangements of the discs, with their corresponding cords, is now an easy matter. First see that the stop-point of the front disc is to the left of the wire stop, whilst that of the back disc is to the right. Then, by references to Fig. 13, it will be seen that whilst cord A is long, B remains short, the cords C and D of the back disc being in the same relative positions.

FIG. 15.—Method of fixing Cord.

Now, if the short cord C be pulled, the back disc will slowly revolve behind the opening in the front disc, thus displaying any photos which it may hold.

In the same way, by pulling the cord B, the front disc revolves, although in the opposite direction, and, when the mount is fixed over the front of the frame, the six photos it contains will be viewed, one by one, through the oval opening at the bottom of the mount. Thus all the photos will have been displayed, and, to view again, the operation has only to be reversed.

MAKING THE MOUNT

Everything is now ready for the mount, which is to be in the form of a cardboard square, with a side of 14½ in., and which, when in position, is to cover the sheet of glass previously mentioned. This mount has to contain seven openings, the position of one of which is of great importance, for it must coincide with the opening made in the front disc. The exact position of this important opening may be easily ascertained in the following manner. Temporarily fitting the square of cardboard in the frame, revolve the front disc until it is brought to a standstill by the wire stop. Then, from the back of the frame, pencil on the cardboard mount an opening exactly corresponding in shape, size, and position to that in the disc. Not quite so much importance need be attached to the shape and position of the other openings, for the reader may well use his own judgment as to what will prove most suitable.

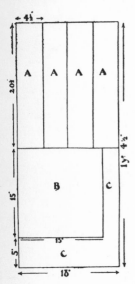

FIG. 16.—Plan for cutting the Plush.

For those unable to devise a better arrangement, Fig. 1 will offer a suggestion, for there may be seen, besides the oval just constructed, four more of similar size and shape, a circle of 3½ in. diameter, above an oval placed lengthwise in the centre.

When these holes have been neatly cut out, the mount and frame are ready for the plush covering.

THE COVERING

A little judgment in the cutting out of the plush will prevent great waste of this somewhat expensive material. As has been already stated, it is necessary to purchase 1⅛ yards of 18-in. plush, and this may be very economically cut in the manner shown by Fig. 16, where, you will notice, the piece provides four strips, AAAA, for the frame, a square, B, capable of covering the mount, and two strips, CC, to be used for odd pieces, edging ovals, &c.

Taking the plush square, lay it face downwards on the tablecloth, and ensure that it is quite smooth. Then, with glue which is quite hot, but not too thin, cover the face side of the mount and place it quickly upon the back of the plush, in such a central position as to leave a $\frac{1}{4}$ in. margin all round. It is advisable to leave it a day before cutting out the plush which covers the openings.

This cutting is done in exactly the same manner as was adopted in the case of the mount on the front disc, viz., cut out a small piece of the plush, and, after making side cuts, turn back and glue the material as shown in Fig. 10.

The frame itself has still to be covered, but this will present no new difficulties. Placing the strips temporarily along the sides, cut them to the shape of the mitres. Then, taking them one at a time, place them smoothly on the glued sides of the frame, being careful to turn back the over-lapping edges behind.

You have not yet fixed the mount in position, and, before this can be accomplished, the photos must be attached to the glass face.

Having selected your six photos, which should be cabinets, turn the mount face downwards with the glass above it. Then taking one photo at a time, put it in position by raising both mount and glass from time to time to ensure its being symmetrically placed. When quite to your satisfaction, fix it to the glass by means of strips of glued paper.

In this way you should cover six of the openings, remembering, of course, that the bottom oval must remain uncovered. Now place the glass in position, and cover it with the plush-covered mount.

Your labours, as far as the construction of the frame is concerned, are now practically at an end, and but one or two finishing touches remain to complete everything. You have not yet supplied the two discs with the photos they are to display. Choosing your thirteen cabinet-sized photos—seven for the back disc, six for the front—remove them from their mounts by the application of cold water.

When quite dry, place them in their respective positions by means of ordinary paste, not forgetting to remove any corners, &c., to enable the photos to fit their sections exactly.

A final touch may be given by providing a back, either of stout paper or cardboard ; but this is not essential, although it greatly helps in keeping dust from the interior of the frame. The fixing of two looking-glass plates, one on each side of the frame, provides a means of attaching it to the wall, and finally completes the frame, which is now ready for exhibition.

Thus at very small cost and trouble, which may, paradoxically, be termed pleasure, you have constructed an ornament both useful and amusing.

CHAPTER VII

A HOME-MADE BOOMERANG

AND HOW TO THROW IT

A FEW words will explain what a "boomerang" is—that wonderful weapon wielded so skilfully by the dusky aborigines of Australia. Used by the natives in war and the chase, it consists merely of a piece of stout wood bent in a curve and having a length from two and a half to three feet, with a breadth of two to three inches. One side is convex, and the other flat, the curved side possessing a sharp edge.

At some time or another every boy has doubtless wished himself the possessor of a boomerang. Well, here are instructions for both making and correctly throwing a small-sized specimen of this strange and primitive but effective weapon.

First procure a piece of well-seasoned hickory, about 1 foot long, 3 inches wide, and 1 inch thick. Then proceed to scald it

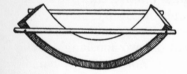

FIG. 1.—Bending the Wood.

thoroughly by pouring several kettlesful of boiling water over it. The hickory will thus be rendered quite pliable, and whilst in this condition it should be bent to the shape shown in Fig. 1. This may be quickly done with the aid of a vice ; but if the reader does not possess one of these extremely useful implements, he can adopt a very simple and equally effective method.

Lay the piece of hickory plank on the table, with half of it projecting over the edge, Fig. 2. Then, firmly holding the half resting on the table in position with one hand, bend down the unsupported half with the other. A glance at Fig. 2 makes this clear.

When the hickory has assumed the correct curve, two side pieces should be nailed on, as shown in Fig. 1. These are fixed temporarily to hold it in position whilst the wood dries.

FIG. 2.—Another Method of Bending.

When thoroughly dry, remove the side pieces, and saw the curved hickory into six strips each ½ in. wide.

The result will be six roughly fashioned boomerangs, and it only remains to trim them into shape with a pocket-knife. One side should be left quite flat, while the other must be carefully rounded, the convex or outside curve being brought to a bluntish edge. The correct shape is clearly shown in the sectional diagram, Fig. 3. Lastly round off the ends, and smooth down the surface of the wood with glass-paper.

Fig. 3.—Section of Boomerang.

The finished boomerang should have the appearance depicted in Fig. 4.

Now go into an adjacent field, or other open space, and try your luck at throwing this curious weapon.

Fig. 4.—Completed Boomerang.

Grasp the boomerang at one end, which should possess cross-cuts to give a grip, and keep the hollow or concave side away from you. Then throw it as if you wished to hit a spot on the ground about thirty yards distant. If possible, give it a slight downward twist with the wrist as it leaves the hand, thus imparting a spinning motion or "screw-back" to the weapon. Instead of travelling straight forward, and then falling to the ground, the boomerang will gradually ascend in the air, whirling round and round, and, taking a circular course, will sweep back towards you, finally depositing itself a few yards from your feet, the retrograde motion being produced by the bulged side of the weapon.

It is not advisable to throw the boomerang in the vicinity of a crowd, as in the hands of a novice its flight is liable to be a trifle erratic.

CHAPTER VIII

HOW TO MAKE A FLAGSTAFF

For National and Family Celebrations

ALTHOUGH there are seldom wanting occasions when a national or family celebration demands the "hoisting of the bunting," it is a comparatively rare thing to find a flagstaff from which the colours can float gaily in the breeze.

There is no need, of course, to have an iron mast with wire rigging and all the stays and cross-trees such as one sees in the finished signal posts used by coast-guards. But a very cheap mast, firmly secured to the ground and of a reasonable height, is all that is required, and can be erected at very small cost.

Obtain a small scaffold pole forty feet in length from any builder, who will sell this for about a penny per foot. A very smart appearance is produced if the pole be planed and varnished; but if this

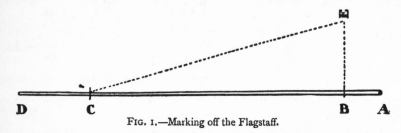

Fig. 1.—Marking off the Flagstaff.

cannot be done, it may be painted with a cheap white paint, obtainable from any oil-shop or ironmonger for about sixpence a pound.

Lay the pole upon the ground and mark it off with chalk according to the following measurements: Mark B, Fig. 1, 4 ft. from the end A, this being the depth to which the mast will be sunk into the earth. From B measure 28 ft. to C, this being the point where the knees must be fitted. The distance from C to D will then be 8 ft.

Two triangular pieces of wood about 4 inches in width must now be made and firmly screwed and bolted 8 ft. from the top of the mast at C. The object of these knees is to keep the shrouds in place and prevent them from slipping down.

The next proceeding is to take the measurements for the shrouds and stay, and for this purpose the staff must be laid so that B is on the spot where the hole will be dug in the ground to receive the mast. Draw the line BE, Fig. 1, at right angles to the pole, and mark off E at a distance of 7 ft. from B. Now stretch a piece of string from C to E, allowing an extra 24 in. for fastening round the pole and splicing. This will give the measurements for one of the shrouds, and as there will be six of these and a stay of similar length, calculations must be made accordingly.

Two-inch rope will prove suitable for the rigging, and a pound of rope (about six feet) can be purchased for sixpence. A finer line for the signal halliards must also be procured, the required length being double the distance from D to B, *i.e.* 72 ft.

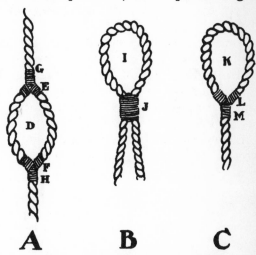

Having obtained the rope, measure off two pieces for a couple of shrouds, each piece being the length of the string stretched from C to E, Fig. 1. At one end of each of these ropes unravel a length of about twelve inches. Then lay these two unravelled ends together, and twist the separate strands of each in such a manner that a loop is made, large enough to go round the mast above the knees at C.

FIG. 2.—Methods of Splicing the Shrouds.

At the ends E and F of the loop D—A, Fig. 2—the remainders of the strands must be forced in and out of the unwound rope, and "served" in the following manner:—

Starting from about a couple of inches above the joint at G, wind thin twine very tightly and evenly down and over the branches of the joint, cutting it short when finished and forcing the end beneath some of the winding. The joint at F must be similarly treated from H, and the serving can then be tarred as a preservative against the ravages of the weather.

Now measure out two lengths on the remainder of the supply of rope, each length equal to two of the shrouds, *i.e.* twice the length from C to E, Fig. 1.

Bend each of these double shrouds in the centre, and bind them as shown at J in Fig. 2, B, making the loop I large enough to pass round the mast as before. When both the double shrouds have been treated in the same way, only the stay remains to be made. The end of this must terminate in an eye-splice, as seen at C, Fig. 2, which can be made in the following manner :—

The end of the rope is bent round to a sufficient length to allow of 6 in. or 7 in. more than the amount required to pass round the mast. Then the strands in the portion of the main rope, M, above the eye K are forced apart with an iron point, and the unravelled ends are

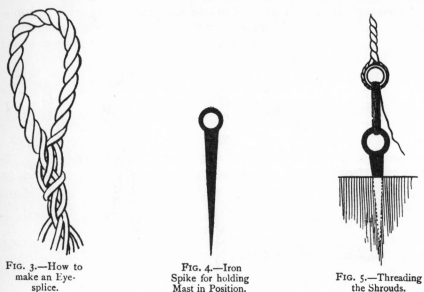

FIG. 3.—How to make an Eye-splice.

FIG. 4.—Iron Spike for holding Mast in Position.

FIG. 5.—Threading the Shrouds.

woven into these strands as shown in Fig. 3. The joint at L must then be served and tarred as in the other splices.

The rigging, being thus completed, should now be fitted on the mast above the knees, the cut-spliced shrouds, A, Fig. 2, being placed first, then the two double shrouds, and the stay last of all.

A truck, or circular piece of wood containing a little pulley wheel called a sheave, can be purchased for about a shilling, and should be fastened to the top of the mast, the signal halliards being threaded over the sheave.

The next thing to be done is to dig the hole, 4 ft. deep, in which to step the mast. When this hole is ready, sink the mast into it and press the earth in very tightly all around, so that the flagstaff will stand quite firm.

Stout iron spikes 3 ft. long, shown in Fig. 4, should now be driven into the ground, three on each side of the mast and at a distance of 7 ft.

The ends of the shrouds and of the stay must be spliced round thimbles, or concave rings of iron, in the manner depicted in Fig. 5. The method of doing this is similar to that employed in making the eye-splice, the only difference being that the loop must fit tightly round the thimble.

Tie the end of a piece of stout line to one of the spikes, and thread this line backwards and forwards through one of the shroud

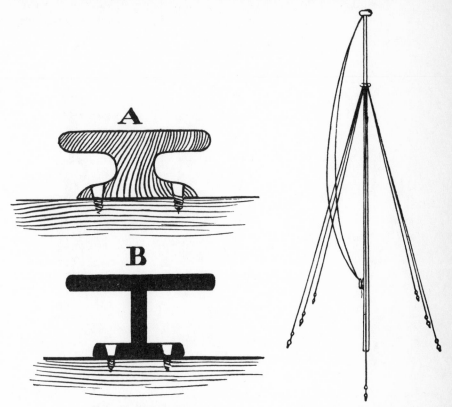

FIG. 6.—The Cleats.   FIG. 7.—Flagstaff complete.

thimbles and the eye as shown in Fig. 5, until the shroud is drawn taut and secured to the spike in the ground. Treat the remainder of the shrouds and the stay in a similar manner, thus fastening the flagstaff in a perfectly upright position.

Nothing now remains but to screw cleats to the mast at a convenient height from the ground. These cleats can be procured either of wood, as shown in section A, Fig. 6, or of iron, as in B, Fig. 6, and the lines of the signal halliards are lashed to them when the flag is floating.

A glance at Fig. 7 will show the flagstaff complete and ready for hoisting the colours. Inland, there are few restrictions as to what flags may be floated, but when the staff is close to the seashore, no flags should be hoisted that may be taken by passing ships for code signals, since serious trouble might be caused if such a mistake were made.

CHAPTER IX

AN AUTOMATIC FOUNTAIN

FOR THE HOME

THE sight of thousands of glistening drops of water lightly tossed into the hot summer air, and the soothing "splish, splash" as they descend to unite once again, cannot fail to exert a cooling and refreshing effect upon the most indifferent onlooker. Yet very few realise that, with a little pleasant labour, we may provide ourselves with such an interesting addition to the home.

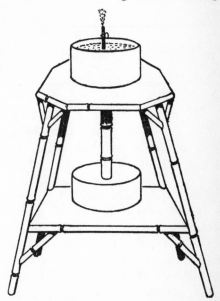

FIG. I.—The Automatic Fountain.

The object of the next few pages is, therefore, to describe the most practical way of making a small fountain, Fig. I, suitable for use in drawing-room or conservatory.

At first sight the article when finished appears to be an artistic flower-stand and fish-bowl combined, but the turning of a tap sets the fountain in motion, causing a small jet of sparkling water to rise to a height of 15 in., and then, breaking into countless drops, to descend into a bowl of gold fish surrounded by cool-looking ferns.

Since the construction of such a fountain may be divided into two distinct parts, the materials required naturally fall under two heads, *viz.*, those necessary for the stand and those required for the making and fitting of two cylindrical zinc tanks which form the fountain proper. The stand consists chiefly of wood and bamboo, of which the following quantities will be required.

WOOD.—1 board, 6 in. by 9 in. by 1 in. . costing about 8d.

BAMBOO (in the form of rods)—

2 rods of 1½ in. diameter . .	„	„	8d.
2 rods of 1¼ in. diameter . .	„	„	6d.
1 rod of 2 in. diameter . . .	„	„	6d.
(or smaller piece, say 2 in. if possible)			
2 rods of ½ in. diameter . . .	„	„	4d.

In the case of the tanks, the materials are more numerous and somewhat more costly, although not beyond the reach of the average

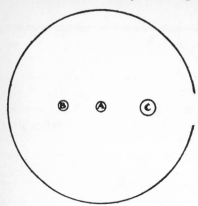

FIG. 2.—The Holes in the Upper Disc.

boy's pocket-money. The first purchase must be the zinc, and much time and trouble will be avoided by buying the metal cut to the required shapes and sizes. For this reason you must obtain four circular discs, each of 10-in. diameter, together with two rectangular strips each measuring 32 in. by 8 in.

With regard to the discs, it is necessary to have holes punched in three of them, and thus the reader must obtain a clear idea as to the position and purpose of these holes.

A glance at Fig. 2, which illustrates the top disc of the upper tank, shows that there must be a central hole, A, of $\frac{1}{2}$ in. diameter, with a similar hole, B, 1 in. to the left, to take the overflow pipe. Then, $2\frac{1}{2}$ in. to the right of the central hole, must be punched one of $\frac{5}{8}$ in. diameter, capable of taking the filler, which will be soldered into it later.

Now, since the holes in the bottom of the upper tank correspond in size and position to those in the top of the lower tank, it is only necessary to describe the punching of one of these discs.

Two holes of $\frac{1}{2}$ in. diameter, placed $\frac{1}{2}$ in. apart, are all that are needed, since one will take the overflow pipe, whilst the other serves for the air pipe. The

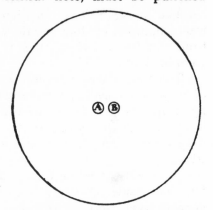

FIG. 3.—Method of Punching Lower Disc.

fourth disc, forming the bottom of the lower tank, for the present needs no holes whatever. Zinc, such as is required for these tanks, is usually sold at the rate of 4s. 6d. per piece of 24 square feet; 2s. should cover the cost of both material and labour in cutting and punching it.

Lead piping of $\frac{1}{2}$ in. diameter will also be necessary, and 5 feet of this, costing about 2d. per foot, should prove sufficient.

A small tap, suitable for drawing off water, must also be purchased. This, if new, will cost about 6d., although an equally serviceable article may often be obtained from a second-hand stall for about half that sum.

The purchases are not yet complete, for you have now to provide yourself with a jet capable of being turned on or off. The hole of this jet should be as fine as possible; indeed, it should be capable of just taking a thin needle. Such jets are often to be seen in tobacconists, where they are used to supply a tiny flame for the convenience of matchless customers. Although, of course, they cannot be obtained from this source, the reader will be able to form an idea of the kind of jet required.

Nothing more remains to be obtained but $\frac{1}{2}$ in. of brass filler with screw cap. This must be soldered into $1\frac{1}{2}$ in. of brass tube of $\frac{5}{8}$ in. diameter, so that the total length of the filler is just 2 in.

With the above-mentioned materials at hand, you are now in a position to commence the more interesting work of construction, the first step in which is the making of the stand.

THE STAND

The stand, 2 ft. 9 in. high, consists simply of an overlapping top supported by four stout bamboo legs in which is fixed, 9 in. from the floor, a shelf; the whole being decorated where required with bamboo.

The top of the stand is the first part to be made, and consists of a square formed by battening together two boards, each 18 in. by 9 in. It should be here stated that considerable importance is attached to the shape of the battens, which must be similar in shape, dimension, and position, to those shown by the dotted lines in Fig. 4.

It now becomes necessary to pencil several guiding lines on the top thus made. Starting from the corners, after drawing the diagonals, points should be made 4 in. from each, and joined. By sawing off the corners thus marked, AB, Fig. 4, the top becomes octagonal in shape, presenting a better appearance than if it had been left square.

Placing the point of a compass at the intersection of the diagonals, C, describe a circle of 5-in. radius, thus indicating the position which the tank will take later.

Holes to receive the legs of the stand may now be bored, and since their exact position is of some importance, a study of Fig. 4, where they are shown at DDDD, should be made. In boring these

holes, they should be allowed to slope gently outwards, thereby allowing for the spreading of the legs.

Having accounted for these four holes, next bore in the centre
of the pencilled circle a hole of 1½ in. radius, the purpose of this
becoming apparent later. The cutting and fixing of the four legs
might now claim your attention, and as each is a 2 ft. 9 in. rod
of bamboo, you should be able to cut two from each 6-foot rod.
Having ascertained that they are all of the correct length, fix them in
the four holes made to receive them. When sure that they are just

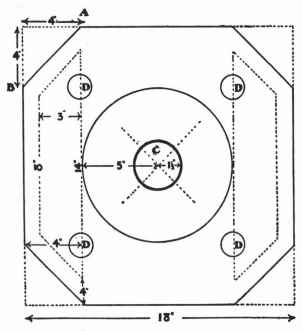

FIG. 4.—The Top of the Stand.

flush with the top, permanently fix them with glue. A 2½ in. nail,
driven from underneath, through each leg into the batten ensures
rigidity, and having filled the open bamboo ends with 2-in. wooden
plugs well glued in, you may turn your attention to the shelf.

The shelf, unlike the top, is a square obtained by battening together
two boards, each 18 in. by 9 in. by 1 in. In this case the battens are
of no particular shape, the only restriction being that they are to be
set back at least 1 in. from all edges.

It is next necessary to mark off from each corner a quadrant of a
circle of ¾ in. radius, Fig. 5, thus enabling the legs, when these pieces
have been removed, to fit flatly against the shelf when it is fixed in
position. Before doing this, however, you must pencil from the

centre two circles, one of 5 in. and the other of 2 in. radius. The smaller circle must then be cut out by means of a keyhole saw; the pencilled circle being left as a guide for the placing of the tank.

This shelf must first be put in position between the legs, 9 in. from the ground, and then firmly secured by two nails driven through

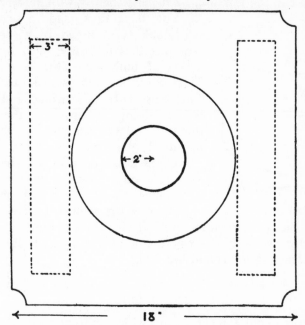

FIG. 5.—Method of Cutting the Shelf.

each leg into its edges. With the stand thus completed, attention must be turned to

THE CYLINDRICAL TANKS

Since it is proposed to utilise the upper of these tanks for the double purpose of a fish-bowl and water-tank, its construction differs slightly from that of the lower vessel.

Taking the wider metal strip, 32 in. by 8 in., lightly pencil a line parallel with its top edge, and 3 in. away from it, Fig. 6. Then, with this as the inner side, curl the strip round in the manner depicted in Fig. 7,

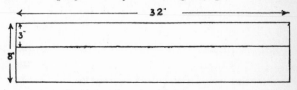

FIG. 6.—Method of Marking the Zinc.

letting one end overlap until the circles formed are just capable of taking the discs which are to form the top and bottom of the tank.

Having thoroughly soldered the overlapping parts, take one of the discs and press it up from underneath until it is level with the pencilled line, when it may also be soldered to the encircling band. Next fit in the bottom disc flush with the bottom of the band, and, having ascertained that the hole for the overflow pipe is in line with the corresponding hole in the top disc, fix it permanently with solder.

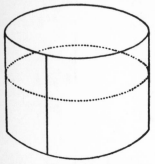

FIG. 7.—Tank made of Zinc.

You have thus made a perfectly airtight tank surmounted by a suitable fish-bowl, so that the easier work of providing a second tank may now be commenced. This work is very similar to the last, consisting only of curling and fastening the remaining zinc strip, and then soldering the top and bottom discs in their places just inside the rim.

These tanks have now to be placed in their respective positions on the stand made to receive them. For this purpose the two pencilled circles on the top and on the shelf will serve as guides.

If the tanks be placed over these circles, they may be kept stationary by nailing to the woodwork of the stand pliable pieces of thin cane closely fitted round the tanks.

THE PIPING

All is now ready for the piping which is to connect the top with the bottom tank. A glance at Fig. 8 shows that two such pipes have to be arranged ; one, AB, being termed the overflow pipe, whilst the other, CD, may be called the air-pipe. Since holes have already been made to carry these pipes through the tanks, very little difficulty should be experienced in getting them into position. The overflow pipe must be fixed first, by pushing the five-foot length of tubing through the proper holes in the upper tank until it reaches the lower vessel, which it must enter by the proper opening until it is within one inch of the bottom. The piping, A, should then be cut off $1\frac{1}{2}$ in. above the upper tank, and soldered at each hole through which it has passed.

The remaining length of piping will be used for the air-pipe, CD, which is pushed from underneath the upper tank until it touches its top. It is then cut so that it is just long enough to touch the bottom tank, after which a point is marked $\frac{1}{4}$ in. from the lower end. The piece must then be drawn down until $\frac{1}{4}$ in. of piping has entered the lower tank, in which position the pipe can be carefully soldered at all the points of entry.

In soldering to the top tank it will become necessary to raise the metal work a little above the stand, thus affording easy access to the part to be soldered. There yet remains to be fixed a pipe, EF, capable of taking the jet for the fountain. This is provided by placing

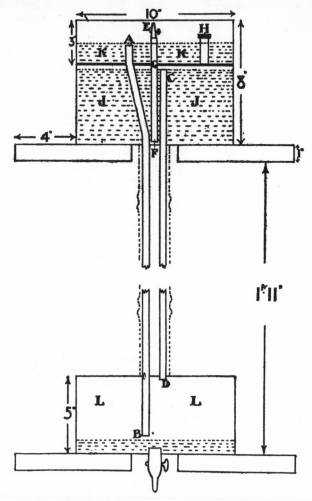

FIG. 8.—A Sectional View of the Fountain.

the remainder of the piping through the central hole, G, in the top tank, and, having pushed it to the bottom of this tank, marking the point of entrance. This done, draw it up a distance of ¼ in., and, having allowed another 2 in. to project above the top of the tank, solder the tube in position. It is the work of a few moments to fix the jet firmly into the open end.

Yet another hole in the top tank remains to be explained. This was made to take the filler, a piece of brass tubing 2 in. long, $\frac{5}{8}$ in. in diameter, surmounted by a screw cap, H, Fig. 8. When this has been soldered in, you must fix a tap into the lower tank in order that it may be emptied when necessary. For this purpose, it will be recalled, a circular hole of 2-in. radius was made in the shelf. By cutting in the bottom of the lower tank a hole large enough to take the tap, this last addition may be soldered into place, thus completing, for the time being, the tanks and piping.

DECORATION

Attention may now be turned to the final step in the construction—the decoration. The edges of the top and shelf present a very bare and unfinished appearance, and this defect may be remedied by enclosing them in pieces of bamboo. Thus, in dealing with the top you have to cut from your rods of $1\frac{1}{4}$ in. bamboo eight pieces, which, when their ends have been mitred, will just fit the eight edges of the top. You must then split from each of these, after the manner described in Chap. XXIV., page 205, the one-third required to make them fit over the edges.

When all are ready, fix them on their respective sides and firmly nail them into position.

After treating the shelf in a similar manner, set to work on the brackets which do so much to strengthen and ornament the article. For this purpose cut sixteen 6-in. lengths from the $\frac{1}{2}$ in. bamboos, and, having bevelled their ends to fit nicely across the corners, fix them by nails driven through their extremities.

It will probably have occurred to the reader that the lead pipes which form the connection between the two tanks, being in such a conspicuous position, not only detract from the artistic appearance of the fountain, but also reveal to uninitiated eyes the secrets of its working, and for these reasons it would be advisable to adopt some means of hiding them. Doubtless many methods of overcoming this difficulty will suggest themselves, but for those who can contrive no better plan, the following is suggested.

From your rod of 2-in. bamboo cut a length just sufficient to cover the offending pipes. This length must then be carefully split down the middle, and all joints removed by means of a sharp chisel.

Then, taking the two halves, fit them together over the pipes, and, having assured yourself that they fit quite tightly, glue them together. In this manner, besides concealing the pipes, the bamboo rod gives the appearance of a strong central support.

In spite of the decorative appearance of the bamboo, there are still parts of the fountain which offend the eye by reason of their unfinished appearance, and for this cause it would be advisable to paint, not only all bare woodwork, but also the zinc of the tanks. This will prove of great advantage, for not only will it render the fountain more in keeping with other articles of furniture, but it also preserves the woodwork from the effects of the water which, from time to time, is sure to be spilled over it.

In choosing the paint you would do well to select a shade of brown to tone with the colour of the bamboo. When the paint is dry, the whole article should receive a coat of varnish, thus enabling it to be cleaned when occasion requires.

How to Make the Fountain Work

The first care must be to ascertain that the taps of both the jet and the outlet are turned off. Having assured yourself that this is so, unscrew the filler top, and, by means of a small funnel, pour water into the upper tank. The liquid will rise, of course, until it reaches the top of the air-pipe, CD, Fig. 8, and will then begin to flow down this pipe into the tank below. Directly the sound of trickling water is heard in the lower tank, it is time to cease pouring and to screw on the filler top very tight.

The upper tank is now almost full of water, above which is a layer of air. Leaving the tank thus, pour water into the fish-bowl. Here the water will rise until it reaches the top of the overflow pipe, AB, when, passing down this pipe, it will enter the lower tank. The entrance of this water from above has the effect of compressing the air in the lower vessel, and water should be poured into the fish-bowl until the air is thus compressed, and will allow no more water to enter the lower tank.

When this becomes apparent, you know that all is ready for the fountain to play. By turning on the jet tap, you cause a small column of sparkling water to be thrown into the air.

Provided the instructions here given have been carefully carried out, the fountain should play continuously for at least two hours before it needs refilling. When undertaking this latter operation, a large bowl must be placed beneath the shelf, and then, by turning the tap, the water can be run off which has been transferred from the upper to the lower vessel.

Why the Fountain Works

How are you going to account for this automatic action? The whole secret is explained if it be remembered that the water from the upper tank and fish-bowls is used to compress the air in the lower tank. Let us see exactly how this is brought about. A glance at Fig. 8 once more will serve to explain the mystery.

You already know that the water, entering the upper tank by the filler, at last reaches the top of the air-pipe, and there stops, thus allowing for a layer of air above its surface.   Then, when the liquid is poured into the fish-bowl, it rises until, reaching the overflow pipe, it finds its way into the lower tank, where the air at last becomes so compressed that no more water can enter. At the same time increased pressure is exerted on the air in the tube, CD, and also on the air above the water in the upper tank. This air, in turn, increases the pressure on the water, and, as its only outlet is by the jet EF, the liquid is ready, directly the tap is turned on, to issue forth as a tiny column.   After reaching a height of about 15 in., the column breaks into countless drops, descending into the fish-bowl. Here the extra water is carried away by the overflow pipe into the lower tank, thus keeping the air in that vessel compressed. In this way the action is continued until all the water in the upper tank has been replaced by air from the lower, and then it is that the fountain ceases to play.

Before the fountain can again be set in motion, it is necessary to empty the lower tank, fill the upper, and proceed as previously described. It can easily be seen that, provided the work of construction has been accurately carried out, such an article not only affords considerable amusement, but may be utilised as an admirable means of displaying ferns and flowers to the best advantage.

CHAPTER X

HOW TO MAKE A MODEL OPERA-HOUSE

THE CHARM OF THE FOOTLIGHTS

THERE must really be some very subtle charm in the glare of the footlights! If there were not, how is it that the fascinating little lady seen in the first illustration finds herself irresistibly compelled to whirl around, as though the motion of her body were seeking to ex-

FIG. 1.—The Ballet Queen on the Stage.

press the happiness of her heart? Yet dance she will; and since such a very delightful young person is not to be denied, no time should be lost in setting to work and making a theatre in which she can exhibit to an admiring audience the nimbleness of her limbs.

The Ballet Queen herself demands attention first, and, as the whole success of the piece depends upon her performance, great care must be exercised in constructing her neatly.

Obtain from the chemist twenty-five artificial straws, the cost of which will be but a few pence, and cut them into lengths of 7 in. To each of these straws glue a triangle, cut out of stiff writing-paper, measuring 7 in. by 3 in., as seen in Fig. 2.

Having put these triangles aside whilst the glue is hardening, take a smooth drawing-board and describe a circle 9 in. in diameter, indicated by the dotted line, Fig. 3. Then trim the edges of a flat cork, such as the stopper of a magnesia bottle, into the bevel shown in B, Fig. 3. Run a strong hat-pin A through the centre of this cork and drive it securely into the centre of the circle marked upon the board, being very careful to see that the pin is absolutely perpendicular.

The ends of the straws to which the paper triangles have been

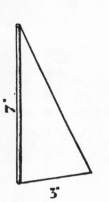

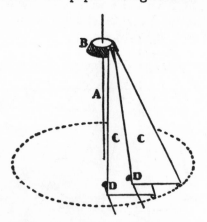

FIG. 2.—The First Stage of the Skirt.   FIG. 3.—Second Stage in Skirt-making.

fixed must now be glued to the bevelled edges of the cork in such a manner that the other extremities of the straws rest on the circumference of the circle a little more than 1 in. apart, as depicted in CC, Fig. 3. Whilst the glue is hardening, the free ends of the triangles should be kept in place by pins, DD.

When the glue is quite hard, withdraw the hat-pin, replacing it by a stout pin, which should be securely fastened in its place with sealing-wax.

MAKING THE BALLET QUEEN

Having thus made the dancer's skirts, the next thing to be done is to construct her body, and for this an egg must be blown by boring a hole with a pin at each end. The empty egg-shell can then be fastened in position upon the cork as shown in Fig. 4, sealing-wax being the best substance to use for this purpose.

For the arms and head, suitable portions of fashion plates should be mounted on post-cards and cut out, being fixed to the egg-shell body with glue or sealing-wax. The backs of the arms will have to be painted in naturally, whilst the back of her head can be coloured to match the locks which cluster about her forehead.

The Ballet Queen is now complete, and may be placed on the base of an inverted tumbler or wine-glass in such a way that her skirts surround the bowl, whilst the pin in the centre of the cork rests upon

FIG. 4.—The Ballet Queen.

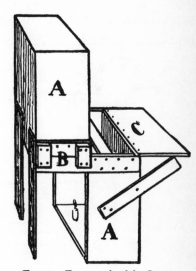

FIG. 5.—Framework of the Stage.

the foot of the glass. A slight touch of the hand will make her revolve quite naturally and freely.

THE STAGE

The next thing to be constructed is the stage, which can be very simply made from the two soap-boxes seen at AA, Fig. 5.

Take one of these boxes and remove one side, nailing in its place a thin strip of wood 3 in. wide, as shown in the lower box, Fig. 5. Then nail or screw a long strip of wood, B, to each end, and fasten the other box upon the supports thus formed, as depicted in the illustration, making a couple of legs to keep the whole contrivance steady.

When the side which was removed has been fixed as a shelf at the front C, supported by two wooden brackets, the fabric of the Opera-House will be complete.

The stage itself must now be adorned with a hood and wings. Cut these from some bright-coloured cardboard—red, for example—and

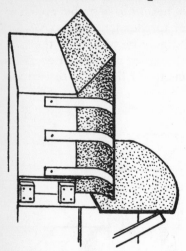

tack the pieces to the inside of the upper box, securing them with strips of card similar to those shown in the side view, Fig. 6. A stage of thick card must also be made, considerably larger than the shelf and curved artistically in front, as illustrated in Fig. 7, which depicts the finished front of the stage.

The making of the scenery is quite simple, and most effective results can be produced with very little trouble. To make a background similar to that shown in Fig. 8, it is only necessary to paste some deep-blue paper against the back and both sides of the stage, and cut the range of hills in outline from

FIG. 6.—Side-wings of Opera-house.

some paper of a darker shade, pasting them in position.

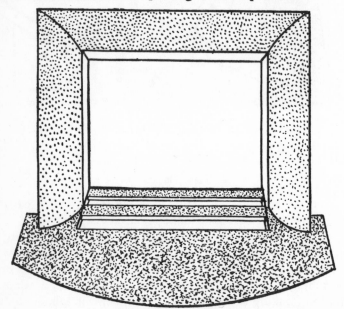

FIG. 7.—The Stage Front.

Stage trees can be made of thick cardboard painted a dark green, and must be glued inside the wings on either side, as shown in Fig. 8, whilst the floor, including the strip of wood already nailed in position, must be covered with paper of the same colour as the stage itself. When this is completed the Opera-House is ready for a performance.

Place three or four stumps of candles in the lower box beneath the strip of wood, Fig. 4, but do not light these until the last moment.

Now set the dancer upon the glass, and place them both on the wooden strip in the stage, first giving the figure a gentle touch to see that it revolves freely. Having extinguished the lights in the

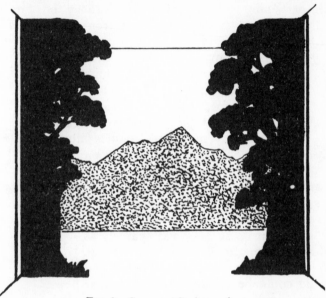

FIG. 8.—Scenery at Background.

room, put a match to the candles ; the hot air arising from them will act on the skirt of the Ballet Queen and make her revolve with a speed that the nimblest of *coryphées* might well envy.

As many figures may be introduced as the stage will hold, and, to improve the effect, the other dancers can be made to revolve in contrary ways by placing the triangles of paper of which the skirt is made, in reverse directions.

With the addition of a little music from a gramophone, if there be one handy, operatic pieces may be represented in a very realistic and charming manner, and, since the Ballet Queen does not know the meaning of fatigue, she will dance merrily on until the footlights grow dim.

CHAPTER XI

MODEL AIR CRAFT

THE charm pertaining to flying machines—be they actual or model—is undoubtedly real, and exists quite apart from any of that sense of exhibition which belongs to actual flight. Perhaps this is because

FIG. 1.—Primitive Air Propeller.

they convey the idea of the frustration of nature's law of gravitation, by which man has always felt himself curbed, and which to-day frequently gains the upper hand with calamitous results. However, great pleasures involve great risks, and, as a corollary, model aeronautics fail to offer the immense joy of exhilaration. But, on the other hand, they possess the advantages of safety.

The earliest type of flying machine consisted of a two-bladed tin propeller spun on a frame by unwinding string, as with a top, and suddenly released. It made its appearance under the name of Maxim's Flying Wonder, but its success was scarcely as wonderful as the name would lead one to expect.

Purchasers, however, soon discovered that a milk-tin lid could be cut into a shape similar to that shown in Fig. 1, and made to revolve rapidly on a string. These spinning frames were adapted after the manner shown in Fig. 2, where A is a silk reel bushed with a tightly-

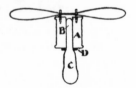

FIG. 2.—Another Form of Air Propeller.

fitting brass tube in its centre hole. Into the top surface of the reel two decapitated French nails are driven. These engage with holes in the tin screw, and the reel is twisted on its spindle, B, by smartly pulling a length of string wound round its circumference. The spindle is provided with a handle, C, and two washers at D, to ease the spinning of the wheel.

DIRIGIBLE AIR SHIPS

Small flying models of dirigible air ships are difficult to design. In the first place it must be understood that a balloon filled with hydrogen gas exerts a lifting effort of ·07 lbs. per cubic foot volume, *i.e.* the difference between the weight of a cubic foot of the gas and of the like quantity of air. Now the load to be lifted by a balloon must include the weight of its silk envelope, and since, for example, for a reduction to half of every dimension, the area (and consequently weight) of the envelope is only quartered, whilst the volume is lessened to one-eighth, it follows that a very small scale model cannot be constructed. As a matter of fact, a specimen of silk weighed $2\frac{1}{4}$ oz. per 16 sq. feet, and with this material the minimum size for an envelope was 6 feet long by 12 in. diameter, cigar-shape. The dissolving of nearly $\frac{3}{4}$ lb. of zinc in dilute spirits of salt would suffice to fill this with hydrogen, the lifting effort of which would be, roughly, 5 oz. Of this weight 3 oz. would be apportioned to the envelope and the remaining 2 oz.

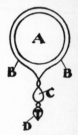

FIG. 3.—Framework for Dirigible.

to the framework supported by two aluminium strips from the balloon and bearing the propeller driven by elastic. It will probably

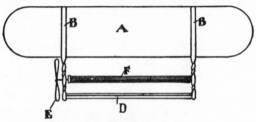

FIG. 4.—Framework for Dirigible.

be found necessary to treat the silk envelope with thin rubber solution (ordinary solution diluted with mineral naphtha), squeezing it carefully afterwards and drying, so as to render the silk less porous. A possible light method of

attaching the framework and motor is shown in Figs. 3 and 4. The aluminium strips, BB, are passed round the balloon, A, and twisted, as at C, to hold the spindle of the propeller, E, whilst it further ends in such a way as to support the T section keel, D. Elastic bands, F, Fig. 4, stretch from the propeller shaft to the farther piece of aluminium, so that when twisted an effective power is given to the propeller.

GLIDERS

The general design for a model air ship of the heavier-than-air type can be arrived at through extensive experiments with gliders. These contrivances, for the reader's better information, comprise a winged structure, which when released from a height does not fall

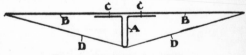

FIG. 5.—The T-Bar in a Glider.

directly to the ground, but descends gracefully at a gentle angle.

One of the simplest of these can be arranged by folding a strip of paper 8 in. by 4 in. in a T-shape, A, Fig. 5, and pinning another strip, B, measuring 7 in. by 2 in. crosswise to CC, with its loose ends restrained

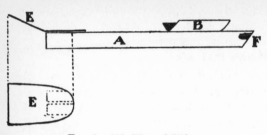

by cotton threads, D, passing through a nick beneath the keel. To the rear end of the T-bar is pinned a smaller piece of paper, E, Fig. 6, at an upward slope, which acts with an elevating effect, when the model is launched downwards, large wings fore-

FIG. 6.—Side View of Glider.

most. The front is weighted with paper fasteners and strips of metal bent double and screwed tightly over the keel, as at F.

ANOTHER MODEL

A more complete model built of cartridge-paper can be seen in Fig. 7. The T mid-frame A of the craft measures $12\frac{1}{2}$ in. long with top 2 in. wide, and keel $1\frac{1}{2}$ in. deep, curved upwards to a point in the front where a small weight, B, of sheet lead is

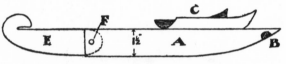

FIG. 7.—Another Model Glider.

squeezed into place. The large wing, C, extends 13 in. across, and is 5 in. wide, being slightly curved, as shown in the figure. Four tags, DDDD, Fig. 8, are formed by cutting slits with a knife so that it may

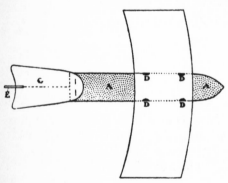

FIG. 8.—Top View of Glider.

slide on the T-bar of the frame. In this way its position is alterable backwards and forwards, so that the best adjustment can be determined by experiment, the front corners being warped upwards to increase the supporting action. At the rear of the craft a tail, E, Figs. 7 and 8, is fixed between the folds of the keel by means of a boot eyelet, F, so that it turns on the latter and serves to keep

the elevator, G, at any required angle. This latter is $3\frac{1}{2}$ in. wide and 6 in. long, and narrows off towards the front. Here it is pinned to the T-bar, whilst its back edge engages with a slot in the tail-piece, so as to be adjustable up and down at different elevating angles.

Twisted india-rubber has been judged the most suitable motive power for model aeroplanes, since it is capable of storing considerable energy, at the same time being very light.

A Hawk Aeroplane

A common flying machine worked by elastics is shown in Fig. 9, and the aerial evolutions of this machine are not unlike those of a hawk. Two small oval blocks of wood, A, B, shown in section at O, are spaced apart by means of the two square pillars, C and D, which

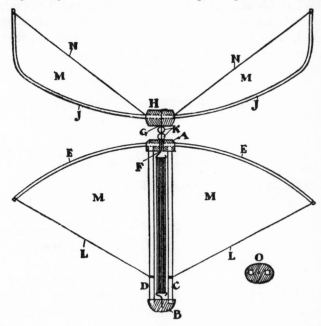

Fig. 9.—A Hawk Aeroplane.

are glued into the holes in A and B. When dry another hole is bored right across A to accommodate the strip of cane, EE, whilst the hole, F, must be made thin and smooth to take the wire spindle, G. The outer end of this spindle is fixed into the cork, H, through which another strip of cane, JJ, is passed, whilst two glass beads shown at K serve to facilitate and smooth the running. The holes should both be blackleaded.

In the wood block, B, another wire hook is fixed, and between this and the hook in the end of the spindle several endless bands of elastic are stretched—the tension not being very great. The more numerous and thinner these bands the better will the machine work. The cane strip, E, is bent round at either side and held to the wood rods, CD, by the threads, LL. The spaces, MM, thus formed are covered with very thin tissue paper—Japanese rice paper being the best for the purpose—which is gummed in place with overlapping edges. Similarly the cane strip, JJ, is curved by means of the threads, NN, the spaces between being covered with tissue paper as before.

The propeller thus formed is wound up about fifty times, and the machine launched in mid-air, where it will continue to support itself until the energy of the elastic is abated. The proportions of the figure are sufficiently accurate to be taken as working measurements, but the chief *desideratum* is lightness, and wherever an opportunity of clipping off unnecessary wood occurs, this should be done, *e.g.* the rods C and D could be grooved with the point of a penknife along the inner edges without reducing their strength.

A Larger Aeroplane

A design for a larger and more realistic aeroplane, one, moreover, which could make a decided flight at its first launch, is given in Figs. 10, 11, and 12. Two spars, A, which run the whole length of the machine, are made of bamboo 2 feet long and $\frac{5}{8}$ in. wide, smoothed by scraping and sand-

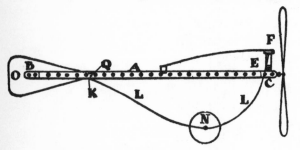

FIG. 10.—Elevation of large Aeroplane.

papering, and drilled with $\frac{1}{4}$ in. holes at distances of 1 inch. When they are screwed to the sides of the blocks, B, C, the cross plane spar is bound in place with carpet thread, and a piece of corset whalebone, E, is fixed to C, with two small screws. To this the front cross spar, F, is tied at GG, Figs. 11 and 12, being thus raised two inches above the frame, and the plane frame is then completed by binding curved ties of cane, HH, Fig. 11, to the extremities

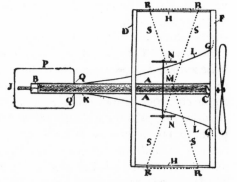

FIG. 11.—Plan of Aeroplane.

of the spars. It is lastly covered with silk, cut slightly large to allow for hemming, and sewn over at its edges to the spars.

Three extra strips of whalebone or cane, somewhat longer than the width of the plane, are sprung into place beneath the silk, thus maintaining it curved like the end braces, HH. A strip of cane some 40 in. long and $\frac{1}{4}$ in. wide by $\frac{1}{8}$ in. thick is split for 22 in. of its length, and the fork is bound to the underside of the bamboo spars at K. The two prongs are curved round as shown at LL, and bound to the front spar at GG, where the whalebone is jointed. A short length of steel wire, M, is bound across the prongs at their lowest part in order to form the spindle for two wheels, NN. These wheels can be made by cutting $\frac{1}{4}$ in. slices from a cork

bung and bushing a hole in the centre of each with brass tubing, whilst a glass bead placed on either side before slipping on the projecting end of the spindle and bending the latter outside all, will keep the wheels in position and allow of easy running. The unsplit portion of the cane beyond K should be whittled down to $\frac{1}{8}$ in. square and then bent as indicated at O, the free end being bound to the top of the frame above K. It must be understood that where one binding, as in this case, and also at GG on the plane spar in the front, will serve to keep three or four members together, it must be used in preference to two on the score of lightness.

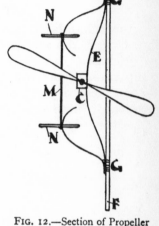

FIG. 12.—Section of Propeller End of Aeroplane.

The cane framework, O, is covered very tightly with silk in the same manner as the main plane. A piece of aluminium wire must be bent to the shape shown in P, and its ends passed through the holes, QQ, and bent over. The end, J, should press on the back edge of the cane framework, O, so that when P is covered with silk on either side of the vertical plane O, it can be moved up or down at any required angle, and will keep in that position by friction.

The propeller can best be cut and shaved down with an even pitch for both blades, from a solid piece of wood 12 in. long. The section measurements could be $1\frac{1}{2}$ in. by 1 in. A boss of wood is left in the centre of the propeller for attachment to the wire spindle, which passes through a smooth hole in C—one or two beads being threaded between the block and the propeller. The wire is bent into as wide a hook as possible between the two bamboo spars of the frame, and endless lengths of thin rubber are crammed on between this hook and that fixed in the back block, B. The elastic should be cut in double lengths, so that when each two ends are bound together, the endless bands so formed stretch lightly between the two hooks.

If, when the propeller is wound up, the bamboo frame tends to bend in any way it can be strengthened by tying tiny cross-pieces beneath the spars at the weakest places. A last refinement to the machine is the drilling of two small holes, RR, in each of the ties, HH, and threading through these a long piece of twine above the silk, according to the dotted lines S. It should only pass the holes with difficulty, and be tied after threading to make it endless, so that by its agency one side of the plane can be warped more than the other, and the machine thus balanced or given a slightly curved path.

YET ANOTHER AEROPLANE

There has been much discussion in "flying circles" as to the respective merits and demerits of the bi-plane and mono-plane types of machine. But without entering upon a lengthy and technical comparison of the two, we will straightway pick upon the bi-plane as best deserving of our attention as model-makers. It may be mentioned, however, that one of the main reasons for this choice is that the "double-decker" looks so much more impressive in flight

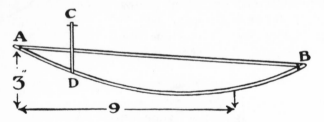

FIG. 13.—Runner for Model Aeroplane.

than does its smaller brother, the mono-plane, and in this direction shows a better return for the labour the model-maker expends upon it.

The materials necessary for the model are both simple and inexpensive, the principal object being to combine lightness with strength and durability.

The first thing required is an ordinary penny cane, and this must be carefully split into strips of about ¼ in. wide. Take two of these strips, and, after cutting them to the length of 16 in., bend them to the shape shown by ADB, Fig. 13. This bend may be much more easily and permanently made if the cane be held to the spout of a boiling kettle.

To strengthen these "runners," as the two bent canes are technically termed, take a couple more strips, and, by the aid of brass pins or small brads, nail them into the position shown by AB, Fig. 13. To make the joints more secure, it is advisable to bind them with thin but strong twine, afterwards coating them with glue or gum.

THE PLANES

This is made of American whitewood, $\frac{1}{16}$ in. thick—obtainable at any dealers in fretwood. Its measurements are 11 in. long and 1½ in. wide, and by being steamed with the kettle—similarly to the cane—the back edge must be given a slight downward droop, Fig. 14. Then round off the corners nicely, and give the surface a thorough sand-papering. This done, the front plane is ready for attachment to the

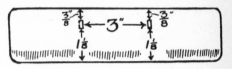

FIG. 14.—The Front Plane.

framework by means of two pieces of cane 1¾ in. long, generally termed "struts." One of these is fixed into position on each of the two "runners" (by pins, brads, or twine binding) as shown at CD, Fig. 13. Then cut two small slots in the front plane, Fig. 14, afterwards fixing it into position upon the framework by forcing the extremities of the two cane "struts" into these slots C, Fig. 13.

Fig. 15 presents a front view of the "runners" and plane, and also indicates how the whole thing must be further strengthened by

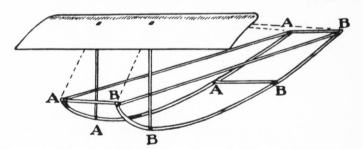

FIG. 15.—Runners and Front Plane with Bottom Struts.

bottom struts AB, connecting the two runners. Four pieces of twine should also be carried from the top of the two upright struts to the ends of the runners, as illustrated by the dotted lines.

The back planes now claim our attention. First select a strip of cane 26 in. long. Measure off 2½ in. at each end. Then, by means of the steaming kettle, bend these ends at right angles, as shown in Fig. 16. Another piece of cane, 21 in. long, also illustrated in the diagram, must now be fixed to the bent ends by means of two small tin joints, one of which is illustrated in Fig. 17. They are made in the following manner :—

First cut a piece of tin to the shape shown by A, Fig. 17, and bend

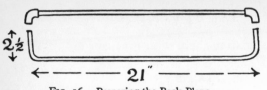

FIG. 16.—Preparing the Back Plane.

it at right angles along the dotted line. Then, with a pair of pliers, clamp the tin tags firmly round the ends of the canes, as indicated by B, Fig. 17.

When the two joints have been satisfactorily made, the result will

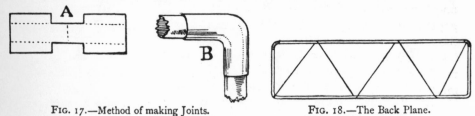

FIG. 17.—Method of making Joints.   FIG. 18.—The Back Plane.

be an oblong framework similar to that illustrated by Fig. 18. This must be additionally strengthened by cross-ties of twine, as shown in the diagram.

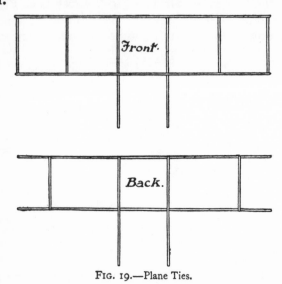

FIG. 19.—Plane Ties.

A second framework, exactly similar to that described above, must next be made.

This accomplished, the two frames are to be fixed together, one above the other. This is done by means of ten "plane ties"—six for the front and four for the back, Fig. 19. These "ties" merely consist of strips of cane, six being 2¾ in. long, and the remaining four 5 in. in length.

The method of securing each "tie" into position is illustrated in Fig. 20:—A piece of fine flower wire is first bound round the end of the "tie" and then carried tightly round the cane of the framework. The protruding ends of the "ties" must be cut off flush with the top of the framework.

The top and bottom frames are now to be covered with stout tissue paper or fine Japanese silk. The edge of the silk or paper must be wrapped round the cane and then glued or gummed. Care should be

FIG. 20.—The Method of securing Ties.

taken that this is executed neatly, or the result will be a thick and untidy "cutting edge" and a consequent erratic flight of the finished model.

It is a good plan to damp slightly the tissue paper or silk before stretching it over the frames. This damping causes the material to slacken somewhat. Then, when it dries and shrinks, the covering will be taut.

FIXING THE BACK PLANES

Our next task is to fix the completed back planes to the rest of the model. This does not present much difficulty. It is accomplished by means of the four long "ties" protruding from the centre

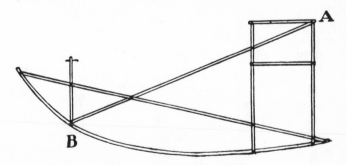

FIG. 21.—Fixing the Back Plane.

of the planes. These are forced over the back portion of the main framework, as illustrated in the sectional view, Fig. 21, and then bound tightly into position with thread.

For additional strength, two long pieces of cane must next be carried from the back of the plane down to the front of the framework AB, Fig. 21.

In order to complete the model, it is now only necessary to instal the motive power. This consists of a propeller 8¾ in. long, which is driven by means of twisted elastic.

THE PROPELLER

To make the propeller, first procure a piece of American whitewood 8¾ in. long, ¾ in. wide, and about ⅛ in. thick. Then with a sharp pocket-knife, carefully whittle it to the shape shown at A, Fig. 22. This done, the partly finished propeller must be given the correct "twist" or "screw." For this purpose the steaming kettle is again employed.

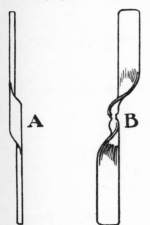

FIG. 22.—The Propeller.

Holding the extreme ends of the propeller in the thumb and forefinger of each hand, permit the jet of steam to play upon the blades at each side of the thick, central portion. When it is judged that the steam has rendered the wood sufficiently supple, turn the right hand slightly outward, and the left hand inward, thus twisting the propeller into the shape shown at B, Fig. 22. This must be done very carefully, so that the twist at one side is exactly equal to that at the other. Otherwise, should there be much discrepancy, the flight of the aeroplane will be as erratic as that of a wild-fowl carrying an overdose of duck-shot.

Having nicely finished off the propeller by sand-papering the rough surface, a slight groove must be cut round the centre to receive the spindle. This consists of a piece of stout wire, one end of which must be wrapped tightly round the propeller in the central groove.

For the propeller bearings cut out a strong piece of tin to the design given in Fig. 23. The two tags, AA, are then clamped by a pair of pliers firmly round the back strut connecting the runners, Fig. 24.

FIG. 23.—Propeller Bearings.

Now obtain a medium-sized glass bead, and slip it on the spindle of the propeller, thrusting this, in turn, through the hole B, Fig. 24, in the bearings just completed. Lastly, bend the extremity of the spindle into a hook.

Now purchase seven or eight strands of catapult elastic, each strand being 12 in. long and $\frac{1}{16}$ in. thick. This can be obtained at most toy-shops, but should the reader experience any difficulty in making his purchase, he should write to Messrs. Gamage, Holborn,

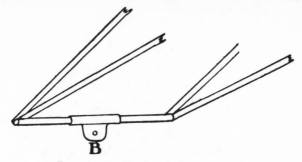

FIG. 24.—The Bearings fixed to Framework.

London, W.C., who stock skeins of elastic, specially prepared for model aeroplanes.

After binding the ends of the elastic firmly together with twine, fasten one extremity to the hook of the spindle. Then carry the other

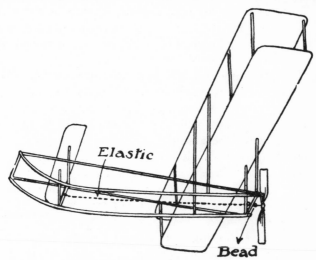

FIG. 25.—The Completed Aeroplane.

end away to the front of the aeroplane, fastening it firmly to the second cross-strut, which must be strengthened if necessary with an additional strut of cane. The complete machine should resemble that shown in Fig. 25.

Our model is at last ready for its initial flight!

With the forefinger of the right hand give the propeller about one hundred turns (in the direction taken by the hands of a clock).   Then, holding the aeroplane well above the head—handling it in the manner shown by Fig. 26—throw it sharply forward in a slightly downward

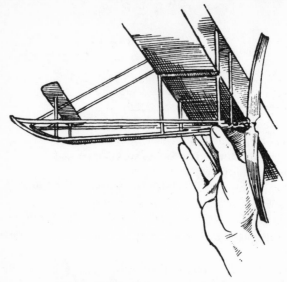

FIG. 26.—How to hold the Aeroplane.

direction.   The little model will at first swoop towards the earth, and then, with propeller merrily buzzing, wing its flight slowly upward and forward.

The model-maker may not be altogether successful at his first trial, but after a time he will be able to launch his little machine on a long and pretty flight.

CHAPTER XII

MODEL BOATS

THERE is much to be said in favour of the paper craft for satisfying the desire every boy experiences to build a ship. They are simply constructed, and no difficulties need arise in carrying out the most extensive naval programme. A plan which was mooted some little time back for rendering these boats water-tight is well worth attention, the idea being to steep them in glue solution coloured yellow by the addition of bichromate of potash. When dried in the sunlight the glue becomes quite insoluble.

FIG. 1.—Paper Boat with Keel.

The provision of cardboard keels, A, Fig. 1, which are weighted, B, with lead glued into the slit beneath the boats renders them very stable, so that it is possible to fit a mast in place and thereon two spars with tissue-paper sails.

A WINDMILL BOAT

A boat propelled by wind power, although without sails, has at least the charm of novelty. The hull itself, Fig. 2, should be carved to shape by means of saw, chisel and plane from a sound piece of 3 in. by 2 in. quartering. When completed it should be floated in water to test its riding powers, and if it floats unevenly, adjustment can be made as required. It must then be dug out carefully with a gouge as thin as possible, except at the stern, where the propeller tube is fitted and the upper edges to which the deck will be screwed.

The keel is of ½ in. wood cut 1 in. deep, and of such length and curve as to continue the lines of the boat when fixed in position by screws from inside the hull. It is also planed bevel, so that whereas the edge next to the boat bottom is ½ in. thick, the lower edge is about ⅜ in.

The mast must be of ash or some other tough wood, and should taper from ½ in. square at the base to ⅜ in. square in a length of 8 in.

A glance at Fig. 2 will now explain the further arrangement of the sailing machinery. Two right-angled brackets, AA, must be fixed at the top and bottom of the mast, and should have two holes, BB, drilled at ¾ in. from the mast. These brackets can be made of stout strips of brass.

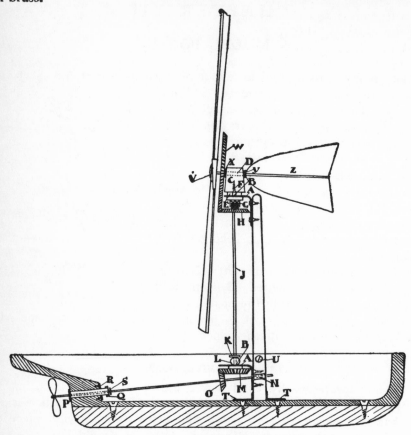

FIG. 2.—A Windmill Boat.

An enlarged view of the mast-head machinery is depicted in Fig. 3, the component parts of which may be described thus :—

C is a round piece of hard wood 1¼ in. deep, in which the hole, D, is bored at a slight tilt and bushed with a tightly-fitting brass tube, the internal bore of which must be ⅛ in. full. Between C and the brass bracket, A, is a washer, E, and a similar washer is placed at the other side of the bracket, separating this latter from the head of the screw, F, upon which the block of wood, C, is pivoted. To this last-mentioned washer is soldered ½ in. tubing, G, which, although not too small for the head of the screw, F, must be of such a size that it will cover the boss of the gear wheel, H, thus forming a bearing for the same.

The gear wheel, H, is mounted upon the vertical shaft of the steel rod, J, to the lower end of which is soldered a washer, K, Fig. 2, before it passes through the drilled ball, L—a friction-saving device— and the lower bracket. Beneath the bracket, on the very end of the shaft, is placed a washer, after which is fastened the bevel wheel, M.

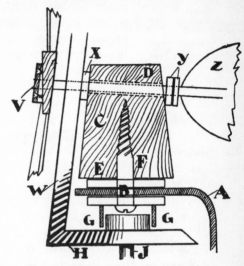

The hole, N, in the mast, which is bushed with brass tube for the propeller shaft, must be bored at a slight angle, and it may be better to hold the mast temporarily in position just forward of the mid-section whilst the place and direction of N is determined, the hole in the boat stern being already bored. If

FIG. 3.—Enlarged View of Sail Machinery.

the shaft is pushed through this latter and then fitted with its gear wheel, O, the direction of N can be easily determined.

In the stern of the boat the propeller shaft passes through $1\frac{1}{2}$ in. of large tube, to the end of which, outside the boat, is soldered a brass cover, P, drilled in its centre to accommodate the shaft. Inside the boat is another cover, Q, which is removable. The tube is kept in position by being soldered to a brass plate, R, through which screws are driven into the hull, whilst the washer, S, keeps the cap, Q, in position. Inside the tube, round the shaft, a thick grease of tallow and blacklead is packed, a water-tight joint being thus ensured.

FIG. 4.—How to secure the Mast.

The lower end of the mast fits into a square socket soldered to metal plates, TT, which are screwed to the bottom of the hull, whilst long screws, U, pass through each side of the boat near the deck and direct into the mast, thus serving to maintain its vertical position as shown in Fig. 4.

The propeller is cut $1\frac{3}{4}$ in. diameter from sheet copper or zinc, in the shape shown in Fig. 5. It must be soldered to the shaft in such a manner that it clears the stern of the boat.

The windmill sails are made from two 14-in. strips of wood cut to the design shown in Fig. 6 (sectional view, Fig. 7), which are mortised

FIG. 5.—The Propeller Blade.

to one another at right angles at their mid-lengths, and then pushed on to the axle. In front is soldered a metal plate, V, Figs. 2 and 3, through which four screws pass into the sails and thus keep them in place. They may also be further secured by stretching a wire and attaching it to the tips of each of the four sails.

Behind the sails is fixed the large bevel gear wheel, W, and a washer, X, after which the axle passes through the tube, D, in the wood block, C. At the other side two washers are placed at Y, after which come the feather, Z, which serves to keep

FIG. 6.—Windmill Sail in Elevation.

the mill opposite the wind. This feather can be cut from sheet metal, and its weight should roughly equal that of the other sails, as this will balance the shaft and save considerable friction.

The deck of the boat must be cut to shape from $\frac{1}{2}$ in. wood and planed down so that its surface is curved, the underneath being cor-

FIG. 7.—Sectional View of Sail.

respondingly hollowed. Square holes should be cut to accommodate the mast and to give an inspection hole for the propeller tube. Hatchway covers can be cut for both of these holes, and arranged to fit tightly.

A rudder can be provided with its post passing perpendicularly through the hull and connected to a tiller of springy metal, whereby it may be adjusted to any required position, Fig. 8.

The boat should be held stern view on, whilst the mill revolves and the propeller's rotation is noted. If its direction be clockwise, the blades must be twisted so that their right-hand edges are turned away from the observer. If they revolve in the reverse direction, the left-hand edges must be turned away.

All that now remains to be done is to tack strips of lead to the edge of the keel until the boat rides steadily, and at this stage comes the recompense for any time spent in hollowing out the hull, for the less this weighs, the more lead may

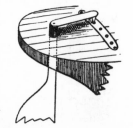

FIG. 8.—The Rudder.

be added, with consequently increased stability. When a couple of coats of paint have been added, the windmill boat is ready to be launched.

CHAPTER XIII

HOW TO MAKE A SUBMARINE BOAT

THE construction of the boat about to be described calls for considerable skill in soldering. The real secret of good soldering is to exercise unstinted care in cleansing the metal, and it should be noted that although scraping with a knife or filing is the best method of cleaning, rubbing with spirits of salt (killed by zinc) is a very good substitute, especially where the surfaces have no awkward corners and are easily accessible.

Two small tin paraffin-oil funnels must be obtained, the inside diameter of which will probably be about 2½ in., whilst a cylinder of sheet tin, 8 in. long, should be made of like diameter.

To the inside of one of the funnels near its tube is soldered a disc of brass, A, Fig. 1, drilled with a ⅛ in. hole in its centre, whilst outside at the end of the tube a threaded brass sleeve, B, is soldered so that the cap, C, may be screwed upon it. This cap C should also be bored with an ⅛ in. hole. Through these bearings passes a straight steel shaft reaching from ½ in. beyond C to the rim of the funnel, and whilst thus placed it is provided with a washer at D. A square piece of

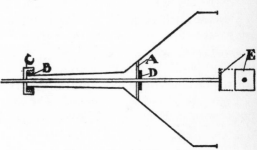

FIG. 1.—Stern of Submarine.

brass, E, is filed until the edges are bevel, and is attached to the shaft.

The funnel is now pushed on to one end of the tin cylinder or shell, Fig. 2, and soldered round. A hole, F, ¼ in. in diameter is cut at one part of the conical surface so that a tin

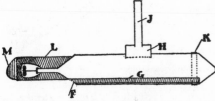

FIG. 2.—The Shell of the Submarine.

cylinder, G, 9 in. by ¼ in. diameter, can pass through and be soldered, whilst its forward end is closed and lies flush with that of the large shell whereto it is likewise soldered.

A round hole must now be cut in the centre of the shell, large enough to accommodate the end of a small condensed milk tin—this forming the conning tower, H. The end of the tin should be cut away in such a manner as to fit the cylindrical form of the shell to which it must be soldered. In the top of the conning tower another hole must be made, and a 6-in. vertical tube, J, about ¾ in. diameter with a closed top, should be soldered thereon.

The clockwork engines of the boat must now be made. Two circles of stout sheet tin, Figs. 3 and 4, should be cut so that they fit readily within the shell. From their circumferences must be cut pieces to clear the small tube, G, Fig. 2, and the inner edges of the conning tower. If the tube and conning tower are correctly placed, a line, PQ, Fig. 3, scratched on the disc from the centre of one gap to the centre of the other should pass through the centre of the disc. Supposing this to be the case, an ⅛ in. hole must be drilled in the centre, and the discs spaced apart and fixed in position by being soldered to the ends of three 7-in. tin strips, shown in dotted line in Fig. 3, and bent L-shape to increase their strength. A straight piece of steel rod passes through the centre holes and outside the disc, Fig. 3, where, after slipping a washer, it is provided with a small pinion, A, from a Dutch clock, whilst inside it has another washer and sleeve, B, Fig. 5, soldered in position. The part which projects beyond the disc shown in Fig. 4 is left long enough to provide a bearing for the

FIG. 3.—Tin Partition.

FIG. 4.—Tin Partition.

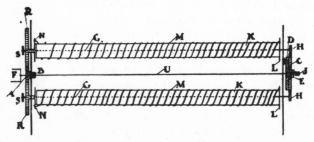

FIG. 5.—The Works of the Submarine.

toothed wheel, C, Figs. 4 and 5, which is provided with a ratchet, D, and a square key shank, E.

The remaining portions of the works will best be understood by a careful examination of Fig. 5, the lettering of which may be explained thus:—

A. Small pinion between the wheels RR. See also Fig. 3.

B. Washer and sleeve fixed at the back of disc depicted in Fig. 3.

C, D, and E. Toothed wheel, ratchet, and key shank, revolving on the centre shaft but not fixed thereto.

F. Square sleeve attached to the central shaft to connect with the propeller.

G. Side shafts.

H. Pinions fixed on the side shafts. Fig. 4.

J. Sleeve on the centre shaft to keep the toothed wheel, C, in place.

K. Tin tube barrels with fixed ends at L. These barrels have spiral springs, M, wound round them. They are soldered to the side shafts, and are therefore fixtures with the pinions, HH.

N. Tin discs to which the other ends of the springs are soldered.

R. Toothed wheels with tube bearings running loose on the side shafts, but having the discs, N, soldered to them

S. Washers on side shafts to keep the wheels, R, in position.

U. The centre shaft.

No measurements are given for the above as they will depend very largely upon the resources of the scrap heap. It may be added that the shaft, U, when pushed forward, connects by means of the sleeve, F, with the propeller, and thus makes this latter revolve.

The funnel, which is to serve for the bow of the boat, must now be dismembered of its tube, and provided with a pointed nose of brass or iron as shown in Fig. 2. It is not soldered to the shell, but remains detachable, in order to allow of winding and oiling the clockwork—the joint being rendered watertight by means of a wide rubber band stretched round the body of the boat, K, Fig. 2.

The propeller tube is packed with a mixture of tallow and black-lead, and the shaft is then fitted with a three-bladed fan, cut from zinc or copper, of about $1\frac{1}{2}$ in. diameter. Its direction of running when the clockwork is set going will have to be noticed, and the blades twisted accordingly. A guard, L, Fig. 2, of sheet metal should then be put in position, and a small rudder, M, attached to this.

The boat can then be floated, the tube, G, Fig. 2, being closed with a cork. The weight of solder is then ascertained which will depress the boat until the conning tower is just above water, and the shell can then be opened and this amount of solder run into place around the tube to form a permanent ballast. All that is necessary to make the boat sink beneath the water until only the top of the vertical tube is showing, is to fill the tube, G, to a greater or less extent with water, and thus increase the specific gravity of the boat.

CHAPTER XIV

A WOODEN "STEAM-ENGINE"

WORKED BY COMPRESSED AIR

IT is an instinctive desire in most boys to construct something which will work, albeit they are mostly handicapped by a lack of tools. In such sorry circumstances, the only plan in making models is to utilise articles of everyday life, and thus as far as possible evade the exacting work.

The following description of a "steam-engine," which, however, can only be worked by compressed air, is based upon the coincidence that most lead pencils fit the holes in thread reels very closely.

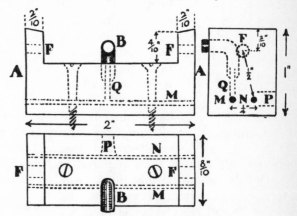

FIG. 1.—Plan of the Model.

The base of the model should be a 6-in. square of wood ¾ in. thick, planed smooth and with upper edges bevelled, cut from deal, or preferably something tougher. On its centre is screwed down a block of hard wood shaped and drilled to the dimensions shown in Figs. 1 and 2, the faces AA being smoothed quite flat by rubbing with a circular movement on fine glass-paper. The holes MN are best bored with a twist bit held in an Archimedean drill, starting from each face and penetrating half-way through in turn, whilst a rather larger hole P is driven from the middle of the nearest side to meet N, and similarly one Q from the top of the block to meet M. Into this is driven a short length of copper or lead tube, bent at right angles, in order to make a

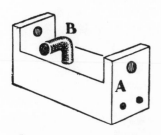

FIG. 2.—Base of the Model.

connection for the air supply B. Screws pass through the block, where they will not interfere with the holes already bored, in order to fasten it down to the base.

THE CYLINDERS

Two thread reels are cut down their length for all but $\frac{9}{10}$ in. to within $\frac{1}{8}$ in. of the centre hole, and for this $\frac{9}{10}$ in. a flat is left $\frac{4}{8}$ in.

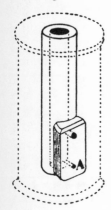

wide, the lower corners being rounded off and the top edges bevelled, Fig. 3, whilst the $\frac{4}{8}$ in. by $\frac{9}{10}$ in. faces are sand-papered in the same way as the hardwood block. Also in the middle of their width and $\frac{1}{4}$ in. from their lower edge, a small clean hole $\frac{1}{16}$ in. is bored with a twist bit through to each thread-reel hole, whilst $\frac{1}{2}$ in. higher a larger hole is drilled *nearly* through. Into these latter $1\frac{1}{2}$ in. round-headed screws are cautiously driven so as to form a thread in the wood, and then, being withdrawn, all but $\frac{1}{4}$ in. of their screwed shank is cut off. The holes FF, Fig. 1, in the hardwood block must be such as to accommodate the shanks of these screws comfortably, but without play, and probably the best way of securing this is to drill slightly smaller than required and finish with a fine round file, afterwards administering black lead to eliminate all but the least

FIG. 3.—The Cylinder.

friction. The engine cylinders, for so the thread reels may be now designated, are completed by closing their central holes at the end where the flat was left, with plugs of wood glued in to a depth of barely $\frac{3}{16}$ in. —*i.e.* not quite reaching to the small hole, Fig. 3.

An unvarnished lead pencil is next procured, which just fits the cylinders and has its lead drilled out for a distance of 1 in., this portion being then cut off, divided in half, and trimmed down to two pieces $\frac{2}{8}$ in. long. Two $2\frac{1}{4}$ in. straight lengths of brass wire, such as the central holes in the lead pencil can just accommodate, are twisted into round eyes at one end and are then cut off at $1\frac{3}{4}$ in. distance from these. Measuring $\frac{7}{16}$ in. from these plain ends,

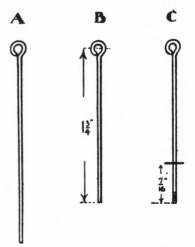

FIG. 4.—The Piston Rods.

two small brass washers are soldered on the rods, which are then screwed to take a small hexagonal nut, Fig. 4, A, B, and C. Both the nut and washer should be appreciably less than the cotton-reel hole in diameter. Probably no die will be at hand to cut the thread on the brass wire, and in this quandary one method is to obtain a nut of the requisite size in iron A, Fig. 5, make three gaps in its thread with a fret-saw—as shown at B, Fig. 5—and then harden by heating in a spirit flame till the bright metal shows straw colour, following by quenching in cold water.

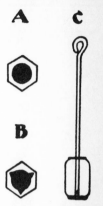

FIG. 5.—Making the Die, A and B, and Piston, C.

This nut-die can be worked on the brass rod by holding and twisting with pliers. The $\frac{2}{8}$ in. lengths of pencil are pushed on the brass rods and held in place against the brass washers by screwing on the hexagonal nuts, Fig. 5, C, thus completing the pistons and rods.

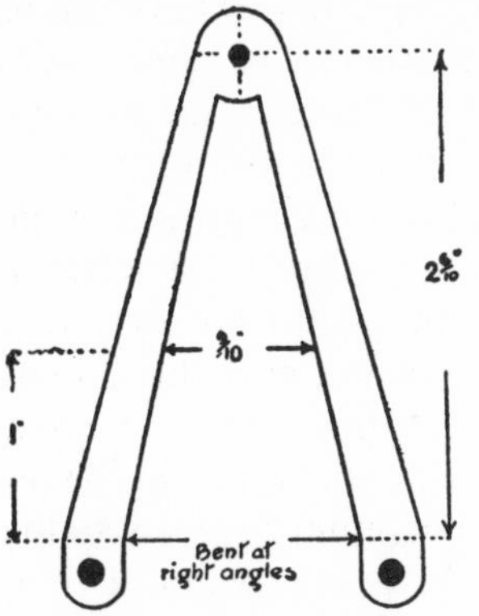

The bearings for the engine are cut and filed up from sheet brass to the shape and measurement shown in Fig. 6, whilst the shaft is a length of $\frac{1}{8}$ in. brass rod, with a brass or lead pulley. A 3-in. to $3\frac{1}{2}$-in. fly-wheel is soldered to the shaft, the ends of which

FIG. 6.—The Bearings.

are bent at double right angles in opposite directions in order to form $\frac{5}{12}$ in. cranks, Fig. 7. WW are small washers soldered on to keep the shaft in position between the bearings.

Supposing the hardwood block — which might be technically termed the "steam chest"—to be already screwed in position,

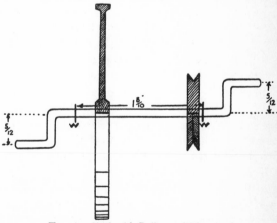

FIG. 7.—Shaft with Pulley and Fly-wheel.

the engine is erected as follows. The bearings are slipped on the shaft from either end and screwed down so as to be properly spaced for the washers WW, Fig. 7, and to enable the shaft to be set vertically above the holes F, Fig. 1.

The eye ends of the piston rods are then passed over the cranks and their plungers pushed into the cylinders, the lower faces of which are then held against the "steam chest" faces AA, Fig. 1, by means of the mutilated $1\frac{1}{2}$ in. screws. These are provided with spiral springs between their heads and the steam chest, Fig. 8, and their thread ends too should be wetted so as to obtain a firm grip in the cylinder walls by rusting.

On spinning the fly-wheel of the little machine with the fingers, it should make at least two or three complete revolutions quietly and smoothly. Inasmuch as the cranks are oppositely placed, the operations of one cylinder—although identical with the other—occur at the difference of time of half a revolution.

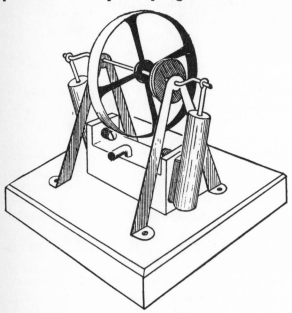

FIG. 8.—The Finished Engine.

Suppose one cylinder to be as far over towards one side as possible, so that the small hole A, Fig. 3, coincides with the hole M, Fig. 1, and a rubber pipe be connected to the bent copper tube B, Figs. 1 and 2, whereby air can be blown down from the lungs. This will reach the cylinder and force up the piston, thereby turning the crank, wheels, and shaft until, when half a revolution is completed, the other cylinder comes into action, whilst the one is in a position to have its air discharged through the exhaust hole, N, Fig. 1. Thus the cycle of operations continues, and so long as air is supplied—preferably not moist from the lungs for any prolonged period—the engine should continue in motion.

If matters work closely and smoothly, and there still appears to be some impediment to the little machine's sweet working, it may happen that the air cannot find exhaust easily enough, and in this case the holes N, Fig. 1, may be carefully enlarged until a good result is obtained.

CHAPTER XV

HOW TO MAKE AND WORK A SCENIC RAILWAY

A PICTURESQUE JOURNEY IN MINIATURE

To many boys, and even grown-up people, the construction of a realistic model is a hobby both instructive and interesting; and, of all models, one of the easiest to make and most pleasing in effect is that of a scenic railway.

Who would not view with pride a miniature railway, which, although only large enough to cover an ordinary dining-table, yet contained almost everything to be seen in an actual journey through a picturesque country?

In order to give a broad idea as to what is to be accomplished in the construction of such a model, perhaps the following description, based on the working of an actual home-made railway, will prove of assistance to those undertaking the task.

The train, motionless in the station, awaits the dropping of a signal to commence its journey.

The signal falls, and the train, gathering speed as it leaves the station, rushes off.

Swiftly gliding round a graceful curve, it rumbles over points until another station comes in sight. Here, should the signal be against it, the train comes to a standstill, but if not, it pursues its course round another bend, the signal going up when it has passed.

A slackening in speed indicates that the train is struggling up an incline. Such is the case, and the train bravely thuds along until a mountain tunnel comes in sight.

Disappearing for a moment, it emerges from the tunnel and, sweeping round another curve, rushes down a straight, steep incline, until, with a fine swerve round a fourth curve, it approaches the station from which it started.

This time, the signal being down, no stop is made, and the train continues its journey to the tunnel station.

Here, the signal being against it, the train comes to a standstill. Should such a miniature train be capable of holding any passengers, this stoppage would afford them an opportunity of making a more detailed study of the surrounding scenery. Steps descending from the station lead to a charming little châlet, with moss-covered walls, gravelled paths, and pretty little bee-hives.

Swiftly flowing by the châlet, its banks lined with stunted trees, is a crystal stream, spanned by a rustic bridge. The origin of this turbulent rivulet may be traced to a spring gushing from the hillside.

The train is now ready to resume its journey, and, as the signal falls, it struggles on its upward way to the tunnel.

The movement of a lever changes the points in the tunnel and, instead of dashing out as before, the train, switched to a branch line, emerges from the tunnel at a different point.

Presently a hollow rumbling sound shows that a bridge has been crossed, and now the train takes a circular course, passing on its way a picturesque windmill, with its long arms slowly revolving.

With a roar, the train dashes under the bridge, over which it has recently passed, and continues its circular journey, until, jumping over points, it is again switched on to the main line.

Reaching the little tunnel station, and finding the signal against it, the train now comes to a stop, having thus traversed the whole of both branch and main lines.

An Inexpensive Toy

Even such an incomplete description of the model will, at first, raise doubts in the minds of many ; to others it will act as an incentive.

Some would argue that the construction of such a realistic toy would dip deeply into the pockets of those attempting it, but great will be their surprise when it is stated that the complete model, including a 5s. 6d. train, need not cost a penny over 15s. Such a statement indeed seems incredible, but the secret lies in the fact that the materials used are mainly those at the disposal of every boy. This very fact alone should lend an additional charm to the construction of this interesting and pleasure-giving toy, for, with the materials easily procurable, the work involved becomes much lighter.

What to use ; its Cost, and whence obtained

Before the construction is commenced, the person undertaking it must form a clear idea as to the materials required, with their approximate cost, and the sources from which they may be most easily obtained.

The following list shows the cost of materials used in the construction of the model just described :—

	s	d
Engine, tender and carriages	5	6
Lines, 25 lengths at 2d. per length (" O " gauge) . . .	4	2
Signals (2)	0	8
2 pairs of points	1	6
Wood, 6d. ; Glue, 6d. ; Sand, 3d.	1	3
Screws (⅝ in.)	0	3
1 lb. French nails (1 in. and 1½ in. mixed)	0	3
7 lbs. Cork	1	0
Moss, for decorating	0	2
	14	9

This list includes almost everything required for the construction of the model, but it does not necessarily follow that this outlay need be made all at once. In fact, it might even be advisable, in some cases, to purchase only part of the quantities mentioned, the remainder being obtained as occasion requires. In buying the train, lines, signals, and points, it would be well to obtain them all from a reliable firm like Gamage, of High Holborn, London.

The best style of engine to procure is one fitted with a self-acting brake, as then the work of automatically stopping the train, by means of signals, is greatly facilitated.

To assist the reader in the selection of such an engine, it might be mentioned that a very suitable engine and tender, called the King Edward VII., No. 1902, Gauge O, can be obtained from Messrs. Gamage for 4s. 6d. This engine, which is of the L. & N.W.R. pattern, has the self-acting brake fixed just under the cab, whilst the starting-lever is conveniently placed inside the cab. When the engine is stationary this lever is up, but, by pressing the thumb upon it, the brake is released, and the train set in motion.

Care should be exercised in the selection of lines, since they may be obtained in several gauges. For such a model the most convenient line to acquire is that of the " O " gauge, which is commonly used and very easily procured. The purchaser should remember, too, that the engine and carriages must be of a corresponding gauge.

A little care in the selection of the wood will save both time and expense. The wood most easily worked, and perhaps the least expensive, is that of which Hudson's soap boxes are constructed. Half-a-dozen of these boxes, each costing a penny, will suffice for the whole model.

Sand is used for varying the surface of the track, at the same time giving it a realistic appearance, and is best obtained in the form of Hyde's Bird Sand, three penny packets of which are all that is necessary. Sand in this form has an advantage over that commonly used, since the shell particles it contains give a more varied aspect to the track.

To represent rockwork, virgin cork is used, and this, like the sand, may be obtained from any oilman. Since this cork is sold by weight, the purchaser would be wise in selecting thin pieces, which are lighter, and more easily nailed, than the thicker strips.

For varying the rockwork, and putting the finishing touches to any little huts, &c., that it may be necessary to erect, small ground cork is invaluable. Your fruiterer receives large quantities of this cork, since it is much used in the packing of grapes. You will therefore have no difficulty in getting a bagful free of charge, and this, with two pennyworth of moss from the florist's, completes your purchases.

Attention must now be directed to the construction of the track. the first step towards which is to decide upon the form the model has to take.

In the case of a scenic railway, this entails the drawing of an accurate diagram showing the suggested shape of the track, the position of the points, signal, &c., together with an indication of the various features of the scenery.

Presuming that the model is to be similar to that already described, the constructor will receive much assistance by carefully studying the accompanying diagram, Fig. 1, for it is the construction of this model that is now to be described in detail. Unforeseen circumstances, however, may necessitate slight alterations, in which case the constructor must use his own judgment.

THE CONSTRUCTION OF THE MODEL

It will at once become apparent to those undertaking the construction of a model of this size, that the work must be divided into sections. Accordingly at this stage, a few words indicating the general treatment of these sections now become necessary.

Having selected your section, which need not necessarily be restricted to the length of a single piece of line, prepare a piece of wood of the right dimensions.

For line of the "O" gauge, the most convenient breadth of the track is 4 in., this allowing a width of $1\frac{1}{4}$ in. between rails, $1\frac{1}{4}$ in. on each side, the actual width of the rails accounting for the remaining $\frac{1}{4}$ in.

Rails are usually sold in $10\frac{1}{2}$ in. lengths, $\frac{1}{2}$ in. of which is taken up by the connecting pins, marked AA in Fig. 2. Fig. 2A depicts the dimensions of an ordinary 10-in. straight length bent to a curve.

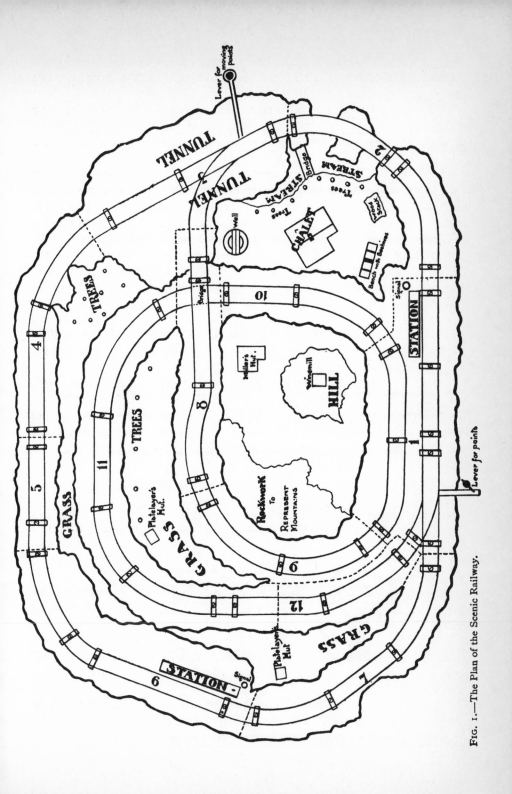

Fig. 1.—The Plan of the Scenic Railway.

There are cases, however, where the track must be widened, but these will be dealt with hereafter.

In order to raise the track to the required height from the table, cross support pieces should be fixed under each end of the section, as

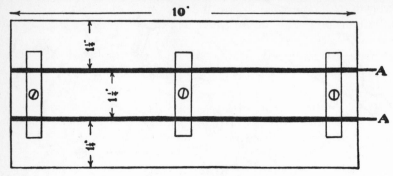

FIG. 2.—Section of Rail with Measurements.

shown in Fig. 3. These, besides raising the track, prevent the wood from warping, so that, in the case of the longer sections, three

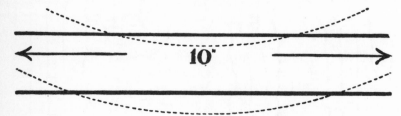

FIG. 2A.—Relative Dimensions of Straight and Curved Rails as usually sold.

supports become necessary, the extra piece being placed under the middle of the section. The height of these supports varies, of

FIG. 3.—Track Supports.

course, according to the section, but for the level track, a uniform height of 2 in. for each support should be adhered to.

When these supports have been fixed, pieces of virgin cork, sloping outwards, may be attached to the sides of the track, thus giving the appearance of rocky banks. These pieces should extend from the table level to a height of 1 in. above the level of the track, and should be made to appear as rugged as possible.

Everything is now ready for the sanding, which requires a little special attention. The upper surface of the wood should be well covered with plenty of *hot* glue, and, whilst still in this state, sand should be freely poured over it. Do not stint the quantity of sand, since any which does not adhere may be shaken off when the glue is quite dry.

In fixing the lines, which is done after the sanding, care is needed to ensure their being properly laid. Place each length of line in such a position that it runs down the middle of the track, the end of the line finishing level with the end of the section, Fig. 2.

It will then be found that the connecting pins AA, Fig. 2, just overlap, so that, when the sections are fixed together, the line becomes even and continuous.

Having previously punched a hole in each of the end sleepers, firmly fix the lines to the woodwork by means of screws.

DETAIL WORK

Now, having ascertained the general treatment necessary for the sections, you may turn your attention to their construction in detail. This calls for constant reference to Fig. 1, which should be conveniently placed before you.

It will be seen that the proposed model has, for the sake of convenience, been divided into twelve sections, some of which require a treatment different from that used for the majority.

Section 1.—The most convenient starting-place is that marked as Section 1 in the diagram, and of which a separate drawing is here given, Fig. 4.

The diagram shows that this serves as the track for both the main and branch lines M and BL respectively, and it therefore becomes necessary to make it wider than the 4 in. previously referred to. An additional 4 in. will afford ample room for the placing of both the main and branch sections of line ; and, as the section is long and level, four supports, each 2 in. high, should be placed in position under it.

For the present, it is only necessary to fix the main line, which consists of three lengths of straight metals, the first of which is in the form of points.

The fixing of the piece of branch line should be left until the main line has been completed, since it is not till then that its exact position can be ascertained.

On the inner side of the third length of line, a rustic station may be constructed, the details of which, of course, must be left to the inventive powers of the constructor.

In the main, it should consist of a platform raised 1 in. above the level of the track, with a sloping approach from the steps at the end of the section. Back the platform by a rough wall 1 in. high, and add the finishing touches by constructing a ticket-office, a little waiting-room, and perhaps a platform seat bearing the name of the station.

All that is now required to complete this section is a signal—at S—the fixing and working of which, however, calls for a little thought and care.

Fix the signal-post securely at the proper distance from the lines,

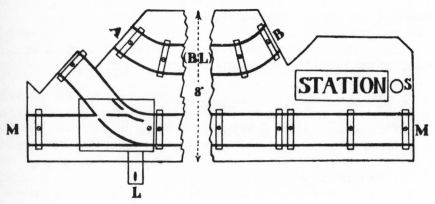

FIG. 4.—Plan of Section 1, showing the Main and Branch Lines.

so that the train may pass without touching it. Now the signal has to be so arranged that, when it is up, the train automatically stops.

To ensure this, a shaft must be constructed of hard, white wire of $\frac{1}{16}$ in. gauge. This wire must be so bent that it contains two cranks ; one being vertical, A, whilst the other is horizontal, B, Fig. 5. The lever C for working the signal D is also contained in this wire, and is bent as shown in the diagram.

Now pass this shaft under the lines, to the signal, so that the vertical crank lies between them, whilst the other crank is at the foot of the post immediately under the signal rod. Care should be taken to see that the vertical crank is at the required height above the lines to enable it to act on the brake of the engine.

A few $\frac{1}{2}$ in. wire-netting staples should now be driven in near the cranks to prevent the shaft from shifting sideways. Next erect the signal, and attach the connecting rod to the horizontal crank beneath it. When this has been done, the signal is quite ready to work.

It will now be seen that when the signal is up, the crank between the lines is vertical, and, coming into contact with the starting-brake of the engine, it brings the latter to a standstill.

By pulling over the lever C the crank between the lines A now becomes horizontal, and the other vertical, thereby lowering the signal.

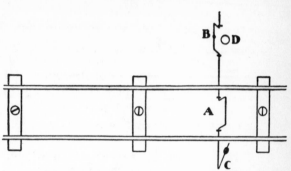

FIG. 5.—Crank Shafts for Brake and Signals.

The train may then be re-started by lowering the self-acting brake.

As the fixing of signals is perhaps the most difficult of all the construction, it would be advisable to limit their number to two, one near each station.

Section 2.—No such difficulties will be encountered in the second section, which consists simply of two pieces of curved line, the track for which, however, has to rise from 2 in. to 2¾ in.

This rise is obtained by increasing the height of the second support by ¾ in., the first support remaining of course at 2 in.

As regards the curved lengths of line, it may here be mentioned that it requires six of them to complete one circle, so that the two lengths referred to in this section cause the track to turn a corner.

Section 3.—You now have to deal with the third, or tunnel section, in which is the beginning of the branch line. As this branch line is to contain a bridge, the rise commenced in the last section must be continued until the outlets for the main and branch lines are 3½ in. and 3 in. respectively. This will necessitate support pieces of the required heights being placed directly beneath the outlets. As regards the line required for this section, a glance at Fig. 6 shows that the straight length of the points, A, with an additional half-length of straight, B, will suffice for the main line. For the branch line, the curved part of the points will suffice. The further construction of the branch line should now be delayed until the completion of the main line.

When the lines of this section have been fixed, large rough pieces of cork may be nailed over to represent a tunnel. These pieces of cork should be fastened to the base of the track, and then joined up to form the tunnel, or, should you prefer it, a skeleton tunnel may first be constructed of wood, and then completed by nailing pieces of cork over it. If a skeleton tunnel be constructed, care should be exercised to ensure that the outlets are in the right places, and also that the lever working the points protrudes through the side of the tunnel

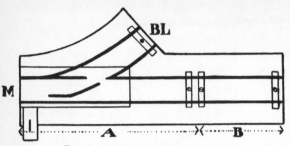

FIG. 6.—Beginning of Branch Line.

as in Fig. 1. Since the further construction of the branch line is to be delayed, the next section to receive attention will be the fourth of those constituting the main line.

Section 4.—Now this fourth section contains two lengths of line, the first of which is curved, at the $3\frac{1}{2}$ in. level, whilst the other is straight, but inclined downwards with a gradient from $3\frac{1}{2}$ in. to 2 in.

In order to meet the difficulty of a level and an inclined length of line in the one piece, it would be advisable to build the whole section on a bed piece, as shown in Fig. 7.

Taking the thickness of the bed piece C as $\frac{1}{4}$ in., the supports D for the level line B must be $3\frac{1}{4}$ in. high, thus bringing the elevation to the $3\frac{1}{2}$ in. necessary to join it to the tunnel section.

To this curved level line must be

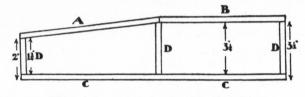

FIG. 7.—Supports for Level and Inclined Track.

joined the straight inclined length A which is brought down to the 2 in. by $1\frac{3}{4}$ in. supports nailed to the bed piece. Since the level line is over 3 in. from the bed piece, a wide space is left between them, and this may be filled in with pieces of cork to give the appearance of caves under the railroad.

Section 5.—The next section, being at the 2-in. level, and containing only one length of straight line, is easily constructed in the same manner as the other level sections.

Section 6.—The sixth section, although still at the same level, calls for a little more labour, as it contains both a signal and a station. This latter will necessitate a wider track for the platform, which, like that in Section 1, is on the inside of the rails, and runs the whole length of the straight piece of line, Fig. 1. This extra width should amount to 3 in., thus bringing the total breadth to 7 in. The line consists of two lengths, the first curved and the other straight.

At the farther end of the platform, the signal should be fixed in precisely the same manner as was that of Section 1. The station, however, should differ in many details from that constructed previously. As it will later be backed by mountainous scenery, it must partake of its rocky nature. In other respects, however, it should be similar to the tunnel station, with a sloping outlet from the platform, a little ticket-office, and a waiting-room. The dimensions of this new station need vary very little from those of the other station.

Section 7.—Having accounted for the sixth section, with its signal, there yet remains one more to complete the main line. This will connect the station section with that first constructed, and, if care has been exercised, all should fit up exactly.

Still at the same level, this last piece of main line is composed of one length of curved rail, to which is joined half a length of straight, which in turn is attached to another piece of curved line. Under the half-length of straight line, a little artificial bridge may be so constructed as to allow for the passage of a small trickling stream.

Section 8.—The main line being completed, attention must next be turned to the branch line—the beginning of which, you will remember, was formed by the points of the tunnel section. Now the curved part of these points had been made to emerge from the side of the tunnel at an elevation of 3 in., the reason for this increased height being to allow for a bridge over and under which the train will have to pass.

It is at this point in the tunnel section, then, that the first of the five constituting the branch line must be commenced.

A glance at Fig. 8 shows at once that this section, like the fourth

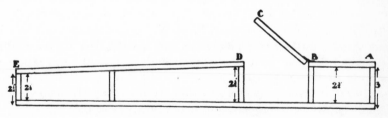

FIG. 8.—Section showing Bridge.

in the main line, contains both level and inclined pieces of track, and the difficulty is overcome in the same manner by building the whole on a bed piece.

Starting from the end near the tunnel, the section is composed of four pieces of line arranged as follows: One half-length of straight at the 3-in. level A, joined by a horizontal bridge of the same length, BC, and also at the same level, with two more lengths inclined from 3 in. to 2½ in. The first of these latter two pieces is a bent piece of straight line B to C, Fig. 9, whilst the other is about four-fifths of

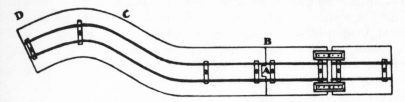

FIG. 9.—Plan of Bridge and Curve.

a length of curved rail, C to D. It will now be seen that, whilst no insuperable difficulties occur, yet considerable thought is required for the successful execution of the subsequent labours.

Since you have here to deal with two half-lengths of line, it might be mentioned that, whenever lines are cut, it may become necessary to insert connecting pins in either one or both of the cut ends. Having cut your bed piece to the required size, fix, at the right end, by means of two ¾ in. supports, one at each end of it, the half-length of straight track.

Assuming, as in Section 4, that the thickness of the bed piece is ¼ in., the track will now be 3 in. from the table level, and will thus join the branch line of the tunnel.

THE BRIDGE

To the piece of track thus constructed must be joined the bridge, which, to allow for the passing of a train beneath, will be hinged, thus enabling it to be raised or lowered at will.

The bridge itself consists, as previously mentioned, of half a length of track cut with a projecting piece as shown at A in Figs. 9 and 10. The object of this projecting piece is to fix the bridge firmly, when lowered, to the remaining part of the section, thus ensuring that the lines shall remain in one continuous length. For this reason it will be necessary to cut out from the track of the adjoining part of the section a piece similar in shape to the projecting piece marked A.

Having made the bridge as directed, it must next be attached, by means of hinges, to the track already constructed. This involves a little extra care, and should be carried out in the following manner :—

First cut two wooden blocks, 3 in. long, ¾ in. wide, and of such a height that, when placed on the track, their upper surfaces are just level with the tops of the rails.

By means of glue and brads, firmly fix one of these blocks on each side of the end of the bridge in such a manner that, whilst half of each block is fixed to the track, the other half projects from it as shown in Fig. 10. These projecting halves should next be fixed in like manner

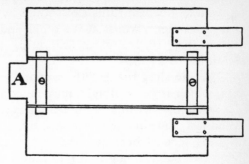

FIG. 10.—Plan of Bridge.

to the track already constructed, care being taken to see that the rails are in line, with a space of an eighth of an inch between them to allow for free movement in raising and lowering the bridge.

It remains to sever the connection and fix the hinges. To do this the blocks should be carefully cut through, level with the end of the bridge, and the hinges adjusted, across the cut, Fig. 11, in which A is

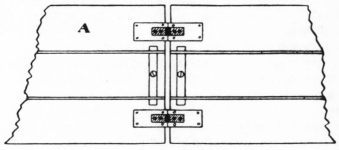

FIG. 11.—Method of fixing the Block to the Track.

the movable bridge portion. In this position, they may be fixed by means of small screws. Desk hinges, ¾ in. long, are the most convenient to use, as they are narrow, and will thus fit nicely on to the blocks. (The reader will understand, of course, that, in order to allow the train to pass beneath, the bridge must be raised, but, after the train has passed, it should at once be lowered, to prevent any possibility of a mishap when the train has to cross the bridge.)

Attention must next be directed to the two remaining lengths of inclined line which complete this section. Of these, the first is a length of straight rail bent as shown in Fig. 9. No difficulty will be experienced in bending this, provided you remove the end sleeper, which need not necessarily be replaced.

To the line thus bent, one length of curved rail should be attached. Cut the track to the required shape, and fix the rails, not forgetting, of course, to allow for the fitting in of the projection from the bridge. Immediately beneath this slot should be placed a 2¾ in. support nailed to the bed-piece, whilst at the other end of the track, a 2¼ in. support, fixed to the ¼ in. bed-piece, will bring the height of the track at the end down to 2½ in.

This finishes the eighth section, so that the construction of the next, which is quite simple, may be commenced.

Section 9.—In this ninth section is continued the curve commenced in the last, together with the descent to the ordinary level of 2 in. As no bed-piece is here necessary, the construction simply consists of fixing two curved lengths of rail to a track of the same shape. To return to the 2-in. level from the 2½ in. at the end of the bridge section, the bearers must be 2½ in. and 2 in. respectively.

Reference to Fig. 1 will show that the curved lengths of line in this and the last section have brought the branch to the first section, so that a length of rail must now be fixed to that piece.

If you refer to the plan in Fig. 1, and to Fig. 4, you will see that sections 9 and 1 join at point A, whilst 10 and 1 meet at point B.

The line required to join A to B consists of half a length of curved, joined to about half a length of straight rail, terminated at B by another half-length of curved. The best manner of dealing with these rails is first to place the curved pieces at A and B in such a manner that they are in line with the rails of Sections 9 and 10, and then connect them by the required length of straight line placed in between.

Section 10.—Having finished this satisfactorily, you are now brought to the tenth section, which leads off from Section 1 at the point B in the same way that the preceding section joined it at A, and terminates at, but does not pass under, the bridge of Section 8.

To bring the track to this point, one length of curved line, with nearly a length of straight, is required. The length of this last piece of rail may vary a little in different models, but, if the construction has been accurately carried out, not more than 6 in. should be necessary. Since this, and the two remaining sections are all at the 2-in. level, the work of construction is quite simple.

Section 11.—The last section but one is, perhaps, the longest in the whole model, since it consists of five pieces of rail, some of which, however, are half-lengths. The track starts under the bridge, so that the first support rests on the bed-piece of Section 8. This means that the support need only be 1¾ in. in height, as the bed-piece will supply the extra ¼ in. required for the 2-in. level.

The first piece of line consists of rather more than half a length of curved rail, *i.e.* a piece containing two sleepers. To this is attached a whole curved piece, which in turn is joined by half a length of straight line. Yet another length of curved rail must be joined to this, and the whole section completed by 8 in. of straight line.

It will then be apparent that but one short section is required to connect the branch line to the points of Section 1.

Section 12.—This short section consists simply of two curved pieces of rail. Should these not exactly join the points, it may be necessary to bend the latter, or even to add or cut off a small piece of line.

If the section be too short, a small piece of straight line should be added to the curved lengths ; if too long, a piece may be cut off from one of them. In this way the whole track is completed, and nothing remains but to add any scenery the constructor may deem necessary.

THE SCENERY

Although the model is now at such a stage that no extra construction is essential for its completion, yet a few finishing touches in the way of scenery will greatly add to its picturesque appearance.

Reference to the diagram shows that there are two large empty spaces, besides several smaller ones, which present an unfinished aspect, and the little trouble required to fill them by suitable scenery is amply repaid by the effect produced.

It is not proposed in the following few words to deal in detail with the creation of this scenery, but rather to place before the reader a few suggestions which may be augmented and put into practice by his own inventive mind.

The first, and largest, of the spaces is that enclosed by Sections 2, 3, and 10, and a start should be made by cutting a bed-piece which, whilst exactly filling up that space, will fit in easily, thus preventing any damage to the surrounding sections upon its removal.

On this bed-piece should be built the various items constituting the scenery, and perhaps the most suitable object to start upon is a little Swiss châlet, pictures of which can be easily procured. Constructed of wood, and placed in a fairly central position, it should consist of a main building, with outhouse adjoining ; the whole being covered by an overhanging roof.

A little doorway, showing the door ajar, might next be arranged. Windows may be represented by marking out the frames and sash-bars with narrow strips of cork. Long, narrow strips of thin cork, glued over the roof and eaves, provide an excellent imitation of logs, and a small chimney, also cut from cork, gives the final touch of completeness to the roof.

The building should then be sanded in precisely the same manner as was the railway track, with the exception, however, of the windows, doors, and chimney, all of which should be left clear.

The finishing touches may be added by placing here and there small pieces of moss, in imitation of bushes and climbing plants, round the walls of the building. This does not exhaust the means of making the scenery as realistic as possible, for a little well, constructed of cork and wood, with a tiny bucket suspended from a windlass, may be placed near by, somewhere at the back of the building.

On one side place a beehive or two, standing on a cork bench, whilst in another convenient spot a wood-stack—such as is seen in the country—may be erected. This is easily accomplished by cutting a number of 3-in. twigs from a privet, and then placing them in layers, first one way, and then another, each layer being well covered with glue.

Close by, a pretty mountain stream can be represented by gluing pieces of silvered glass to the bed-piece ; the banks of the stream being of a rocky nature, and interspersed with moss. Stunted trees lining the banks are admirably represented by cutting small knotty pieces from a privet bush, and then placing them in holes bored about 1½ in. apart. Small pieces of cork glued to the silvered glass will give the appearance of stepping-stones, and the rivulet may receive its final touch in the form of a rustic bridge with raised sides and steps leading to and from it.

A few gravelled paths from the châlet, with mossy banks here and there to disguise any bare patches, are sufficient to make this scene complete, unless, of course, the constructor should wish for any additional ornamentation of his own design.

The other large space should now claim your attention. This space, you will find, is enclosed by Sections 10, 8, 9, and 1. As before, a bed-piece, taking the shape of the space, should first be cut. On this, in a fairly central position, may be constructed of cork, a small hill, from which a tiny winding path, leading to the plain below, might be added to increase its picturesque appearance. On the hill may be placed a small windmill, the construction of which, however, will be dealt with later.

The rest of the space should partake of the same rocky nature, so that the hill can be backed by miniature mountains. Here and there may be placed small huts—say, for instance, a miller's dwelling, similar in design to the châlet, and situated near the windmill.

The windmill is best constructed of cigar-box wood, which is easily worked. The form the building is to take will be left to the constructor, who may either decide on the stationary type, or that in which the whole mill revolves upon its own foundations. Arms which actually rotate add greatly to the natural effect, and for this the works of a small clock are indispensable. A band passing round the spindle of the arms and the spindle of the clockwork will, when the latter is set in motion, produce the desired effect.

There now remain a few odd spaces here and there in the model, which may be utilised for the planting of a tree or two, or for the erection of a few platelayers' huts.

The inventive mind will, no doubt, devise many additional improvements when the whole model is at this stage, as, for instance, the erection of telegraph poles at the side of the track, or the placing of a signal-box here and there.

Even should such details be neglected, the model is now at such a stage that it may be regarded as complete, and, although the pleasure derived from its construction has passed, many an amusing hour may be spent in fitting it up for the inspection of friends, or for your own quiet enjoyment.

CHAPTER XVI

A MINIATURE MILL

AN easily made realistic model, the construction of which may be simplified or complicated almost indefinitely at will, is that of a windmill with a see-saw in the foreground. Picturesqueness plays but a small part in modern life, and these landmarks are constantly disappearing from the schemes of countryside scenery—in many cases to be superseded by incessantly thumping gas-engine plants. However, a few words will suffice to recall their general construction—the

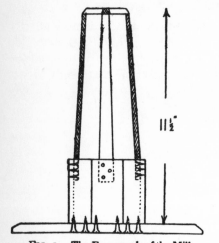

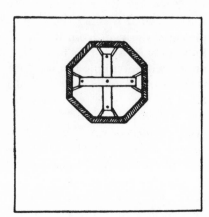

FIG. 1.—The Framework of the Mill.　　　　FIG. 2.—The Base of the Mill.

square or octagonal house of white stone, surmounted by a steep conical wooden structure, on the summit of which a saucer-shaped cap, free to turn with the wind, shelters the paraphernalia of gear wheels and sail shafts which rotate the grinding stones below.

There will be no necessity to make the model capable of turning with the breeze, as, its base being a square foot of deal, the whole foundation is movable, albeit a calamitous circumstance in the case of structures founded on the earth. The lower part will be octagonal and thus built up of eight 2-in. by 4-in. pieces of wood, which are bevelled on their inner edges, so as to set flush together, and fixed in position by screws passing upward through the base, Figs. 1 and 2. To the inner parts of four alternate sides are screwed stout upright strips, joined by cross braces at the top, Figs. 1 and 2. These do not stand quite perpendicularly and form the framework for an extinguisher arrangement of cardboard. To this use an obsolete kaleidoscope tube might be turned, or it may be made in the

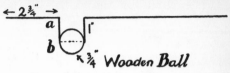

FIG. 3.—The Crank and Wooden Ball.

orthodox fashion by pasting brown paper round a suitable shape.

The foregoing remarks indicate how the framework is to be erected, but this must not be done until some machinery is in place.

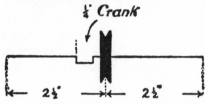

FIG. 4.—Box Pulley on the Crank.

A foot of stout iron wire must be bent to the shape shown in Fig. 3, the wooden ball being placed in position before the bends A, B are made. Another piece is bent with a ¼ in. crank, and has a small box pulley of 1-in. diameter driven into position, Fig. 4.

A hole P is drilled in each of the octagon faces, A, B, Fig. 5, distant ¼ in. alike from the top and front edges and bushed with short pieces of brass tube to take the wear of the little shaft shown in Fig. 4. This is threaded through—the crank being nearest B—and the two octagon faces are then screwed into position on the baseboard, small washers being lastly soldered on the shaft to butt against the brass bushes and thus prevent the former getting out of place.

Similarly, holes are drilled in the faces C, D, ½ in. from the edges nearest A and 1 in. from the bottom edges, and the shaft, Fig. 3, is placed with its longer part extending through D, whilst washers are soldered on to maintain a position with its crank directly below the shaft, Figs. 4 and 5.

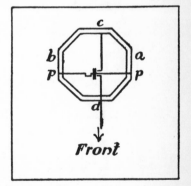

FIG. 5.—Positions of Cranks in the Base.

The ¼ in. crank is connected with the wood ball, B, on the lower shaft, by means of a metal connecting-rod of strip brass, twisted in the middle as shown at A, Fig. 6.

It will thus be seen that for every complete turn of the upper shaft, a movement of twice ¼ inch.—*i.e.* ½ inch—is given to the connecting-rod and thence to the wood ball, this only meaning a small movement of the lower shaft, owing to the length of its crank. The wood ball joint would not be necessary were it not that the shafts are at right angles to one another.

The shaft for the mill sails passes through holes near the top

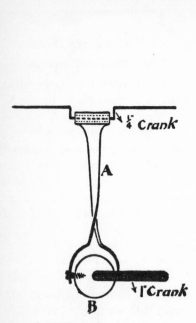

FIG. 6.—Small Crank with Wood Ball.

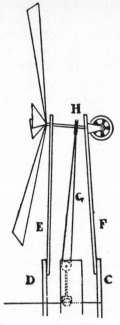

FIG. 7.—Section of the Mill.

of the uprights E and F which are affixed to D and C, Fig. 7, and points slightly upwards towards the front in order to give a tilt to the sails. This is the practice in actual mills, because the action of the breeze is found to be more effective. As on the other shafts, washers are fitted to keep it in place between the bearings, and also a wooden pulley wheel, H, similar to that used on the shaft depicted in Figs. 4 and 7. The two pulleys are connected by an endless gut band G—e.g. a violin string. The sails of the mill are each 8 in. long, tapering at the peripheral ends, being carved as in Fig. 8, in order

FIG. 8.—A Mill Sail.

to represent the adjustable vanes of a real mill—whereby the embraces of zephyrs and hurricanes are alike received with equanimity. They are attached to the top shaft by the medium of a boss, A, indicated in Figs. 9 and 10, which is fixed in place by a brass plate B soldered to the shaft C, and through which two or three screws pass into the boss. The narrow ends of the sails are screwed to the projecting pieces D, D, D, D of the boss.

At the opposite end of the mill shaft, but screwed to the upright,

FIG. 9.—Plan of the Boss.

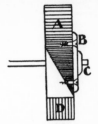

FIG. 10.—Section of the Boss.

J (attached to C), Fig. 11, is a cardboard wheel 2 in. diameter, built up round a silk reel, K. There are six vanes, which glue into slots cut diagonally across the reel, and a ring of cardboard, R, engages with a slot cut in each vane, to keep the latter firm. Fig. 12 shows the same idea in section.

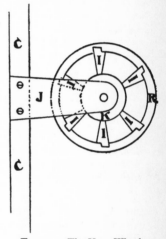

FIG. 11.—The Vane Wheel.

Supposing the three shafts to turn easily in their bearings, and their connections to engage properly, when the mill is turned—whether by wind or hand —the pulley on its shaft revolves, and hence, through the endless band, the lower pulley. This means that the $\frac{1}{4}$ in. crank makes complete revolutions, and consequently that the bottom shaft oscillates backwards and forwards through part of a revolution. The extremity of its front projecting end rests upon a third bearing, A, Fig. 13, which should take the form of a barrel, tree-stump, or any other object upon which see-saws are commonly poised. To the shaft itself is fixed a 6-in. strip of wood, B, to represent the see-saw itself, and on its extremities—in order to strike a note of realism—two tiny dolls are secured in a sitting posture.

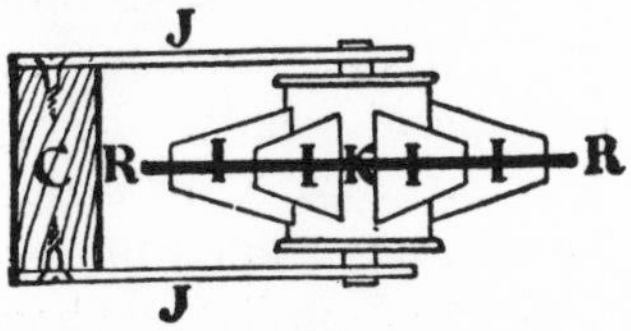

The cardboard covering for the mill house will best be screwed to the uprights in two halves—clearance holes being cut for the sail's shaft, and may be painted grey or stone colour, whilst the sails receive a coat of white. For the absolute summit of the mill house, a 5-in. diameter circle of brown paper is cut along one radius, C, Fig. 13, and

FIG. 12.—Section of Vane.

then overlapped so as to form a cone, which is then glued to the top of the edifice.

The two octagon sides at the back of the model on either side of C, Fig. 5, need not be permanently fixed, but can be kept in position

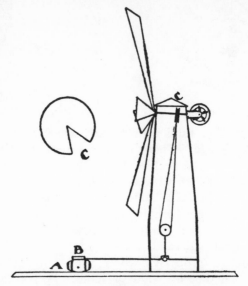

FIG. 13.—Section of Mill complete.

by means of hinges to the baseboard, so that they can be let down to view the mechanism within. Such finishing touches as sand and moss on the baseboard, or imitation windows in the walls, the planting of trees, or the erection of out-buildings, can be applied *ad lib.*, and may be relied upon to add greatly to the appearance of a realistic model.

CHAPTER XVII

THE BICYCLE BLONDIN

A NOVEL TOY FOR CHILDREN

THE small bicycle of wire framework with V-grooved wheels ridden along a tight rope by a tenacious monkey is well known to every one acquainted with children's toys. The sight of one of these little contrivances careering down an inclined string has always led the writer to wonder whether some other power than gravity might

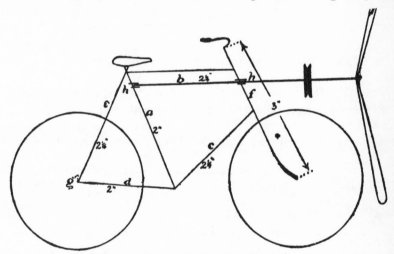

FIG. 1.—Skeleton Design of the Bicycle.

not be employed, and the following scheme is the result of his speculations.

The connection of any motive power on the bicycle to its wheels, by the turning of which it might be propelled, involves many difficulties, and it will therefore be advisable—not to mention novel—to utilise a propeller in front after the fashion of an aeroplane. This will be driven by means of an electric motor, the current being supplied from the wire over which the bicycle runs.

The machine itself should be built up with soldered joints according to the design sketched in Fig. 1. The stay A and the front member

F are each cut from sheet brass and have $\frac{1}{8}$ in. holes drilled at HH, whilst the other bars are made of stout brass wire. E and D, Figs.

FIG. 3.—Fork for Front Wheel.

1 and 2, are almost like a hairpin in shape and carry the spindle at G, Fig. 1, for the back wheel.

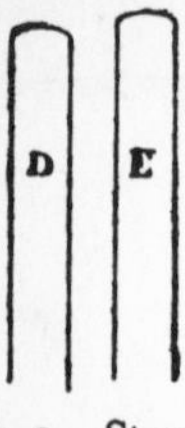

Both the wheels are $2\frac{1}{2}$ in. diameter, with V-grooves, and the front one, of course, runs in the fork, Fig. 3, of the member F. Short lengths of metal tube are inserted in the holes HH, and through

FIG. 2.—Stays for Back Wheel.

these—an easy fit—a knitting-needle for the spindle is placed. The pieces of tube are soldered in position to A and F, Fig. 1, and miniature washers soldered on the knitting-needle prevent its working backwards and forwards. No length need be left extending beyond A over the back wheel,

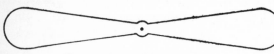

FIG. 4.—Shape of Propeller Blade.

but it should reach forward on a level with the edge of the front wheel.

A metal pulley wheel is next pushed on the spindle, and then, on the very extremity, is soldered a propeller with two $2\frac{1}{2}$ in. blades—cut from thin sheet tin, copper, or brass to the shape shown in Fig. 4. These blades are twisted, and also bent forwards equally from the

FIG. 5.—Propeller Blade twisted to the required Angle.

centre, to the extent shown by AA, Fig. 5, to clear the front wheel. Lastly, wire handle-bars and a tin saddle are soldered in place.

The bicycle is suspended by a piece of string, tied to the top bar, B, along which it is shifted until the machine hangs horizontally. At this point is soldered a 14-in. length of stout brass wire bent to the shape of an inverted V, and to the two ends of this are soldered brass plates, each drilled with a couple of holes, Figs. 6 and 7.

FIXING THE ELECTRO-MOTOR

These brass plates will be the means of support for an electro-motor of the type depicted in Fig. 8, mounted on a wood base, and fixed as indicated by the dotted lines in Figs. 6 and 7. This motor should cost about five shillings. It must be furnished with a V-pulley, and if that on the propeller spindle, which has not yet been definitely fixed, cannot be brought vertically above the same, the motor shaft must be lengthened by driving on the required length of tightly-fitting tube. Then, on the latter, the pulley can be soldered and that on the upper spindle sweated in position.

The wire V-support of the motor should be further attached to the bicycle, and thus so far strengthened, by a cross-piece soldered to the two limbs and the frame rods A or C, Fig. 1, as the case may be.

The next business is to flatten a 7-in. length of brass wire for an inch at one end, drill two holes, and bend at right angles, afterwards fixing it to the underside of the motor's base by screws which cannot possibly touch the metal part of the machine itself.

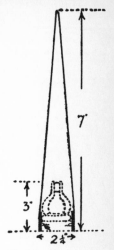

FIG. 6.—Support for Electro-motor.

Round one screw, before it is driven home, twist the bared end of some insulated wire, which is then cut off to a length sufficient to reach one of the motor terminals, where it has its free end bared to connect up. The other terminal is connected to the nearest arm of the V-support.

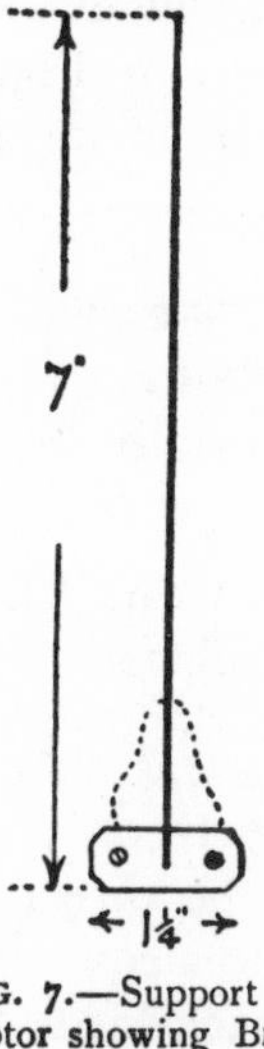

The bicycle having been constructed, it only remains to erect its track and power station. The fact must be realised that electricity needs complete circuits in which to work; in the present instance the current may be supposed, on leaving one pole of the battery, to travel *via* the wire on which the bicycle runs to the latter's frame and the terminal connected thereto; then round the motor coils to the other terminal, which is joined by insulated

FIG. 8.—The Electro-motor.

FIG. 7.—Support for Motor showing Brass Plate.

wire to the rod collector beneath the base, and thence—how back to the other pole? Inasmuch as water is a fair conductor of electricity, one method suggests itself, viz. that of running the model over a bath and allowing the collector to dip below the water's surface, thus providing a return path for the current. This arrangement will be described first. An alternative scheme would be to provide a metal tongue hinged beneath the base in place of the rod collector, and allow it to rest upon a wire stretched at a suitable depth from the track wire. This also will be considered.

Suppose Fig. 9 to represent the mid-section lengthwise of a household bath, and that AB are lengths—say 9 in.—of broom-handle fixed

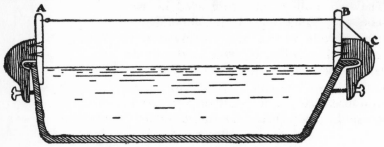

FIG. 9.—Fitting the Track Wire over the Bath.

in a vertical position by means of wood clamps attached in the manner shown. Steel piano wire—if copper be not available—will be suitable for the track, and should be hooked at one end to engage with an eye in the vertical rod, A, whilst the other passes through a hole in B and thence round a cleat, C.

THE BATTERIES

The number of batteries required is difficult to judge—especially as this depends in a great measure upon their condition—but certainly three bichromate cells should be tried or—more economically—four Sac Leclanchés. Ordinary cells of the latter type have very poor recuperative powers, but the Sac Leclanchés are capable of a constant output provided a sufficient number be used. The advantage of their employment is that they do not deteriorate when out of use. The cells are joined up in series—*i.e.* zinc A to carbon B—and thence the connections are *via* two 2-way switches, C being the track wire, D the water or second wire, Fig. 10. By this means the direction of the current through the motor can be changed and, consequently, its rotation, so that the bicycle may be propelled backwards or forwards at will.

If the machine cannot be run over water, the wooden rods must be somewhat taller with a second wire stretched parallel to and below the first, but absolutely insulated from the latter.

In this connection it may be noted that the wooden fittings must first be thoroughly varnished or soaked in melted paraffin wax. The second wire corresponds to the water in the connections of Fig. 10, whilst a wide flap of metal hinged below the motor baseboard takes the place of the wire collector which was dipped into the water.

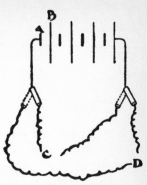

FIG. 10.—Two-way Switch for Electro-motor.

The two pulleys are connected by an endless gut band—*e.g.* a banjo string—and the bicycle wheels are placed on the track wire by unhooking the latter and tightening afterwards. The finishing touch is to find an intrepid cyclist for the mount—preferably a monkey of wire and wool, or a teddy bear—as these seldom evince any qualms of fear.

CHAPTER XVIII

A HANDY MOTOR CAR

MADE FROM BOXES

IT is probably the ambition of every one to have a motor car, and for those who are unable to realise this desire to its fullest extent, the following instructions have been written, so that any practical boy can construct a car for himself. It has been called "A Handy Motor Car" for a very good reason, as its speed will depend rather upon arm-power than upon horse-power; but the machinery is neither complicated nor expensive, and is not very likely to get out of gear.

FIG. 1.—The Handy Motor Car.

The most expensive part of the car will be the wheels. Old bicycle wheels are the best for the purpose, although substitutes may be found in the shape of perambulator wheels. A visit to a cycle repairer's will reveal the fact that the cost in any case is not heavy, whilst an extra shilling or two will induce the man to fit them with strong axles. A glance at Fig. 1, which represents the finished car, will explain the following instructions.

The two front wheels A and B run freely on the axle C, which is fastened to the block A, Fig. 2, by two strong staples, BB. In the centre of this block a hole is bored, through which a bolt C passes upward and through another block of wood D. As shown in the illustration, a washer is placed between the two blocks of wood, and thus prevents friction that might otherwise prove disastrous to the car.

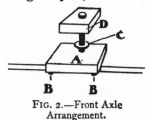

FIG. 2.—Front Axle Arrangement.

Before proceeding further it will be necessary to make the tonneau or body. This should be constructed as shown in Fig. 3, from a box of ½ in. wood about 5 ft. in length, from 18 in. to 2 ft. in width, and 1 ft. deep, that should be either purchased or made.

A foot from the front of the box two braces, *i.e.* strips of wood, AA, Fig. 3, should be nailed or screwed upon the sides, whilst similar braces, BB, must be placed a foot farther back. Between these two braces a portion of the sides must be cut away as shown by the dotted lines. The front of the box should now be covered by a piece of wood stretching from CC to AA.

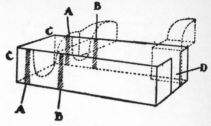

FIG. 3.—Tonneau of Car.

The driver's seat is the next consideration. This should be formed of a piece of wood stretching from side to side of the car and about 1 ft. in width. Sides and back can be made as shown in the finished car, Fig. 1. In the back of the box a width of 10 in. should be cut down the centre D, Fig. 3, to allow of entrance to the back seats.

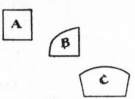

FIG. 4.—Portions of Seats.

These back seats are made of squares of wood A, Fig. 4, which are fastened over the ends and corners of the body as shown in the diagram. The sides B and the backs C must be screwed in their respective positions.

FIXING THE FRONT AXLES

Having completed the body of the car, the front axles are now ready to be fixed. A glance at Fig. 5 will show very plainly how to do this. The block of wood D, Fig. 2, is screwed to the bottom of the box in the centre, in such a way that the axle swings free on the bolt. Now, at either side of this block of wood, cut holes in the bottom of the box of sufficient size to allow the feet to be pushed through, so that they rest on the axle of the

FIG. 5.—Steering Arrangement.

wheel. By this means the driver is enabled to steer the car with his feet.

The back wheels are fastened to the body of the car by wooden cleats as shown in Fig. 6. These should be screwed on very firmly. At this stage of the proceedings, the car may be given a trial run,

FIG. 6.—Cleats for Back Axle.

the driver taking his seat with his feet upon the front axle, whilst some kind-hearted friend pushes him from behind. If all goes well, the question of constructing the driving machinery may then be tackled.

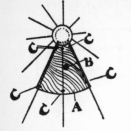

FIG. 7.—Block for Back Wheel.

Triangular pieces of wood similar to those shown at F, Fig. 1, and constructed of wood 1 in. thick, so shaped that they will fit between the spokes of the rear wheels, must now be fastened in position with staples, as shown in Fig. 7. When they are in place, a hole ⅝ in. in diameter, B, should be bored, at a point half-way between the centre and the circumference. Into this hole a bolt with two nuts and washers must be fastened very securely in the manner shown in section, Fig. 8.

THE CONNECTING RODS

The next things to be made are the connecting rods. They should be of wood, long enough to stretch from the back wheels to a point just short of the front wheels. Two inches from the end of each of these connecting rods holes must be drilled of sufficient size to permit the end of the bolt shown in Fig. 8 to pass through. They can be further strengthened by inserting pieces of iron tubing just large enough to pass round the bolt. A heavy washer should be placed at the end of the bolt outside the connecting rods, and a nut then screwed over the end of this bolt.

Two lengths of wood, at the lower end of which the connecting rods are attached, similar to those used for these connecting rods, must now be pivoted to either side of the car at DD, Fig. 1. The length of the connecting rods must be such that the crank bolt is in a forward position when the upper handle E, Fig. 1, is at its farthest extremity backwards, whilst when the handle is pushed forward as far as it will go, the crank on the back wheel is thrust rearwards.

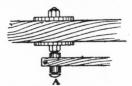

FIG. 8.—Connection for Back Wheel.

The motor car is now complete, and if the foregoing instructions have been carefully carried out, the maker should have a handy road machine for his use.

Of course the painting and decoration can be done according to taste, a deep green or a fine crimson being very suitable colours. The seats may be covered with cushions, whilst a bicycle-horn placed at the driver's side will enable him to clear such traffic as may impede his progress.

CHAPTER XIX

THE WONDERS OF A JACK-KNIFE

HOW TO MAKE MECHANICAL TOYS AND NOVEL INVENTIONS

THE love of making things is a part of human nature. There is a certain charm about whatever you make yourself that never attaches to anything that has been bought. It is your own handiwork—you know all the difficulties of the task, and how they were overcome—bit by bit it has grown under your hands, and when it stands complete you feel the thrill of success.

Now, while the desire to make things is so inherent in some natures, that the moment people see the simplest bit of mechanism their fingers twitch to make it, a second thought damps their ardour. "What about tools?" comes the question. "I could never hope to make that clever thing without a big chest of tools."

To a certain extent this may be true, but, on the other hand, it is quite possible to make scores of ingenious articles and mechanical toys with a simple jack-knife. At any rate, just to do the finishing, only a saw, screw-driver, file, and a bradawl need be occasionally resorted to.

Let it be presumed that you possess a good strong steel jack-knife—one with several blades of different sizes, all well sharpened. Perhaps you can secure a combination knife, in which the other tools I have just mentioned are included. In any case the knife is the main thing.

Wood is the principal material employed in jack-knife carpentry. For special articles you will want lengths of thin white wood, such as can be obtained in any timber yard. It is, however, possible to make all manner of things out of the waste of the household, for there is scarcely a home in which old wooden boxes, cotton reels, rollers, and other apparently worthless materials are not discarded, and out of them you can make some of the cleverest things, as will be shown.

A BOX OF DOMINOES

To begin with the simplest articles. The game of dominoes is very popular, and a set can be made very easily. Any odd pieces of wood, provided that they are all $\frac{1}{4}$ in. thick, 1 in. wide, and 2 in. long, will do, although every piece must be exact in measurement. Carefully smooth each piece to size, using one perfectly-shaped piece as a model by which to gauge the others. Twenty-eight pieces must be so treated to make up the set. Now with a blacklead pencil score a line on the right side, dividing the face into two equal parts. Starting with double blank, the next is blank and one dot, blank and two dots, right up to the double six. Each dot will be a circle of a quarter of an inch in diameter. Make each dot or circle perfectly round. Now take your knife and cut out these circles with the point of a small blade, hollowing the wood and graduating the hole. Paint the dividing lines and the dots with black, and colour each domino with a walnut stain.

You will want a box in which to keep the domino set. Take two pieces of wood, $5\frac{3}{4}$ in. wide and $2\frac{1}{4}$ in. deep for the sides, and two pieces, $2\frac{1}{8}$ in. wide and $2\frac{1}{4}$ in. deep, to serve for the ends. Make five grooves at the ends of these pieces so as to dovetail them

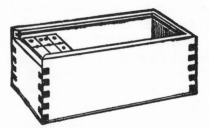

FIG. 1.—Dovetail for Domino Box.   FIG. 2.—Domino Box complete.

together, Fig. 1. The bottom of the box will be made of a piece of wood 2 in. wide and a little over 7 in. long to fit. Then the lid will be $\frac{1}{8}$ in. thick and $2\frac{1}{4}$ in. wide. Make a groove inside the box a quarter of an inch from the top, into which the lid will slide. Stain and varnish the outside of the box, Fig. 2.

PICTURE FRAMES

Nearly every one has a picture or two worth framing, as well as photographs with which they would like to adorn their walls. You can easily make frames for them with your jack-knife. Cut out four strips of wood from a piece of $\frac{3}{8}$ in. board $1\frac{1}{2}$ in. wide, the lengths being determined by the size of the picture to be framed. Next take four more strips of wood, $\frac{3}{4}$ in. wide, and nail these, one on each of the former strips, keeping them neatly to the edge, by this means forming the groove into which the picture will be fitted.

After measuring the size of your frame, carefully cut a mitre at each end of the four strips, so that when fitted together they form perfect right angles at each corner, Fig. 3. Securely nail or glue the corners together; get a piece of glass cut to fit the groove of the frame, and cut a piece of wood $\frac{1}{4}$ in. thick for the back, which will be held in position by a few brads knocked in flat. This frame can be

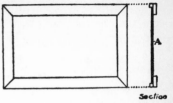

Fig. 3.—Picture Frame.

decorated by enamel or wood stain, walnut, or any suitable colour.

AN OXFORD FRAME

A more artistic frame is the Oxford, which must be cut of solid $\frac{3}{4}$ in. quartering. Cross grooves $\frac{3}{4}$ in. wide at 1 in. from each end, and half the thickness of the wood, must be cut, and each piece will then fit one over the other, thus making a perfect frame with projecting ends 1 in. in length, Fig. 4. The groove for the glass and back can be made either by cutting out with the knife, or by nailing small strips on the back,

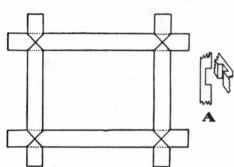

Fig. 4.—An Oxford Frame.

as explained above. If desired, a fancy design can be cut on the face of the frame.

A TEAPOT STAND

A very useful and artistic present for the home is a teapot stand,

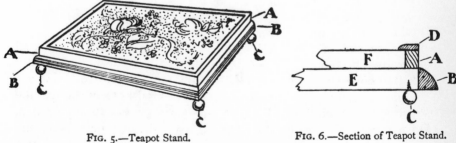

Fig. 5.—Teapot Stand.   Fig. 6.—Section of Teapot Stand.

Figs. 5 and 6. Take a piece of wood, E, 8 in. by 8 in. and $\frac{3}{4}$ in.

thick; procure a fancy pattern enamelled tile F—6 in. square is a very usual size—and lay it on the wood in the centre, leaving a margin of 1 in. all round. Get four pieces of wood, AD, rounded on one edge, and mitre them to hold the tile down, nailing them securely to the board. Ornament the edges of the board itself with a simple pattern, B. Procure four ¾ in. brass screw knobs, C, and fix them underneath, one at each corner, to form feet; then stain or polish the sides after all is fixed together.

A PIPE-RACK

Take a piece of wood 3 in. by 12 in. and ¼ in. thick, and cut out fancy corners in semicircular or other shape at each end.

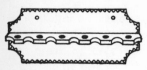

Obtain a second piece of wood, the same length and thickness, but 2½ in. wide, and cut in it six holes at equal distances apart and ¾ in. in diameter. Glue and nail the edge of this slip to the centre of the first piece of wood, Fig. 7. The front edge of the

FIG. 7.—A Pipe-rack.

pipe-rack can be ornamented with a zigzag or other pattern with your knife, and stained to whatever colour is desired. Two holes should be bored in the back, by which the article may be hung to the wall.

A JAPANESE FIDDLE

This novel musical instrument can be made thus. Procure an old cigar-box; clean off all the paper and detach the lid. Next take a broomstick, A, Fig. 8, 3 ft. long, slice it in half, and smooth up the flat side; round off the top, and bore a hole, B, 1½ in. from the extremity, into which a wooden peg, C, will be screwed. This peg is to hold a musical string— a D violin string, or a wire. At the other end of this stick cut a groove the length of the lid of the box, and nail the lid to the stick, keeping it in the centre.

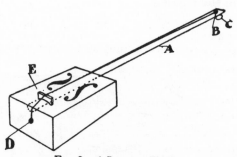

FIG. 8.—A Japanese Fiddle.

In each side of the lid cut an S-shaped hole 3 in. long and ¼ in. wide, similar to those in the face of a violin. Nail the lid to the box, and drill a hole in the end of the box directly in line with the end of the stick. Here insert another peg, D, ½ in. long, to

hold the other end of the string. Make a small movable bridge, E,
of wood 2 in. long, to hold up the string. Tune up the string to
any note on the piano, and the instrument can then be played with
an ordinary violin bow.

A Cage for Tame Mice

Procure from the grocer a light wooden soap-box, ABCD, Fig. 9,
about 20 in. long, 9 in. deep, and 12 in. high. Divide this off
by a thin wooden partition, E, about 8 in. from the end, AA. Put
in a floor, F, about half-way up, and with your knife cut two entrance

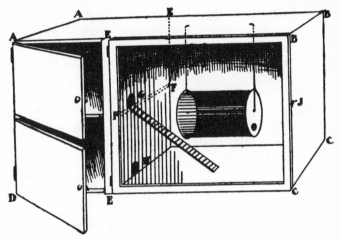

FIG. 9.—Cage for Tame Mice.

holes, G, H, in the partition, top and bottom. Close in the front of
this compartment with two doors, one above and one below. Now
make a frame for the front, and cover it with strong bird wire,
securely fixed with staples. Put hinges on this front, and a small
fastening, J, to open and close.

Place a small sloping piece of wood from the bottom of the cage
to the hole, G, in the first floor to serve as a staircase for the
mice, attaching little cross pieces, $\frac{1}{2}$ in. apart, as foot-boards. If
desired, a wheel for exercise can be added. Cut two round pieces
of wood, 4 in. in diameter, with a hole $1\frac{1}{2}$ in. in diameter, to admit
a mouse. Nip off a number of pieces of wire 4 in. long, and
fix them in each circle of wood near the edge, as so to form a
wheel, which can then be made to hang from the ceiling of the
house by means of two pieces of wire fixed at the centre of
each end, and bent up to allow the wheel to spin round.

OLD AUNT SALLY

A great deal of fun can be obtained from the game of Aunt Sally, Fig. 10, and very little trouble need be expended in making a life-like representation of that venerable old lady.

Obtain a stout block of wood some 11 in. wide, and twice as long; draw rough outlines of the face upon the various sides of the wood, and then whittle it down until some resemblance to a human head is obtained. The assistance of paint will be required to emphasize the appearance, whilst a hole bored in the mouth will serve to contain the clay pipe with which Aunt Sally is wont to regale her leisure moments. The addition of a little coloured wool or tow should give an almost

FIG. 10.—Old Aunt Sally.

life-like appearance, whilst a strong hook driven into the back of the head will serve to keep the figure suspended on a tree or a wall. The sticks for throwing can be made by cutting some old broom handles into lengths of 12 in., and neatly rounding the ends with your knife.

THE WRESTLERS

A very clever and novel illusion is the wrestlers, Fig. 11, which can be easily made with a jack-knife. Get two ordinary clothes' pegs; cut off the bottom prongs, AB, of each and fix them to the sides of the pegs by means of brads, so that they work quite freely, thus forming the legs. Next get two pieces of wood, CD, 3½ in. long, ½ in. wide, and ⅛ in. thick. Fix them by brads to the top or shoulder parts of the pegs, so as to form the arms, and thread pieces of black cotton through them at EE to the leg of a chair or table, holding the other end in your hand. By simply

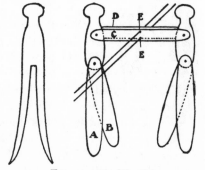

FIG. 11.—The Wrestlers.

moving the cotton with your finger you can make the men wrestle on the floor quite naturally, or dance most quaintly, according as you wish.

BUILDING BRICKS

As a simple exercise to test your skill with the jack-knife in really smooth work, try to make a box of building bricks. The wood for this can be obtained from any old pieces of board lying about the house. The only thing is that they must be of uniform thickness. For simple bricks, Fig. 12, cut your wood into six lengths, each of 1, 2, 4, and 6 inches. For triangular pieces to be used on top of the house, all you have to do is to mark a triangle on a 4-in. piece, and cut away along the lines. To form arches mark a 4-in. piece with an exact semicircle and cut round the line.

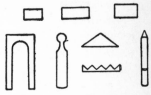

FIG. 12.—Building Bricks.

If you are more ambitious, you can exercise your powers on cutting columns and ornamenting them with capitals. In the accompanying sketches, Fig. 12, are several designs of ornamented columns, all of which can be cut with a little care. Be careful in measuring. Every brick, whatever its size, must be perfectly smooth and exact in measurement. Churches, town-halls, and various other buildings can be copied for models. Stain all the pieces an even colour.

NIGGER NINEPINS

FIG. 13.—A Nigger Ninepin.

This is quite a novelty in the way of toys for the youngsters of the family circle. Ordinary ninepins is a good game, played by both young and old; but nigger ninepins appeals to the humorous side of play. Get ten pieces of thick wood, 6 in. high and 2 in. deep—longer sizes look more attractive. Draw with your blacklead pencil the simple outline of a nigger boy, as shown in Fig. 13. Cut the wood round at the top for the head, then slope gradually away to the foot. The cutting must be plain and bold. Ensure that each figure will stand by making the bottom quite smooth. When all the cutting and shaping is done, paint the face black, the jacket and vest yellow, and the pants red. Add a number from 1 to 10 to each figure. An ordinary round wooden ball completes the set.

A CHARMING DOLLS' HOUSE

Every boy who has a young sister and is clever with his jack-knife should certainly make an up-to-date dolls' house, which will give an amount of pleasure that no other article could equal. Although at first sight it may seem a big undertaking, it is a capital bit of knife work. Take any strong wooden box without a lid. When stood on one end it should measure 2 ft. 6 in. high, 2 ft. wide, and 1 ft. from back to front. First divide it by means of a shelf in the centre, securely nailed to the sides. Then divide each of these compartments with a piece of thin wood, thus forming four rooms—kitchen, parlour, and two upstair bedrooms.

For the front, take a piece of wood the same width as the whole box, but four inches higher, and nail a fancy piece of wood on the top to form a cornice. Next cut four squares to form windows for each room, and make a small groove at the back in which to fix the glass. These windows should be ornamented by carving out with your knife two small columns for the sides and an angular piece for the dripstone over each window, also a piece of wood to form the window-sill. Glue all these pieces on strongly.

The door can be cut in the lower part of the front and ornamented with columns and dripstone like the windows, whilst two small steps should be glued to the bottom part of the door opening. A piece of wood must then be cut the same size as the doorway, and made to open on small brass hinges. The knocker consists of a small brass screw ring, and the handle is a brass cabinet knob, such as may be obtained from any ironmonger. The front is fastened to the house by two small hinges placed on the left-hand side, and is kept closed by what is called a cabin hook and eye fixed on the right-hand side.

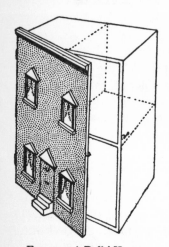

FIG. 14.—A Dolls' House.

Paper the inside of the house with odd pieces of wall-paper, and put linoleum on each floor. Thoroughly clean the outside of the box, and stain or paint it red. The front should be painted to imitate the front of an ordinary house. Pick out the ornaments round the windows and door, and the cornice at the top with white paint; the rest can be painted red, and lines indicating brick work drawn in with a blacklead pencil or white paint. The inside of the front should be painted pure white. When the house has been varnished it will appear elegant and neat, as in Fig. 14.

THE MECHANICAL SHOEBLACK

This is an extremely clever bit of mechanism, yet it can all be executed with your jack-knife. It consists of three parts—the man having his boots cleaned, the kneeling shoeblack, and the propeller worked by the wind, as seen in Fig. 15.

Take a piece of wood about 12 in. long, 3 in. wide, and ¼ in. thick to form the base on which the figures are placed. Now take a thin board, ⅛ in. thick, and draw upon it, with a blacklead pencil, the

Fig. 15.—The Mechanical Shoeblack.

figure of a man, A, Fig. 15, standing with one leg raised and the foot placed upon the shoeblack's box. This man should be about 6½ in. high.

The shoeblack, B, is cut in three separate parts—the kneeling body with one arm resting on the box C, the right arm D, with a long brush in the hand, and the head with shoulder and elbow all in one piece. Fasten the elbow to the arm by means of a piece of string or wire with a knot each side to hold them together. Then connect the head to the body in a similar way, so that the two parts will work freely.

The third portion of the mechanism consists of a post, E, cut out of a piece of wood, 7 in. long and ¼ in. square, securely fixed upright 1 in. from the end and side of the base board. The fan or propeller, F, is made by cutting a small circular piece of wood 1 in. in diameter, and securely fixing round it five wind flaps, each 3 in. long and 1½ in. wide, slightly tilted as shown in the picture.

Now get a piece of stout copper wire, cut off two pieces 1¼ in. long, and form a hook at each end. Fix one, G, near the top, and the other near the bottom of the post. Take another piece of wire, H, about 8½ in. long, fix one end to the propeller, pass it through the two hooks in the post, and form a bend as seen in the diagram on a level with the shoeblack's brush. The other end should be pointed and allowed to rest on a small piece of glass, ¾ in. square, glued to the base. Connect another piece of wire, K, to the end of the shoeblack's brush, and hook it to the bend you have already formed in the propeller wire. Outline the coats and faces of the two figures with a blue and red pencil. When the article is placed in the wind it will work quite successfully.

A Working Railway

This is a working model which can be made with a jack-knife. It consists of a locomotive engine and a number of trucks, worked

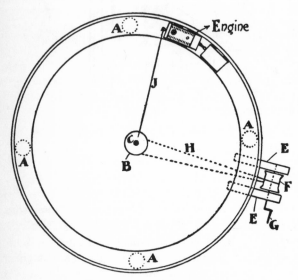

FIG. 16.—A Model Railway.

by means of a handle which causes the whole train to run round a track on an ordinary dining-room table, Fig. 16.

To make the track, secure sufficient match boarding perfectly clean and smooth, out of which, when nailed together, cut a large circular disc 4 feet in diameter. Next get a broom handle, and cut off four pieces 2½ in. long, and glue them upright on the underside of your base board to form legs, AAAA. Bore a hole ¼ in. in diameter, exactly in the centre of the board; take two small cotton reels and a piece of wooden curtain rod about 3 in. long, which will easily pass through the centre hole. Glue the end of one cotton reel, B, to the rod, C, pass the rod through the centre hole of the base, and glue the other reel, D, Fig. 16A, to the part of the rod projecting below, leaving just sufficient space to enable them to turn round freely.

On the outer edge of the underside of the board nail two small pieces of wood, EE, projecting far enough and sufficiently wide apart to carry another reel, F, fixed on a pivot, which will work freely with a handle, G, made of stiff copper wire. Now take a piece of stout cord to form a band, H, which will pass round the reel underneath the centre of the board and over the reel on the outside edge, so that when the handle is turned the whole apparatus will work freely.

A track or lines will be laid as near the outside edge of the base as possible and 3 in. apart, and can be formed of thin lath wood securely nailed down. Be careful to keep the rails in a perfect circle, quite even, and the exact distance apart from the centre reel all the way round.

Having made the track, now proceed with the locomotive. For the base you will require a piece of wood 7 in. long, 3 in. wide, and ½ in. thick. For the body of the engine get a piece of cornice pole 3½ in.

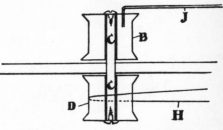

FIG. 16A.—Reels for working the Railway.

long, and nail this to the base, keeping it about ¾ in. from one end. The funnel can be formed out of a piece of broomstick about 2 in. long, curved at one end to fit on and fix over the circular body.

The air drum is made of another piece of broomstick 2 in. long, cut circular at the top and glued on to the body. Near the front of the body fix two small bracket supports, whilst at the back the cabin can be formed out of wood cut to fit the base, with two windows in front. Form the coal tender at one end of the base of the engine, leaving a space of about one inch between it and the side of the cabin. Two small pieces of wood can be fixed to the front and rear of the engine to form buffers, and four small wooden brackets about 1½ in. long should be fixed under the base to carry the wheels.

The four wheels are formed by cutting away the centres of two cotton reels, so as to leave the outsides and sufficient of the centre to rest on the rail. Join the wheels with axles made of very stout wire, which must pass through the brackets under the engine.

The trucks are made from cigar-boxes cut to size, and the

wheels are identical to those used for the engine. Connect the trucks to the engine with small hooks, and paint the train a shade of green or red picked out with white lines.

To make the train go round the track, secure a piece of stout wire, J, Fig. 16A, and fix it firmly to the reel in the centre of the base, connecting the front part to the engine with a hook. By turning the handle the model will work perfectly.

BOATS AND SHIPS

Having procured a suitable block of wood, mark the outlines of the boat in pencil, and cut away the outside portions, smoothing

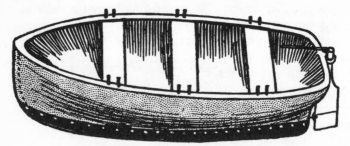

FIG. 17.—A small Rowing-boat.

the work when finished with glass paper. A strip of lead should then be nailed on to form a keel. Cut out the rudder from a piece

FIG. 18.—A Paddle Steamer.

of a cigar-box, and secure it to the back of the boat with two small staples and pins to hook on and off. If you wish to make a rowing-boat, Fig. 17, hollow out the inside and make seats from small pieces of lath wood neatly glued in place. The hull should be left solid for a sailing boat, whilst the masts and sails can be rigged according to the style of boat desired.

Far more imposing, however, is the paddle-steamer shown in Fig. 18. The body of the vessel should be cut out and a funnel formed of a thin piece of metal tubing. The paddle-wheels, B, may be made from two cotton reels, A, with eight pieces of lath wood, B, securely fixed round them to form paddles. Two small wooden brackets, CC, should be fixed at each side of the centre of the steamer, and the axle, E, of the paddle-wheels made of ¼ in. round stick will pass through holes in the same brackets. A mast with proper rigging should be placed towards the bow of the boat.

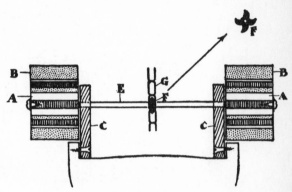

FIG. 19.—Machinery for the Paddle Steamer.

The cabin may be erected on the back part of the vessel with windows and roof, and sufficiently large to contain the inside of an old alarum clock. Connect the spring wheels to the axle of the paddle-wheels by means of a small piece of chain, G, working on a cog, F, so that when the clock is wound up it will immediately set the paddle to work and thus propel the steamer. A section of this boat is shown in Fig. 19.

ACROBATS AND MOVING ANIMALS

These little toys are easily made with a jack-knife. With a pencil, sketch in simple outline the figure of a man in gymnastic attire, Fig. 20. Cut the body, the head, arms, and legs separately, and make the head and limbs rather long. Drill a small hole in the centre of the neck at the shoulder and at the bottom of the body, and fasten the head and limbs together by means of a piece of thin twine with a knot at the end to prevent it falling off. The figure is able to stand upright by having a groove, A, made underneath the feet. Prepare a board—say 8 in. long and ¾ in. thick, having grooves, B, in it to hold up the figure. It is surprising how many strange and comical attitudes can be struck by the figure on moving the head or arms, and the free leg.

Such figures can be made to move by means of strings. Fasten the string near where the limbs are put on, letting it hang down with a

FIG. 20.—The Acrobat.   FIG. 21.—Mechanical Elephant.

small weight at the end. By pulling one or more strings at a time very amusing effects are produced.

Various animals, dogs, cats, donkeys and especially elephants, make capital mechanical figures. The head and trunk of the elephant, Fig. 21, should be in one piece, and the string placed far back in the head, so that the trunk and legs move alternately.

Such are some of the clever and amusing mechanical toys which can be made with a jack-knife. Start with the simplest things here described, and with a little practice you will be able to produce more difficult ones.

PART II

INDOOR HOBBIES

CHAPTER XX

BLACK AND WHITE DRAWING

FOR PLEASURE AND PROFIT

THAT the "great artist is born, not made" is a truism none will deny, yet it may be argued with a great deal of right that many boys not naturally possessed of any considerable talent for drawing may, by carefully following out certain rules and practical instructions, produce results both pleasing and profitable.

It should be borne in mind that many young artists of ability fail to make satisfactory progress owing to the lack of encouragement and assistance which they might receive from those who have made names and fortunes by their skill with pen and brush.

Interviews with celebrated artists have been published times without number, for the purpose of revealing the methods by which they have achieved success, but in reality very little information concerning the methods so successfully employed has been brought to light.

As can be readily understood, there is no short and royal road to success as a black and white artist, but in the present chapter some suggestions are given which have been used with great effect by one of the most popular "black and white" men of the day, and by utilising the information thus given, any boy who can draw should be able in a very short while to produce sketches that would be readily purchased by the art editors of practically any monthly or weekly periodical.

When it is remembered that at the present time, there are dozens of young men earning incomes ranging from £300 to £2000 a year by drawing for the illustrated press and trade advertisers, no further encouragement should be necessary to induce the young artist to put his skill to the test in this direction.

THE ART OF DRAWING

Before embarking on any serious attempt at black and white work, the student should make himself familiar with the principles of drawing. Nearly every large town boasts a good Art School, and the first and soundest step is to attend some of the classes and pursue a thorough course of study under an experienced master, beginning with the plaster casts and finishing with life models.

"Draw, and keep on drawing," is an excellent rule ; and the student should confine himself to the simple media of charcoal and chalk.   All attempts at wash work may be left until thorough proficiency in outline has been attained.

Having acquired the ability to memorise figure studies, a start may be made on a composition of some kind.   It is a good plan to pick up some simple incident in a story and attempt an illustration. Begin by working out the subject in a strong manner, keeping the lines free from all uncertainty and wavering, by this means gaining that strength of treatment which will eventually become your most valuable and treasured characteristic as an artist.

Let every touch show determination.

It is a distinct advantage to cultivate a particular style.   Those famous exponents of line work, Phil May, Charles Dana Gibson, and Fred Pegram won places for themselves in the world of art by the styles they perpetuated.   The distinctive wash drawings of men like Maurice Greiffenhagen, W. Hatherell, and Cyrus Cuneo have formed a standard that no modern artist can afford to ignore.

CHOICE OF MATERIALS

Every artist shows a particular fancy in his selection of working materials, or, in other words, evinces a preference for certain makes of whites and blacks, brushes, pens, cardboard, &c.   One will prefer his white paint to be of a dead and chalky nature ; another will invariably employ a more sticky substance.

A lengthy controversy has raged during recent years concerning the use of blacks and their respective qualities of reproduction, but as the point has never been satisfactorily settled, each artist championing his own particular choice, it must be left to the student to discover by experience which suits his style the best.

Lamp-black is the most favoured, as, by working in a little gamboge, a certain warmth of tone can be obtained.   Moreover, when blended with white for body colour work, this mixture has the advantage of preventing that undesirable greyness which is so prejudicial to satisfactory reproduction.

Persian black, manufactured by Roberson, of Long Acre, London, although somewhat more expensive than other blacks, produces splendid results—especially when utilised in pure wash work, by which is meant the gaining of proper effects without the use of

Chinese white. Another good one is ivory black, which is a favourite colour with many professionals.

The Chinese whites sold by Winsor & Newton, Reeves, or Rowney, can be tried and judged according to the results obtained. They cost from 4½d. a tube and upwards, but it is sometimes found better to purchase white in bottles.

Having procured his colours, the student should next obtain three sable-hair brushes, sizes Nos. 3, 5, and 7. One or two flat hog's-hair brushes, such as are used for oil painting, must also be bought. These will be found extremely useful for "body colour" work, an explanation of which will be given hereafter. In making a selection preference should be given to short-haired brushes similar to that shown in A, Fig. 1. Should these not be obtainable, get brushes like that shown at B, and cut down the hairs at the point indicated by the dotted horizontal line.

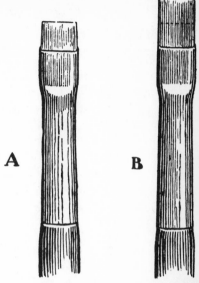

A   B

FIG. 1.—Hog's-hair Brushes.

The only other requisites are a few pencils, a piece of soft rubber, some drawing-pins, Conté crayon and carbon chalks, together with a supply of card which, for either wash or line, can be bought at any artists' colourman. The board generally chosen for both purposes is ordinary white mounting-board.

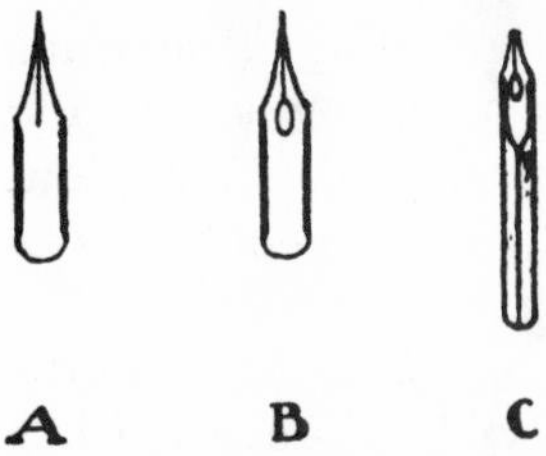

For erasing and fetching up lights in chalk work, plastic rubber is the best material.

The best nibs for pen-and-ink or line drawing are those of the shape and size depicted in Fig. 2. That shown at A is made from extremely fine and flexible steel, and will produce lines of every possible gradation of thickness. It should not be used, however, until some degree of proficiency has been attained ; for in unpractised hands its fineness may lead to splaying the point.

A   B   C

FIG. 2.—Types of Nibs required.

For practical purposes the pen shown at B will be found the most useful. The old-fashioned steel crow quill illustrated at C is still favoured by many artists.

The most satisfactory ink is that known as " Waterproof," which is preferable to ordinary Indian ink inasmuch as it never clogs the pen nor results in " missing " lines.

HUMOROUS ILLUSTRATIONS

Humorous drawings, roughly speaking, may be divided into three main divisions; those broadly comic, such as appear in the

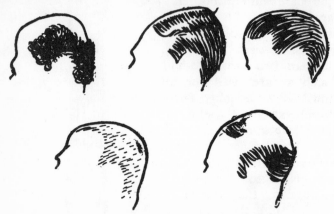

FIG. 3.—Profile Outline of Humorous Heads.

cheap illustrated press; caricatures or pictorial exaggerations, and the more detailed and artistic humorous illustrations such as are published in *Punch* and the better-class magazines. For the latter kind of work

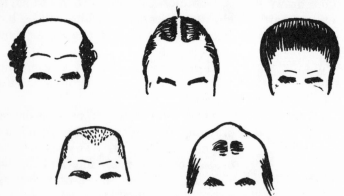

FIG. 4.—Full View of the same Humorous Heads.

a thorough knowledge of the technicalities of art, as well as the power of humorous representation, is essential.

To achieve success in any of these branches, a keen appreciation of the humorous side of things is of paramount importance, for no matter how fine a draughtsman the artist may be, he will never shine as a humorist if he lack the faculty of appreciating the ridiculous.

FIG. 5.—Side View of Eye Expressions in Humorous Faces.

The preliminary training of the would-be comic artist will necessitate perpetual observation of the marked characteristics of human beings, and of every kind of animal. Such points

FIG. 6.—Full View of Eye Expressions.

as peculiarities of facial expression, of features and appearance, should not only be noted, but be drawn and drawn again until they can be accurately reproduced at a moment's notice. The habit of carrying a sketch-book is recommended

FIG. 7.—Side View of Noses in Humorous Faces.

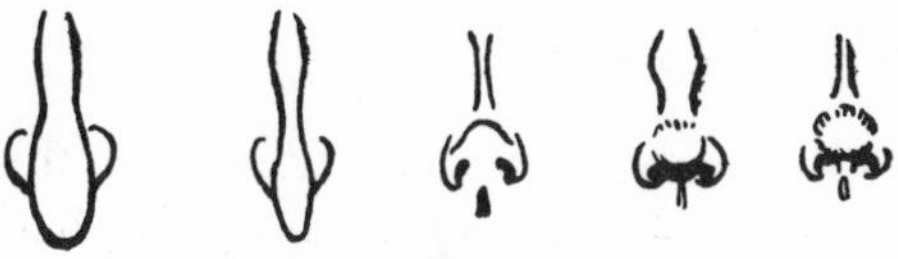

at this stage, and in a very little while, it is safe to say, a most extraordinary collection of eyes, ears, noses, boots, hats, mouths, and so on, will be acquired.

FIG. 8.—Full View of Noses.

The different points of view from which such objects can be viewed and reproduced must also create lasting mental images, so that the young artist will be able, whilst retaining in his mind the appearance of a nose in profile, for example, to represent

FIG. 9.—Side View of Humorous Mouths.

the same feature as if he were standing with its owner face to face.

FIG. 10.—Full View of Humorous Mouths.

In the subjoined illustrations, Figs. 3 to 14, examples are given of prominent characteristics shown in profile and full face.

FIG. 11.—Side View of Humorous Ears.

FIG. 12.—Full View of Ears in Humorous Faces.

In the complete drawing shown in Fig. 15 is introduced one

FIG. 13.—Boots for Humorous Figures.

marked feature from each of the above sketches. It will be noticed

FIG. 14.—Boots (Full View) for Humorous Figures.

that the artist has adopted a free style, altogether lacking in un-

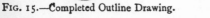

FIG. 15.—Completed Outline Drawing.   FIG. 16.—Complete Figure in Solids and Tints

necessary detail, with a result both striking and effective.

In the next picture, Fig. 16, almost made up as before, the reader will notice that the coat is put in with solid black (generally done with a brush), white lines being left to indicate the creases in the garment. The artist indicates the tint he requires—which may be made either with dot or line—by pencilling the part in blue, and the printer fills in the space with dots or lines—according to which gives the better effect.

A

FIG. 17.—Hand drawn in Detail.

For comic work scanty detail is required in the drawing of hands, although more time should be given to a study of these members than to any other portion of the human anatomy. Many otherwise passable artists make a terribly poor show when it comes to depicting "hands."

B

FIG. 18.—Hand drawn for Comic Purposes.

Some idea of a hand correctly drawn in detail is given in Fig. 17, while Fig. 18 shows the same hand drawn for broadly comic purposes. This method can be applied generally in treating other portions of the body, for feet and their coverings usually prove an equally formidable stumbling-block to the uninitiated.

The principles thus outlined may also be adopted for the comic representation of animals.

CARICATURING

Celebrities with marked facial expressions and prominent characteristics lend themselves readily to the art of the caricaturist. It should be borne in mind that the main intention of the caricaturist is to give a pictorial representation in which, while retaining a general likeness, certain peculiarities are exaggerated in order to make the person or thing look ridiculous.

All idiosyncrasies should be noted, and then accentuated on paper, the entire face or figure being drawn in with as few strokes as possible. At first only heads should be attempted, and a good photograph is the best model from which to copy. The point which is to form the basis of the caricature should then be studied most carefully and exaggerated only to such an extent that no part of the original likeness is marred or destroyed.

Figs. 19, 20, and 21 are fair examples for the amateur to copy. The former depicts the late Sir Henry Irving, whilst Figs. 20 and 21 show how normal features, A, may be exaggerated, B, for caricaturing purposes.

FIG. 19.—Caricature of the late Sir Henry Irving.

More ambitious students, anxious to qualify in the higher branches of humorous illustrating, cannot do better than become regular subscribers to *Punch* and its American contemporary *Puck*, a vigorous and clever journal in which the political cartoon is coloured.

A FEW NOTES ON PEN-AND-INK ILLUSTRATIONS

Assuming that the fundamental principles of drawing from life have been thoroughly mastered, a start may now be made with drawing for the illustrated press. First work out the subject in pencil with rough sketching from models, if circumstances permit. A brother or sister can generally be pressed into service for a few minutes.

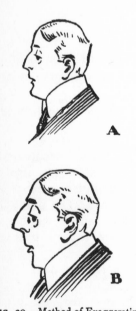

FIG. 20.—Method of Exaggerating Features.

FIG. 21.—Another Example of Exaggeration

Now trace off the most pronounced features of the drawing on a piece of transparent paper, and, with a soft pencil, coat the back thoroughly with lead. Pin the tracing-paper thus prepared on to the white card-board and go over all the lines again with a steel point, such as can be obtained from any art colourman. The result will be the transmission of a faint impression to the card.

Line in the outline with ink ; work in the shadows and afterwards add the lines for tone. Fig. 22 shows the various stages of the work up to this point.

There are several ways of lining for shadows, depicted in A and B, Fig. 23. When a tone is required, it is advisable to make the shadows more solid, as shown in Fig. 24.

Not infrequently, when engaged in the task of submitting specimens of your work to art editors, you may be met with the criticism that your sketches lack colour, by which is meant, not that they should

FIG. 22.—Completed Line Drawing.

possess coloured tints, but that they are devoid of those contrasts of light and shade so essential to an effective drawing. This is

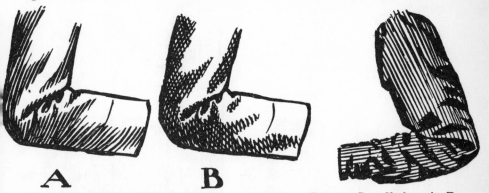

A   B

FIG. 23.—Linings for Shadows.   FIG. 24.—Deep Shadows give Tone.

exemplified in Figs. 25 and 26, which represent the same man, but whereas the former is flat and lacks colour, proper tone is given to the latter by the deeper shading and cross hatching. This principle applies to all drawings.

Experience and practice alone will overcome the difficulties pre-

FIG. 25.—A Drawing which lacks "Colour."

FIG. 26.—The Difference made by "Colour."

FIG. 27.—A Figure swamped by the Background.

FIG. 28.—The Background rectified.

sented in attempting to draw backgrounds. A great deal of discretion is necessary, since no part of the background must be allowed to in-terfere with the subjects in the foreground.

In Fig. 27 is shown an example of a background swamping the figure which alone should have pro-minence in the picture; the next illustration, Fig. 28, shows the same picture correctly drawn.

When drawing for the cheaper publications, it is as well to keep faces free from all shading, obtain-ing different expressions solely by the outlines of the features, as ex-emplified in Fig. 29. The reason why shading should be avoided is that the rapid printing by the rotary machines on common paper tends to clog the lines.

FIG. 29.—Expressions obtained by Inline.

FIG. 30.—Specimen of Work for Book or Magazine Cover.

When it happens that some part of a drawing, perhaps a head or an arm, does not meet with the approval of the editor, it is not necessary, in order to meet his requirements, to redraw the sketch in its entirety. By careful erasures or by covering the lines with Chinese white the offending portion may be obliterated and after-wards drawn again; or in the event of a fairly large alteration being re-quired, a slip of white paper may be pasted on and the correction made in such a manner that the new lines will meet those already made.

For book and magazine covers a strong and heavy method of working is generally used. An example of this is seen in Fig. 30.

DECORATIVE WORK

There is often a demand for decorative work for borders and headings, or to supplement an ordinary sketch. A simple method for applying flowers and twigs for decoration is shown in Fig. 31. Fig. 32

shows a decorative scroll, A representing the elaborated form of the

A

B

FIG. 31.—Flowers and Twigs treated ornamentally.   FIG. 32.—A decorative Scroll.

simple design B. Fig. 33 suggests a way of working a ribbon for a title heading, the actual material being first pinned to the board in the manner depicted and the drawing thus made from the model.

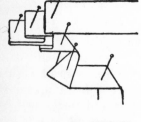

FIG. 33.—Working a Ribbon for a Title-page.

WASH OR HALF-TONE WORK

This also may be divided roughly into three main sections: pure wash, by which is meant all the different tones and effects obtained by a greater or less amount of water being mixed with the black; body colour, by which is understood the mixing of black and Chinese white to form the various tones; thirdly, a combination of the previous two.

In the last mentioned, chalk and pure colour may be utilised for the working out of the design, the finishing touches being put in with body colour. From this last method the most satisfactory results may be obtained.

PURE WASH

It is not an uncommon practice with some artists to commence the design in black chalk, blocking in the form or shape of shadows and working over the half-tones in pure colour. Another method is to outline the sketch in pencil, putting in the shadows with pure wash, deep black, or, according to the requirements, softening the edges of the shadows and then taking a wash over the whole. In both cases the detail work is put in afterwards. High lights can be added when the drawing is otherwise complete. The use of Chinese white for high lights is occasionally supplemented by scratching with a pen-knife.

BODY COLOUR

To commence body colour, take a quantity of black and Chinese white upon the palette, just as if you were about to paint in oils. The method of mixing is practically the same as for oil work, except that on the palette the combination must be made a shade darker, since it dries slightly lighter upon the card.

It must also be borne in mind that as water colours dry very quickly, the different tones should be worked in rapidly while the mixture is wet. When once the colour has dried upon the board, never disturb it ; but should the result not be a success, wipe off the faulty part with a sponge or soft rag, and repaint the portion.

A good plan is to work up faces and hands with Conté crayon or carbon pencil when the rest of the picture has been completed. An example of the working of a crayon pencil on a face is given in Fig. 34.

It is the practice of some artists to outline their drawings in waterproof ink, and to cover the line of the workings with the different tones. The object of this mode of procedure

FIG. 34.—Working Crayon Pencil on a Face.

is to ensure that any alteration that might be necessary may not destroy the original scheme of the drawing.

COMBINATION WORKING

By this is meant the commencing of work in the pure, *i.e.* with water and black, and finishing up the lighter tones with body colour. After all this the final effects may be obtained by the use of chalks.

A style of working favoured by some artists is the following :— Mix in a saucer enough black and white to form a light grey ; add a little gum arabic, and stir well. Only sufficient gum should be used to ensure the composition being slightly sticky. Now take a sponge and, dipping it into the mixture, smear it evenly over the cardboard intended for the drawing. When the coat is dry the drawing should be made upon it in black chalk.

Next work with either pure or body colour, but instead of adding lights, procure them by damping the part required to be lightened with the point of the brush and wiping away the composition swiftly with a soft rag. This will not only give the required lights, but produce a generally softening effect.

FIG. 35.—Method of Working Lights on Tone Ground.

In using this grey tone it will be found that when drawing faces, hands, and delicate parts of drapery, the tone already on the card will produce a half-tone, so that when the darker portions are put in, the high lights can be obtained by the use of Chinese white, as depicted in Fig. 35.

An ingenious method of working in backgrounds of trees, grass, &c., is outlined in the following paragraphs.

Should scrub, bushes, trees, or grass be required, it is advisable to make the backing of a dark shade, and to work on the branches, leaves, and twigs in a light body tint.

For trees, procure a sable or hog's-hair brush, with the bristles splayed at the top as shown at A, Fig. 36. Taking the colour into

A

FIG. 36.—A Method of Working Foliage.

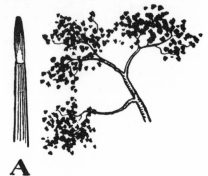

A

FIG. 37.—Adding Leaves to the Branches.

the brush and holding the latter at right angles to the card, dab on the foliage in the manner depicted. A little practice is necessary before a satisfactory result can be obtained.

In A, Fig. 37, is shown a sable brush with a flat point (old worn sables are best for this). Working in the branches and twigs first, and holding the brush as above described, dab on the leaves after the fashion described. This will prove most effective for leaves and foliage in the foreground.

The flat hog's-hair or sable brush shown in A, Fig. 38, has been greatly splayed out and cut away. By taking the end of the brush

A

FIG. 38.—Grass-work done with Brush.

dipped in the colour, and passing it lightly upwards over the surface of the board, the effect of grass as shown in the illustration will be given.

CHAPTER XXI

BENT-IRON WORK

ORNAMENTAL ARTICLES FOR THE HOME

THE number of artistic and ornamental objects that can be made in bent iron has given this handicraft increasing popularity as an indoor hobby. With a small and inexpensive outfit the beginner may embark at once upon more or less ambitious designs, and make frames, screens, letter-racks, and many similar ornaments with a certainty of success.

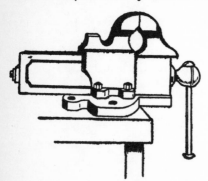

FIG. 1.—The Hand-vice.

FIG. 2.—Flat-nosed Pliers.

FIG. 3.—Round-nosed Pliers.

The establishment of the workshop is the first consideration, and the following list of tools and appliances will serve for a guide as to what must be purchased.

FIG. 4.—Tinman's Snips.

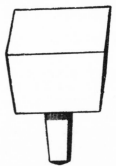

FIG. 5.—Square-headed Anvil.

Hand-vice, Fig. 1	approximate cost	8s. od.
Pair of flat-nosed pliers, Fig. 2	„	1s. 2d.
Pair of round-nosed pliers, Fig. 3	„	1s. 2d.
Pair of tinman's snips, Fig. 4	„	1s. 5d.
Small square-headed anvil, Fig. 5	„	8s. 6d.

Tinman's bull-nosed hammer, weigh-
    ing ½ lb., Fig. 6   .   .   .   approximate cost   1s. 6d.
8-inch flat file @ 1d. per inch, Fig. 7 .   „   8d.
Hand-drill and bits, Fig. 8 .   .   .   „   5s. 6d.

A bench drill may be added to the above list at an approximate
cost of twenty-five shillings, but as, for all practical purposes, the

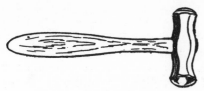

FIG. 6.—Tinman's Hammer.

FIG. 7.—Flat File.

FIG. 8.—Hand-drill.

hand-drill will be found sufficient, this more expensive tool can be
dispensed with.

MATERIAL

Flat Staffordshire iron is the best material to use, and can be
purchased in 12-foot lengths from any iron-
monger. Ask for " ⅜ in. width, 16 gauge," as
this will be the easiest size to manipulate for
small objects. At the same time procure 1 lb.
of ⅛ in. diameter rivets with a shank of ¼ in.,
illustrated in Fig. 9. These rivets cost 8d. per lb.

SECTION

FIG. 9.—Small Rivet.

THE SCROLLING IRON

In addition to the tools already mentioned, the scrolling iron shown in Fig. 10
is an essential part of the outfit, and must
be made at home before starting work.

Take a 12-in. length of flat iron, measuring ¾ in. by ¼ in., and hold it in the fire
with the pliers until it is red-hot. Place
the red end upon the anvil, which should
be gripped securely in the vice, and hammer
until the iron is beaten flat, as seen in Fig. 11. When cool, the

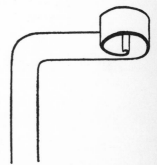

FIG. 10.—Scrolling Iron.

top and sides must be filed to the shape indicated by the dotted lines.

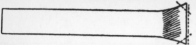

FIG. 11.—Iron prepared for scrolling.

Heat this end of the iron again, and, taking a firm hold with the round-nosed pliers, bend it into a hook, Fig. 12. Make this hooked end red once more, and with a complete turn of the pliers curl it according to the scroll shown in Fig. 13.

When the scroll is perfectly cold, the centre of the iron bar must be heated and bent vertically at right angles, to the shape de-

FIG. 12.—The Iron turned in a Hook.

FIG. 13.—The Scroll completed.

picted in Fig. 10.

This scrolling iron is of vital importance ; the greatest care, therefore, must be exercised in following the directions given above.

THE WORKING DRAWING

A working drawing is made to the exact size of the finished object, with charcoal upon brown paper. It is, however, unnecessary to duplicate the drawing of scrolls that exactly resemble one another in size and shape, as will be noticed when the method of making a frame is hereafter described in full detail.

PAINTING

On no account should Brunswick black be used for painting, as it gives a shiny, inartistic surface to the iron. When all the scrolling and riveting has been done, a couple of coats of Berlin black can be applied, this liquid imparting a dull colour to the metal.

HOW TO MAKE A FRAME

The following explanation of how to make the simple frame shown in Fig. 14 will serve to demonstrate the method of working and bending the iron to make up any design.

FIG. 14.—A simple Frame.

THE BASE

The base, or iron frame to which the scrolls are attached, is made from Staffordshire sheet iron, No. 18 gauge, a piece of which, measuring 3 ft. square, can be purchased for a few pence from any ironmonger.

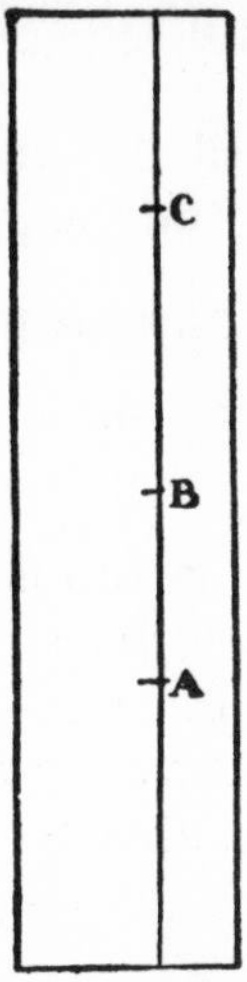

Cut a strip 2 ft. 4 in. by $\frac{5}{8}$ in. and rule a line from end to end with a metal point, dividing the strip into two unequal portions of $\frac{1}{4}$ in. and $\frac{3}{8}$ in. respectively, as shown in Fig. 15. Upon this line mark off three points, ABC, A being 8 in. from the end; B, 6 in. from A; and C, 8 in. from B.

At each of these points cut out V-shaped pieces with an apex angle of 90°, at the same time cutting the ends to angles of $22\frac{1}{2}$° as in Fig. 16. The

FIG. 16.—Strip prepared for the Base.

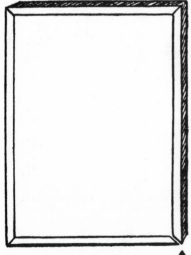

FIG. 15.—Strip for the Base of the Frame.

portions between these incisions must then be turned at right angles to the remainder of the iron, and the whole strip bent at the V-shaped cuts as shown enlarged in Fig. 17. The two ends can then be riveted together at A with an angle iron according to the method illustrated in Fig. 18.

Another way of joining these ends is to cut an additional $\frac{1}{4}$ in. in the original strip, indicated by the dotted lines at A, Fig. 16, which must be riveted to the other extremity of the frame, thus obviating the use of angle irons.

FIG. 17.—The Base completed.

FIG. 18.—The Angle Iron.

SCROLLING

A full working drawing, Fig. 19, of such scrolls as are not repeated in size or shape, must be made before beginning the work. The length of iron required for each scroll can be exactly ascertained by measuring the drawing with a piece of string, as in Fig. 20, where A is the length of string required to make the scroll B. Measure and cut the lengths of iron for all the scrolls before proceeding further.

Hammer and file the ends of the irons

to be scrolled in the manner already described (Fig. 11), and, heating the metal again, curl these ends very slightly, as depicted in Fig. 12, tak-

FIG. 19.—The Working Drawing.

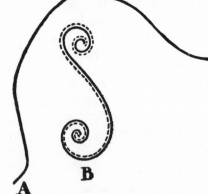

FIG. 20.—Measuring a Scroll with String.

ing care that the hook thus made is just sufficient to catch the scrolling iron at the point A, Fig. 21.

When this has been done, allow the iron to cool slowly, but on no account plunge the hot metal into cold water.

FIG. 21.—Making a Scroll.

FIG. 22.—Completing the Scroll.

Fix the scrolling iron firmly in the vice and clip the hook of the iron to be scrolled against the point A, Fig. 21. Seizing the other extremity with the pliers, bend the iron as shown in Fig. 22, taking it off repeatedly to compare with the working drawing until the desired outline is obtained. This comparison cannot be made too often, for the whole beauty of the finished work depends upon the care devoted to the scrolling.

RIVETING AND CLIPPING

When all the scrolls have been made, put the centre frame upon the working drawing and place the scrolls in their respective positions. Then, with a piece of chalk, mark off the spots where rivets are to be placed, indicated at X, Fig. 14. Holes must be drilled in the sides of the frame at these chalk marks to receive the rivets.

The scrolls must now be replaced and a pointed piece of chalk thrust through the holes drilled in the frame to mark the places where corresponding holes must be drilled in the scrolls.

FIG. 23.—Riveting on the Vice.

The method of riveting is exceedingly simple. The rivet has only to be passed through the two holes and have the protruding end burred, or beaten flat. In certain cases, however, the relative positions of the different parts make this difficult, and upon these occasions the following plan may be adopted with success. Place a thick piece of steel in the vice as shown in Fig. 23, and, standing the rivet thereon upon its end, pass it through the scroll and the frame and burr it in the ordinary way.

FIG. 24.—The Clip.

A clip is employed instead of a rivet when two scrolls meet in the manner shown in Fig. 24. This clip is made from a piece of sheet iron, cut to the size required and bent as in Fig. 25. When placed around the scrolls with ends overlapping, it serves to keep them perfectly firm and steady, and at the same time gives a neat and workmanlike appearance.

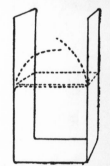

FIG. 25.—Making a Clip.

It frequently happens that three pieces of iron have to be riveted together, as can be seen from a glance at D, Fig. 14. In this case, place the flat end of the scroll E between the frame and the large scroll, and pass a rivet through both pieces at D.

THE SPEAR

The spear-shaped ornament at the top of the frame, F, Fig. 14, is the only piece of iron that remains to be worked before the frame is completed.

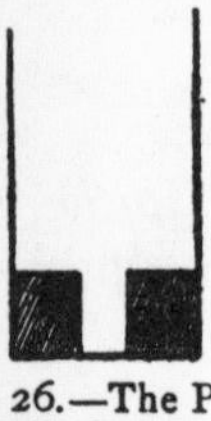

Take a piece of metal of the length required and file one end to form a pin $\frac{1}{4}$ in. long, depicted in Fig. 26. Flatten 1 in. at the other end with a hammer, place the iron in the vice, and file this flat portion to the shape required, indicated by the shaded lines in Fig. 27.

FIG. 26.—The Pin in the Spear.

When this has been done satisfactorily, make the end red-hot, place the iron once more in the vice, and, taking a firm grip with the flat-nosed pliers, give a half turn as illustrated in Fig. 28.

A hole must now be drilled in the frame to receive the pin in the lower end of the spear. When placed in position, the projecting end of this pin should be burred and the sides of the spear clipped to the adjoining scrolls so that the work when finished will appear as in Fig. 14.

FIG. 27.—Making the Spear-head.

THE BACK

A wooden back, to fit into the iron frame, can be fastened with pegs or nails passed through holes drilled in the sides of the base. This back will serve to keep the glass and picture in position when they have been inserted, and must not, therefore, be fixed until the frame is completely finished.

ROSETTES

It is not unusual to place brass or copper rosettes in the centres of the scrolls. When it is intended to do this, the ends of the irons must not be beaten flat when being prepared for scrolling, but must be turned in a complete circle as seen in Fig. 29. The rosette can then be fastened in this circle with a bolt and nut, shown in section, Fig. 30.

FIG. 28.—The Spear.

CROSS CORNERS

A cross corner is illustrated in Fig. 31, where two pieces of iron

are crossed to make a sharp angle. This is done by making two half-joints, Fig. 32, with a flat file, and hammering one piece of iron into the joint in the other piece. The riveting of the various scrolls will serve to keep the joint firm, although, if the work be done neatly, there will be no fear of the irons coming apart.

FIG. 29.—Scroll made to hold a Rosette.

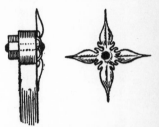

FIG. 30.—A Rosette.

SCROLLING IN BRASS

Scrolling may also be done in brass, that metal costing four times as much as iron. Extra care must be expended upon the work, as

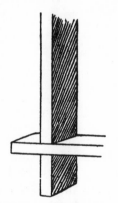

FIG. 31.—Cross Corner.

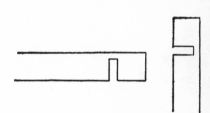

FIG. 32.—Cutting the Cross Corner.

each piece of brass must be annealed before any attempt is made to hammer or scroll.

The method of annealing is very simple. The brass is made red-hot and allowed to cool gradually in a slightly warmed oven. The metal may be hammered when cool, but before being placed in the scrolling iron it will have to be annealed again, and whenever the surface shows the least sign of cracking or splitting the process must be repeated without delay.

A few useful designs for bent-iron work are shown in Figs. 33, 34,

35, and 36, which will furnish the beginner with patterns for practice. A very slight knowledge of drawing will enable the metal-worker to

FIG. 33.—Design for Bent-iron Screen.

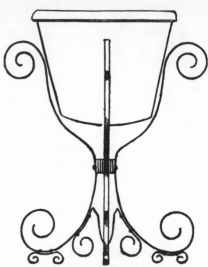

FIG. 34.—A Flower-pot Holder.

elaborate these patterns or execute entirely original ideas with skill and taste. The only point particularly to notice about the construction of the umbrella-stand—if the instructions previously given have been

FIG. 35.—A Simple Design for an Umbrella-stand.

FIG. 36.—Design for a Window Ornament.

carefully carried out—is that the pan at the bottom should be well weighted with lead ; otherwise the affair will incline to top-heaviness

CHAPTER XXII

FRETWORK

A POPULAR WINTER PASTIME

FEW hobbies make a smaller inroad into the weekly pocket-money than Fretwork. When once the initial outlay of about five shillings for the purchase of the frame and table has been made, there is little else to buy except wood for working up the designs. Expensive outfits may, of course, be purchased, but the work turned out with a three-shilling saw is quite as good as that produced by an expensive treadle machine.

THE FRAME

Frames are made in several sizes at prices ranging from two shillings upwards. A glance at Fig. 1 will illustrate how these sizes are reckoned. The distance from C to D, *i.e.* the length of the actual saw, is always the same, but the length of the arm from A to B, varying from 12 in. to 20 in., determines the size.

A 14-in. frame is the best to start with, as a larger saw is apt to be unwieldy in the hands of one not accustomed to its use.

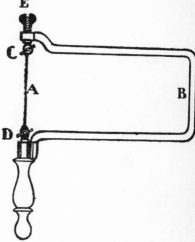

FIG. 1.—The Hand Fret-saw.

THE SAWS

The saw is fastened into the thumb-nuts, C and D, Fig. 1, with the teeth pointing downwards.

When purchasing saws, examine the teeth carefully to see that they are made as in Fig. 2, and not after the

FIG. 2.—A good Saw.

pattern depicted in Fig. 3. The reason why the former are the best to use may be briefly explained thus: The continual friction caused by the passage of the saw up and down through the wood makes the metal very hot and takes the temper out of the

187

steel. When the teeth are close together, as in Fig. 3, this heat becomes so intense that the saw either snaps or bends in the wood, thus rendering work almost impossible. Another very good reason for this selection of saws is, that when the teeth are close together they become clogged with sawdust, whilst this inconvenience is entirely obviated by the use of saws of the pattern illustrated in Fig. 2.

The Drill

This tool, shown in Fig. 4, can be purchased with the necessary bits for a few pence, and is used for drilling the holes through which the saw is threaded.

Fig. 3.—A
bad Saw.

Fig. 4.—The
Drill.

Table and Clamp

The piece of wood with a V-shaped incision shown in Fig. 5 is called the table, and all the sawing is done upon it. With clamps

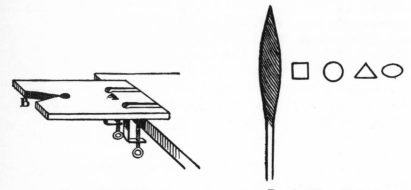

Fig. 5.—The Table.

Fig. 6.—Files with Sections.

passed through the holes at A it can be fastened to a bench or strong table and kept immovable for working upon.

Files

Two or three files as shown in Fig. 6 should be obtained at a cost of about twopence each.

Sundries

Several sheets of glass-paper, some strong pins, and a tube of liquid fish-glue will complete the outfit.

WOOD

The beauty of a piece of fretwork depends to a very large degree upon the wood in which the pattern is worked, and a certain amount of taste must be exercised in its selection. The following list of the principal woods used will serve to help in the choice of material.

The usual thickness of these woods is $\frac{3}{16}$ in. or $\frac{1}{4}$ in., and they may be purchased from most cabinet-makers at very low prices.

Mahogany.—This wood is of a rich, dark red colour, and will take a good polish, although, as a general rule, wood should be left unpolished.

Walnut.—The colour of this wood is well known. The material is so easily worked that it proves exceptionally suitable for making fretwork furniture.

Satin Walnut.—This is one of the most popular of fretwoods, and is of a fine brown colour. Owing to its softness, it is employed more than any other wood, and has the additional advantage of being sold in greater widths than other material.

Oak.—This wood looks handsome when made up, but it is very difficult to cut on account of its toughness.

Birch.—A light brown wood, easy to cut and fairly popular amongst fretworkers.

Cedar.—The Spanish cedar, of which cigar-boxes are usually made, is very soft, and can be sawn with the greatest facility.

Rosewood.—This is the best, and at the same time the dearest, of all woods, and will take a fine oil or may be French polished with great success. Being hard, the wood is slow to cut, but amply repays any trouble expended upon it.

Holly.—This is a white wood, and when made up resembles ivory.

Bird's-eye Maple is of a yellowish colour, and, owing to the pretty mottling of the grain, is very popular.

WORKING A PATTERN

Fretwork designs are frequently sold with the pattern shown in half portions only, and in such cases the design must be duplicated upon tracing-paper. An example of this is seen in Fig. 7, which, together with Fig. 8, illustrates a pipe-rack.

The first thing to be done is to paste the design to the wood, always remembering that the paste must be applied to the design, and not to the wood. Flour or starch make the best paste, as they hardly warp the wood to any noticeable degree.

When the design has become perfectly dry upon the wood, drill holes in all the parts that have to be cut out. Hold the drill perfectly

FIG. 7.—Half Design for the Back of Pipe-rack.

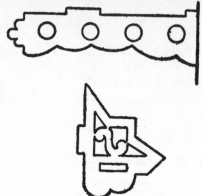

FIG. 8.—Side and Shelf of Pipe-rack.

upright; it will thus help to start the saw vertically. The right, A, and wrong, B, methods of holding the drill can be seen very plainly from a glance at Fig. 9.

Now loosen either the

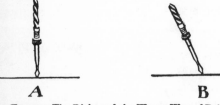

A   B

FIG. 9.—The Right and the Wrong Way of Drilling.

top or the bottom thumb-nut of the saw frame, insert the free end of the saw into one of the drilled holes, and then screw it back into the nut. Having thus threaded the saw, place the wood on the table in such a way that the portion to be cut lies over the V-shaped incision B, Fig. 5.

Seat yourself at the table at such a height that an easy action can be obtained, as seen in Fig. 10.

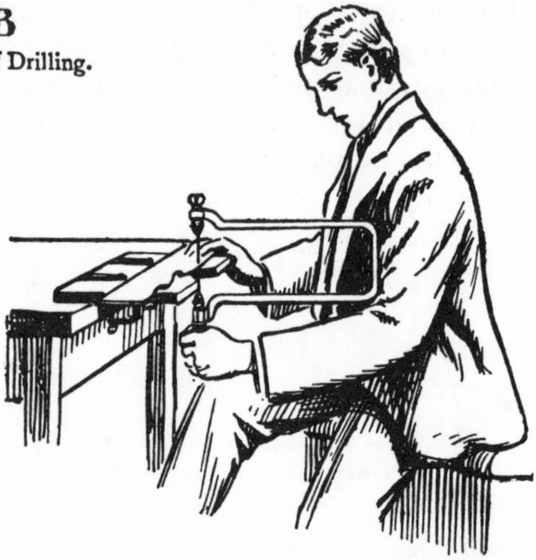

The whole design should

FIG. 10.—Correct Position for Working.

now be cut out, piece by piece, the outline not being commenced until the interior has been completely finished.

The paper design can be removed from the wood by sand-papering. Soaking with water is almost certain to warp the wood, and therefore cannot be recommended.

When all the cutting has been done, any unevenness can be removed with a file, although great care must be taken to see that the sharp outlines of the pattern are in no way destroyed.

In delicate designs it frequently happens that small pieces get snapped from the wood. This misfortune is easily rectified by gluing the pieces in place and sand-papering the join very carefully.

The tenons and mortices in the different pieces must be fastened and glued into one another in the usual way, the use of pins, driven into the wood and cut flush with the surface by means of pliers, being advocated rather than that of nails.

SOME REMARKS ON SAWING

The point of most importance with regard to sawing is that the saw must be held absolutely vertically. It is impossible to be too emphatic in impressing this upon the beginner. However carefully the pattern traced upon one side of the wood may be followed out, unless the saw has been held vertically, the reverse side of the wood will present no similarity to the pattern.

Do not hurry the saw—let it take its time. Manœuvre it skilfully with a steady pressure, so that all the angles may be cut sharply.

Fig. 11.—Method of cutting Angles.

The design in Fig. 11 will demonstrate how this should be done. The saw is inserted at the drill-hole (*x*)

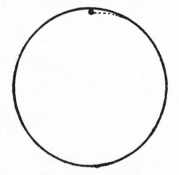

Fig. 12.—How a Circle should *not* be cut.   Fig. 13.—How a Circle should be cut.

and the outline followed from A to B. Having reached B, the

clumsy craftsman will jerk his saw up and down until he has made a hole large enough to turn it and saw from B to C; whereas the proper plan to follow when B has been reached is to draw the saw backwards to A, thence to the drill-hole, where there will be room to turn, and down past C to B, thus giving a perfectly sharp and clean point to the angle. This system applies to all inside and outside angles.

In cutting a circle, do not drill a hole near the cutting line, as seen in Fig. 12, but make it nearer the centre of the circle, Fig. 13, taking the saw as shown by the dotted line in such a manner that the outline of the circle is perfect.

PLURAL CUTTING

Plural cutting, *i.e.* cutting two or three pieces of wood together where the pattern is repeated in several separate parts, should not be attempted by the beginner. It is much better to saw each piece by itself, duplicating the design by tracing it upon paper. If two or three pieces of wood are cut together, it will generally be found that the pattern of the lower pieces bears no resemblance to that cut in the upper.

When proficient, however, the fretworker may attempt plural cutting, and in that case should screw or nail the pieces of wood before starting.

WORKING IN BRASS

The use of brass for making objects such as finger-plates is very

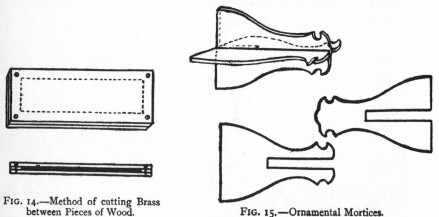

FIG. 14.—Method of cutting Brass between Pieces of Wood.

FIG. 15.—Ornamental Mortices.

popular amongst more advanced fretworkers, as metal, when mounted on some good polished wood, presents a handsome appearance.

The brass, which must not be more than $\frac{1}{32}$ in. thick, can be procured from most good ironmongers.

FIG. 16.—Back of Letter-rack.
Supports to be fastened at A, A, A.

FIG. 17.—Supports for Letter-rack.

Special saws with the teeth close together are necessary for the

FIG. 18.—Frame for Photo or Looking-glass.

FIG. 19.—Half Design of Bracket.

work, and can be purchased for 4d. per dozen. In adjusting them the tension screw E of the frame, Fig. 1, must be tightened until the saw emits a high note when twanged with the finger.

Having obtained the design to be cut, procure two pieces of deal, ⅛ in. thick, and place the sheet of brass between them, nailing or screwing them firmly together as shown in Fig. 14. Paste the design upon the top piece of wood and drill the necessary holes.

Upon proceeding to saw in the usual way, it will be found that the pieces of wood serve to prevent the trembling which the direct

FIG. 20.—Half Design of Shelf for Bracket.

FIG. 21.—Support for Shelf.

FIG. 22.—Half Design for Brass or Celluloid Finger-plate.

application of the saw to the simple sheet of brass would inevitably produce.

Screw-holes, of course, will also have to be drilled at those places where the brass will be secured to the wooden background.

The foregoing remarks apply to working in such materials as xylonite or celluloid, but none of these fancy stuffs should be attempted until great proficiency has been attained in plain woodwork.

ORNAMENTAL MORTICING

In the making of certain ornaments large mortices similar to those shown in Fig. 15 are frequently introduced. These must be very carefully cut, and should then be glued in the ordinary way.

DESIGNS

Designs for fretwork can be obtained from many books and periodicals. The craftsman need have no fear, indeed, of lacking designs, and Figs. 16 to 22—original designs by Mr. Sid Pride—will give an idea of several of the many articles which may be sawn and fitted together.

CHAPTER XXIII

WOOD-CARVING

AN INEXPENSIVE HANDICRAFT

THE instinctive pleasure experienced by most people in cutting or whittling with a sharp knife, makes Wood-carving an ever-popular hobby, whilst the moderate outlay required for tools and material counts as a very great point in its favour, since it places the handicraft within the reach of the most limited pocket-money. Artistic designs, neatly and skilfully executed, can be worked into many useful and handsome ornaments which will serve to decorate the house to an appreciable extent.

TOOLS

The tools required for wood-carving, although few and inexpensive, must be chosen with great care. Complete sets may be purchased from most dealers, but quite as good work can be produced with no more than a dozen gouges and chisels as with a larger assortment of implements.

FIG. 1.—A Flat Gouge.

Four flat gouges varying in size from ⅛ in. to ½ in. should be purchased at a cost of about one shilling each. These tools are very similar to chisels, having a slight curve, as can be seen in Fig. 1.

A gouge with a very "quick" curve, Fig. 2, and several of intermediate degrees, all ⅜ in. size, must be obtained. The "quick" curved gouges are technically known as "veiners," as they are frequently used for carving the veins and small grooves in foliage.

FIG. 2.—A "quick" curved Gouge.

FIG. 3.—Straight-ended Chisel.

Chisels can be bought, either with straight ends, Fig. 3, or with diagonal edges as in Fig. 3A, the latter being known as "skew" or corner chisels. One of each description, both in ⅜ in. and in ¼ in. size, must be included in the outfit.

A V-tool, Fig. 4, is indispensable, and should be obtained in ¼ in. size.

Curved chisels and gouges as shown in Fig. 5 are frequently recommended in handbooks on carving, but the beginner need not take them into consideration, as the ordinary straight type of tool is quite sufficient for every description of work. An exception, however, may

FIG. 3A.—A Skew Chisel.

be made in the case of the back-bent gouge shown in Fig. 6, as this will often prove of the greatest service.

FIG. 4.—The V-tool.

The punch, Fig. 7, is used for stamping the background in cases where the pattern has been carved in relief.

A mallet is essential for practically all work with chisels. Professional carvers usually use a round-headed mallet, but the ordinary carpenter's mallet will prove equally serviceable.

FIG. 5.—Curved Gouge.

SHARPENING TOOLS

Carving tools require a much sharper edge than do the chisels and gouges used by carpenters. The long tapering bevel shown in section, Fig. 8, is essential to the carver, and rather than allow a carpenter or cabinet-maker to put

FIG. 6.—Back-bent Gouge.

an edge on his implements, it is far better for the wood-carver to learn to whet his tools at home.

As will be observed from a glance at Fig. 8, the blade should be sharpened on both sides. The cutting edge must, of course, be kept absolutely straight and free from notches or irregularities.

FIG. 7.—The Punch.

Gouges, owing to their shapes, are naturally more difficult to sharpen than chisels. After the outside of the edge has been ground on the oilstone, the inside must be sharpened on a slip, the *stone* being rubbed against the *metal*, as by so doing there is little chance of cutting the fingers.

FIG. 8.—Bevel for Carving Tool.

The edges of carving tools should be finished off on a strop or piece of buff leather, and be constantly stropped and kept ready for use.

THE TABLE

An ordinary kitchen table is very suitable for a carving bench, but, to ensure stability, the legs must be firmly clamped to the floor with angle irons.

To the table a flat piece of wood must be clamped, to which in its turn the wood to be carved will be glued. The simplest method of gluing these pieces of wood is the following: Pass the glue-brush roughly over a sheet of newspaper and press this against the lower piece of wood; then glue the carving wood to the newspaper and leave the glue to harden.

When the carving is finished, the two pieces of wood can be separated with the point of a knife, as the newspaper splits very easily, and thus allows the pieces to come apart.

MATERIAL

The material used for wood-carving depends almost entirely upon the pattern that is being worked. Foreign oak, which is generally free from knots, is, perhaps, the most suitable for large designs, although walnut, mahogany, chestnut, pear, and lime are all handsome woods and may be worked into effective panels.

Spanish mahogany being the harder of the two varieties of that wood, is frequently chosen on account of its extreme durability.

What may be termed fancy woods, such as sycamore, holly, or ebony, are used principally for small work, as they can rarely be procured in large pieces.

For the first attempts at carving, a cheap soft wood is desirable, and American white wood answers the purpose admirably. Being free from knots, it proves an easy material upon which to learn the use of the tools.

Woods become seasoned by storing, and it is advisable, therefore, to stock in a dry place such woods as are likely to be used. Each piece should be carefully inspected when bought, as any cracks or flaws render the material utterly useless for carving.

A SIMPLE EXERCISE

The simpler the design the easier will it be for the beginner to turn out good work, and a plain pattern similar to that shown in Fig. 9 will be very suitable for the first attempt at wood-carving.

Take a piece of American white wood, 1 in. thick and 1 ft. square, and trace the design upon it with carbon paper.

Now, holding a chisel or gouge perfectly upright in the left hand, follow the outline of the pattern, striking the tool sharply with the mallet to the depth of about ⅛ in. The chisel will serve for the straight lines, whilst the curves can be worked with gouges of suitable sizes.

Having completed the outline, cut away some of the surrounding wood with a gouge, thus making the work appear as in Fig. 10. All the background or waste wood can then be cut away with a flat gouge and levelled uniformly. The design will then appear like a fretwork overlay.

FIG. 9.—Pattern for Beginner

FIG. 10.—Outlining the Pattern.

The depressed portion or background will require to be punched all over, any slight irregularities being by this means effectually concealed.

The pattern, which is in relief, must now be moulded, and here the difficulties of carving really begin. Where possible, the wood should be cut with the grain, every precaution being taken to keep the outline clear and distinct. The berries must be neatly rounded and the leaves worked as well as possible, although it must ever be borne in mind that carving from nature should only resemble the original in a broad similarity, and not in any intricate imitation.

Sharp outlines can always be obtained by undercutting, *i.e.* cutting down and inwards. With judicious care, undercutting may be most successfully employed for all stalks and stems—in fact, wherever a very clear and defined relief is required.

The first attempts at wood-carving are sure to prove disappointing, for there is a knack in handling the tools and working the wood that must be learned by experience. The art can be acquired with care and attention, however. Such simple instructions as can here be given will serve as an introduction to this most fascinating hobby, in the pursuit of which many pleasant hours may be passed with profit and amusement.

CHAPTER XXIV

BAMBOO CARPENTRY

OF all the many branches of carpentry none affords more pleasure nor provides better results than what may be termed bamboo carpentry. Doubtless, from time to time, many readers have seen various articles, the making of which comes under this heading; and all will agree that such articles have immediately attracted attention by their dainty appearance and general utility. In the following pages, therefore, it is proposed to place before the reader some ideas as to the making of three very useful pieces of household furniture; namely, a pedestal coal-vase, a simple hat and coat rack, and a handy little music cabinet.

In case any misconception still exists as to what is meant by the term "bamboo carpentry," it might here be stated that this work largely calls for the use of bamboo, grass matting and wood, which is used for the framework of the various articles. Herein lies one attractive feature of this work, for these materials are very cheap and can be very easily procured.

Bamboo and matting are to be obtained at a very small cost from any furniture dealer or draper, whilst it is often unnecessary to incur the expense of wood from the timber yard, since that important item may be more cheaply obtained from the various assortment of boxes at the disposal of your tradesmen.

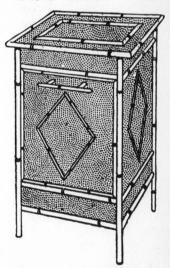

FIG. 1.—A Pedestal Coal-vase.

A PEDESTAL COAL-VASE

The first article to receive consideration is the pedestal coal-vase, Fig. 1, the making of which is quite practicable. Standing almost 3 ft. high, this attractive piece of furniture, besides serving as a coal-box, may be utilised as a table for cards and draughts, or as a stand for flower vases.

The coal is contained in a box attached to a swinging front, so nicely balanced as to keep shut whether full or empty, and, when required for use, to swing out and remain at rest in a convenient position. As to the materials required, they are few in number and slight in cost, consisting, as previously described, chiefly of bamboo and wood.

Should the reader be possessed of a box corresponding in dimensions to those of the proposed vase, he will be saved much time and trouble, but as it is highly probable that it will be necessary to make a box, the following particulars will prove of use. The body of the vase will be 2 ft. 6 in. long, 12 in. deep and 12 in. wide, and to construct this the following materials will be required :

Wood.—1 board, 4 ft. 6 in. by 12 in. by $\frac{3}{4}$ in. ⎫ To be bought
    1 board, 3 ft. 9 in. by $10\frac{1}{2}$ in. by $\frac{3}{4}$ in. ⎬ from any timber
    1 strip, 1 ft. 9 in. by $2\frac{1}{3}$ in. by $\frac{3}{4}$ in. ⎭ yard for 1s. 5d.
    1 board, 1 ft. 4 in. by 8 in. by $\frac{5}{8}$ in. to be cut from the lid of a Nestlé's milk box.

Matting.—$1\frac{1}{4}$ yards, costing about $8\frac{3}{4}$d. per yard.

Bamboo.—3 six-foot rods, $1\frac{1}{4}$ in. diameter, costing $3\frac{3}{4}$d. per rod.
    2   „   „ $\frac{1}{2}$ in.   „   „ $1\frac{3}{4}$d.   „

Miscellaneous.—A 2-in. brass hinge and some sheet iron for lining the coal-box.

With these materials at hand, you may commence the construction by making a rectangular box with open front and no top, Fig. 2. For this purpose boards of the following dimensions will be required :—

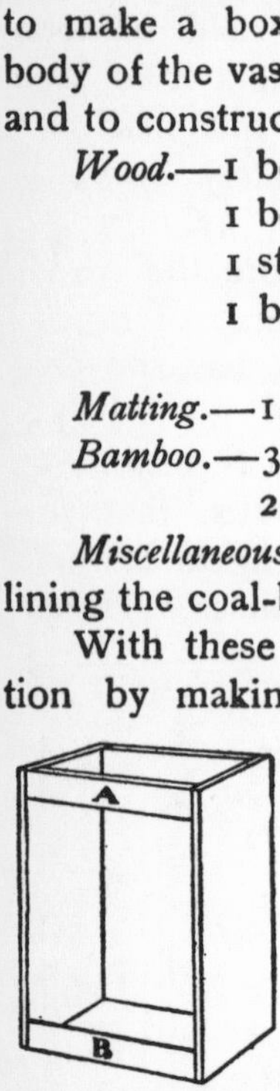

FIG. 2.—The Outer Case.

Two sides, each 21 in. by 12 in. by $\frac{3}{4}$ in.

Back, 21 in. by $10\frac{1}{2}$ in. by $\frac{3}{4}$ in.

Board for swinging front, 16 in. by $10\frac{1}{2}$ in. by $\frac{3}{4}$ in.

Top and bottom front pieces A and B, Fig. 2, each $10\frac{1}{2}$ in. by $2\frac{1}{3}$ in. by $\frac{3}{4}$ in.

The bottom front piece should be bevelled inside as shown at C in Fig. 3.

FIG. 3.—Bevelled Bottom of Front Piece.

Having cut the boards as instructed, nail them together in the form of a box, placing the back and two front pieces between the sides. You must next fix the bottom, which is a square of $10\frac{1}{2}$ in. cut from the wood of the Nestlé's milk box. In this manner the front of the box is left open to allow for the swinging front of the box, to which will be attached the coal receptacle.

This front may now be prepared from a board which must measure 16 in. by $10\frac{1}{4}$ in. by $\frac{3}{4}$ in. Before describing the construction of the box to be attached to this side, it would be well to mention that for all nailing a bradawl should first be used, French nails, not exceeding 2 in. in length, being driven into the holes thus made. Now, since the shape of the coal-box is a very important matter, considerable care must be taken in cutting the boards with which it must be built. The easiest method of obtaining these boards is to take them from a Nestlé's box, the wood of which will be about ⅝ in. thick. The shape of the box depends entirely upon the shape of the two sides, and for this reason a careful study should be made of Fig. 4, which shows these measurements. It will be noticed that the side is 9 in. wide, with edges 13 in. and 15¼ in. respectively.

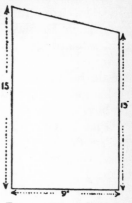

FIG. 4.—Side of Coal-box.

The back, which is 13 in. by 9 in., should be carefully fixed between the two sides, thus producing an incomplete box. In this

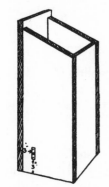

FIG. 5.—The completed Coal-box.

condition it should be attached to the front already prepared, the best manner being to drive screws through this front into the two sides. The coal-box will then be complete, as shown in Fig. 5, except for the bottom, which is provided by nailing in a board 9 in. wide and 8⅜ in. long.

It will be readily understood that, when the coal-box is complete, it must contain a stop so placed as to prevent the swinging front from moving too far forward or too far backward, and this stop must now be placed in position immediately behind the front top piece A, Fig. 2, of the outer case. It consists simply of a piece of wood 10½ in. by 4 in., and shaped as shown in Fig. 6. This, if fixed in position immediately behind the front piece of the case, will project 1½ in. below it, and will form an admirable stop for the swinging front.

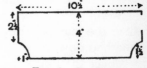

FIG. 6.—The Stop.

FIXING THE COAL-BOX

You have now made the coal-box and the case to contain it, so that the next thing is to fix it in position. This must be done in such a manner that, although swinging easily forward, the front will quite as easily return to its vertical position. This clearly calls for the use of pivots, which must be arranged in the following manner :—

On each side of the coal-box select a spot 3 in. from the front and 3 in. from the bottom edge, Fig. 5. At this point fix a brass plate, such as may be obtained by cutting off the two leaves of a 2-in. brass hinge. Each plate will contain three holes, two of which must be used to screw it to the woodwork. Then, if necessary, the middle hole must be enlarged to enable it to take a $\frac{1}{4}$ in. screw of 10-in. gauge, this hole being continued through the woodwork of the box.

Place the swinging front temporarily in position, and from the inside bore a small hole through into the outer case so as to mark the exact places where the screws will come later. Glue washers round these holes, when the coal-box has been removed. The permanent fixing of this front should not yet take place, but will be done later by screwing from the inside of the box into the outer case, thus enabling the box to swing backwards and forwards, as on pivots.

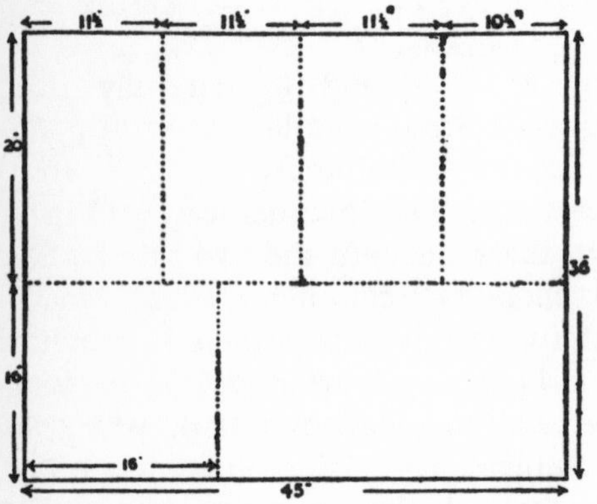

FIG. 7.—Method of cutting Bamboo Matting.

THE MATTING

A very important feature in the decoration of the article thus made is the matting, the fixing of which must now be taken in hand.

The length of matting, which is one yard wide, necessary for the purpose is $1\frac{1}{4}$ yards. From this piece cut three strips as shown in Fig. 7, each 20 in. by $11\frac{1}{2}$ in., and another of the same length but only $10\frac{1}{2}$ in. in width. A square, 16 in. by 16 in., will be necessary for the top, whilst the remaining piece, 29 in. by 16 in., should be reserved for future use.

The method of fixing is quite simple, consisting only of covering the wood with plenty of hot, but rather thick glue, after having done which the matting should be quickly placed in a central position and smoothed down.

Cover the four sides in this way, remembering, of course, that the matting for the front must be divided into three pieces—one large piece for the coal-box front, and two narrow strips for the top and bottom cross-pieces. Later, when the square top is fixed, it should be similarly covered.

THE BAMBOO WORK

The bamboo work, which, besides serving as ornamentation, provides the cabinet with its four legs, must now be dealt with. These legs are the continuation of the bamboo rods covering the four corners of the outer case ; it will therefore first be necessary to cut four pieces, each 27 in. long, from the rods of 1¼ in. bamboo. The 6-in. legs are marked off on these pieces by saw-cuts through a third of the circumference of the rods. If the bamboo can be split up from the point, an easy method is obtained of fixing it to the corners, and at the same time allowing 6 in. of the whole rod to serve as legs, Fig. 8. This splitting may be easily done by inserting a sharp chisel in the slit, and thus evenly removing the strip, 21 in. long, taking care that the joints are well cut out. The lengths can now be made to fit over the corners of

FIG. 8.—The Bamboo split in order to make the Legs.

the coal-vase, and, after boring holes to take nails, they may be permanently fixed in position, Fig. 9.

It may here be mentioned that proper bamboo nails, with scarcely any head and 2 in. long, may be obtained from any ironmonger, and these should be placed as near the joints as possible.

The next task will be to decorate each side with three strips of bamboo placed horizontally between the corner posts. The position of these is determined by those on the front face, and, as will be observed in Fig. 1, one hides the bottom

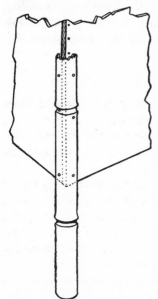

FIG. 9.—Section of Bamboo-covered Corner.

edge of the top front piece, whilst the other two are similarly placed along the edges of the bottom front piece. As far as possible use the strips cut from the bamboo rods for this purpose, bevelling the ends to enable them to fit neatly over the bamboo with which they come in contact. Having treated each side in this fashion, provide the front of the coal-box with a framing of smaller ($\frac{1}{4}$ in.) bamboo, using half-round pieces with mitred edges.

An attractive appearance can be given to the vase by decorating the front, sides, and back with diamonds, formed of half-round pieces of $\frac{1}{2}$ in. bamboo with mitred ends. As to the size of these diamonds, the reader must use his own judgment.

When the coal-box has been fixed in position in the manner previously described, the top of the vase should receive attention.

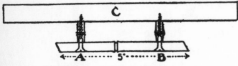

FIG. 10.—The Handle.

This top is formed of two 8-in. boards, making a square with a 16-in. side. After gluing on the matting, make edges with $1\frac{1}{4}$ in. mitred bamboo rods from which the third has been removed, and finish the decoration by an 8-in. square formed of half rounds of small mitred bamboo.

Although now nearing completion, one or two little touches are still necessary to render the vase as practical as possible. Thus the fixing of a handle to the swinging front amply repays any pains that may be spent on the work. Cut a piece of $\frac{1}{2}$ in. bamboo to the shape shown in Fig. 10, and bore holes at A and B, countersunk to allow for the heads of thin 2-in. screws. Next cut two knots, each 1 in. long, and, by means of a small bradawl, bore a hole through the joint to take the screws, after which the handle may be fixed to the front C, as shown in the diagram.

A coal scoop holder, similar in design to the handle, may be arranged on the right side of the vase, and should be of such dimensions as to take the coal scoop at your disposal.

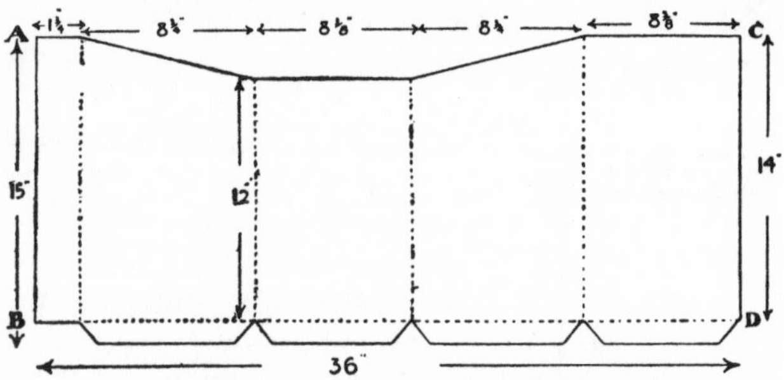

The Lining

Nothing now remains but to

FIG. 11.—Sheet Iron for lining the Coal-box.

provide the coal-box with a suitable lining. The dimensions of the sheet-iron box used for this purpose will be $8\frac{3}{8}$ in. deep, $8\frac{3}{4}$ in. wide, with front and back 12 in. and 14 in. respectively, and it should be made of a piece of iron sheeting of the shape and dimensions shown in Fig. 11. Should the construction of this lining prove too difficult, it can easily be put together by any tin-worker for a few pence.

When the sheet iron has been bent inwards at the places marked by the dotted lines, the box, without either top or bottom, is completed by riveting the side flange, AB, to the side, CD. The bottom is formed of a sheet 8¼ in. by 8⅝ in. riveted to the bottom flanges, thus completing a very strong and suitable lining.

The vase may be kept much cleaner and brighter by covering its whole surface with varnish, in which case care should be taken that the liquid finds its way into all crevices and into the pores of the matting. This renders it easily washable, and ensures for the coal-vase a long and serviceable life.

HAT AND COAT RACK

Another very useful and equally ornamental article is shown in the hat and coat rack, Fig. 12, a glance at which will immediately satisfy the reader that the making of such a thing is both simpler

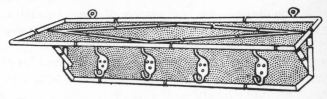

FIG. 12.—Hat and Coat Rack.

and less expensive than was the construction of the coal-vase. Requiring no floor space, it is suitable for either a hall or a room, and the sum of 2s. 6d. is the only expense involved.

As before, the materials consist mainly of wood and bamboo. Of the former two boards will be required, one measuring 3 ft. by 6 in. by ¾ in., and the other 2 ft. 9 in. by 8 in. by ¾ in., the cost of these being about 3d. each.

Half a yard of 36-in. matting, together with the piece left over from the last article, will amply meet the requirements, whilst only two 6-ft. rods of ½ in. bamboo are needed to complete the decoration. Besides these materials purchase four penny coat-hangers similar in pattern to those shown in Fig. 12.

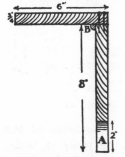

FIG. 13.—Method of fixing Boards together.

In the first place see that the boards are of the stated dimensions. Then, from two corners of the wider, mark off points 2 in. up the sides and along the bottom. A saw-cut along the lines joining these points will remove the corners, A, Fig. 13, and it will be possible to join the boards together.

This is done by securely nailing the narrower board to the wider back after the manner shown in B, Fig. 13. Care should be taken to see that the angle thus formed is a perfect right angle, and that the holes for the 2-in. French nails have been previously bored.

You must now fix the matting in the way described for the coal-vase. To do this, cut the ½ yard into three strips, 5½ in. by 35½ in., 5 in. by 35½ in., and 7¼ in. by 35½ in. respectively, and, having cut the two corners of the last-mentioned strip, place them temporarily in a central position, whence it will be seen that a ¼ in. margin is left all round. Fix the strips permanently with hot glue, and, whilst it is drying, turn your attention to the cutting of the bamboo rods. First cut lengths from the 1¼ in. bamboo to correspond with all the edges of the rack. Then, with the exception of the rod intended for the back of the shelf, split from each the third required to enable it to fit over the edges of the wood. For the back edge of the shelf split the length into two half-rounds and fix one of them flatly along it. The remaining half-round should in turn be split in half, and one of the pieces thus obtained fixed in the angle formed by the shelf and the back, B, Fig. 13. In this manner it will just cover up the edges of the matting beneath the shelf and on the back board. Having edged the rack with bamboo, you might next arrange for brackets to strengthen the shelf, and also to form an attractive feature of ornamentation. These brackets, similar in shape to that shown in Fig. 14, should be placed across the angle and have their

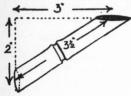

FIG. 14.—Shape of Bracket.

mitred ends fixed to the *matting*—not the bamboo—of the shelf and back.

The upper surface of the shelf may now receive a little ornamentation in the shape of a diamond made of half-rounds of small mitred bamboo, Fig. 12. This done, nothing remains but to fix the hooks. It is better to mark off 4½ in. from each end, and then divide the intervening space into three equal parts. At each of the four points thus obtained, fix a hook in a convenient position by means of screws. With the varnishing and fixing of the looking-glass plates, each screwed to the back about 6 in. from the end, the rack is completed and quite ready for use.

A USEFUL MUSIC CABINET

Although not quite so simple in construction, the music cabinet, when finished, surpasses in appearance both the coal-vase and the coat rack.

Before commencing the construction, Fig. 15, which shows the cabinet when complete, should be carefully studied. It will then be seen that the article consists of two chief parts, the music cabinet proper, and a drawer separated by a space suitable for the displaying of fancy flower-vases, knick-knacks, &c. In estimating the materials required, it should be borne in mind that the whole cabinet stands about 3 ft. high, whilst the music cabinet proper is 16 in. wide, 14 in. high, and 11 in. deep. The drawer slide, although of the same width and depth, is but 4 in. high, whilst the top overlaps on three sides by 1½ in. A liberal estimate of the materials required is given below; the most important being wood, matting, and bamboo.

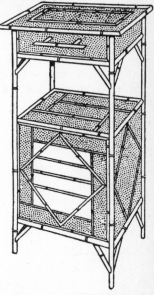

Wood.—In this case it is quite unnecessary to incur the somewhat heavy expense of purchasing wood from the timber yard, since most of it may be cut from Nestlé's boxes, the tops and bottoms of which are generally in the form of boards 17 in. by 12 in. As the sides may also be utilised, such boxes will be found exceedingly useful.

FIG. 15.—A Music Cabinet.

Matting.—Provided judgment and economy be exercised in cutting, it will be found that one square yard of matting will be amply sufficient.

Bamboo.—Having studied Fig. 15, the reader will readily understand that bamboo rods are to form a large item, and for this reason he would do well to equip himself with five 6-foot rods of 1¼ in. diameter, and an equal number of ½ in. diameter.

With the exception of nails, glue, a sheet of glass, and a lock, little else is required.

The first step in the actual construction is the making of two rectangular boxes, the larger serving for the music cabinet, whilst the smaller forms the drawer slide. If the external measurements of these be given, the reader should find very little difficulty in putting them together.

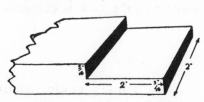

FIG. 16.—Ends of Strips for Door-frame.

The larger box is 16 in. wide, 14 in. high, and 11 in. deep, the front being left open for the door, which is to be fixed later. This door is provided by first constructing a flat frame of 2-in. strips just large enough to fit the opening. The ends of each strip should be cut as shown in Fig. 16, and the joints fixed together with glue and a few screws. The frame should then be set on one side, until the time comes to provide it with glass and finally fix it in position. Before leaving this part of the cabinet, it would be well to fit it with, say, three shelves. These should be placed at equal distances from one another, care being taken that their front edges are at least 2 in. from the extreme front of the cabinet. They are best secured by nails driven into their edges through the sides of the cabinet.

This brings us to the drawer slide, and since its height is only six inches, its dimensions will be 16 in. by 6 in. by 11 in. When the box, with the excep tion of the front, has been completed, nail to the front and two side edges of its top, strips of wood 1½ in. in width and of the required length. This will cause the top of the whole cabinet to overlap on three of its sides.

A drawer to fit the front opening in the slide must now be constructed. For this it is only neces- sary to nail together

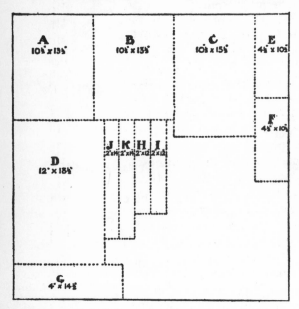

FIG. 17.—Method of measuring Matting for the Cabinet.

strips of the required width and length, fitting in a squarely-cut bottom.

At this stage the interior parts of the boxes might be stained. The object of doing this is to take off the bare appearance which the plain wood would otherwise present. A tablespoonful of perman- ganate of potash dissolved in a pint of hot water gives a very effective oak-coloured stain. This should be applied to the back and edges of the cabinet door, the interior of the cabinet proper, and both sides of the shelves.

All the plain woodwork of the drawer should be similarly treated, but in the case of the slide it is only necessary to stain the interior to a depth of 2 in. from the front.

Attention should now be turned to the matting, and, as previously mentioned, a great deal depends upon the manner in which the strips are cut. For this reason a careful study of Fig. 17 must be made, as this shows the most economical way of using a square yard of matting. From this figure it will be seen that the pieces A and B are for the sides of the cabinet proper, C is for its top, and the large piece, D, is to cover the extreme top of the cabinet. The sides of the drawer slide are covered by pieces E and F, whilst G is used for the front of the drawer. There yet remain four small pieces to be accounted for, and of these H and I cover the sides of the door frame, whilst J and K are used for its top and bottom.

FIG. 18.—Method of cutting Corner Posts.

All of these pieces should be placed centrally in their respective positions, leaving a $\frac{1}{4}$-in. margin all round, and then fixed with plenty of hot glue. The bamboo work, which may next claim attention, will give very little trouble if the following instructions be complied with. It is best to deal first with the four corner posts, and, as each is just three feet long, two six-foot rods of $1\frac{1}{4}$ in. bamboo will provide the four.

Taking one of the posts thus obtained, measure 6 in. from the bottom, and at this point make a saw-cut through one third of the circumference; 14 in. above this repeat the operation, and, having treated the other three posts in a similar manner, carefully split out the thirds from between the two cuts. Another saw-cut, 10 in. above the last, should now be made on each post, and the third of bamboo, 6 in. in length from this point to the top, may then be split out. It will be understood, of course, that all saw-cuts should be in line with one another, Fig. 18, or difficulties will arise. The rods thus prepared may then be firmly nailed to the corners of the boxes, care being taken to keep the holes square.

The article now begins to take a definite shape, and is ready to receive decoration. This must be commenced by ornamenting the edges of the tops of both boxes with $1\frac{1}{4}$ in. bamboo from which the third has been removed.

In dealing with the edges of the boxes at the bottom, the work is a little simpler, since they only require half rounds of $1\frac{1}{4}$ in. bamboo nailed flatly along them. In the case of the pieces under the door and drawer, it must be seen that their top edges are just level with the inside of the boxes, so that the movements of both the door and drawer shall be free.

This finishes all work with the wider bamboo, and leaves the decoration with that of $\frac{1}{2}$ in. diameter to be dealt with. Starting with the extreme top of the cabinet, arrange for a rectangle of 15 in. by 18 in. of half-round pieces with mitred ends.

Next treat the drawer front in the same way, after which the top of the music cabinet should be decorated as shown in Fig. 15. The ornamentation of the sides of this part of the cabinet should take the form of diamonds similar to those shown in the figure, unless the reader devise a more suitable design.

The door frame might next have its extreme front edges covered by mitred half rounds, whilst the bamboo along the inner edge should be allowed to overlap an eighth of an inch in order to hold the glass which is to be fixed later. A handle, similar in design to that shown in Fig. 10, will be found very useful for the drawer, although in this case instead of only being 5 in., it may measure double that length.

The sixteen brackets across the angles formed by the posts and boxes must now be considered. Each is about 4 in. long, with ends mitred to enable them to fit across the corner. In fixing, bore holes through the mitred ends, and nail to the bamboo posts and the woodwork of the boxes.

A lock having been so fixed to the door that its bolt may shoot into a small groove in the sides of the cabinet, a sheet of glass is all that is required to complete the door. This glass, cut to size, should be placed in a frame, where it is held in position by thin wooden beading nailed round the back.

In hanging the door, ordinary hinges cannot be used owing to the projecting bamboo. It therefore becomes necessary to use pivots. Having first fixed on the lock side a $\frac{1}{2}$ in. strip of wood as a door stop, place the door in position, level with the front of the cabinet.

Bore holes through the top and bottom of the box into the edges of the door—these holes being about $1\frac{1}{4}$ in. from the corner post. The pivots are then formed by driving French nails, $2\frac{1}{2}$ in. long, into the holes thus made, where it will be seen that the door opens without meeting with any obstruction, since the shelves are set back 2 in. for this purpose. By varnishing the whole cabinet your labour is complete, and your home provided with a very useful article of furniture.

CHAPTER XXV

POKER-WORK

THE LATEST HOBBY FOR DECORATING USEFUL AND FANCY ARTICLES

ANY one with a taste for decoration and skilful with his fingers should certainly make a trial of Poker-work. As the name implies, it is the decoration of objects by means of a red-hot "poker." In its initial stages, a simple poker with a sharp point was the instrument used, and, indeed, some workers even now use only a red-hot steel to produce plain, bold designs which are most artistic and effective and possess great merit.

But this early method is very laborious and is now old fashioned. If you want to do the best up-to-date Poker-work, it is advisable to procure a proper outfit, such as can be obtained of some well-known firm, Gamage's in London, for example, for about fourteen shillings. The outfit contains the principal apparatus and tools required, consisting of a glass bottle, with connecting cork, spirit-lamp (for heating the points), rubber bellows and tubes, cork handle, and platinum point.

FIG. 1.—The Lamp in Use.

OUTFIT

A glance at Fig. 1 will show how the lamp apparatus is operated. The bellows are held in the left hand and worked by means of the connecting tube attached to the lamp itself, whilst the point is held in the right hand by its cork handle and placed in the flames until properly heated. Benzoline is the spirit used.

There are several other outfits on the market, differing in construction and cost, but the beginner would do well to start with the simplest and cheapest.

In order to obtain the various effects shown in different examples of Poker-work, from the simple background to a perfect picture with figures, several platinum points are needed, which may be briefly described thus :—

The first is the flat point, Fig. 2, which is used for burning away backgrounds. Usually manipulated on its flat side, it can also be worked on its edge when making lines.

FIG. 2.—The Flat Point.

Another is the round sharp point, Fig. 2A. This will help in producing flower sketches of a natural kind, or making strong incised lines.

A third point is in the shape of a horn, Fig. 2B. It is a very useful instrument, as the convex side can be used for shading as well as for background work, whilst its sharpness will help in producing dots and fine lines.

FIG. 2A.—Round sharp Point.

Other points in an ordinary outfit are claw-shaped and extra fine, a shading point, a knife point, and a smoke-diffusing point, which last blows away the fumes of the burning wood and gas from the worker's face.

Some of these points are used for the most difficult kinds of Poker-

FIG. 2B.—Horn-shaped Point.

work. It will be found best to start with just one or two simple implements of your own making, then, as advance is made with the hobby, you will gradually get the particular point you want for the execution of more ambitious designs.

A small clamp to hold your work to the table or bench is useful, also a wire brush to clear away charred remains.

MATERIAL

Suitable kinds of wood on which to work are very necessary, if you would like your efforts to appear to the best advantage. White wood is very popular, and can be obtained of all dealers, in different lengths and sizes, as well as in made-up articles. Until you are fairly efficient, it is advisable to keep to panels or the decoration of boxes, stools, or racks, the making of any of these presenting great interest, especially if you possess any skill in the handling of tools.

Chestnut, cedar, sycamore, pear, and elm are all good woods to work upon. Choose pieces free from knots or other blemishes that would detract from the design, and where the grain of the wood will add to your work, select such material.

PRACTISING THE PATTERNS

Before attempting any design, practise simple lines, curves, and shading, Fig. 3. Being able to do these with ease, you can then begin upon a simple, bold flower, in which one or all of the points will be required. Sketches of the first exercises to practise, together with geometrical examples and flowers, are shown in Fig. 4.

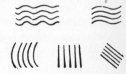

FIG. 3.—Simple Lines for Practice.

You will next practise how to produce backgrounds. These are of various styles. Dots, semicircles, diagonal strokes, crinkled marks, and wide and open lines are among the best patterns, Fig. 5.

It is a good plan to make your own sketches, and it will be as well to start with a design of conventional flowers. Draw it in pencil

FIG. 4.—Burning-point Exercises.

FIG. 5.—Poker-worked Backgrounds.

on the wood, and then burn it in by the aid of the poker or point. See that the wood is well sand-papered before you start, and get your design in the exact position. The specimen pattern for a clothes-hanger, Fig. 6, is a nice bit of simple work. Or you might try a part or whole of the design on a cabinet frame. Another nice piece of work is that for an engagement slate, the design of which may be traced out clearly on the wood and worked carefully inch by inch until it is accomplished.

FIG. 6.—Clothes-hanger.

Still progressing, you can next attempt a pretty pattern of roses for a blotter. The darker parts of the leaves must be secured by neat shading.

If you are not quite skilful with a pencil in drawing, designs already made on tracing-paper can be purchased, and these you can easily transfer to the wood.

RELIEF AND MOSAIC WORK

Another branch of this hobby is relief Poker-work, a specimen of which is shown in the panel frame, Fig. 7. You will notice that in this work the design stands out in relief, and carving tools will be

FIG. 7.—A Relief-work Frame.

FIG. 8.—Specimen of Mosaic Poker-work.

required for producing the raised effect. The small frame illustrates a very nice bit of relief work.

Finally, the latest branch of Poker-work takes the form of mosaic. A glance at the accompanying specimen, Fig. 8, will show that the aim is to produce the effect of mosaic pavement. The design is carried out in lines, the darker parts being shaded, whilst colours are used to imitate variegated marbles.

Poker-work can be done on leather, velvet, and similar substances, as well as on wood, and very charming effects are produced by the artistic treatment of these materials.

CHAPTER XXVI

REPOUSSÉ WORK

THE ART OF ORNAMENTING METAL

AT the present time it is quite the fashion to ornament metal. Not only are our houses and public buildings thus adorned, but numberless articles in common use are made beautiful by being embellished with designs in metal-work. Repoussé is the name given to one kind of this work, and is a French word, meaning to beat back, drive, or punch with a tool, this being precisely what the worker does with his metal. Any one can learn it, and will, from the beginning, find the hobby really fascinating, even if only able to execute a simple piece of work, whilst to ornament different articles will prove a source of great pleasure.

THE OUTFIT

Scarcely any other technical hobby requires fewer things to start with ; a hammer and a nail being all that the first efforts demand. The hammer is used to strike the nail against the metal in order to produce the pattern desired. Indeed, many simple designs have been executed in repoussé work with only these two primitive tools.

It is advisable, however, to start with a fairly good kit of tools, so that as the difficulties of the work arise they may be encountered successfully. Procure, accordingly, a round-headed hammer, with a somewhat flexible handle, and half-a-dozen tracers. These are small steel or iron tools, 3 inches long, one end of which is shaped like the edge of a screw-driver. Each of these tracers will have a different point or edge, one being flat, another irregular, a third circular, a fourth with a broader edge.

For working the backgrounds, secure two or three "matting" tools. These are of different patterns—one will be round in shape,

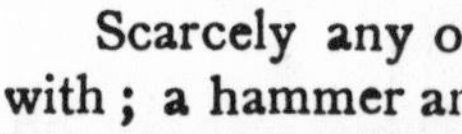

FIG. 1.—Matting Tool. 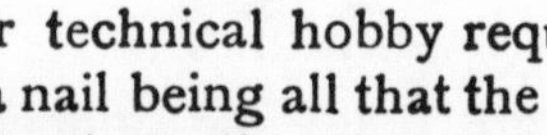   FIG. 2.—Triangle Matt. 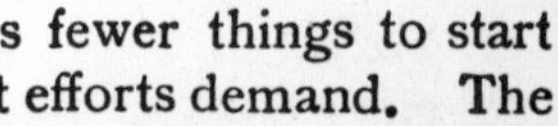   FIG. 3.—Matt for Background.

with four oval indents, Fig. 1, another will have a star for a pattern, a third will bear a triangle, Fig. 2, whilst, for closer background work, a matt can be procured with a design of small circles, Fig. 3.

Pressed Work

As a preliminary to real Repoussé work, it would be as well to have a little practice in pressed work. For this purpose, get a few foils or some pieces of extremely thin sheet-metal. Lay one of these on a pad of cardboard, blotting-paper, or very soft wood, then roughly sketch on the metal, by means of a hard pencil, the pattern you intend to work. This design may be a row of leaves or a network of tiny circles or cubes—anything to form a pattern. Then take a stylus, or some other simple tool with a point, and press it all over the marked pattern on the metal. This design is merely pressed in, and, although the relief is very low, some pretty pieces of decorated work can be thus produced.

Chasing

Growing accustomed to working on metal by these first exercises, you can proceed to chasing. For this some of the tools just described are required, although before you can use them it is necessary to know something about the metal, and how it should be worked.

Material

The favourite metals are brass and copper. Either can be obtained in sheets, and at first only comparatively small pieces should be purchased. The metal must be very thin, though not so thin that it breaks beneath the pressure of a tool.

When metal is obtained from the ironmonger, see that it is not too brittle. State the purpose for which it is required, and he will give you the best kind for the purpose. It should neither be too thin nor loose in texture, but an even sheet that will receive pressure clearly. Then it must be such that it will keep its colour and not tarnish or assume unsightly tints. Always bear in mind that the thickness of the metal should be governed by the height of the relief in the pattern —a thicker kind of brass or copper will be needed for high relief.

While copper and brass are the two metals chiefly used, pewter, iron, soft steel, and tin-plate can all be worked, whilst gold and silver are also employed for very delicate designs.

Hammering tends to harden metal—a process sometimes necessary. On the other hand, by placing metal under an extreme heat it is softened, although by heating a sheet of metal to red-hot temperature and then plunging it in water it is made excessively hard and tough.

THE PAD

For the surface on which the metal must be placed whilst it is being worked, get a perfectly smooth piece of board, about a foot square and at least an inch thick. Having procured a piece of sheet-metal, fasten it down so that it will not move while you are at work upon it. There are two methods of doing this. In the first, the sheet is taken large enough to fold over the board all round the edges, where several screws are inserted to hold it securely. The second way is to lay the metal sheet flat upon the board and screw it down firmly. Whichever plan you adopt, be sure that the metal sheet is quite smooth—there must be no buckling up or inequality, as this would hinder the work and injure the pattern. Should the sheet be uneven, go over it with a flat iron or an iron tool, that will do duty as a burnisher. Emery paper is also useful for securing a good surface, whilst, for polishing, a chamois leather or a little whitening can be applied.

HOW TO USE THE TOOLS

Learn to handle the tools with nicety. The tendency in chasing and repoussé work is to be clumsy, dealing heavy blows that only smash the thin metal or knock it out of shape. Put the end of the tracer down on the drawn line, and give a gentle tap with your hammer so as to cause a clear indent in the metal. Remember that if you want to make a long line or an extended curve, you must not tap spasmodically, or first hard and then softly—this will make a very uneven, irregular line. You must learn to keep up a series of running taps by continually moving the tracer. By this means the line will, when finished, prove perfectly even.

As to the use of the tools, the various tracers are to be employed for indents corresponding to their shape—fine or broad, round or irregular. The matts are to help in forming backgrounds, and can be selected according to the design.

HIGH RELIEF

To obtain high-relief repoussé work you must make a bed of pitch, consisting of 8 parts pitch, 20 parts fine sand or brick dust, 4 parts resin, and 1 part tallow. Heat these materials in an old can, and when thoroughly mixed pour them on a board. The metal plate being placed on the pitch, beat out the

FIG. 4.—Wooden Beater.

hollows, which form the relief, by means of a hammer and a wooden beater, Fig. 4. Of course, while working, bear in mind that the hollow parts you are making will appear as relief in the metal when turned. A cushion placed under the board will facilitate the work and lessen the noise.

The pattern to be followed is drawn on the brass or copper with a lead pencil, pen and ink, or India ink and camel's-hair brush. Begin with a simple conventional design similar to that shown Fig. 5. Geo-

FIG. 5.—A simple Design.　　FIG. 6.—An Ash-tray.　　FIG. 7.—A Finger-plate.

metrical designs, such as cubes, diamonds, zigzags, circles, ovals, &c., also form good patterns for the beginner.

As you proceed and become dexterous with your tools, you will want to attempt more ambitious designs. Many good examples can be obtained from wall-papers and the scroll-work on cabinets and house decorations. Better still is it to draw your own patterns on articles, such as ash-trays, Fig. 6; finger-plates, Fig. 7; dishes, vases, tankards, and other fancy or useful articles which lend themselves for decoration by repoussé work.

CHAPTER XXVII

BOOK AND PERIODICAL BINDING

HOW TO PRESERVE CURRENT MAGAZINES

WHEN the completed parts of a periodical or magazine have been collected, the question of binding them neatly and serviceably arises, frequently creating a difficulty which a little care in observing the following instructions will soon remedy.

Having obtained the numbers necessary for a volume, the paper

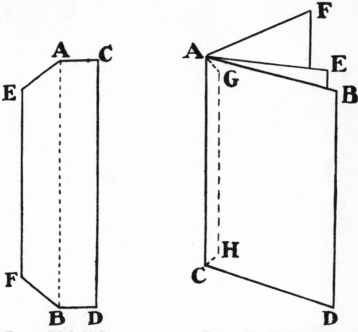

FIG. 1.—Tab for binding a loose Page.

FIG. 2.—The Tab fastened to loose Page.

covers of each part must first be removed and the temporary binding undone. This will be quite simple, as in most cases the folios are merely glued to the back of the cover. If there should be any difficulty, a little steam will effectually soften the glue. The threads with which the folios have been sewn can then be cut and removed.

Folios usually consist of four sheets which are folded into eight paper pages, and when printed on both sides, make sixteen pages of type.

As a guide to the binders, each folio bears a capital letter at the bottom of the first page, so that, beginning with A, the binder places folios B, C, D, &c., in their proper order. Before proceeding, however, it is advisable to glance at any full-page illustrations there may be, as in periodical publications these are frequently inserted irrespective of the letterpress. When possible, these illustrations should be removed and placed where they properly occur in the book.

The method of binding transposed illustrations and loose pages is very simple. A strip of white paper, one inch wide, should be cut and folded down the middle as in Fig. 1, where the dotted line AB shows the fold. The half ABCD must be evenly pasted to the back of the loose page in such a manner that the inside edge of the page is flush with the folded line AB. When this strip of paper is firmly stuck, the page should be inserted in its destined place and the protruding slip ABFE pasted against the back of the opposite sheet as shown in Fig. 2, where AB and AE indicate the folded sheet, whilst FA is the loose page with the slip GH pasted to the page ABCD.

STITCHING

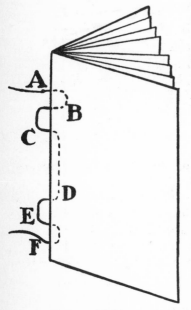

FIG. 3.—Stitching.

Each folio must now be stitched. Cut as many twelve-inch lengths of strong white thread as there are folios, and in each length make a knot about two inches from one end. With the help of a needle, pass a thread through the first folio about $1\frac{1}{2}$ inches from the top, at A, Fig. 3. Thread it in and out at B, C, D, E, and F, as shown in the figure, taking great care in each case to keep to the exact crease of the sheet. The remaining folios are to be treated similarly, the utmost precision being exercised to ensure all the stitches being made at corresponding spots in each folio.

Fly-leaves of white paper must be made for the front and back, doubled and stitched so that one leaf may be stuck to the inside of the cover, whilst the other half will remain free.

The folios should now be arranged in order, the "Contents" and "Index" put in their respective places, and the whole book carefully checked to make sure that the pages follow in numerical order.

FIG. 4.—Folios held in Clamp.

Having placed the tops and stitched edges of the folios level and flush with one another, grip them together with a single clamp as illustrated in Fig. 4. This serves to keep the folios from moving whilst they are undergoing the next process, that of being threaded on the tapes. There will be three of these clamps required, and they should be after the pattern shown in Fig. 5, the distance between A and B being 3 in. and AC measuring $2\frac{1}{2}$ in.

Cut two pieces of broad tape, 8 in. long and 1 in. wide, and thread one piece through the loops formed by the thread at C, Fig. 3, and the other piece through the loops at E. The stitches must then

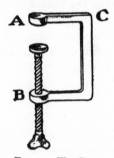

FIG. 5.—The Clamp.

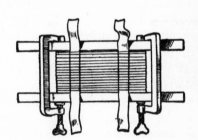

FIG. 6.—Binding the Folios.

be drawn taut, the knot at A enabling this to be done securely. They should then be similarly tightened at E and at F.

When this has been done, take two smooth strips of wood, each measuring 18 in. in length and 4 in. in breadth, and place one on each side of the book, flush with the threaded edges as shown in Fig. 6, screwing a clamp fairly tightly at each end. When the ends of the thread at A and F have been cut to an inch in length, the book is ready to be glued.

GLUING AND COVER-MAKING

Glue for bookbinding should be very thin and applied liberally with a fine brush. Having given a generous coat of glue to the backs of the folios, threads and tapes included, place a strip of canvas or coarse linen over the "tacky" surface. This canvas should be wide enough to allow a margin of one inch to overlap each side for attaching the covers. The glue should now be left to dry for twenty-four hours.

In the meantime the first steps may be taken towards making the covers. Obtain two pieces of pasteboard or stout cardboard, a quarter of an inch larger each way than the book to be bound. These pieces of pasteboard must be perfectly flat with the corners accurately squared.

FIG. 7.—The Book completed.

When the glue on the back of the book is dry, remove the clamps and boards, and place the covers in position. The tapes and canvas margin must now be firmly glued to the insides of the covers, and left to dry under a steady pressure.

For the back of the binding a strip of fine canvas or coloured cloth should be cut 2 in. longer each way than the book and wide enough to stretch 3 in. over each cover, as shown in Fig. 7. Glue this evenly to the pasteboard, bringing over the ends at the top and bottom and gluing them inside the cover. Pieces of marbled or coloured paper are then pasted over the remaining portions of the cover, care being taken to make a clean edge where the paper overlaps the canvas.

It only remains to paste one of the leaves to the inside of the cover at the beginning and end, thus hiding the pieces of tape and ends of canvas and paper. Books thus bound will last for years and prove an ornamental addition to any library.

CHAPTER XXVIII

HOW TO MAKE A SIMPLE STENCIL

AN EASY METHOD OF COPYING DESIGNS

THE primitive stencil here described will be found useful for reproducing diagrams, ornamental borders, simple sketches, designs, and in some cases, bold printing.

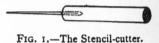

FIG. 1.—The Stencil-cutter.

The tools and materials required are neither numerous nor expensive. The first, the stencil-cutter, is depicted in Fig. 1. It consists merely of a needle with its head buried in a small stick of wood, which does service as a handle.

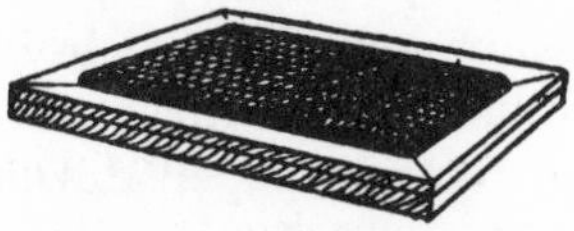

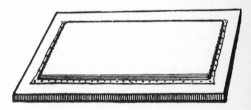

FIG. 2.—Printing Ink-pad.

The second requisite is a printing-pad. This may be made in a very elementary fashion by procuring two pieces of stout black material, e.g. felt, stretching them tightly over a perfectly flat piece of board and nailing the cloth to the underside.

As, however, successful results depend almost entirely upon the use of a well-made pad, that depicted in Fig. 2 will doubtless appeal to the amateur stenciller. The cost of making it should not exceed threepence.

First procure a piece of board 7 in. by 4 in. by ¼ in., and a second piece 6 in. by

FIG. 3.—The Felt nailed to the Base.

3 in. by ⅛ in. This latter should be carefully glued above the former, leaving a ½ in. margin all round. Next stretch over the raised portion two thicknesses of any absorbent black material, tacking the edges firmly down on the lower board as shown in Fig. 3.

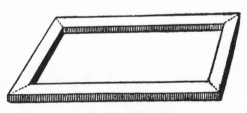

FIG. 4.—The Mitred Frame.

Mitre together four lengths of wood—two pieces 7 in. by ½ in. by ¼ in. and two pieces 4 in. by ½ in. by ¼ in., after the style of a picture-frame, Fig. 4, sand-papering the inner edges sufficiently to allow of this frame being forced down upon and stretching over the felt pad. Glue the base and frame together, and fasten at the corners with nails AA, Fig. 5.

FIG. 5.—Section of Pad.

If a larger pad is required, increase the sizes accordingly.

THE STENCIL

Obtain a sheet of smooth-surfaced paper—oil paper answers excellently—and, with a soft pencil, sketch out upon it the diagram or design you wish to reproduce. Fig. 6 depicts a simple subject upon which the novice might try his 'prentice hand.

The diagram having been satisfactorily drawn, take a prepared needle, or stencil-cutter, and proceed to prick a number of small holes along the pencilled outline. A much better final result will be obtained if the paper is placed upon a piece of blotting-paper during this "pricking-out" process. The minute holes thus made will then be cleaner and more defined.

Next take four drawing-pins, and pin the stencil tautly over the inked pad.

Unless you happen already to be an amateur photographer, it will be necessary to buy a squeegee from a photographic dealer, the cost of this being sixpence. Having made the purchase, place a clean sheet of paper on top of the stencil, and run the squeegee lightly over it.

The gentle pressure thus applied will cause the ink from the pad to ooze up through the pinpricks, and so on to the clean paper.

FIG. 6.—An Example of Stencilling.

In this manner any number of reproductions may be obtained.

By the same process it is quite an easy matter to reproduce the more simple illustrations from those magazines having paper with a glossy surface. Of course, the more complicated the illustration the greater is the amount of patience required by the stenciller to prick it out with his primitive stencil-cutter.

CHAPTER XXIX

PHOTOGRAPHY

SOME VALUABLE HINTS ON THIS INDOOR AND OUTDOOR PASTIME

THE popularity which photography has unceasingly enjoyed since its vogue extended from a profession to a recreation is sure evidence of the interest which it is able to arouse. Not only is the devotee charmed by the circumstance of being able to secure pictorial mementos of days which he has lived, but he has the additional pleasure of watching the gradual appearance of pictures upon the creamy surfaces of the plates. Nevertheless, fascinating as this pleasure may be, it will assuredly wane, unless the photographer pursue inquiries into the why and wherefore of his hobby.

The ignorance which exists respecting the less known byways of photography is surprising, and is never more surely realised than when a person asks whether a particular photo will be damaged by being copied, as though a sitter's physiognomy risks damage—except in the amateur's initial endeavours—by being portrayed. And yet such a question may be propounded by one who has handled a camera and dabbled with pyro in the ruby light. No excuse could be found for the publication of instructions on the lines of the simpler hand-books, all of which are reliable and may be read with profit by any camera fiend; but the following notes are intended to describe various contrivances and schemes which have been evolved during the course of an amateur photographer's existence.

The subject-matter seems divisible into two broad classes—that which might be followed in a practical manner at home, and that in which expeditions would be advantageous—and the latter, being the less comprehensive, will be broached first.

OUTDOOR PHOTOGRAPHY

Some of the most disappointing results encountered in outdoor work are obtained in the photography of panoramic views. Valleys, for example, which to a spectator present all the charms of varied colour and expanse of view, when photographed appear little more than mere stains on the paper. The truth of the matter would seem to be that the picture presents the appearance of a mosaic, and, since the virtue of these productions lies mainly in the colour, a monotone portrait has no recommendation. The long approved method of judging the suitability of a view for photographing, is to regard it through a pair of smoked or blue glasses, and thus take into consideration only the composition of the picture, and not its colouring.

Not only is photography obliged to render natural objects in monotone, but, unless special precautions be taken, the colours are not rendered correctly according to their shades. For example, a light red will appear as darker than a medium blue, because the former colour has less effect upon the photographic plate. This is the reason that a ruby light is used in the dark room. A measure corrected of such errors is to take the portrait through a yellow screen, whereby the more influential colours, *e.g.* blue, are handicapped, a blue object reflecting but few yellow rays, which alone are allowed to pass by the screen. On account of this screen's action in levelling or equalising the effect of the light-rays, it is termed Isochromatic. However, ordinary plates cannot well be used for this work, seeing that they are but slightly sensitive to the yellow rays, and prolonged exposure will be necessary. The remedy lies in the employment of Iso- or Ortho-chromatic plates, which, by the dyeing of the emulsion, have been rendered specially sensitive, and accordingly need to be developed by a very safe dark-room light—for instance, green and ruby glasses superimposed.

A Long-extension Camera

When the landscape is panoramic—that is to say, when the separate objects of interest cannot be approached near enough to secure photographs on a reasonable scale—the advantage of a long-extension camera is appreciated. The majority of lenses on focussing cameras consist of two back and front elements—either of which can be used separately—and possess foci of approximately double the length of that of the original lens. These, then, can be utilised if the camera bellows be extensible, and the picture so obtained would be twice the usual scale. The stops must be reckoned at twice their marked value, for example, F 8 becomes F 16, and consequently the exposures are increased.

Another method of lengthening the focus of the lens, supposing that it does not consist of two elements or of a longer extension than twice the normal required, is to place the lens of negative focus in front. Such a lens is concave, or thinner at the centre than at the edge, Fig. 1. The power of this is reckoned by the formula $\frac{1}{F} - \frac{1}{F} = \frac{1}{F_2}$, where F is the focus of the camera lens, F that of the negative lens required, and F the resulting focus. For example, supposing the camera has an available extension of 20 in. and its lens a focus of 5 in., it is required to add a concave lens in front, whereby a sharp picture will be obtained at the full extension. Substituting these figures in the above formula—

FIG. 1.—Concave Lenses.

$\frac{1}{5} - \frac{1}{20} = \frac{1}{F_2}$ *i.e.* $\frac{4}{20} - \frac{1}{20} = \frac{1}{F_2} = \frac{3}{20} = \frac{1}{7\frac{1}{3}}$, so that the required lens must be of $7\frac{1}{3}$ in. focus or, say, $7\frac{1}{2}$ in. It is better to choose one erring on the side of weakness, because otherwise the resulting focus would be too long for the camera extension, whereas the latter can always be shortened.

A TELEPHOTO ATTACHMENT

A telephoto attachment consists of the addition of a negative lens behind the ordinary lens, the two being separated by a distance roughly equal to the latter's focus. The effect of such an arrangement may be tested by making two cardboard tubes, A and B, Fig. 2, and mounting the negative lens, say 3-in. focus, in one end of A, whilst within B is placed a cork ring, D, into which the brass mount of the camera lens, E, can be screwed. The tube with the negative lens is fixed into the front panel, C, and this being extended to the full, the B tube is slid backwards and forwards until the object appears fairly sharp.

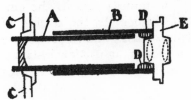

FIG. 2.—Telephoto Attachment.

The magnification is very considerable and illumination correspondingly dull, whilst focussing will be found somewhat difficult. In attempting an exposure by this method, the best plan will be to hold a hat in front of the instrument and utilise this as a shutter, because the least vibration, which is prone to happen at long extensions, blurs the picture absolutely. Although with such a home-made, uncorrected optical system the resulting photographs are scarcely likely to give complete satisfaction, the experiment is well worth making. The alighting of a bird upon a chimney-pot, witnessed through such an instrument, becomes a really startling event.

Respecting the exposures necessary for these enlarging arrangements, it is simple to remember that with a telephoto lens the exposure is reckoned according to the usual system for distant objects, and then multiplied twice by the magnification. For instance, supposing the exposure necessary for a house were one second, and then through the telephoto lens the image of a chimney-pot becomes three times the size, the new exposure would be 1 × 3 × 3 = 9 seconds. On the other hand, when the focus of the camera lens is lengthened by the addition of a concave lens in front—to double or treble its original value—then the stops shown become double or treble also, and F 8 has to be read as F 16 or F 24, as the case may be.

An advantage of long-focus lenses which should not be lost sight of in considering their properties, is that the image obtained is not distorted. To take extreme examples, the freak pictures of people with seven-league boots, or monstrous noses, and tiny ears

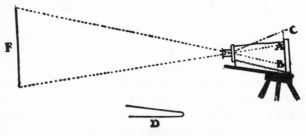

FIG. 3.—Tilting the Camera.

could never be secured but by short-focus lenses and approaching very near to the subject.

The photography of lofty buildings and kindred subjects involves many troubles for the tyro camera-man—supposing, at least, that he cares the slightest for parallelism in the vertical lines of his pictures. When an object is so high that its image is cut off by the lower edge of the plate, the natural remedy is to tilt the camera. However, upon doing this, the lines, which should all be perpendicular, are found to converge towards the object's summit. If the camera be provided with lens panel and back, which can be swung on pivots, and thus always made to assume a vertical position, the bellows themselves may be tilted as far as necessary without distortion of the image. The only point to be noticed is that the lens may need considerable stopping down, because, as shown in Fig. 3, it is in reality being asked to cover a plate of unusual size, of whose surface, however, only the part AB is being utilised. In this figure, BC is the size of plate which the lens is actually covering, although when tilted at the angle shown in D the object F is received upon the portion AB, as already described.

A rising front to a camera performs the same service as the swinging of back and front, but the range is more limited, and is mostly used when—the camera being in its normal horizontal position—a slight increase of sky and decrease of foreground or similar change of the view appears to be called for. Nevertheless this arrangement may necessitate the lens being stopped down.

When trying to secure photographs against brilliant sunshine, it is always an advantage to shield the lens by holding a book or piece of cardboard horizontally in front. With a focussing camera there is no difficulty in seeing whether the screen cuts off any part of the picture, but in the case of a hand camera this, of course, falls to guess-work or experience. Moreover, with a focussing instrument the bellows also ought to be shaded, seeing that the minutest puncture will form the element of an efficient pin-hole camera, where the sun is concerned as the sitter and an inexplicable halo constitutes the resulting photograph.

Another trouble arising on sunny days is to give the landscape adequate exposure and yet allow the sky no time to render an absolutely dense image of itself on the negative. This difficulty is readily overcome when exposing, by uncapping a lens, lifting the cap upwards and closing downwards, thus limiting the exposure of the top portion of the picture. When an ordinary shutter is employed, the best safeguard is to use an Iso screen and yellow sensitive plates, whilst, if the exposure be at all prolonged, screening with a book during part of the time may also be resorted to.

HALATION

Halation occurs in a negative where there are abrupt contrasts of light and shade, the reason being that the bright pencils of light, A, Fig. 4, pass the gelatine, D, and are reflected from the back surface of the plate, E, at the slight angle, C, thus darkening the emulsion, D, where it should only be affected by the subdued rays, B, as will be seen from the diagram.

Celluloid films are not subject to this halation trouble, and are said to be non-halative, because they have practically no thickness,

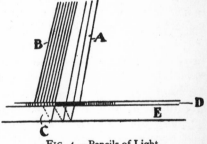

FIG. 4.—Pencils of Light.

and therefore offer no facilities for reflection from a back surface. In the case of glass plates, halation is prevented by coating the back of the glass with a black or red pigment, which tends to absorb the light rays passing the emulsion, so that they cannot be reflected.

STEREOSCOPIC PHOTOGRAPHS

The taking of stereoscopic photos does not necessitate the use of a special camera, provided attention be confined to still-life subjects. The property of two pictures which renders them suitable

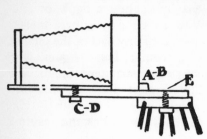

for viewing in a stereoscope is that they shall have been taken from two distinct points of view, differing by a distance equal to that between the eyes of an average person. In ordinary life it is the image through one eye regarded by the brain simultaneously with the slightly different image obtained through the other eye that renders a landscape in relief, and hence,

FIG. 5.—Auxiliary Board for Stereoscopic Pictures.

incidentally, a person possessed of but one eye cannot appreciate the solidity of objects. A view to such a person presents a similar appearance to one painted on canvas in the eyes of an adequately endowed mortal.

If the object, a stereoscopic picture of which is required, be one of still life, the two views may be secured successively, and the camera moved an inch or so from its original position for the second exposure. This is not a difficult matter if a hand camera be in use, resting upon some support such as a brick wall, or if the tripod of a stand camera be so placed upon a level surface that each leg can be moved a measured distance in the same direction.

The arrangement of an auxiliary board, Fig. 5, is a very practicable solution of the difficulty of stereoscopic picture-taking. The ledge, AB, is screwed in place against the camera back, see also Fig. 6, and serves to make it impossible for the instrument to be turned round whilst moving from one end of the slot, CD, to the other. This slot is 2¾ in. long, and is large enough to contain a thumbscrew, which can pass into the bush beneath the camera. The auxiliary board can be screwed to the tripod by means of

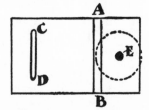

FIG. 6.—Plan of Auxiliary Board.

the bush, E. Needless to say, both exposures should be as nearly the same as possible, or the resulting pictures will not be of equal density, whilst the prints must be so mounted that the picture taken by the camera towards the right is viewed by the right eye, and *vice versa*.

Coloured Lights

Photography, regarded as an indoor pastime, involves many operations conducted in a red or a yellow light. These illuminants are said to be non-actinic, because, although capable of making objects visible to the human eye, they do not chemically affect the silver compounds embodied in photographic plates and papers. Consequently all dealings with these materials up to the time that the picture has been developed and the superfluous sensitive salts of silver dissolved away, whereby the picture is fixed, can be carried out in this coloured light.

The Dark Room

A dark room is doubtless most economically and comfortably illuminated by means of daylight, although in such cases the screening must be most carefully arranged. In any case the window ought not to face bright sunlight directly. The glazing may be of orange glass, whilst shutters of ruby and green must be kept handy and superimposed where necessary. With these arrangements the orange lights can be used for working bromide papers; the superimposed ruby is useful for work with ordinary plates; whilst orange and green or orange, ruby and green can be used for fast orthodox plates.

Among artificial illuminants, oil and candles are probably in commonest use, objectionable and uncomfortable though they prove in practice. Electric light, however, is singularly free from all the objections that can be raised in connection with other forms of illumination, nor can it be considered expensive when batteries are used,

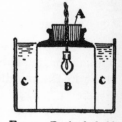

Fig. 7.—Device for holding a Coloured Light.

especially now that metal filament lamps of such high efficiency are obtainable.

Probably the cells best adapted for electric light in the dark room are those of the Sac Leclanché type, as these provide a very constant current and do not deteriorate during intervals of rest, as do bichromate cells, where the zincs have to be removed from the electrolyte after every spell of employment. With a Leclanché battery of about 4 cells, a 6-candlepower lamp can be lighted, and that intermittently by means of a switch fitted in the circuit.

As for the screening of the lamp, one of the simplest and most efficient arrangements is shown in Fig. 7. The flexible wire passes through a large cork, A, which is used to stopper a jam jar, B, and by this arrangement the lamp hangs inside. The jar is coated with black paint round the top edges so that no white light can escape in that direction. The whole apparatus is then stood within a larger glass bowl, C, which contains saturated bichromate of potash solution. This should reach to a point just above the black line on the jam jar, so that when the lamp is lighted illumination can only be made through the orange solution. This affords reasonable safety for ordinary plates, and is perfectly adapted for working bromide paper.

A dark room lamp for electric light and fitted with glass screening can be made with a wooden box measuring about 9 in. by 7 in. by 6 in. These dimensions are not, of course, strict, but the glass surface should be roughly half a square foot in area. Thin strips of wood are nailed round three sides of the box to form grooves for the glass, and the fourth side is cut away for about ¾ in. at A, Fig. 8, to allow the glass to slide into place between the grooves, B. This strip of ¾ in. is also provided with a piece on its under edge, so that it can be replaced in position when the sheet of glass has been inserted. The glass should be orange, or a deep yellow, in order to give ample light for the development of bromide papers, whilst for plates a sheet of thin red paper can be pinned in front to reduce the illumination. The box is covered with black paper or painted, whilst in the middle of the top side a hole, C, is bored large enough to take a cork, cut down the middle, and arranged to grip the flexible wire between its halves.

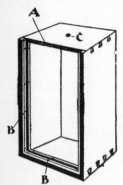

FIG. 8.—Lamp-box.

A Focussing Camera

For copying photographs or pictures, *i.e.* for photographing them on the scale of actual size or thereabouts, a focussing camera is necessary. Even with this, however, the process is not very simple if an attempt be made to pin the object against a wall and bring the camera into position by means of the tripod, whilst greater complications ensue if the illustration of a book be under treatment, and the whole volume has to be manœuvred into focus. As this is an interesting branch of photography, it will repay the beginner to construct a stand similar to that shown in Figs. 9 and 10.

The backboard, A, has two extension pieces, B, screwed to it, of such a length that when A is folded forward upon the hinges at C, it rests flat upon D, so that the paraphernalia can be neatly packed away. A slot, E, Fig. 10, is cut in the middle of the backboard and through this passes a bolt from the shelf, F, Fig. 9, which slides up and down in the grooves, G, and may be fixed at any required height by the tightening nut, H. In this way a support is formed for an open book, or, if necessary, the bolt may be loosened and the shelf removed, so that large pictures can be pinned to the board. The latter should therefore measure about 15 in. by 12 in.

The camera stand, D, slides in the grooves, J, and has a hole, K, through which the tripod screw may pass into the camera bush. Its

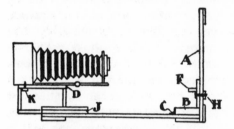

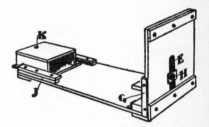

FIG. 9.—A focussing Camera.　　　FIG. 10.—Base of focussing Camera.

height is governed by the size of the backboard, and should be such that the camera lens, in its normal position, reaches to the centre of the board. The length of the baseboard depends upon the focus of the camera lens, but may be about four times as great.

Correct exposure and suitable development are important factors in photographic copying work. When focussing, attention should be paid to the reflection of light from the picture, and care must be taken that this does not strike direct into the lens, and thus cause excessive exposures in certain parts. Especially slow plates should be employed, and in estimating the exposure by Watkins or other approved meter system, allowance must be made for the extra extension which causes the stop values to be increased. Developers compounded of hydrokinone alone prove very useful in giving bright contrasting negatives, although the greatest density possible is to be sought on account of the bluish tinge of the silver deposit. Really, however, the actual developing agent does not greatly signify, seeing that slow plates allow of exceptional latitude, and if the exposure be approximately correct and development carried to its full extent, a pleasing negative can hardly be missed.

Contrast of light and shade can often be considerably improved during copying operations by employing various methods successively. Supposing the original under treatment to be a yellow-faced photograph, in which the light parts are approximately white, but the dark portions yellow, by making the actual exposure through a pale blue or purple glass, the yellow portions are severely handicapped, seeing that they do not reflect many of those blue rays which alone affect the sensitive plate, and consequently approach more nearly in their action to dark masses. Then again, the illumination should be subdued—indoors for preference—so that the exposure with nominal F16 and a slow plate may reach half-an-hour or more, but should certainly be the minimum possible.

Development, on the other hand, ought to be carried as far as possible, so that when the negative is dried, it appears almost opaque. It may then be treated with Farmer's Reducer (fresh hypo solution tinted a distinct yellow with potass. ferricyanide solution), which attacks and dissolves the thin parts more quickly than the dense—thus still further increasing the contrast. After a thorough washing, supposing the photo still to appear weak, intensification by mercury may be adopted. Perchloride of mercury (which must be bought in the presence of a witness and signed for as poison at the chemist's) is made into 5 per cent. solution, rendered acid with several drops of hydrochloric acid, and, when applied to a negative, bleaches its black deposit. The negative is reclaimed by darkening either with hypo solution, or with metol. hydrokinone developer. In all such chemical operations staining is very prone to occur, but it can be prevented by ample washing and cleanliness throughout.

Lastly, another plan to improve contrast occurs in the printing of the positive, for which gas-light paper is the most effective. If print-out paper be used, printing should be conducted in the shade, and under pale yellow glass, the process being made to extend over several days.

Respecting photography of line subjects, *e.g.* black diagrams on white ground, a special treatment of intensification may be meted out to these negatives with advantage. They are treated, after thorough washing, with a solution compounded as follows :—

Potass. ferricyanide	.	.	3 parts.
Lead nitrate .	.	.	2 parts.
Acetic acid .	.	.	3 parts.
Water .	.	.	70 parts.

In this solution the negative is bleached yellow, and may be dried at once after washing, if desired. However, it will certainly present a better appearance if further treated with ammonium sulphydrate solution, wherein it becomes darkened.

The employment of methylated spirits for dispelling the washing water in white negatives preparatory to rapid drying is fairly well recognised. However, as this method is generally applied to important photographs which can ill afford to be spoiled, it is well to point out that the spirit ought to be discarded after twice using, as otherwise small spots of unequal drying will occur in the film and spoil the printing value.

Whilst considering the chemical treatment of plates it might be noticed that Farmer's Reducer applied over an extended time and changed occasionally will completely dissolve the image from a negative. By this means spoiled plates may be converted to plain gelatines, which further may be cut down to $3\frac{1}{4}$ in. square, and after staining with aniline dyes used as tinted cover glasses for lantern slides. Alternatively the gelatine films can be hardened in alum or formalin, and employed when dry for pen-drawing or writing announcement slides.

LANTERN SLIDES

Photographic lantern slides of standard size consist of pictures printed upon $3\frac{1}{4}$ in. square plates, bound up, when dry, with gummed strips of silk or paper round the edges and cover glasses. These prevent the scratching of the film by constant use. The plates only differ from those employed for negative making in so far as their film is thinner, so that the densest parts are not opaque, and the emulsion is slow. Some makes need such a long exposure that they can be worked by ordinary gas-light, like gas-light paper, whilst others must be worked by yellow light, and can either be printed in contact through the negative by exposure to a candle, or some other artificial illuminant.

A large reflector formed by pinning white paper upon a board, A, Fig. 11, is supported on the window-sill at an angle of about 45° by means of strings, B, to the top frame. The negative, C, is sup-

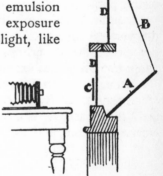

FIG. 11.—Making Lantern Slides.

ported level with the camera lens on the window with its film towards the room, being fixed to the pane, D, by strips of gummed paper. On the ground-glass screen of the camera a 3-in. square is marked, so as to make certain, when focussing the negative, that the picture required is reduced or enlarged as far as necessary. The $3\frac{1}{4}$ in. square lantern plate must be held in a special carrier, in the dark slide, and should receive exposure judged by some accurate meter method, unless many slides are being made at one time, when, of course, the wastage in trial and error will not be so noticeable. The use of Ilford Special plates, and reckoning by Watkin's Meter, makes the exposure equal to the light value when copying equal sizes at nominal F16. Seeing that the plates and stop can be kept constant, the exposure will only vary according to the light value and the camera extension.

Camera extension—

1	focal length	(*i.e.* 7 in. if lens is 5-in. focus)	.	.	$\frac{1}{2}$ light value
$1\frac{3}{4}$	,,	(*i.e.* 8 in. if lens is 5-in. focus)	.	.	$\frac{3}{4}$,,
$2\frac{3}{4}$	,,	(*i.e.* 10 in. if lens is 5-in. focus)	.	.	light value

If the operator be once accustomed to this method he will probably make all slides thus. The results obtained seem to approach the ideal nearer than when contact printing, whilst the exact portion

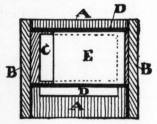

FIG. 12.—Frame for Lantern Slides.

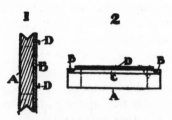

FIG. 13.—Frame for Slides.

of the photograph required may be focussed upon the lantern slides by a judicious use of the camera's rising front. Moreover, should the vertical lines in the original negative be not all parallel, the error can be rectified, perhaps entirely, by tilting the back of the camera when focussing and exposing.

A negative can be very conveniently held in front of the window by means of a frame constructed after the manner shown in Fig. 12. The base, A, is a rectangle cut from $\frac{5}{8}$ in. wood with V-grooves top and bottom, and an aperture slightly larger than the negatives to be held. At the two sides $\frac{1}{4}$ in. strips, BB, are screwed with the inner edges bevelled under, in order to form slides for the frame, C. The edges of the latter are bevelled and blackleaded so as to slide in B, whilst along the top and bottom edges are screwed strips, DD, far enough apart to accommodate the negative, E. The central hole in C is slightly smaller than the latter. The whole frame is supported by means of the V-groove, which engages with two V-shaped bars across the window, and the negative can be moved within certain limits in two directions, vertically in the slides, B, and across in the slides, D. Fig. 13 serves to explain this more clearly.

BROMIDE ENLARGEMENTS

Whilst the window is fitted for lantern slide work, with the reflector outside and the negative holder within, we may consider a method of screening the rest of the window so as to render it dark for making bromide enlargements. Hitherto we have been able to utilise the camera dark slides for holding the lantern plates, so that they were not exposed to daylight before entering the camera, but the paper for enlargements is usually too big to be dealt with thus, and consequently the camera's position has to be reversed with its back—after the ground glass screen is removed—adjoining the negative holder.

The whole room is then converted to a camera by having the window darkened. Of course, if enlargements are only required the size of the camera, *e.g.* half plate, the paper may be placed with the film towards a plain half-plate sheet of glass and loaded thus into the dark slides. A blind of adequate size to cover the window glass is cut from good black cloth, and at the part opposite the upper panes has about a square foot removed, A, Fig. 14. This place is, as it were, patched with safe red fabric, and the blind is then mounted on a spring roller above the window sashes, whilst through its bottom hem is passed a long wood lath, B. The projecting ends of this latter engage with vertical wood slides screwed to

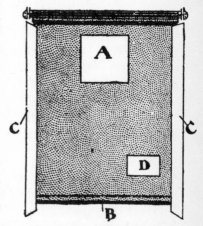

FIG. 14.—Blind used for Screen.

the beading, and strips of black cardboard, C, are also tacked in place in such a way as to overlap the edges of the blind. When this is pulled right down a second rectangular hold, D, is cut to coincide with the negative holder, care being taken that this is in proper position for equal illumination from a reflector. The edges round the aperture can be fastened to the negative frame with drawing-pins. If a little light escapes round the back of the camera when this is pushed against the negative, it may be muffled up in the focussing cloth, the two upper corners of which are pinned to the blind.

As to the actual enlarging, a vertical easel or drawing-board should be stood a little distance from the camera, and provided with a sheet of white paper of the same size as the required enlargement, its mid-point being opposite the lens. The negative having been previously centred, focussing is carried out by racking the camera in and out and moving the easel backwards and forwards until the image is of the correct size and shape. It is advisable to use the lens as wide open as possible during these operations, and then stop down to about F16 for actual exposure. This exposure is tested by pinning a strip of bromide paper across the easel, where a typical part of the picture will appear, e.g. not all sky or all grass, but introducing contrasts of light and shade, and then exposing in several sections of ten, twenty, thirty, and forty seconds each. This is effected by holding a sheet of cardboard in front of the sensitive paper before the camera shutter is opened, and then withdrawing in four or five steps at intervals of ten seconds. Possibly no idea of the accurate exposure can be gathered, and then such a strip will be exposed with intervals of perhaps ten to fifty seconds. Upon development for a standard time, e.g. two to three minutes (depending upon the developer employed and slightly upon the temperature), and fixing, the nearest expanse can be two minutes, whereupon a second strip may be exposed with variations round this time until the right exposure is estimated. Then the large sheet of bromide paper is pinned in place and exposed accordingly.

When bright sharp enlargements of a good black tone can be produced from one's favourite negatives, this branch of photography becomes as fascinating as any other. However, generally speaking, it should be left for the winter, seeing that it must be carried out by daylight, and to spend hours in a darkened room in summer time seems a pity. Moreover, the cloudy skies of winter diffuse a more even though subdued light, and the difficulties of exposure are to that extent simplified.

Photography, like any other hobby, exerts greater fascinations as one's knowledge increases, but it differs from most others inasmuch as it fascinates from the very first, without tuition and without bent.

CHAPTER XXX

HOW TO PATENT AN INVENTION

HINTS FOR AMBITIOUS BOYS

OPPORTUNITIES for inventors were never so great as at the present day. In olden times technical knowledge was limited to the few who had time and money to prove their theories and make experiments ; but now that science and mechanics are marching steadily onwards towards perfection, there is ample scope for every intelligent person to add his quota to the cause of the common good.

That this fact is very generally realised can be proved by the great number of applications that are filed every week in the Patent Office, where inventions of all kinds are registered and protected from unscrupulous imitators.

The Patent Office is in charge of the Comptroller-General of Patents, Designs, and Trade Marks, who acts under the control of the Board of Trade. All communications should be addressed to him at the Patent Office, 25 Southampton Buildings, Chancery Lane, London, W.C. Every reasonable assistance short of legal advice is readily given by the officials of the Patent Office, whose uniform courtesy has smoothed the path of many a diffident inventor.

It should be clearly understood that a patent is taken out at the entire risk of the inventor, and, if his papers are all correct, few inquiries are made, as the Office does not guarantee the validity of any patent. The official search made after the specifications have been filed only extends over a period of fifty years, and, unless the invention be of a frivolous nature or to accomplish an illegal purpose (such as machines for lottery-working, &c.), a patent is invariably granted.

There are two modes of applying for a patent :—

(i.) By application for a provisional patent, which, in not less than six months, must be followed by the completed specifications necessary to obtain the final patent.

(ii.) By depositing the completed specifications without any preliminary application.

The Provisional Patent

Although at first sight the routine for taking out a provisional patent appears rather complicated, the procedure is really of a very simple nature.

Applicants must sign a special form that can be procured at a few days' notice from any Post Office, or may be had direct from the Inland Revenue Office, Room 6, Royal Courts of Justice, Strand. This form requires a £1 stamp to render it valid, and must bear the real name of the applicant, making no mention of any trade or business name.

All forms and specifications must begin with a short descriptive title for the invention, setting forth its principal object ; *e.g.* " Improvement in Construction of Concrete Houses." They should be couched in plain, straightforward language, unadorned by any "fancy" terms or unnecessary phrases. The inventor's name should not appear on the specifications.

Application for one patent only can be made on a form, but analogous or alternative descriptions are considered as identical and integral parts of the application.

As soon as his provisional specifications have been accepted by the Patent Office, the inventor is "provisionally protected" for a period of six months, which should be employed in making further experiments and thoroughly testing the soundness of his deductions and calculations.

During the six months the inventor must also institute a careful search to discover whether his invention has been anticipated. In the Patent Office Library (open from 10 A.M. to 10 P.M.) a large collection of material is obtainable and every assistance is rendered by the officials.

Completed Specifications

Completed specifications must be lodged within six months of the first application. The inventor, however, is advised to wait until this period has almost elapsed, as the early publication of his specifications may give hints to others enabling them to succeed in forestalling him.

The completed specification is designed to inform the public of the precise nature of the monopoly desired, and to give a full description of how the invention will be worked. It must be begun upon a proper form, to which a £3 stamp should be affixed, and may be continued upon foolscap sheets.

The nature of the invention must be so worded that skilled persons may immediately grasp its object. Claims, *i.e.* short paragraphs, should appear at the end of the specification describing exactly what parts the inventor desires to patent, as, in a new invention, many old devices may be employed which it would be unreasonable to expect to protect. Moreover, if the invention consists solely in the combination of existing devices, it must be clearly stated that the patent is only sought to cover this combination.

The description of the method of working the invention must be absolutely *bona fide*, and the practical directions should be exact and sufficiently simple to be easily understood by the workmen employed by the Patent Office.

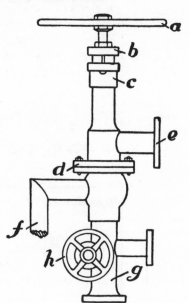

FIG. 1.—Type of Drawing to accompany
Specification.

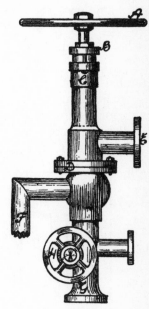

FIG. 2.—A wrongly-drawn Diagram.

DRAWINGS AND SPECIFICATIONS

All drawings accompanying the specifications must be in simple line, Fig. 1, and not have any shading as shown in Fig. 2, which illustrates the same machine incorrectly drawn. The lettering should be clear and legible, not less than $\frac{1}{8}$ in. in size, and solid as illustrated in Fig. 3, rather than of the description depicted in Fig. 4. As the original diagrams are reduced in size when photographed for reproduction, they should be disposed on the illustration sheets with due regard to economy of space. as

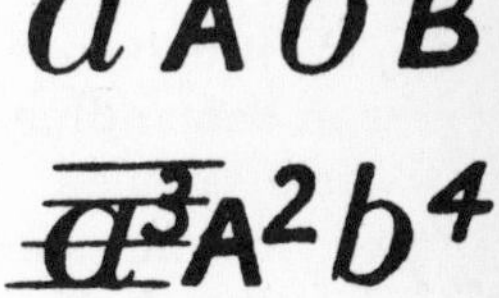

$$a \ A \ b \ B$$

$$a^3 \ A^2 \ b^4$$

FIG. 3.—Correct Lettering.

seen in Fig. 5, and must not be sprawled over the page, Fig. 6. If diagrams have already been lodged with the application for

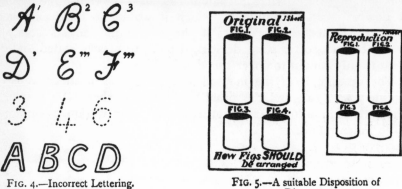

FIG. 4.—Incorrect Lettering.

FIG. 5.—A suitable Disposition of Diagrams.

provisional protection, there is no need to submit copies with the final specification.

As soon as the completed specification is received by the Patent Office, the papers are handed to an examiner, whose business it is to ascertain whether any invention *claiming* to accomplish the same

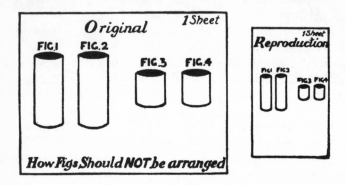

FIG. 6.—Ill-arranged Diagrams.

object has been filed during the past fifty years. If a similar claim be found, the inventor is allowed two months in which to amend his claim, or, if persuaded that the former invention was a failure, he may persist in demanding a patent for his own.

When satisfied that the applicant has fulfilled all that he has claimed in the specification, the Comptroller accepts the patent, publishes it in the official Journal, and, affixing the seal, finally completes the business.

CHAPTER XXXI

HOW TO MAKE A HECTOGRAPH

A SIMPLE DEVICE FOR DUPLICATING LETTERS AND SKETCHES

A HECTOGRAPH, or copygraph, is such an extremely useful article, and so simple to make, that no boy should be without one. By its aid letters, drawings, leaflets, catalogues, &c., can be rapidly duplicated as many as a hundred times.

The first thing to be procured is a receptacle for the hectograph, and for this purpose the lid of a tin biscuit-box is admirably suited.

The ingredients are : glycerine, 9 ounces ; water, 6 ounces ; sulphate of barium, 3 ounces ; powdered loaf sugar, 1½ ounces ; and Nelson's gelatine, 1½ ounces. The glycerine and sulphate of barium may be purchased at the chemist's, whilst the grocer will supply the sugar and gelatine.

Next obtain an old saucepan or tin canister and pour the ingredients into it, mixing them well together. Then set it aside for twenty-four hours, in order that the gelatine may dissolve and assimilate with the other ingredients. After this, stir the composition well with a stick of firewood or an old spoon, and place the saucepan on the kitchen stove, where the heat is not too fierce. In half-an-hour or so its contents will have melted. Continue to stir the sticky mixture, however, until it is reduced to a thick, treacly liquid.

Then place the lid of your biscuit-box on a perfectly level surface, and pour into it the contents of the saucepan. In all probability a number of bubbles will form on the top of the graph. These must be removed by drawing a piece of paper lightly over its surface.

Leave the hectograph in a cool place, and in a short time it will become set and ready for use.

Write the matter to be duplicated upon a smooth-surfaced sheet of paper, employing a new nib and the special hectograph ink which can be purchased at any large stationer's for ninepence a bottle. Let the writing dry without using the blotter, then lay the paper face downwards upon the graph, rubbing it gently with the tips of the fingers, to ensure its entire surface coming in contact with the graph. Leave it thus for one minute, then carefully remove it by peeling off from one corner.   It will now be seen that a reverse copy of the writing remains on the graph.

Without loss of time take a clean sheet of paper, and lay it upon the hectograph.   Rub it lightly with the finger-tips, then peel it off immediately.   An exact copy of the writing will have been transferred to it, and by placing other blank sheets of paper upon the gelatine surface as many as a hundred copies may be obtained.

Yet another method of making a hectograph is as follows:—

Take 2 ounces of fine Russian glue, 4 ounces of cold water, 6 drops of carbolic acid, and just sufficient Paris whiting to make the solution milky.

Place the glue with the water in a jam jar, and dissolve it over a slow fire.   Then stir in the carbolic acid, glycerine, and Paris whiting, in the order here given.

When all is thoroughly assimilated, pour the composition into the biscuit-tin lid, and leave it to set.   When it has done so, the hectograph will be ready for use.

If the reader prefer, instead of buying his ink, he may make it by dissolving aniline dye in water and adding a little methylated spirits. Another good ink may be manufactured by thinning Judson's dye with methylated spirits.   The ink must not be made too thin, however, but should be left rather thick.

When the desired number of copies has been taken from the graph, its surface should be washed clean by means of a sponge dipped in warm—not *hot*—water, and as soon as it is dry it will be quite ready for further use.

CHAPTER XXXII

LEAF-SKELETONS

AN INTERESTING AND UNIQUE COLLECTION

IT is not a very difficult task to obtain the skeletons of leaves, and the delicate white veins, or "bones," of different leaves, interlaced in an entirely distinct manner from one another, make an interesting and unique collection.

The first thing required for the "skeletonising" process is some lime. A pennyworth of this may be purchased from any colour-merchant, though it is stocked at the majority of oil-shops. After this the reader must take a walk into his garden, and pluck a few leaves with which to commence operations.

Upon returning indoors, he should procure an empty jam jar—the three-pound size is preferable to the smaller variety—and place about a quarter of the lime in it, afterwards filling it half-full of water. This done, he must stand the jar and its contents in a saucepan of water, and then place the whole on the fire.

Very soon the water in the saucepan will commence to boil, and shortly after the lime-water in the jam jar will boil also. Give the lime-water a thorough stir with a stick of wood, and then drop in one or two of the leaves, continuing to stir *very gently*.

At the end of two or three minutes—the time varies according to the style of leaf, strength of lime, &c.—take out one of the leaves, and lay it flat on the table. Then, with a small mop, made by binding a thickness of rag on the end of a short cane or wooden knitting-needle, Fig. 1, gently proceed to rub the surface.

It will now be found that the green, fleshy part of the leaf comes clean away, leaving the delicate tracery of veins beneath.

FIG. 1.—The Mop

Having cleaned the green epidermis from one side, turn over the leaf, and repeat the process on the other, until nothing but the white skeleton of the leaf remains.

If the green fleshy substance is at first difficult to remove, the leaf should be replaced in the jam jar, and boiled a trifle longer. Care must be taken, however, not to leave it there too long, as the lime will ultimately attack and destroy the veins themselves.

FIG. 2.—A Skeleton Leaf.

Having "skeletonised" a number of leaves in the above manner, give them a thorough wash in cold water, then lay them upon a sheet of paper, and place them in the sun to dry. In addition to drying them, the rays of the sun will bleach the leaf-skeletons a spotless, bone-like white, adding greatly to the beauty and delicacy of their appearance.

The best method of displaying the specimens is to place them in a case lined with black velvet, the dark background of which will show up the delicate tracery of the veins to advantage. Cases similar to those used by butterfly collectors will be found to answer admirably. The skeleton of each leaf can be fixed into position by a small band of black paper pinned over the stalk and the opposite point, as illustrated in Fig. 2.

CHAPTER XXXIII

TAXIDERMY

THE STUFFING OF BIRDS AND ANIMALS

IN a large subject such as taxidermy, which includes the stuffing of elephants on the one hand and the mounting of insects on the other, it is clearly necessary to describe the treatment of the more general objects likely to come into the province of one who takes up the art as a hobby. Having acquired a certain amount of skill in stuffing and mounting birds and quadrupeds, the student of taxidermy will feel competent to undertake the treatment of whatever may come in his path.

NECESSARY OUTFIT

The tools required for taxidermy are few and such as can be found in most households.

The knife, shown in Fig. 1, should be about 10 in. long, with a cutting edge of half that length, and the tip sharply pointed.

FIG. 1.—The Taxidermist's Knife.

Two pairs of scissors will be required—one pair with pointed blades, and the other with blunted ends, Fig. 2.

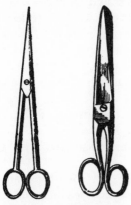

FIG. 2.—The Scissors used in Taxidermy.

FIG. 3.—The Pliers.

FIG. 4.—The Goffering Iron.

A pair of bell-hanger's pliers, Fig. 3, and a goffering iron, Fig. 4, for forcing the padding into the limbs, will complete the outfit.

STUFFING A RABBIT

As the first specimen to be stuffed will be rather of the nature of an experiment, some easily procured animal should be obtained, and the beginner cannot do better than start work upon the body of a rabbit.

Place the rabbit upon a table with its hind feet towards you, and, inserting the point of your knife a little below the vent, make a long slit up the skin to the centre of the breast. Take great care not to cut too deep, as by doing so the walls of the abdomen will be perforated, and this must be avoided if possible.

Now insert the knife in the slit thus made, and, beginning with the left side, commence separating the skin from the flesh, sopping up any blood with sand or sawdust. Work steadily in this fashion down to the hind-legs, and then, when you have reached this spot, force up the knees one after the other, through the opening, cutting through the bones at the knee-joints.

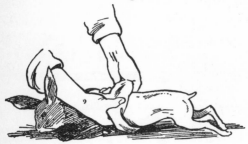

FIG. 5.—Skinning a Rabbit.

Clear away the chief muscles of the legs and separate the skin all round the tail. A slight pull will slip the tail right out of the skin as neatly as a finger is withdrawn from a glove.

The skin must now be gradually turned inside out and rolled up as it is detached from the carcase of the rabbit, as shown in Fig. 5. Cut the forelegs at the elbow joints and work the skin over the shoulders and head, taking the utmost care not to cut the skin in passing the eyes and mouth. Plenty of sawdust should be used to prevent the fur getting soiled with blood.

When it has been entirely removed, brush the inside of the skin with arsenical soap, paying especial attention to the interior of the limbs. You must also be sure that none of this poisonous soap gets to the outside fur.

The next thing to be done is to sever the head from the carcase and boil it until all the flesh and brains fall away, leaving the bare skull. The lower jaw must then be tied in position with a piece of thread or cotton.

You will now require a strong piece of wire long enough to stretch the whole length of the rabbit, with three or four inches to spare. Bend one end of this wire into a ball and fasten it in the brain-pan of the skull with some plaster of Paris, Fig. 6.

By this time the skin can be turned right side out. Cut wires to fit into the legs and pad them out properly with cotton wool. The tail may be treated in a similar manner.

FIG. 6.—Adjusting the Skull.

Fit the skull into the head, and wrap sufficient cotton wool around the central wire of the body to fill the skin, but not enough to stretch

FIG. 7.—The Mounted and Stuffed Rabbit.

it. When this has been done satisfactorily, sew up the opening down the belly, and pose the specimen as naturally as possible, Fig. 7.

STUFFING A BIRD

The first thing to be done with a bird is to fill the mouth and nostrils with cotton wool, in order to prevent the escape of various fluids which discharge after death. Until the *rigor mortis* or death stiffening has passed off, nothing further can be done. A very short time, however, will suffice for this stiffness to disappear.

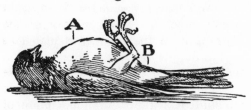

FIG. 8.—Bird prepared for Skinning.

Upon passing your finger over the abdomen you will find a bald or almost bald spot, B, Fig. 8, near the vent. From this spot make an incision with the point of the knife or scissors, as far as the sternum, A, taking care not to pierce the walls of the abdomen.

FIG. 9.—Wrapping the Bird in Cotton.

Now press and push, rather than pull, the skin from the flesh until the thigh bones appear, being careful not to let any of the feathers get soiled with blood.

The thighs must be severed with pliers from beneath the joint, and the stump of the tail and wing bones broken before anything further is done.

Now, starting from the tail, skin very carefully upward and past the wings to the neck. Turning the skin inside out, the neck will come clear quite easily until the base of the skull is reached. At this point the membranes of the eyes may be cut and the eyes removed, a sharp wire being driven through the sockets and into the brain. The brain must then be fetched out through the base of the skull by means of a wire hook, its place being filled with cotton wool forced through the sockets of the eyes.

A dummy body of cotton wool should be constructed around a stiffened wire, smaller wires being made for the legs as in the case of the rabbit. When all this is properly arranged the belly may be sewn up and the legs and wings placed in a natural position.

The stuffed bird will now appear a most disreputable object, a very discouraging result after all the care expended upon the operation. But the finishing touches have yet to be made before the specimen is fit to be mounted.

FIG. 10.—Stuffed Bird complete.

Take a piece of stout thread, and, beginning with the head, wind it tightly round the body, smoothing down the feathers as you proceed, until the bird is tightly wrapped in the manner depicted in Fig. 9. When the specimen is thoroughly dry, this thread can be unwound, and the plumage will be found perfectly smooth and natural.

With a little artistic setting the stuffed bird may then be mounted on a twig or stand, as seen in Fig. 10, and the taxidermist's task will be complete.

CHAPTER XXXIV

PEBBLES, AND HOW TO POLISH THEM

AN ARTISTIC WAY TO PRESERVE THE TREASURES OF THE SEASHORE

WHOEVER has been to the seashore and strolled along the beach where the outgoing tide has left the stones all wet and glistening, must have been struck by the singular beauty, both in colour and marking, which many of the pebbles exhibit. Unfortunately, no sooner do the stones become dry than their beauty disappears, leaving dull and uninteresting pebbles in place of what were glistening gems.

By polishing these pebbles, however, the beauty of their colour and veins can be fixed and retained for ever. Not only this, but with a little ingenuity and taste they can be converted into trinkets of no mean value. Bracelets, brooches, and many such trifles dear to a sister's heart ; cuff links and tie pins which are more acceptable to the male mind—all these can be made by the lapidary, as the stone-cutter is called.

It has already been mentioned that, unless they be wet, pebbles show very little of the markings which make them so handsome. After a certain amount of experience, however, a practised eye is able to judge fairly accurately what will be the appearance that a stone will present when cut and polished. There are occasions, of course, when even an expert is at fault, but this is only a matter of chance.

Local jewellers at seaside resorts have discovered that it pays them to pronounce, favourable judgment upon the "finds" which visitors produce for their inspection, and it is no uncommon thing for an enthusiastic holiday-maker to take some stone which he fondly imagines to be an agate or cornelian, and be told by the jeweller to call again in a week's time, when his stone will be ready, cut and polished. Upon paying his visit at the time appointed, the pebble will be ready for him, as also the bill, but there is scarcely need to add that the cut and polished stone seldom has any connection with the pebble he picked up himself. Amber, agates, and other stones *can* be found on our shores, but the enthusiast who hopes to pay for his railway fare, board and lodging with the proceeds of his stone-finding is doomed to disappointment.

One of the most beautiful, and at the same time common, stones to be found on the beach, especially in the south of England, is chalcedony. This is so clear and almost transparent that it seems well worth taking home as a specimen. But, alas, the very fact of its being so clear makes it useless for the pebble-hunter's purpose. A few markings in a stone are essential, as the real beauty of polished work lies in the patterns and markings which variegate the surface. After a time the eye is accustomed to picking out stones on the beach which are really worth cutting, such as moss agates, ring agates, or cornelian.

The markings of a pebble can always be discovered by wetting it, and this is the reason why a walk along the beach, where the waves are breaking, will serve to reveal the stones which are worth troubling about.

<h3 align="center">THE LAPIDARY'S TOOLS</h3>

A very simple lapidary's polishing machine can be made after the pattern shown in Fig. 1. Take an ordinary reel, A, such as is used

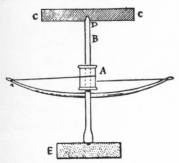

FIG. 1.—A simple Polisher.

for thread, and through the hole in the centre place a pencil of wood, B, one end of which must be reduced to a fairly obtuse point. In the centre of a block of wood, CC, which is just large enough to be held conveniently in the right hand, make a funnel-shaped hole, D, of sufficient size to contain the pointed end of the pencil.

A slab of sandstone, E, will now be required, and in its centre a small cup must be scooped out, the use of which will appear later. Now make a long bow, similar to those used for old-fashioned drills, and pass the cord around the reel as depicted in the diagram.

With this simple contrivance a pebble can be polished with great ease, the grip of the sandstone being quite sufficient to give the stone a clean face. The method of fixing the pebble to the lower end of the pencil will be described in due course.

A more complicated lapidary's bench is shown in Fig. 2, but the construction of such an apparatus would prove too difficult for any but a carpenter to undertake. ABCD is the tray or table upon which the work is done. The handle E when turned causes the large wheel F to revolve, and this communicates its action by means of a belt to the small spindle G. The remainder of the apparatus is very simple, the lap H being fastened to the shaft bearing the spindle which revolves very rapidly when the handle E is turned.

The laps, of which four will be required, should be about ten inches in diameter, and varying in thickness from two inches in the centre to one inch at the circumference, Fig. 3. One will be of lead, another of beech-wood, a third of pewter, whilst the remaining lap must be made of deal covered with common felt stretched tightly and tacked to the other side.

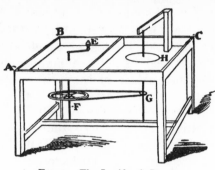

FIG. 2.—The Lapidary's Bench.

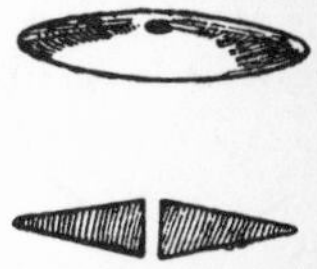

FIG. 3.—The Laps.

Several pounds of emery powder, some lumps of rotten-stone, and an old plate-brush will complete the outfit. One or two jars of clean water should be within easy reach of the bench.

HOW TO POLISH A PEBBLE

As many pebbles are too small to be held against the revolving lap, it will be necessary to fasten them with cement to a stick which can be held between the fingers conveniently. This can be done after the manner shown in Fig. 4. A mixture of pitch, resin. shellac, and beeswax, which any oilman will concoct for the purpose, should be applied to the end of a small stick, and the pebble pressed into the mixture as illustrated in the diagram.

This device will explain how the pebble should be fastened to the end of the pencil in the apparatus described in Fig. 1.

The first process to be undertaken is that of grinding. Place the lead lap in position and smear upon its surface a paste made of emery and water. Then cause the lap to revolve and press the pebble very hard against the lead. As the emery is forced into the metal, apply more paste until, in a short while, the lap has become a fine rasp. The constant revolution will grind away the surface of the stone. When, in your opinion, sufficient has been removed, continue the use of the lead until the emery has entirely disappeared.

FIG. 4.—A Pebble cemented to a Stick.

The next thing to be done is to smooth the pebble, and this is performed with the beech-wood lap. Place this upon the spindle, scatter a little well-damped silver sand upon its surface, and then treat the pebble in the same fashion as with the lead lap until all the sand has disappeared, and the surface of the pebble has become quite smooth.

All that remains to be done is to face the pebble. This must be done with the pewter lap, upon the surface of which not a grain of sand or emery should be allowed to fall. A number of small lines should be scratched upon the surface of the pewter lap

somewhat after the manner shown in Fig. 5, these serving to contain the rotten-stone, which must be applied by wetting the lap very thoroughly in water and then revolving it slowly against the stone. When this has been done satisfactorily, the pewter lap will be covered with a thickish paste.

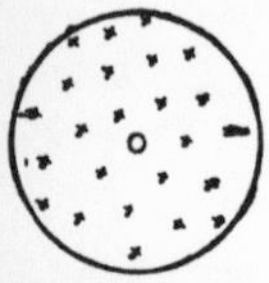

FIG. 5.—Pewter Lap.

The pebble must be very carefully scrubbed in a bowl of water so that there is not the least chance of any grit coming near its surface. This is most important as, should such a grit appear, the entire polished surface of the pebble will be scratched and ruined.

The result of this stage of the work will be that the pebble presents a hard and glassy appearance. The final touches to the work are given by pressing the pebble against the felt lap and revolving the latter until a fine polish is obtained.

PEBBLE-CUTTING

The question of cutting or splitting a pebble in order to polish the inner surface is a matter of considerable difficulty, and beginners will do well to have the stones cut by a professional lapidary.

The only thing of sufficient hardness to cut a pebble is a diamond, and it need scarcely be remarked that the purchase of diamond "bort" is expensive. This diamond "bort" is composed of the cuttings of smaller diamonds, which are useless for jewellers' purposes. Prices vary, but as a general rule it may be taken that "bort" cannot be purchased under six or seven shillings per carat.

This material should be mixed with paraffin into a paste with which the edge of a cutting disc is smeared. These cutting discs, which must be purchased from a lapidary, are made of soft steel, into which the hard grains of the diamond are forced when in contact with a pebble. The cutter, therefore, is really a diamond-toothed saw, and when revolved rapidly against the pebble, it will cut its way through at the rate of something like half-an-inch per hour. The difficulty attending this process, the expense of purchasing diamond "bort," and the extreme improbability of the beginner being able to cut the pebble straight, make it advisable to let this part of the work be done by a professional.

The question of setting polished pebbles does not come into the lapidary's province, and had better be left to a jeweller. Experience will enable this man to suggest the most appropriate method of setting the pebbles, and mounting them in whatever forms seem suitable.

CHAPTER XXXV

SECRETS OF SCIENCE

AMUSEMENT IN THE HOME "LAB."

OF the numerous hobbies with which boys while away their leisure hours, none is more instructive nor more amusing than that of scientific experimenting. Although very popular with a large number of people, it cannot be claimed that this hobby is commonly indulged in, and this for a special reason.

Many, although longing to make this a part of their recreation, find that it is beyond their reach. They will either tell you that the necessary apparatus is not always forthcoming, or that they are not sufficiently acquainted with experiments suitable for home performance. This, unfortunately, is often but too true, and that it will be the aim of this short chapter to overcome these difficulties, and to encourage the innate curiosity of youth by describing a few of the most instructive, yet pleasing, secrets of science. Whilst to the uninitiated some of these experiments will appear as little less than miracles, yet the experienced experimenter will be able to account for them in the most matter-of-fact way, thus mystifying his friends and at the same time providing himself with a valuable means of instruction.

Having some idea of the preparation entailed by the pursuit of this hobby, and realising that parents resolutely set their faces against such trivial matters as explosions in the drawing-room, the reader will naturally conclude that for the sake of peace and quietness a private retreat is essential.

How much happier you feel when assured that the making of a good mess will not provoke the ire of your well-wishing parents, and how nice to guard your scientific discoveries from the irreverent remarks of the unbelieving!

Most boys are able to command the use of a small unused room, a cellar or even a lobby, which, at very little cost, may be converted into a most useful laboratory; for, as every lover of science will tell you, a laboratory is indispensable.

The following few words then, are intended to convey to the

reader some idea of fitting up and equipping a small, inexpensive laboratory suitable for any experiments he may conduct during his scientific research.

A good stout table to serve as a bench is the first necessity, but should this not be forthcoming, a satisfactory substitute will be found in a bench constructed as described below.

Procure two stout deal boards, 4 ft. long, 8 in. wide and 1 in. thick, which, at 1½d. per ft., will cost a shilling.

Securely fasten them together by means of three or four cross pieces, thus forming the top of your bench, ABCD, Fig. 1.

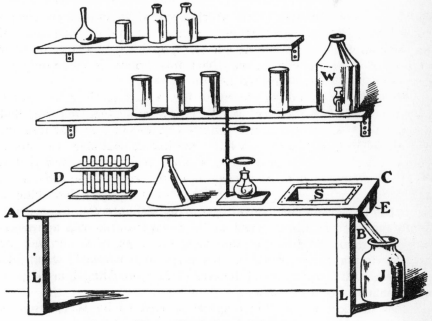

FIG. 1.—The Beginner's Laboratory.

As most experiments necessitate the use of a sink, your bench must be provided with one. Ingenious readers will, no doubt, invent many different methods of construction ; but for those who cannot devise a better plan, the following course is recommended :—

Make a wooden box 1 ft. long, 1 ft. wide, and 4 in. deep, and line the interior with lead sheeting, being careful to use no solder. To a hole in the bottom of the box fix a waste-pipe in the form of a piece of composition tubing, so arranged as to empty into an old pail, or, better still, a jar, J, Fig. 1. To those unwilling to undertake the construction of such a sink, a good, though less permanent, sub-stitute is found in a square meat or biscuit tin well coated two or three times with enamel. This substitute will after a time, however, suffer greatly from the action of chemicals, so that any extra labour involved in the construction of the wooden sink is amply repaid.

When finished, let the sink into a corner of the bench, so as to be conveniently near the water-supply, W, Fig. 1.

You have now to fix your bench in position, and this is done by first nailing to the wall, at a convenient height from the floor— 3 ft. 6 in. should be sufficient—a stout block of wood which is to act as a rest, E, Fig. 1.

Next support the bench in front by two wooden legs, LL, and firmly fix the back to the wall support. In this way a very serviceable bench may be erected, although the finishing touches to the laboratory have yet to be added.

Shelves, of course, are necessary, and two or three should be fixed above the bench. Of these, the lowest should be the widest, in order to contain the larger bottles and a water-supply, which, should no water be available, must be provided.

This is very easily accomplished by purchasing a stone beer-jar of a gallon capacity, which, with a wooden tap, can be cheaply procured, and will serve as an excellent water-supply, W, Fig. 1.

APPARATUS REQUIRED

It has previously been stated that many would-be followers of this hobby find their ardour damped by their inability to obtain the necessary apparatus. They should, therefore, derive much benefit from a list showing a typical outfit with which every beginner should be equipped. Although in the few experiments to be later described, the use of many of these chemicals, &c., may not be necessary, the young scientist should provide himself with as many of them as possible, since they are constantly needed for any experiments occurring in elementary science.

In most cases the following articles may be obtained from any local chemist, who, if he has not them in stock, will order them.

List of Beginner's Apparatus with Approximate Cost

	s.	a.
1 doz. test tubes	0	3
1 test-tube stand (to hold 6 tubes)	0	6
2 test-tube brushes	0	2
2 narrow 6-oz. beakers	0	8
2 8-oz. flasks	0	8
½ doz. corks for flasks	0	2
¼ lb. narrow glass tubing	0	6

			s.	d.
1 retort-stand fitted with 2 iron rings			1	3
1 spirit-lamp, or, if gas be available, Bunsen burner . . .			0	10
2 pieces iron wire gauze			0	4
1 evaporating basin			0	3
1 crystallising dish			0	4
1 thistle funnel (narrow bore)			0	2
1 Wolff's bottle, with 2 necks			1	0
2 small gas jars			1	0
Yard and metre rules			0	9
Crucible tongs			1	0

List of Chemicals

4 oz. sulphuric acid			0	6
4 oz. hydrochloric acid			0	6
4 oz. nitric acid			0	6
$\frac{1}{2}$ oz. red oxide of mercury			0	2
1 oz. sulphur			0	1
$\frac{1}{4}$ oz. sodium			0	3
1 oz. granulated zinc			0	1
1 oz. manganese dioxide			0	1
1 oz. calcium carbonate			0	1

As it is quite unnecessary to make this outlay all at once, the various articles should only be purchased as occasion requires.

Now it will be found that many other pieces of apparatus, although not essential, greatly assist in bringing difficult experiments to a successful conclusion. Thus, a small triangular file is invaluable for cutting glass, whilst a ribbed funnel with filter papers greatly adds to the ease of filtration. Then, again, for the collection of gases by displacement of water, a beehive shelf, on which to stand the inverted gas jars, saves much time and trouble.

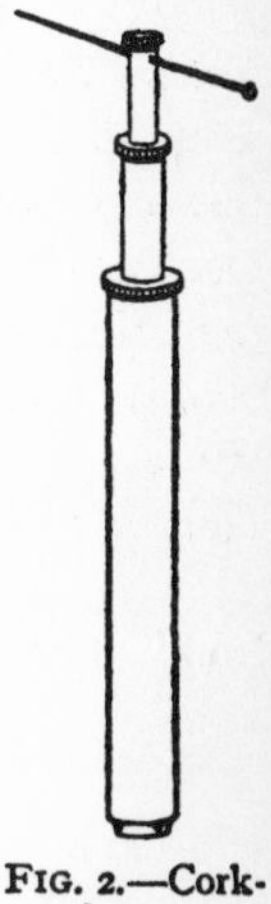

It is frequently necessary to fit corks with one or more pieces of glass tubing, and this can only be accomplished by cork-borers, which consist of tubes having one end sharpened and the other milled, Fig. 2. A suitable set, containing three borers of different sizes, may be purchased at very small cost, and will be found a valuable acquisition.

Very little more is required to complete the beginner's outfit, which will be found admirably suited to the experiments he may have to perform. As the success of

Fig. 2.—Cork-borer.

an experiment largely depends upon the manner in which the apparatus is handled, one of the first lessons the novice has to master is the knack of fitting up his apparatus in a thoroughly workmanlike manner.

Accuracy, carefulness, and cleanliness are characteristics which every would-be scientist must acquire, since deficiency in any one of these qualities may render hours of labour futile.

It must become a duty, therefore, to see that all apparatus is carefully cleaned both before and after experiments. Wet test-tubes, flasks, &c., should always be inverted after washing, to drain all water away, or they may be lightly passed through a Bunsen flame, thus quickening the process of drying.

In course of time it will be found that the ironwork of various pieces of apparatus becomes rusty. In such cases it should be immediately cleaned with a paraffin rag.

Then again, wire gauze is often greasy, especially when new, and it should be placed over a Bunsen or spirit-lamp flame until all signs of grease have disappeared.

To many the boring of a cork seems too simple a matter to call for description, whilst the bending and cutting of glass tubing appears ridiculously easy.

Such, however, is not the case, and the successful performance of these details needs practice.

The method of fitting a cork with one or more bent tubes should receive particular attention, since it is needed for so many experiments.

Having selected the glass tubing, take a cork-borer and, holding the cork in the left hand, press the borer against it at the required

spot. If only one hole be needed, it should be made through the middle of the cork, A, Fig. 3, but should an extra hole be required for a

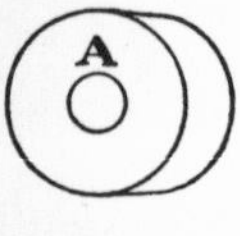

FIG. 3.—Cork bored with Single Hole.

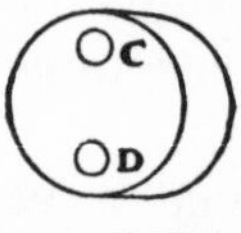

second piece of tubing — such as a thistle funnel, the two holes

FIG. 4.—Cork bored with Two Holes.

must be bored near the sides of the cork, C and D, Fig. 4.

Work the borer from side to side after the manner of a bradawl, taking care to exert an even pressure all the time. When the borer is almost through, press the cork against the bench, thus finishing off with a neat hole, and avoiding an untidy, jagged opening.

CUTTING AND BENDING GLASS TUBING

It may be necessary to cut your tubing to the right length. This is done by placing it on a flat surface, and then making one or two circular niches with the triangular file at the place for breaking. Placing a hand on either side of these niches, break the tube by pressing the hands towards you. Although quite thick tubing will break cleanly in this way, it is advisable to hold the glass in a duster, and to make a circle of niches, thus lessening the danger of cuts.

Should it be necessary to bend glass tubing, it must be heated in the ordinary white or yellow gas flame, as the Bunsen flame invariably produces a bad bend, similar to that shown in B, Fig. 5. Heat two or three inches of the glass by holding it lengthways in the white part of the flame, constantly revolving the tube to ensure that it becomes evenly heated. When the heated part of the glass begins to sink, the tube is ready to be bent, and so, taking it from the flame, gradually bend it to the required shape.

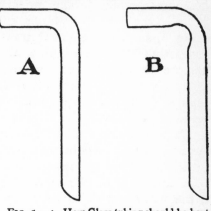

FIG. 5.—A, How Glass tubing should be bent.
B, How it should *not* be bent.

Do not lay it down until quite cool, for, should the hot glass suddenly come in contact with the cold bench, it will inevitably crack.

After removing the lamp-black with a duster, the tube is ready for use, but care should be taken when fitting it in the hole of a cork, not to lever it in by the bend, as this is now its weakest part.

For some experiments a fine glass jet is needed, and this may be obtained by heating a glass tube in the manner described above ; only, instead of bending the tube, its two ends should be drawn apart, Fig. 6, and, when cool, broken off in the thinnest part.

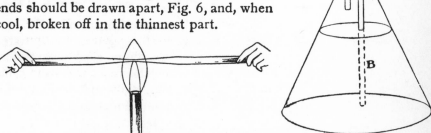

FIG. 6.—How to form a Jet.

FIG. 7.—A Wash-bottle.

The young scientist should also become familiar with the fitting up of a wash-bottle, a simple apparatus used for containing distilled water, with which it is often necessary to wash out test-tubes, beakers, &c.

This useful piece of apparatus consists of a wide-mouthed flask fitted with a cork through which has been bored two holes.

A short tube, bent as shown at A in Fig. 7, is fixed in one of these holes, whilst in the other is inserted a long tube B, reaching almost to the bottom of the flask. This latter tube is bent as shown in Fig. 7, and has the end C drawn out to a fine jet.

Partly fill the flask with water, and fix the cork in tightly. It will then be found that, on blowing down the tube A, the increased pressure within the flask forces the liquid up the longer tube, whence it issues in the form of a fine, powerful jet, capable of cleaning flasks, test-tubes, &c.

The laboratory, thus equipped, should now be ready for use, and the youthful scientist may turn his attention to experimenting.

Since text-books on elementary science are now so common, it would be out of place, in this short chapter, to devote any space to the numerous experiments to be found in them. The following few pages are intended, therefore, to furnish the reader with a few interesting and amusing experiments not to be found in any ordinary work on science.

THE INCONSISTENT EGG

An egg which will sink in one bottle of water, float in a second, and hang midway in a third, may rightly be termed inconsistent; and yet, with very little trouble, the reader may put an ordinary egg through these performances.

For this experiment the requirements are few and simple, consisting only of a fresh egg, some salt, water, and three glass jars, two of which are of the same capacity, whilst that of the third is about equal to the combined volumes of the other two.

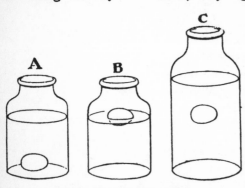

FIG. 8.—The Inconsistent Egg.

Partly fill the first, A, Fig. 8, with pure water; the second, B, with a strong solution of salt and water, and leave the third, C, empty.

Gently drop the egg into A, when it will immediately sink, then, removing it from the jar, try the same with B. Despite all your efforts, the egg will persist in rising to the surface, until in despair you remove it, and gently lower it into the empty bottle C.

Now pour in some of the contents of both bottles, A and B, until with a little more from one or the other, the egg will be seen to rest midway between the surface and the bottom. Then, by the addition of pure water, it may be made to sink, whilst more salt water will cause it to rise again.

How will you explain this to your wondering friends?

It is really very simple; the egg sinks in the pure water because it is of greater density than the liquid, it floats on the brine because its density is less, and is suspended midway when its density is just equal to that of the solution.

THE PERFORMING FISH

It is quite evident, of course, that such a fish must be of your own manufacture, and since the success of the experiment depends upon this home-made creature, some little care must be exercised in its construction.

Take a fresh egg, pierce a small hole at each extremity, and then empty its contents by blowing through one of the holes.

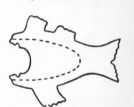

FIG. 9.—The Fish's Head.

By means of a pencil, provide the fish with two large eyes, and then seal up the front hole with a little wax, Fig. 9.

Next cut out two pieces of flannel to the shape of a fish, and sew them as indicated by the dotted line in Fig. 10. Then, having weighted the body with a few lead shots, fix the shell halfway in the sack, the pierced end being inside.

FIG. 10.—The Fish's Fins.

With the aid of a little sealing-wax, stick the sack to the shell, and your fish is complete. Place it in a glass jar filled to the brim with water, and ensure its being so weighted that, although floating on the surface, the slightest touch causes it to descend. You must next cover the jar with a piece of india-rubber, or some other elastic substance, and all is ready.

FIG. 11.—The Performing Fish.

By pressing the india-rubber cover on to the liquid, a little water is forced through the hole into the shell, and, increasing the weight of the fish, causes it to plunge. Directly the increased pressure is removed from the water, the air imprisoned in the shell repulses the invading water, and the fish, thus lightened, shoots to the surface, Fig. 11.

In this way, by regulating the pressure on the water, the performing fish seems to obey your slightest wish.

SENSITIVE MATCHES

Many have no doubt witnessed the sight of children who, fleeing in horror from the scene of washing operations when a piece of soap is produced, yet return with rapidity at the tempting offer of a piece of sugar.

Strange to relate, matches will behave in precisely the same manner as these naughty children.

To demonstrate the truth of this, fill a bowl with water, and on its surface arrange several matches in the form of a star. Then, taking a small piece of soap, previously sharpened to a point, immerse it in the

FIG. 12.—Matches do not like Soap:

water at the centre of the star. It will be seen that the matches, regarding the soap with apparent horror, seek refuge at the side of the bowl, Fig. 12.

How can they be enticed back? It is easily done by dipping a piece of sugar into the middle of the bowl, when the greedy matches will at once be seen to cluster round the tempting bait, Fig. 13.

This interesting experiment is based on what is scientifically known as the superficial tension of liquids, from which we learn that objects passing

FIG. 13.—But they run after Sugar.

over the surface of a liquid appear to travel as if the latter were covered with a very thin elastic membrane.

When the soap became dissolved in the water, the elasticity of the centre of the membrane was lessened, thus carrying the matches away from the centre to the edges of the surface. In the case of the sugar, the water which it absorbed produced a current from the sides of the bowl to the centre, and it is this current which carried the matches with it to that central spot.

BURNING A CANDLE IN A LAMP GLASS

You all know, do you not, what happens if a lamp glass be placed over a lighted candle?

It burns for a moment, and then, as the gaseous products of combustion gradually settle at the bottom of the glass, the flame soon becomes extinguished, Fig. 14.

How can this difficulty be overcome; for it is often necessary to protect a candle from the draught by placing a lamp glass over it.

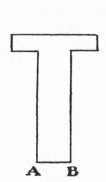

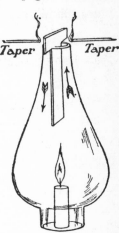

FIG. 14.—The Candle Flame extinguished in a Lamp-glass.

FIG. 15.—The Cardboard T.

FIG. 16.—The Current of Air in the Lamp-glass.

There are more ways than one of accomplishing this, but perhaps the easiest is the following. First cut out a piece of cardboard as shown in Fig. 15, the width of AB being equal to the diameter of the top of the glass.

Fix the cardboard thus cut in the middle of the glass, which should then be placed over the lighted candle. It will at once become apparent that, instead of being extinguished, the candle burns with a bright, steady flame.

By placing the piece of cardboard in such a position, you have divided the glass into two compartments, down one of which passes fresh, cool air, whilst the vitiated heated air issues from the other. The presence of these two currents may be clearly demonstrated by holding a lighted taper over the different compartments, and noticing the direction in which the smoke or flame moves, Fig. 16.

EFFACEABLE INK

There exist many inks the marks of which entirely disappear when subjected to the action of light, whilst it is common knowledge that even ordinary ink-stains will disappear under the bleaching action of a solution of chlorine, although there is more than one way of reviving the marks thus obliterated.

It is quite possible, however, to manufacture for yourself, in the easiest manner possible, an ink which may be effaced without leaving the faintest trace.

Since the ingredients for this ink are to be found in almost every

FIG. 17.—Use of Effaceable Ink.

household, the difficulty of procuring expensive materials is at once dispensed with. It is only necessary to dilute a little starch to the consistency of cream, and then add a few drops of tincture of iodine. By so doing, you have formed, from a chemical point of view, iodide of starch, and this will constitute your ink. Dip a pen into this ink, and write a few words on an ordinary piece of paper, Fig. 17. The writing, which immediately dries, is of a dark brown colour, and appears quite clear. Taking a pocket handkerchief, or a clean piece of rag, lightly rub the writing, when, to the astonishment of your friends, it will be found to disappear as easily as chalk-marks vanish from a blackboard.

THE SWINGING PENDULUM

Nearly every one knows how a glass filled with water may be inverted without the slightest fear of the liquid being spilt.

All you have to do is to fill the glass to the very brim with water, and then cover it with a sheet of strong paper in such a fashion that every bubble of air is excluded. No matter how you shake it, the water remains within the glass. This somewhat surprising result, of course, depends upon the fact that the atmospheric pressure on the exterior of the paper exceeds the pressure exerted by the water on the other side of it, and so the liquid is confined to the glass.

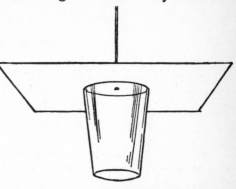

FIG. 18.—Glassful of Water adhering to a Sheet of Paper.

A very striking and amusing application of this principle is afforded by the swinging pendulum. Take a card large enough to

FIG. 19.—The Swinging Glass.

cover the glass, and in the middle make a pin-hole, through which must be pulled a piece of thread knotted at one end. To render the card quite air-tight, carefully cover the knot and hole with a little wax. Then, taking a glass, or, for the first attempt, an unbreakable vessel, fill it with water as described above, and, having fitted the card over the top, attach the other end of the thread to a hook in the ceiling, Fig. 18.

In this way you have made a pendulum, which may be freely oscillated, Fig. 19, without any fear of damage to the glass, especially if you have previously taken the precaution of greasing the rim, and thus augmenting the force of adhesion.

The few experiments which have been here described by no means form an exhaustive list of those which, with a little ingenuity on the part of the reader, may be worked up from some of many interesting truths met with in the pursuit of science as a hobby.

CHAPTER XXXVI

ADVERTISEMENT-WRITING

A HOBBY FOR PLEASURE AND PROFIT

ADVERTISEMENT-WRITING may, to many, savour more of drudgery than of pleasant diversion. Let those of whom this is true at once abandon all thought of it, for one of the first essentials of success is that unquenchable enthusiasm which only a real love of the work can beget.

If, on the other hand, the delights of advertisement creating appeal to you irresistibly, you are happily possessed of the one qualification which bridges the gulf between the born advertisement writer and the mere space-filler.

Some idea of the golden harvest of which this hobby shows promise may be gathered from the fact that good advertisement writers can earn upwards of a guinea an hour for as much of their leisure time as they care to devote to the pursuit. When it is borne in mind that many advertisers spend as much as £1000 on advertising one piece of "copy" (as the text of an advertisement is called), it can be readily understood that it *pays* them to get the best text that money can buy; consequently the successful devotee of this hobby finds himself concerned with how to do all the work he can get, rather than how to get all the work he can do. Furthermore, advertisement-writing is a hobby which opens the door to many of the best-paid posts in the commercial world, for really gifted advertisement writers are even rarer than gifted artists, and their importance as business-multipliers is being recognised more and more every day.

Before entering into the technicalities of advertising, we must first gain a clear idea of the fundamental principles of publicity. Advertising is, first and last, a means of increasing the demand for the article advertised. It is *not* a channel for airing the smartness, wit, or learning of the writer. It is *not* a means of ventilating one's grievances. It is *not* conducted to disparage other people's goods. The use of advertising is simply and solely to sell two articles where one was sold before—and to keep on doing it. In so far as it accomplishes that end, directly or indirectly, the advertisement is a good one ; in so far as it fails, it is bad. To this golden rule there is no exception.

270

The Mystic Word

The mystic word "Advertising" embraces a host of sale-stimulating channels, principal among which are the press and printed matter.

Press advertising is subdivided into three great families—"readers," "insets" and "displays."

"Readers" are so called because they are set like the regular reading-matter of the paper, with the obvious purpose of leading the reader to suppose the advertisement to be a *bona-fide* item of news.

"Insets" are printed matter supplied by the advertiser, and bound or slipped in the newspaper or magazine.

"Displays" are the ordinary form of displayed advertisement familiar to all.

In writing our advertisement copy, we must seek to incorporate attractiveness, lucidity, grip, and conviction—but first of all attractiveness, for, unless the advertisement attracts, its other qualities are nullified.

Too many beginners write an advertisement as they would write an essay. Essays are written to the man who *wants* to read them. Advertisements are written to the man who wants to *dodge* them. It is a pretty big job for cold type to do—to win a man away from his newspaper, and to nurse him from frigid indifference to warm, money-spending enthusiasm !

There is no golden road to success in advertisement-writing, but there are golden rules, and they may be summarised thus :—

1. Don't commence writing until your enthusiasm bubbles over ; if you do, your copy will fall hopelessly flat.

2. Unearth the selling points of the article to be advertised— *i.e.* those features which give it a commanding advantage over similar goods. That selling point may be the price, or the quality, or some novel feature—but whatever it be, it *must be found*, and used to full advantage.

3. Keep your text brief, entertaining, and perfectly lucid. Imagine yourself an ideal salesman speaking to your customers over the counter instead of through the press.

4. Aim at originality, but *not* at the cost of dignity or tone. Develop a style of your own, but avoid freakishness.

5. Don't cram your advertisements. Don't use type so small that glasses would be necessary to read it.

6. Don't make the amateur's mistake of defacing your advertisement by a preponderance of ugly, heavy type—it has the same effect that an aggressive, unpolished salesman would have upon a customer.

7. Avoid employing a great assortment of types, which are no more attractive than a loudly-dressed person. If you seek to emphasize *everything* you will emphasize *nothing*. This is exemplified in Fig. 1, which demonstrates that the advertisement writer has emphasized nothing but the weakness of his display. The text is absurdly exaggerated ; the superlatives kill each other ; the ambiguous reference to Museums is in the worst taste ; the omission of prices is disastrous. Newspaper readers would instinctively avoid such an announcement and mistrust the advertiser.

FIG. 1.

Generally speaking, no more than two type-faces, or at the most three, should be drawn upon.

A few of the principal type-styles (or "faces," as they are technically termed) are given here, but unless the aspirant is well coached in names and sizes of types, he will do well to leave the choice in the hands of the printers.

Nonpariel Modern.	Habit is a cable; we spin a thread of it every day, and at last we cannot break it.
Minion Modern.	Habit is a cable ; we spin a thread of it every day, and at last we cannot break it.
Bourgeois Modern.	Habit is a cable ; we spin a thread of it every day, and at last we cannot break it.
Long Primer Caslon Old Face.	Ambition makes plans. Determination carries them out.
Pica Caslon Old Face.	Ambition makes plans. Determination carries them out.
Small Pica Modern Italics.	*Ambition makes plans. Determination carries them out.*
12-point Cheltenham Old Style.	Procrastination is the thief of time.
18-point Cheltenham Bold.	**Satisfaction is Stagnation.**
36-point Windsor.	**Satisfaction is Stagnation.**
12-point Condensed Haddon.	Ambition makes plans. Determination carries them out.
24-point Plantin.	Satisfaction is Stagnation.
24-point Morland.	**Satisfaction is Stagnation.**

36-point Condensed Sans Capitals.

SATISFACTION IS STAGNATION.

24-point Caslon Old Face Titling.

Satisfaction is Stagnation.

Most type-faces are supplied in several sizes, or "points," and practically all have Italics.

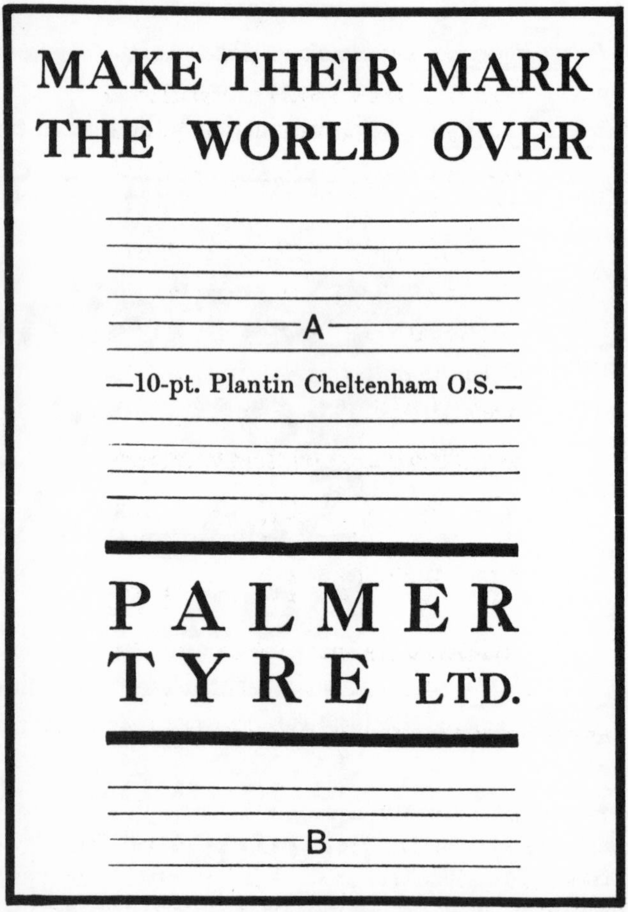

MAKE THEIR MARK THE WORLD OVER

————— A —————

—10-pt. Plantin Cheltenham O.S.—

PALMER TYRE LTD.

————— B —————

FIG. 2.

In getting up a display advertisement, we prepare what is technically known as a "lay-out" or "dummy," *i.e.* a sketch-plan showing how the advertisement is to be set, Fig. 2. Rule on a sheet of paper a diagram showing the exact space allotted to the advertisement. Upon this diagram indicate the position to be devoted to the various features of the announcement. The title must be the first consideration, since upon this and the illustration (if any) the attractiveness of the advertisement has principally to depend. Next, consider the posi-

MAKE THEIR MARK THE WORLD OVER

The sun never sets on Palmer Cord Tyres. There are more in service, and more brought into service day by day, than any other three makes combined. They are the tyres of SPEED, "LIFE," RELIABILITY, DURABILITY. They are priced as low as the best can be. To get Palmer Cords is to forget all tyre worries. Their reputation is olden and golden.

PALMER TYRE LTD.

London: Shaftesbury Avenue, W.C.

FIG. 3.

tion of the block and name display, if any be used, but don't lose sight of the importance of *any* one feature of the advertisement, be it title, sub-title, name-display, block, copy (or text), price-paragraph, or caution against substitution—the whole must be as inter-dependent as the links of a chain.

If there be much text, it is not essential to write it in the space apportioned ; it may be written on a separate sheet, its location being indicated by initials as shown in the example, which, for simplicity's sake, is letterpress only, *i.e.* no blocks of illustrations are used in it. When set up the advertisement will appear as in Fig. 3.

The beginner should provide himself with at least two scrap-books, in the first of which to collect striking advertisements noticed in the newspapers and magazines, in the second to keep a record of all his own advertisements. He should never fail to jot down in his pocket-book any good idea that may occur to him, no matter to what advertised article it relates.

The channels open for converting one's advertising ability into hard cash are almost innumerable. Perhaps one of the best ways to make a start is to watch the advertising columns of your local newspapers, note the leading advertisers in lines of business with which you are acquainted, and try to draw up a set of advertisements of greater selling force. Do not be in a hurry to submit these to the advertisers ; it is better to set them aside and see how they appeal to you after, say, a month or two. If you are then entirely satisfied with them, take them along to the advertiser and invite him to try them in the newspapers, even if he pay nothing for them—for your first object must be to assemble a set of published advertisements with which to lever other commissions. After the first announcement or two, the advertiser will, if there be merit in the copy, ask you to provide more, and you will have your first regular client.

If you chance to be employed in a firm who advertise, you have a golden opportunity of making a start : watch the style of advertising your firm favours, and try to go one better. When you feel you have really achieved this, submit your suggestions to the advertising manager. Don't be disheartened if he declines them, especially if he gives you his reasons for so doing ; keep on trying until you *do* succeed. You will lose nothing by it.

Your own particular business acquaintances, or your parents' tradesmen, may give you the opportunity of writing some of their advertisements or circulars, and so augmenting your specimen file.

The better your advertisements become, the sooner you will be able to ask half-a-guinea or a guinea per advertisement, or even the professional two guineas. When you achieve that, it will be time to place your specimens before the leading advertising agencies, and the general advertisers in the big newspapers and magazines, or to submit advertisement suggestions to them : although they usually retain their own staff of advertising men, they are always keenly on the alert to discover new talent, and if you can show them how to advertise their goods in a really fresh and original style, you will have no difficulty in getting a highly remunerative contract from them.

All advertisers, great and small alike, are always in the market for ideas, and think no price too big to pay for a good notion, for a new picture, poster, booklet, or advertising scheme.

A really striking catch-phrase (or "slogan") is literally priceless. For example, who shall say the advertising value of such famous slogans as these ?

"Try it in your bath !"

"Touches the spot !"

"You press the button ; we do the rest."

"Every picture tells a story."

"Grateful and comforting."

"Worth a guinea a box."

"The world before your eyes."

Couplets and verse also command high fees. No advertiser would hesitate to send a handsome cheque for couplets as good as these :—

"They come as a boon and a blessing to men,
The Pickwick, the Owl, and the Waverley pen !"

"Why does he look at the hands of the clock so ?
To see if it's time they were bringing his OXO."

A thorn in the side of many advertisers is substitution. At great cost, they create a demand for their particular brand or article, and then the dealer tries to persuade the customer to accept some other kind, which gives him more profit. A good phrase or advertisement directed against this substitution evil is as priceless as a good catch-phrase—and no whit less elusive. An example will, perhaps, assist you to invent some of these phrases.

"Be sure they *are* Carter's !"

Poster ideas are equally precious; those reproduced in miniature, Figs. 4, 5, 6 will be recognised by all as familiar friends.

He won't be happy till he gets it!

This really brilliant idea has linked "Pears' Soap" for all time to the forceful catch-phrase, "He won't be happy till he gets it!"

FIG. 4.

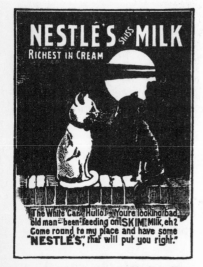

A masterpiece, lending itself admirably to posters, newspaper, and magazine advertisements, printed matter, railway enamelled iron signs, &c. Its good-humoured appeal is irresistible, and its story has strong selling force.

FIG. 5.

A poster which helped to make Bovril one of the best-known firms. "Alas! my poor Brother" became a household phrase.

FIG. 6.

Unfortunately the advertiser's idea of a good notion does not always coincide with one's own. But an occasional success amply repays for a run of disappointments.

Good ideas for insets, folders, tram-car slips, enamelled iron advertise-

I

ARREST

YOUR

ATTENTION etc

FIG. 7.

A BRIEF
ACCOUNT
OF
etc, etc

FIG. 8.

ments, printed novelties, and advertising in any form always find ready acceptance.

THE FINEST

I've ever had

FIG. 9.

It is always easy to point out how things should not be done.

Three examples of bad advertising are shown in Figs. 7, 8, and 9. The style of the first of these is to be condemned for several reasons; its tone would be greatly resented by many ; it is "hackneyed" ; it uses space extravagantly, and, in short, is characteristic of the beginner's work.

The style of Fig. 7 is still in favour with many advertisers, but it has, nevertheless, had its day long ago. The pun exhibits no humour ; the drawing is not attractive, and the whole advertisement presents a distinctly dry and uninteresting appearance.

The advertisement shown in Fig. 9 is a good example of ill-assorted ideas. Imagine the effect of the pun upon the mind of a sufferer—clearly it would never sell pills. The sick man seeks sympathy and advice—he is in no mood for boisterous humour and suggestions of the ring.

In these three examples it will be noticed that the strength (or rather weakness) of the advertisement lies in the pun. The days of punning are over, and plain, attractive, and clever sketches and catch lines—dependent more on real humour than upon artificial plays on words, are what induce people to read advertisements and buy the goods they announce.

PART III

COLLECTING

CHAPTER XXXVII

COIN COLLECTING

HOW TO START, WHAT TO BUY, AND HOW TO KEEP A COLLECTION

WHILST being the oldest, coin collecting is one of the most fascinating and instructive hobbies that any one can take up. It appeals to the intelligent as well as to those who make little pretence to learning; it charms the eye, for coins and medals possess wonderful artistic merit and beauty; it gives new life to history, making one acquainted with almost every great man and royal personage who has moved the world, while the strange designs and curious effigies to be met with afford perpetual delight and interest to the young collector.

MAKING THE CABINET

Before making your collection, it is important to have a proper receptacle in which to house the coins, otherwise they are liable to be damaged, and can never be kept in chronological order or sequence, which adds so much to the interest of a collection when being examined or shown to friends.

If you are at all skilful with tools, it is cheaper and more interesting to make your own cabinet. A nice-sized cabinet for a beginner is one that would hold about 250 coins. The top, bottom, and four sides would be made out of about ½ in. deal boards, the measurements being, width 12 in., depth 10½ in., and height 4½ in.

FIG. 1.—A useful Coin Cabinet.

There should be six or seven trays or slides, Fig. 1. These trays should be pierced with round holes of various sizes. The wood, of course, must be pierced to only half its depth, so that the coins may rest in the holes. Two trays should have holes a little larger than the size of a farthing, two trays with holes slightly larger than a penny, and one tray with holes larger than half-a-crown.   These sizes can easily be measured and marked with a pencil on the wood before it is cut.

Get strong, clear, sound wood for the cabinet, and carefully measure all the pieces to see that they form a good and even box.   Plane each piece well.   If you cannot dovetail the pieces one into the other, use nails, or even strong glue.   The top should have two hinges, so as to lift up when open ; the front of the cabinet should also be hinged, to allow of it dropping down in order to remove the trays.

The trays slide in grooves on each side.   Mark the sides with pencil, accurately measuring the distances, before you glue on the grooves, which consist of small pieces of wood measured and cut to fit each side-piece.   If the young coin-collector experiences any difficulty in constructing a satisfactory cabinet, he should study the chapter on Carpentry, pp. 3–33, which will provide him with useful information.

In the centre of each tray, place a small round brass knob, by

FIG. 2.—A larger Cabinet.

means of which the tray can be pulled out for an inspection of its contents when finished. A small brass handle may be placed in the middle of each side ; if desired, a lock should be screwed on, fastening the top to the front. When unlocked the top can be raised, and the front lowered, thus enabling each tray to be removed as required. Any ironmonger will supply these brass fittings. The wood should be nicely stained in oak or mahogany, colours which may be obtained from any oilman.

This small cabinet is intended for the very modest beginner.   If a larger article is desired, all you have to do is to increase the number of drawers, Fig. 2, to twelve and upwards, and, of course, increase the size of the sides.   Such deeper cabinets look better with doors, instead of a let-down front, and to arrange this you simply measure the depth of the front, also the width, and divide the width down the middle to form opening doors.   These should then have a lock, the top being made a fixture by being fastened down.

Instead of using a book as a catalogue to their collection, many collectors cut out or buy from dealers a number of different-sized labels, circular in shape, and write on each a description of the coin which lies upon it when placed in its proper hole in the tray.

How to Treat and Keep Coins

Many coins are real works of art, and even the most common ones should be carefully treated. The proper way to handle a coin or medal is to hold it by the edge between the thumb and forefinger, as in Fig. 3. The face of the coin should never be touched. The warmth of the hand or ordinary perspiration is almost sure to leave a mark on a coin if handled horizontally. Perfectly new coins and copper medals—that is, in what is called "mint" condition—have a beautiful freshness about them, and this brilliance, if

FIG. 3.—How to hold a Coin.

untouched, is succeeded by a rich "bloom," or deeper colouring, highly prized by collectors. Many a good coin and medal has been depreciated in value by careless or rough handling.

Keep your coins in a perfectly dry place. Dampness not only discolours them, but the verdigris thereby caused will destroy the coin itself.

Never clean your coins or medals with metal polish.

Do not drill holes in them or mark the edges.

If a coin or medal looks dull, rub the surface very gently with a soft silk handkerchief.

Handle your specimens carefully, lest they be dropped and irretrievably damaged.

Beware of counterfeits, especially high-priced coins

How to Select Coins

One great mistake made by most young collectors is starting to collect without any definite idea or object. Any coin of any country that is offered to them is bought, and the result is a miscellaneous collection of scarcely any historic or national interest. Then, no thought being given to the price, one coin costing several shillings and another coin costing only a few pence, the haphazard collection having more than absorbed all the young collector's spare cash, is hardly worth anything.

To avoid such disappointments, have a clear object in view before starting your collection. Try to look over the coinages of several countries and see if one or other appeals particularly to your fancy. Perhaps there is a foreign country you are interested in very much— for example, France, or Germany, or Italy—or some period of British or other history. By a little judicious inquiry you can learn how far it is possible for you to make a fairly complete collection of coins and medals relating to it.

As a rule, there is no collection of such close interest as one consisting of English coins. Certainly no collection is more easy to start than this. A good collection of British coins is full of delight, especially to one who has an interest in the history of our land. Beginning from the present year, the collector can go back step by step to Anglo-Saxon times. There opens before him a splendid portrait gallery of royal personages, with all the changes in Government and rule during the centuries that have gone. History is made a living panorama, and one becomes as familiar with the kings and heroes of bygone times as with notabilities of the present day.

WHERE TO START

I would confidently advise you to begin with a copper and silver coin of King George V. You can get them at face value, and fresh from the Mint—and endeavour to keep them in perfect condition. Gold coins may be collected later.

The first thing that should be noticed is that the King's head is to the left, in contrast to the "facing" of the previous monarch, King Edward VII., whose portrait faced the right. This change of direction in the head is a rule followed with every successive King or Queen.

Edward VII.—Coins of good King Edward, "The Peacemaker," will always be prized. The head is in much lower relief than hitherto. Take note of the inscription with the words, "Brit: Omn:" meaning "all the British possessions." Do not fail to get the little one-third of a farthing dated 1902.

Victoria.—Very interesting is the series of portraits of Queen Victoria during her long reign. The first issue was in 1838, and is known as the "schoolgirl head," as the face represents the youthful Queen, her hair tied with a double ribbon round her head, whilst at the back is a drooping knot of hair.

A strange error was made in the design of the first florin, or two-shilling piece. The words "Dei gratia"—"By the Grace of God"—were omitted. Only after some of the coins were struck was the mistake discovered, and the error so greatly displeased the Queen that these coins were "called in." The piece is now known as "the graceless florin," or "the godless florin," and a copy of it is well worth keeping.

The first Victorian penny, half-penny, and farthing are splendid coins, especially the penny. It is thick and of good metal, the engraving is fine, and the colour beautiful. The second issue, with the "charity girl" head—the hair being coiled round and tied with a hanging knot, is more like the present-day thin coin. It is well worth noting that in the second bronze issue a lighthouse and a ship were added, one on each side of the figure of Britannia, but in the third issue both these symbols were omitted, thus reverting to the early design.

JUBILEE SILVER

The Jubilee silver coin is very regal in appearance, the draped head being surmounted with a crown. The necklace, ribbon and medal on the bust, however, make the design rather tawdry on the whole.

I notice in my collection a peculiar difference in the size of the head on the shilling pieces— that of 1887 is small and narrow, that of 1892 is altogether broader. Such differences in the one kind of coin are worth noting and add much interest to a collection.

FIG. 4.—The "Tea-tray and Poker" Double Florin.

The four-shilling piece, Fig. 4, in this series is called "the Tea-tray and Poker" piece, the four shields with arms and the four sceptres between suggesting the two domestic articles mentioned. The two-shilling piece is similar in design on the reverse.

The third issue of Victorian silver coins gives the Queen's head as a widow—a good design by Sir Thomas Brock. The head is thickly draped, only a small portion of a low crown being shown in front. On the reverse of the half-crown, two-shilling piece, and shilling, the design of the arms on shields is very effective.

There are no fewer than three farthings of this latest issue—the same design, but different metal— a bright, a dull, and an almost black farthing. The alteration in the appearance of the metal was made so that the bright farthing might not be confused with the half-sovereign.

FIG. 5.—The "Curtain" Half-crown.

William IV.—Perhaps the most interesting coin of this reign is the half-crown. It is known as the "Curtain" half-crown, Fig. 5, because the reverse has a design of a handsome open curtain surmounted by a crown, the national arms being displayed in the centre of the drapery.

George IV.—There were three issues of silver and two of copper in this king's reign. The "Lion" shilling, Fig. 6, showing a lion standing on a crown, is well worth securing. More expensive and far less common is the "Lion" sixpence, the same design reduced for the smaller coin.

FIG. 6.—The "Lion" Shilling.

George III.—Owing to the various issues of coins in this long reign, which extended from 1760 to 1820, there is good scope for the collector. The later copper coins are very fine, the two-penny piece of 1797 being a splendid example. The penny is noble compared with the penny of the present time, and the half-penny and farthing are equally handsome. The issue of 1806 is almost as attractive.

Owing to the scarcity of the silver currency, the Government issued in this reign Spanish dollars, counter-marked with the portrait of the King. Tokens were also struck by the Bank of England, for the curious amounts of three shillings and eight-pence. There is also a strange Irish Bank token for ten-pence.

George II.—The two issues of this King's reign are distinguished as having the "old head" and the "young head." With the head laurelled

FIG. 7.—A George II. Shilling.

and the bust wearing armour, the obverse looks like a purely Roman coin, especially with its inscription in Latin. The reverse of the shilling, having roses and plumes in the corner spaces between the arms in separate shields, Fig. 7, is striking. With regard to the copper money, only half-pennies and farthings were struck.

George I.—One of the most interesting things about the coinage of this monarch is that the gold coins bear for the first time the title F. D. (*Fidei Defensor*), *i.e.,* "Defender of the Faith." The silver coins bear all kinds of symbols to indicate whence the metal was derived. We have S.S.C. for the South Sea Company, plumes for Wales, and the letters W.C.C. for the Welsh Copper Company, &c. The reverse of the farthing is the same as that of the very rare and famous Queen Anne farthing.

Anne.—Most collectors have a partiality for Queen Anne coins. The head is well modelled, and is a change from the series of kingly portraits. On the gold coins is the design of an elephant and castle, while the silver ones bear roses and plumes. With regard to the copper coinage, several kinds of farthings and half-pennies were struck, but they were patterns, although it is held by some authorities that they were in currency.

William III.—In 1696 the Government decided to call in all the hammered money and to recoin by striking the silver pieces. Mints were set up in Exeter, Bristol, Norwich, the Tower of London, and Chester. The cost was nearly £2,700,000, and it took two years to perform the immense task. You can tell where many coins were minted by their having the first letter of each of these well-known towns on them. Where there is an elephant and castle, the

silver came from Africa, plumes indicate Wales, and roses the West of
England. On the half-penny and farthing Britannia
is shown either holding up the palm branch, or
resting it on her knee.

FIG. 8.—William and
Mary Shilling.

William and Mary.—The heads of both the
King and Queen, Fig. 8, on the coins of this
reign render them of special interest. The arms
of Nassau were added to the shield. Two different
metals were used for two issues of half-pennies and
farthings—tin and copper, the tin coins having a plug of copper in the
centre.

MONEY OF NECESSITY

James II.—Intensely interesting are the various coins of this troubled
reign. The money minted in England—gold, silver, and tin—bears
the bust of the King and an ordinary inscription in Latin. Sometimes the bust is in armour and undraped. The edge is inscribed
" Nvmmorvm Famvlvs." After the King's abdication, what is called
" money of necessity " was issued, and there being no silver or copper
bullion available for the purpose, resort was had to all kinds of mixed
metals. The term " gun money " is applied to those Irish crowns, half-
crowns, sixpences, groats, pennies, and half-pennies. The design on
the reverse is peculiar. In the centre, resting on two crossed sceptres,
is a large crown, over which is " XXX," meaning thirty pence,
and under it " July," while on each side is " J.R.," the whole
being encircled by an inscription in Latin giving the title of His
Majesty.

Charles II.—In collecting this King's coins you will notice two
varieties in make—one hammered, the other milled. Thomas Simon

FIG. 9.—Charles II.
Two-Guinea Piece.

was the engraver, but the preparation of the dies was
entrusted to Roettier. The marks of value and the inner
circle appear in some pieces, whilst others are without them, and a third kind have marks of value, but
no inner circle. The gold coins are distinguished
by an elephant and castle, or an elephant alone,
Fig. 9, under the King's portrait ; the silver coins
bear the same symbol, or plumes, or a rose. The
copper coins were made of Swedish metal, and there are farthings
of tin.

Oliver Cromwell.—Although these coins are somewhat expensive,
they are amongst the most interesting from an historical point of view
that you can obtain for your cabinet. Cromwell's head, as Protector,

appears on the obverse side, and his arms, a lion rampant, St. George's Cross, the Irish Harp, and the Cross of St. Andrew, are seen

as part of the design on the reverse side, Fig. 10.

FIG. 10.—A Cromwell Shilling.

The Commonwealth.—These coins are of peculiar interest, for in place of a ruler's head we have, Fig. 11, the shield of St. George and the inscription "The Commonwealth of England," the Irish Harp, and, together with the date 1653, the motto "God with us." Unlike the wording in other reigns, English is used instead of Latin.

Charles I.—This hapless monarch has exerted a very great fascination over coin-collectors, and there is an immense variety of pieces to be secured bearing his effigy. In the dress of his Majesty there is distinct variation—some designs show the King wearing the robes of the Garter, whilst in others he is in ruff and armour, and also in a falling lace collar. A fine design is that of the King mounted on horseback.

FIG. 11.—A Commonwealth Shilling.

The mint marks deserve notice. Among them are the open book and crown, three pears, the lion, castle, rose, &c.

The coins issued during the Civil War have the legend altered into words meaning "The Protestant Religion, the Laws of England, the

FIG. 12.—Charles I. Oxford Crown.

Liberty of Parliament," Fig. 12. A farthing token was issued—the only copper coin of this reign.

SIEGE PIECES

The young collector should not forget the Siege Pieces. These are of various shapes—octagonal, lozenge-shaped, and round. The Newark piece, Fig. 13, can be obtained for a moderate sum. Silver was the chief metal used, college and family plate being melted for the purpose.

James I.—It was in this King's reign that copper currency was first adopted in this country, a farthing token being issued. It bears two

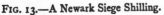

FIG. 13.—A Newark Siege Shilling.   FIG. 14.—A James I. Sixpence.

sceptres through a crown, and on the reverse is a crowned harp. The sixpence, Fig. 14, is the only coin that bears a date, and the value is indicated by "VI." at the side of the King's head. Besides the gold coinage, there were two issues of silver coins.

Elizabeth.—The coins of "Good Queen Bess" are always in demand, and they were all struck at the Tower Mint. Two unique coins found in no other reign are among the number—the three-halfpence and the three-farthing pieces. Two methods of making coins were adopted — the hammered money was struck by the old

FIG. 15.—An Elizabeth Sovereign.

process, and milled money was made by the new invention of mill and screw. The Queen's head is adorned with a crown, Fig. 15, and she wears a quaint ruff round her neck. In some examples on the side of her bust is a rose. The gold sovereign or double rial shows the Queen enthroned, and the rial depicts her in a ship.

Philip and Mary.—The portraits of the King and Queen, each separate and facing each other, are admirable on these coins. A crown is placed above and between their heads, and the date 1554 is divided each side, Fig. 16. On the reverse is a fine shield, bearing in its six divisions the various heraldic symbols relating to England and Spain.

FIG. 16.—A Philip and Mary Shilling.

Mary.—The sovereign issued in this reign is the earliest dated gold coin of the English series. The silver coins of Mary alone are the groat, Fig. 17, half-groat, and penny.

Edward VI.—Every young collector is enamoured of the coins of this reign, for they show a splendid full-face portrait of the

FIG. 17.—A Mary Groat.   FIG. 18.—Edward VI. Shilling.

youthful King, Fig. 18. On comparing the coins of this issue with those of the previous reign, various alterations will be noticed. From the Conquest a cross was used on the reverse side of the coin, but here it is occasionally left out, and dates are added. The marks of value are put on the obverse of shillings, sixpences, and threepenny pieces.

Henry VIII.—There is a goodly number of specimens to be collected which relate to " Bluff King Hal." Strange to say, Henry used

FIG. 19.—A Henry VIII. Shilling.

the last portrait of his father on the first issue of the groat and half-groat. He placed his own likeness in profile on the second issue, although in later series the full face is shown, as in Fig. 19. Then the numerals VIII. are often found after the King's name, although later they are changed to the Arabic figure 8. Another change is the use of Roman letters in place of the Old English for the inscriptions.

Henry VII.—Several striking features may be mentioned about the money of this King. We have the first definite attempt to reproduce on the coins a proper portrait of the monarch. It is a good one, distinguished by the mass of hair on each side of the face. Then the silver issues are differentiated by the style of crown worn—in one example it is open, in another it is arched. One issue has the King's head in profile. The penny contains a full-length

FIG. 20.—A Sovereign Type Halfpenny of Henry VII.

figure, Fig. 20, of the monarch, and is technically known as belonging to the " Sovereign type."

Richard III. and Edward V.—Various interesting mint marks are to be noticed in specimens of the coins of these reigns. Some pennies have an " S " on the King's chest, which indicates Bishop Sherwood of Durham, while a " T " is to be found on the York pennies, in allusion to Archbishop Thomas Rotherham.

GOLD ANGELS

Edward IV.—Interest also centres round the mint marks on Edward IV.'s coins, which are added to, so that a relative knowledge of the dates of the coins which bear them can be inferred. Edward IV. was the first ruler to issue gold coins from local mints, among them being a new coin termed the "Angel." It got its name from the design on the obverse, which shows the Archangel Michael standing on the Dragon, into the mouth of which he is thrusting his spear. Groats were struck at London, Coventry, Norwich, York, and Bristol. In order that the new restored gold noble might not be confused with the old one, a rose was stamped on both sides.

Henry VI.—Attention should be paid to the different marks which were placed on the coins of this reign. They were inserted not only on the bust of the King, but also between the words of the inscription on both sides. The trefoil, annulet, pine cone, &c., are to be seen on the gold pieces, and the rosette and mascle, cross and pellet, &c., on the silver pieces. A strange error is to be met with in the later coins—

FIG. 21.—A Henry VI. Angel.

"HENBIC" instead of "HENRIC" being given. An "Angel" of this King is shown in Fig. 21.

Henry V.—Quite fascinating is it to study the peculiarities in the head of this famous King on his coins. In one specimen the monarch is given a bulging of the neck resembling an egg. Then the hair is close and thick, and the portion beneath the crown sticks out nearly straight.

Henry IV.—Special interest also attaches to this King's portrait, which closely resembles that of his predecessor, Richard II. On looking carefully into the inscriptions, it will be noticed that in the name of "London" the curious Old English "N" is adopted.

FIG. 22.—An Edward III. Noble.

Richard II.—The gold nobles of this reign were issued with and without the addition of a flag. In the middle of the reverse of the gold pieces the letter "R" is placed instead of "E."

Edward III.—The inscriptions found on this monarch's coins, Fig. 22, especially the gold, are full of interest. They are in Latin, and among them are (translated into English), " He shall be exalted in glory "—referring to the King—" I have made God my Helper," and " O Lord, rebuke me not in thine anger."

William I. and William II.—It should be the aim of the beginner to work backward to William the Conqueror, so as to make the chain

FIG. 23.—A Penny of William the Conqueror.

of his collection complete. Only one coin was issued by the Conqueror—the silver penny. There are three types of this—the bonnet, the canopy, and the pax. The bust is either full face, Fig. 23, or in profile. Strange head-gear adorns the monarch—it is intended for a crown, but resembles a bonnet. The coins of the two Williams are difficult to distinguish from one another.

ANGLO-SAXON COINS

Having made a fair collection of English coins from the present monarch to William I., the enthusiastic collector will desire to push on to Anglo-Saxon times. Here he will find a wide field in which to enjoy his taste for research. Of course, these early attempts at coinage in our country are not so successful from an artistic point of view as those afforded by later centuries. Yet the smallest collection of these ancient specimens of money has a charm of its own.

Wessex was the place where the most extensive minting was done. The penny and the half-penny were the only coins issued, and the designs on them vary but slightly. On the obverse is the particular King's head, together with his name and title, and on the reverse is given a cross in varied pattern ; the moneyer's and the mint names being added. Some of these early coins can be bought for a few shillings, while others are high priced because of their great age and scarcity.

The names of archbishops and Saints figure on these Anglo-Saxon coins. The Archbishops of York and Canterbury are most common, whilst St. Eadmund, Fig. 24, and St. Martin are favourites.

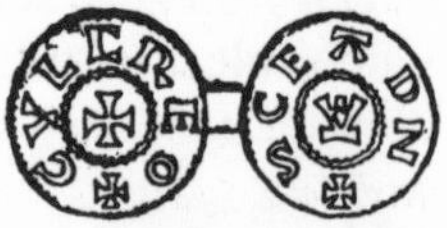

FIG. 24.—St. Eadmund Penny.

Kent, Mercia, East Anglia, and Northumbria also had their mints, and from them were issued the silver penny and the gold and silver sceat.

Going back to times preceding the Christian era, there are coins of gold, silver, copper, and tin, which were the work of the early Britons. Even a few of these pieces add immense interest to an English collection, being an introduction to the fine series of coins of later date.

Colonial Coins

The Colonies form a most intimate part of the British Empire, and to the English collector they afford the means of additional interest, as their coins and tokens are closely related.

The Isle of Man was at one time independent, and in the hands of the Stanley family. In 1709 the Earl of Derby, as Lord of Man, struck a penny and a half-penny. The obverse bears the Stanley crest—an eagle and child on the cap of maintenance, with the motto, "Sans changer." The reverse is the celebrated badge of the island—the three legs joined, Fig. 25. In Queen Victoria's reign, long after the Isle

FIG. 25.—Isle of Man Halfpenny.

had been merged into Great Britain, a half-penny was issued with the Queen's portrait and inscription on one side and the three legs on the other.

The Channel Islands, represented by Jersey and Guernsey, have had a coinage worth acquiring. Three lions on a shield, Fig. 26, is a device common to both islands, and Queen Victoria's head adorns the obverse in some cases. "Doubles" is the name of the money.

FIG. 26.—A Guernsey Form Doubles.

Malta has a nice little coin of the curious value of a third of a farthing. George IV., William IV., and Queen Victoria have their portraits on respective issues.

British North Borneo has a fine series of copper coins, with a striking coat of arms shown on one side.

Some interesting coins were struck for the Ionian Islands in 1819. Britannia seated and holding an olive branch is shown on one side, and the winged lion of St. Mark, with "Ionikon Kratos," inscribed on the other.

India has a varied series of coins. Those brought out by the East India Company bear the arms of the Company and the heart-shaped bale mark. Then there are the Madras coins, bearing on one side a tall pagoda and stars. The Bombay half-anna shows a balance, between the scales being the word "Justice" in Arabic characters. Both the silver rupees and their divisions and the divisions of the anna in copper bearing Queen Victoria's head or the arms of the East India Company are interesting specimens to possess.

Ceylon has a striking coin bearing the device of an elephant,

Fig. 27, and a later issue shows a palm-tree. Malay has a unique design—a bantam cock.

FIG. 27.—A Ceylon Stiver.

Sarawak, on the north-western coast of Borneo, has long been governed by an English Rajah, and so the portrait of "J. Brooke, Rajah," appears on the obverse of its copper money.

Sierra Leone has a fine dollar for the collector. A huge lion is seen pawing the ground, whilst at the back of the coin a white man's hand grasps the hand of a negro.

Several interesting devices will be found on the early coins of Canada, as well as the tokens. One has the figure of a native countryman standing full length ; it is backed by Britannia sitting, holding the horn of plenty and pointing to a ship. One of the Upper Canada tokens bears a sloop in full sail.

Prince Edward Island, St. Helena, and Newfoundland half-pennies are worth collecting for their kinship to the ordinary English namesake.

The coins of America, while it was yet a British possession, are of great interest. Among them are the Rosa Americana penny and twopence, which take the name from the noble-looking rose, Fig. 28. The Higley or Granby token of 1737 is very quaint, with its stag standing bolt upright, and the curious legend, "Value me as you please," while the reverse has three hammers crowned and the words, "I am good copper."

FIG. 28.—A Rosa Americana Penny.

The early coins of Bermuda are very rare, and bear on the obverse the original name of the place "Sommers Islands," with the picture of a large hog, behind which is seen an old three-decker ship with sails set and flags flying. The Barbados halfpenny has for its principal design a large negro head with coronet and plumes, together with King George seated in a chariot drawn by two horses prancing across the waves like Father Neptune.

TOKENS

A delightful bypath of English coin-collecting is that of tokens. During the latter end of the eighteenth century when there was a scarcity of copper money, an Act of Parliament was passed which legalised the issue of trade and other tokens. Pennies and half-pennies were the principal coins which were struck, and while engaged in his hobby the young collector will meet with a number of these numismatic curios which he would do well to secure. They are most interesting because of the strange designs which adorn them.

A COPPER PICTURE GALLERY

My own collection of halfpenny tokens forms a picture gallery in copper. Let me describe just a few of them. The Scotch token bears a full-length portrait of St. Andrew on his Cross. The Irish has a bust of St. Patrick wearing a mitre, and the Anglesey halfpenny has the head of a Druid. Among the portraits are those of Nelson, the Duke of Wellington, Sir Isaac Newton, Howard the philanthropist, Lackington the bookseller, John Wilkinson the ironmaster, William Beckford, and others.

Numbers of towns and cities issued these tokens. Chichester token shows its cathedral with a fine portrait of Queen Elizabeth, and Norwich depicts its castle. Various industries displayed their symbols on their tokens—the stage-coach halfpenny shows a mail-coach being driven at full speed, while the whale fishery halfpenny has the picture of fishermen in the act of harpooning a great whale.

Even places of recreation issued tokens—Pidcock's famous exhibition issued a halfpenny on one side of which was a large elephant and on the other a rhinoceros; then the Bath token has a pretty picture of its botanical garden, a great cedar, and the hyssop growing out of an old wall, as mentioned in the Scriptures, with appropriate texts. There is even a public lottery halfpenny token, showing a blindfolded figure drawing lots.

FOREIGN COINS

While to the young British collector the coins of his own country will always claim prior attention, he will enlarge his knowledge and increase his pleasure in the hobby if he be able to extend his field of operations by securing coins of foreign countries. Let him beware of picking up a few odd specimens here and there without regard to continuity. It is far better to select a particular country and make a collection in proper order.

France is the first country that appeals to the collector who wishes for a wider view of his subject. As a rule, French coins are splendid examples of the numismatic art. Starting from Louis XVI. and coming to the present Republic, a fascinating series of historic value can be obtained. Coins were struck illustrating all the phases of the great Revolution and the story of the rise and fall of Napoleon. Very curious indeed it is to note the different changes of Government. There is the restoration of the monarchy under Charles X., and later on Louis Philippe's head appears on the coins, followed by Napoleon III., until different designs of the head of Liberty grace the money as at present in use.

Germany also presents a fascinating area with a long and wide list of coins. The great number of small German states and free cities have each had a special coinage. Some bear the portrait of the king or grand duke, others have coats of arms or shields, the diversity in the designs of which may be studied for many pleasant hours.

The coins of Spain, Portugal, and Italy also appeal to the young collector who has in any way studied the history of these great countries. The heads of the various monarchs from reign to reign, together with the changes of dynasty and government depicted on the coinage, offer a rich harvest of research. With regard to the Italian coins, mention should be made of the Papal series. Some of these bear the portraits of successive Popes, whilst others show the different arms of these Pontiffs, together with the keys of St. Peter surmounted by the Papal tiara.

There are some good coins to be found in the Russian series, in which you get the double Russian eagle, where instead of the Tsar's head, only the initial of his name, surmounted by the Imperial crown, is given. Closely allied to the Russian are the large numbers of coins struck by the different Balkan States—Bulgaria, Roumania, &c. With a little care and at very small expense a diligent young collector can gradually secure a big cabinet of these excellent coins.

Mention may also be made of the Dutch issues, the older coins of the eighteenth century being extremely quaint and well worth collecting.

American coins from the time of the Act of Independence have quite a charm of their own. Liberty is the persistent allegorical figure stamped on them, first with the classic head and later on the full-sized figure. Then the countries of South America, such as Peru, Argentina, Brazil, &c., have each a good coinage.

Those who delight in really uncommon-looking coins should turn their attention to those issued by China, pierced with holes for stringing together, or the strange Japanese sen, bearing a grotesque dragon. More curious still are the native Indian coins, both copper and silver, thick and lumpy, bearing the sacred pineapple and inscribed with Hindustani and other languages. These coins make a peculiarly attractive addition to one's cabinet.

I have mentioned all these groups of coins to show how widely each collector's particular taste can be gratified. But whatever you

do, choose one or two countries and get all the coins you possibly can.
A small complete collection is always of greater value than a big
assortment of odd specimens. Think before you buy, and get
a fellow-collector's opinion about the price you are asked to pay.
Learn all you can glean about every coin you acquire, and you will
find the collection a perpetual source of pleasure.

CHAPTER XXXVIII

STAMP COLLECTING

OUR KING'S HOBBY

STAMP collecting as a hobby has, during the last fifty years, grown in popularity to an extraordinary extent. Immediately upon its introduction into Great Britain from France, it took a hold upon the public fancy, and from that day keenness in philately on the part of both juveniles and grown-ups has not abated; indeed, it may safely be assumed, as year succeeds year, that the number of devotees to a hobby as interesting as it is instructive, as profitable as it is pleasant, will go on increasing.

Mr. Frederick J. Melville, one of the leading authorities on stamps and stamp collecting in this country, estimates that Great Britain and Ireland can boast no less than 500,000 enthusiastic philatelists. More than 70 per cent. of schoolboys are keen collectors. An idea of the extraordinary growth of the hobby may be gained from the number of books relating to it ; one collector's library alone containing nearly 3000 volumes. To what, then, must we attribute this world-wide popularity ?

The answer probably lies in the fact that there is something in stamp collecting above the ordinary—something which is definite and helpful—something from which can be gained much that is beneficial.

Let me briefly outline one or two of the pleasant results that may be obtained from taking up this fascinating pastime. To begin with, every collector will agree that there is, above his hobby as a means of supplying him with pocket-money, an extraneous interest—an attraction due very much to the general idea suggested by works of art, and a desire, developing gradually as he proceeds in his pursuit, to obtain specimens of every kind and class to help towards completion.

Were this alone all that could be said in favour of stamp collecting, to the most inappreciative it would indicate that importance and value are attached to it, but a practical acquaintance with the science quickly brings to light other facts, which must serve to raise it above the ordinary level.

A Helpful Pastime

At the start the beginner realises, perhaps for the first time, how incomplete and faulty is his knowledge of both history and geography ; then, before long, he finds that his new hobby has given a very remarkable stimulus to the study of these subjects, so invariably presented in a dry form, and he gains in a pleasant manner a deal of information concerning our possessions, both foreign and colonial, as well as enlightenment concerning countries of whose very existence he was, perhaps, not previously aware.

Besides this, and probably of far greater importance, is the amount of general knowledge and information to be gathered. Affording, as it does, acquaintance with variety of colour and design, together with portraiture of eminent people, philately also gives, in the natural course of events, instruction in the various processes of printing and engraving. The different kinds of paper used in the manufacture of stamps are brought under notice, and a deal can be learnt concerning water-marks and other methods employed for the prevention of forgery or imitation.

A glance through any fairly comprehensive collection will show that there are lessons without number to be learned from the pictures of fauna, of flora, and of physical and natural features illustrated in the postal productions of the respective countries to which the stamps belong. The desire to collect stamps of beautiful designs may safely be fostered even among those most scantily blessed with this world's goods, for, as it happens, it is not, as a rule, the elaborate typographical specimen which costs a deal of money ; on the contrary, the great rarities are frequently noteworthy for crudeness and lack of artistic merit.

All this and more may be justifiably claimed for stamp collecting. In all cases it should lead to a cultivation of the powers of observation, the faculty of arrangement, and a general inculcation of neatness and method. Another inducement which may naturally appeal to many boys is the prospect of adding materially to their supplies of pocket money, for with very little trouble and expenditure of time, the hobby can speedily be established on a paying and lucrative basis. Sale and exchange become, quite naturally, duties of even amateur collectors, and unlucky indeed must be the one who fails to make fair and legitimate profit on his transactions.

The fortunate possessors of old collections ought especially to be in a position for making a grand start, for the value of many specimens issued thirty or forty years ago is now so great that large sums are offered for them every day.

STARTING A COLLECTION

No hard and fast rule can be laid down for starting a collection. The three most generally accepted methods are purchasing, research among family papers—for which parental permission should always be obtained—and judicious requests from stamp collecting and other interested friends.

With regard to purchase, a glance through the advertisement columns of any popular boys' paper will reveal ample particulars of reputable firms dealing in every philatelic accessory from gummed paper mounts to entire collections.

The young collector must from the start understand how important it is not only that his stamps should be properly and decently arranged, but that in the manner of choice of album, management of specimens, &c., he should be guided in the right direction.

The value of a very large number of old collections is spoiled by the manner in which the specimens have been put into the book, many, perhaps valuable stamps, having been securely fastened down on the original pieces of paper. The query naturally arises, "Should stamps always be taken from the paper on which they were at first stuck?" The answer requires some amount of careful consideration.

Individually, a stamp is never lessened in value by its being kept on the original envelope. In this condition the whole is called an "entire." The disadvantage is, of course, that these "entires" take up much more space than do the ordinary adhesives—space which the average collector can ill afford ; but when we take into consideration the fact that, particularly in the case of the octagonal embossed of Great Britain (1847), and the earlier stamps of some of the European States, the value of "entires" is generally considerably more than when the stamps have been cut out, we shall feel that the disadvantage accruing from "entires" is hardly one of much weight.

Having then decided upon what we shall keep on the original paper and what we shall remove, the next question that arises is, "What is the best manner in which to clean them?"

To the youngest enthusiast it must be apparent that a stamp on the back of which is an irregularly shaped piece of paper torn from the original envelope would not increase the artistic appearance of the collection, and this means that in almost all cases the superfluous paper must be removed, although this will not apply to rareties or stamps of doubtful origin. This subject may be briefly dealt with under the heading of

CLEANING

By "cleaning" I do not mean the employment of certain acids to bring back the faded colour of a stamp or the removal of old age signs. These tasks fall more to the lot of the experienced philatelist and the dealer ; but it is requisite for the amateur to know the best and easiest method of getting his specimens into a condition fit for placing in the album.

Perhaps the commonest method of removing paper from the back of stamps is to immerse them in water. Now, experiment and experience only will show what stamps may and what may not be treated in this way. For example, it is not advisable to adopt this method with the bi-coloured stamps of Russia, as the colours run very easily.

Personally I think it is quicker to clean large quantities of common stuff thus, as the work may be done expeditiously by simply placing the specimens face upwards in a shallow vessel containing tepid water. This will gradually sodden the " back paper," so that it may be removed without trouble by a pocket-knife. Thus drawn off by the action of the water, the back of the stamp is quite moist and sticky on account of the loosening of the gum. Leave the stamp to dry in this condition, and what follows ?

The gum hardens as the paper becomes dry, and the stamp curls up resolutely, refusing with the pertinacity of a bull-dog to unroll and lie flat. To overcome this trouble, except when a rarity is being dealt with, the moist paper should be placed face downwards on a piece of clean dry blotting-paper, a similar piece being put on the top. Now, by pressing on the paper and frequently removing the stamp as the gum dries, the adhesive may be entirely taken off, leaving the specimen in a beautifully clean condition. Careful treatment in this way ensures a neat and nice-looking collection.

Not infrequently it happens that, by the careless application of a stamp to the envelope when it was originally stuck on, some part of the specimen has become creased.

TO REMOVE CREASES

In such a state it does not present a very attractive appearance, and if sale or exchange be attempted under this condition, the amount obtainable is certain to be diminished. Should you find, then, that some among your collection are like this, the above method of cleaning is particularly useful. Once the back paper has been removed, and while the stamp is thoroughly damp, pressure of the fingers on the upper sheet of blotting-paper will quickly straighten out all obnoxious creases, and the stamp may then be put in the book in a perfect state.

But what is to be done in the case where the colours are liable to run ? Well, the difficulty is first to settle what colours run most and to what countries the stamps belong. Care should be taken particularly with the stamps of Russia and most of the late issues of our own colonies, for, being printed mostly in aniline colours, a soaking in water will cause the ink to spread over the surface of the stamp with disastrous results.

Especially is this so with most green stamps, with which the following method may be adopted : to remove the superfluous paper, thoroughly soak a pad of blotting-paper in water, and on this place the stamp face upwards. The moisture will, in time, detach the back without in any way injuring the specimen, which may then be dried in the manner already described. Having undergone the process of " cleaning," the stamps are now ready for insertion in the album, so the next point demanding attention is

MOUNTING

It has already been mentioned that many old and otherwise valuable stamps have been irretrievably spoiled by being gummed bodily, if one may use such a term, into a book.

By the use of an ingenious and simple device this hurtful habit has happily been done away with.

Any firm that makes a business of selling stamps also sells " stamp mounts," *i.e.* little slips of gummed paper about 1 in. long by ⅝ in. wide. By folding this over ⅜ in. from the top a hinge is formed.' If now, the smaller part be wetted and applied to the back of the specimen, and the longer end be stuck into the book, the stamp is on a hinge, and may be examined with ease both back and. front. Upon the longer strip of gummed paper attached to the leaves of the album may be entered minute but important details concerning the identity of the stamp, *e.g.* its perforation, water-mark, or any other peculiarity.

The value of being able to have all the necessary information to hand when it is required will be more appreciated when we bear in mind how frequently it happens that there are two stamps identical as regards their general appearance, but differing in small particulars of real importance to the philatelist. Thus, they may be of the same face value and of the same colour, yet one may be perforated sixteen and the other fourteen ; one may be water-marked Crown C.C., the other Crown C.A. ; one may be of wove paper, the other possess a chalky surface.

Now comes the subject of albums. I should not advise the beginner to purchase one directly he starts collecting, as his ignorance or lack of experience, so far as stamps are concerned, may probably lead him to insert the stamps in the wrong places. To commence with, and until 200 or 300 have been obtained, the stamps can be classified into their respective countries, and then put in envelopes suitably marked on the outside as to country, issue, &c.

Let us presume the beginner has done this, and now has quite a respectable assortment. His first duty will be to examine the issues he possesses of a certain country and see whether among them there are two or more alike. If he finds this to be the case, then it behoves him to take the greatest care in selecting the best specimen.

The duplicates once taken away, the next difficulty is to divide the remainder into their respective issues, and then to settle which were produced first. To help him in this direction the collector can fall back on two things—the album and the catalogue.

THE ALBUM

In most albums there are prints and illustrations, with accompanying information concerning the stamps. However, in some albums, the actual book is devoid of illustrations, under which circumstances the young philatelist must rely on the help and information provided by

THE CATALOGUE

I am digressing somewhat from the subject of albums in dealing with this, but it is necessary to say something about the catalogue before we go any further, as it is almost essential that one should be used in conjunction with the album.

The Catalogue that I can heartily recommend both for the novice and the more.experienced collector is issued in two parts—Stanley Gibbons' Priced Catalogue of Stamps of the British Empire, 2s. 6d. net., or post free, 2s. 9d. being Part I. ; whilst Part II. of the same firm's Priced Catalogue deals with the Stamps of Foreign Countries, the price being 2s. 6d. net., or post free, 2s. 10d.

From these invaluable books all the knowledge required can be gathered, for the illustrations and letterpress will assist in fixing the accurate dates of the various issues.

As regards the actual insertion of stamps in the album, a start is made naturally enough with the earlier issues. Should the collector not possess any of these, the spaces must be left blank for their reception at a later date. The first stamp of an issue to be inserted is, of course, the lowest in face value ; then the next in face value, in ascending order, is placed by its side ; but if this particular one be wanting the space for it must be left blank.

In this way the gaps can be filled in as the philatelist becomes possessed of the missing specimens. It will be as well to put aside all duplicates, as these can either be sold or exchanged in order to increase the growth of the first collection.

HOW TO COLLECT

A word or two on the subject of "packets" will be of use both to the collector who intends making a speciality of the stamps of one particular country, and to him who desires to collect more widely and include among his specimens stamps of every country.

It is hardly necessary to name the many periodicals in which appear advertisements for the sale of packets of stamps. They are found in almost every boys' paper. I do not advise any one to answer such advertisements indiscriminately. They will soon learn from the treatment they receive at the hands of the firms with which they deal where their money is best laid out.

The "lots" sold at sixpence are usually more cheap than selected. They frequently consist of 1000 mixed stamps, and doubtless out of these quite a fair percentage will be new to the beginner.

An answer to an advertisement will in many cases bring from the firms supplying the packet, sheets of stamps "on approval." One is invited to sell them on commission—that is to say, if the purchaser disposes of a shilling's worth of the firm's stamps from the approval sheets, he is allowed by that firm a discount of threepence or fourpence in the shilling. That discount he can either take in cash or in stamps, whichever he prefers. The remaining stamps, of course, must be sent back. Most firms adopting this method of business deal most fairly and generously with their customers.

Approval sheets are usually made up of stamps above the average of those found in the packets, so this method of purchase, as it provides the collector with better stamps, is dearer. Still, the usual price of stamps on the sheets is not abnormal.

WHAT TO COLLECT

Thirty or forty years ago, before stamp collecting had attained to anything like its present popularity and widespread attention, one might not unreasonably have expected, by the outlay of a few pounds, to gather together specimens of almost every stamp in existence.

How different the condition of affairs to-day ! Matters have gone to the other extreme, and the philatelist who is not possessed of a fortune might as well attempt to form a complete collection of the world's postage stamps as to walk across the sea. It is impossible to say really how many stamps have been issued since the introduction of the adhesive in 1840, but the number and the rareties are such as to render it impossible for any one to gather for himself a perfectly representative collection.

There have been, during the time that stamp collecting has been in vogue, many famous philatelists and many famous collections, but I never yet have heard of any one getting together every known specimen.

The collector as a rule worries himself but little about making such an effort ; so long as he plods along, adding to his number as he goes, he is fairly satisfied. Yet it would be idle to deny that it is a work of no little magnitude to collect specimens of all the common varieties, and as the average person desires rather to make a pleasure of philately, than a burden, he will do well to settle on some definite line of action soon after his collection begins to assume fairly large proportions.

Of late years "specialising" has met with general favour, and the man who has marked out his path in philately with the fixed intention of possessing himself, sooner or later, of a complete set of all the stamps of one particular country, certainly derives more satisfaction from his pursuit than he who collects in a haphazard fashion. Of course, the stamps of different countries appeal to different people.

In the matter of "specialising" no direct advice as to the selection of countries or special issues can be given, but the following branches are suggested:

1. Early Colonials down to about 1870.
2. Company stamps.
3. Issues of our own country.
4. The stamps of the early German States.
5. The collection of "entires," *i.e.* envelopes with the stamps affixed.
6. Stamps of Africa—particularly of the British Colonies and Protectorates.
7. Indian Native States.
8. North America.
9. West India Islands.
10. Russian, German, and Scandinavian locals.
11. South American States and Republics.
12. Oriental stamps of crude and peculiar design, *e.g.* Afghanistan, China, Persia, Japan, Faridkot, &c.

"Specialising" does not involve the rejecting of a postage stamp belonging to a country outside the chosen area, for all such can easily be exchanged. Once the collector has made up his mind as to what he will devote attention and spare money to, the next thing that needs consideration is the question of

SPECIMENS

I doubt whether anything requires more care in this line than the collecting of the finest specimens available, for so much must be taken into consideration before a choice can be made.

It is only by long experience that, in many cases, a decision can be made off-hand, but swift comprehension of the smallest details will rank first and foremost amongst the acquirements of the modern philatelist.

To the beginner the first points that would probably lead him towards making a choice between stamps would be the strength of colour and absence of obliteration mark, for the clearer and less heavily post-marked a specimen is, the more it is to be desired. This, then, is the initial thing to take note of. Pick out, whenever a choice is possible, stamps which are true in colour and clean in general appearance. A careful examination must then be made, not only with the naked eye, but with the aid of a magnifying glass, in order to discover if a stamp is in any way damaged, that is, torn or creased, or whether it has been "faked" or mended.

Thoroughly satisfied with the results of this scrutiny, the perforations must now be looked to (in the case of a perforated stamp), as the absence of one or two of these considerably lowers the value. It is essential that not one should be missing ; and although it is not always possible to obtain a perfect specimen, whenever there is an opportunity of choice, it pays to exercise a little care before making a decision.

By means of the gauge the perforation can easily be ascertained. As difference in perforation often signifies difference in value, especially with old Colonials, it is necessary that as much care as possible be exercised.

Again, the copies we are examining may have "rouletted" or "serpentine" perforations ; even more care is essential in judging between two of this kind than in the case with the ordinary perforations. On the other hand our two stamps may have no perforations at all. These are known as imperforate, or imperf., as it is generally written. In this condition the important point to be attended to is the "margin," i.e. the amount of paper beyond the limits of the actual print of the stamp.

There are many collectors who go even further than this in making choice of specimens, for they place a greater value on the stamp if it still has the gum on the back with which it was first issued ; *e.g.* an unused penny stamp in the same condition as that in which it was sold at the post office would be described by the collector as having the "original gum," or with "o.g."

The last and only other point to be mentioned is that concerning the term "cut to shape," for perhaps the worth of some stamps cannot be lowered more than by "cutting them to shape." An example will make this more clear. In 1874 our own country issued embossed stamps, imperforate, the design being octagonal. In "good condition" those stamps are "cut square," *i.e.* the stamp itself is on a rectangular piece of paper, but to remove the plain paper by cutting round the edges of the stamp and leaving it in its printed octagonal shape, is to cut it to shape and to fall into the error which you are here warned against.

Many of the early and most valuable issues of Ceylon have been treated in this way, and consequently utterly spoiled ; for a copy of any rare stamp "cut to shape" is worth but the merest fraction in comparison with the value of the same stamp "cut square."

In view of the fact that many rare stamps have been successfully forged, it is often an advantage to keep a specimen of that issue to which the stamp forger is known to have devoted a deal of his attention, on the original paper, that is, the envelope or cover on which it was first stuck. The great test as to whether or not a stamp is on its original paper lies, of course, in the postmark. If that on the envelope or cover corresponds with that on the adhesive, you may be fairly sure the specimen is genuine and has passed properly through the post.

Many philatelists go even beyond the keeping of the stamp on the "original" ; they keep the envelope intact. In this case it is called an "entire." The obvious disadvantage of collecting "entires" is the amount of room they take up, but for those who have a fancy for this mode of collecting, it is well worth the extra trouble entailed in keeping them in the best condition.

Of course there are other details that the expert should take into consideration before making a selection between two similar stamps of great value, but for the average collector, attention to such matters as have briefly been outlined will be quite sufficient. It is perhaps hardly necessary to add that the water-marks of two stamps—if they have any—should be examined before the two specimens are classed as being the same. Not even a beginner can be excused making this fatal oversight.

What a Perforation Is

Perforations are a number of small holes, or cuts made in the paper dividing the stamp on the sheet, and are intended to be a means of severing the stamps easily. Now, although the greater number of stamps are at the present day perforated by little circles of paper cut out in rows, there are one or two other kinds of perforations which the stamp collector will doubtless come across sooner or later. Small holes pricked in the paper constitute what is known as a pin perforation, while if there are little slits between the stamps to enable them to be more easily separated, these stamps are said to be "rouletted." However, should the cuts be made in small curves, the perforation is known as "serpentine."

Of course, such stamps as have no perforation, *e.g.* the early issues of our own country prior to 1854, and many early Colonials, have not this distinction, having simply been cut from a sheet in the manner previously indicated, and in this condition they are called "imperf." Although the beginner will hardly find it necessary to go so far as to "specialize" in perforations, yet it is essential that he should have a perforation gauge, and be able to use it. By means of this useful article he is enabled to tell the exact gauge and size of the perforation of the stamp with which he is dealing. The stamp is placed on the card, and with whatever perforation on the gauge that of the stamp corresponds, then that stamp has the perforation indicated on the numbered gauge.

Another method by which the same result may be arrived at is by counting the number of holes that are cut along the edge of the stamp in the space of two centimetres. Reliable perforation gauges may be obtained from almost any stamp dealer for sixpence. Those supplied by Messrs. Stanley Gibbons, London, are specially to be recommended.

A few trials at judging the perforation of stamps will show that the vertical perforation is often dissimilar to the horizontal. Any comprehensive catalogue shows the different value of stamps of dissimilar perforations.

Water-marks

The presence or absence of a water-mark in numberless cases makes the difference between a value of a few pence and of as many pounds. It frequently happens that of two stamps of the same design, colour, and face value, one may be water-marked and the other may not, in which cases it may reasonably be assumed that the value of the two specimens will not be the same.

To decide which of the two is the rarer, the collector must fall back either on his own knowledge or on the catalogue. In the latter he will see values quoted for both stamps.

Now as to what a water-mark consists in no comprehensive answer can be given, as there exists a very wide diversity of design in this direction. Take, for example, stamps of Great Britain. Crowns, both large and small, garters, large and small, sprays of flowers, anchors, orbs, &c., have been successively used at various times; Crown CA and Crown CC, denoting respectively Crown Agent and Crown Colony, have done service in different parts of the Empire; the elephant's head or a star appears in the stamps of India. Wavy lines, crossed lines, and the fleur-de-lis have been utilised by various European countries.

It is sometimes a matter of trouble to decide whether a stamp is water-marked or not, or, if the water-mark is very faint, to make out the design. The following little device may be of use in helping to overcome the difficulty: from a small sheet of cardboard cut out a piece measuring a trifle more than the dimensions of an ordinary sized stamp—for larger specimens the part cut away would have to be proportionately bigger—and on one side of the sheet, round the rectangle thus removed, gum four strips of very thin wood, so that each strip projects somewhat beyond the edge of the part cut away. If the card be held so that the stamp placed in the small rectangle will not fall through owing to the strips of wood underneath, then, by holding the whole up to the light, the water-mark of the stamp may be quite clearly discerned. Should this method fail, by placing the specimen on a flat square of black glazed earthenware—a black fireplace tile will do admirably —and pouring over it a few drops of benzine colis, the design will show up clearly and distinctly.

CHAPTER XXXIX

AUTOGRAPHS

THE SIGNATURES OF FAMOUS MEN

THE genuine autographs of great men are, by the earnest collector, priced above rubies, for they disclose the true character of individuals who otherwise might be sadly misjudged by succeeding generations.

History would be but a dim bird's-eye view of past events were it not for the illuminating torch of the pen which discloses the brain and heart of king, statesman, author, poet, soldier, and ecclesiastic, together with others who have played important rôles on the stage of life.

The value of an autograph is considerably enhanced when it is attached to a holograph, such as a complete letter or manuscript. A detached autograph of Henry Fielding the novelist, for example, is worth no more than £5 or £6, whereas at a recent sale at Sotheby's the original agreement for " Tom Jones," together with the receipt for the £600 which he was paid for that masterpiece, fetched no less a sum than £1015. The signature of Charles I., again, is worth from two to three guineas in an ordinary way, yet a single half-page letter from that monarch fetched £66 at the same sale. The signature of Beethoven fetches, as a general rule, about £3, 3s., but an autograph MS. of " The Jolly Beggars " was sold for £205.

The value of autographs mainly depends upon seven points :—

(1) The importance of the writer.
(2) The circumstances that caused the letter to be penned.
(3) The period and age of specimen.
(4) The subject and its influence on current affairs.
(5) How many such writings are in the market.
(6) The person in which the letter is written.
(7) The span of life enjoyed by writer.

It is obvious that when an author has lived to a ripe old age and written prodigiously, his autograph is not nearly so valuable as when he has come to an untimely end, almost at the beginning of his career.

The epistles of such men as Chatterton, Shelley, and Keats are extremely rare, for the reason that the men all died young. Their autographs therefore run to a much higher figure, as a rule, than do those of

Dickens, Thackeray, and Sir Walter Scott. These last may be usually bought for a few pounds each, whereas the letters of the former can rarely be purchased under £20 apiece.

However, there is no hard and fixed rule for the auction of autographs. The novice will, no doubt, be extremely puzzled by the extraordinary value given sometimes to the writings of inferior and little-known men, while those of individuals, whose genius and power have been universally acknowledged, can often be purchased for a few shillings.

Two letters by Richelieu were recently bought for a florin, and an epistle penned by Napoleon from Cairo was purchased at 20s. At another sale a letter of Charles Dickens reached £500. When this sum is contrasted with some of his other letters priced from 10s. to 70s. although of equal interest, the uninitiated is naturally perplexed.

The only explanation of such inconsistencies lies in the fact that, in the matter of autographs, the whim of fashion and fancy is as prevalent as in matters of dress. Among these fluctuations the experienced collector stands firm, and these are times of great advantage to him when probably for a few shillings he may obtain an autograph which time will prove to be of great price. He who is governed by this whirlpool of enthusiasm, which very soon dies out, will find himself stranded with an almost useless collection with which he can only part at great loss. A little thought will prove that the calligraphy of a reigning actress or danseuse is but a flippant possession.

Of course, there are times when a collector is obliged to be mercenary and be guided by the prevailing taste, but he should always have the ultimate welfare of his treasures at heart.

For this reason, it might be well to purchase a few autographs of some temporary favourite and sell them again at a profit before the public interest decreases, for by so doing the collector may procure with the money gained a far more valuable possession.

Writers of repute often suffer periods of ignominy and desertion, their autographs for a time being mere drugs in the market ; but the collector knows well that by and by these will once more assert their power, and so, unmoved by the fickleness of others, he remains loyal, gathers in the rejected letters, and is anon rewarded for his fidelity.

FORGERIES

Counterfeit letters and documents are so cunningly manufactured that, unless a collector be very careful, he will amass many unauthentic autographs. In order to protect himself from unscrupulous dealers, he will be wise to study reliable catalogues, frequently attend auction sales, and keep a watchful eye on competition. He should be wary of all advertisements.

A clever process of forging an autograph is as follows. From some old book a fly-leaf is torn and spread over the letter to be copied, which is laid upon a glass slanted surface, behind which a powerful lamp is placed, Fig. 1. The letter is traced upon the blank paper in ink mixed with crystals of sulphate of iron, diluted with water. This is dried, subjected to a damping of muriatic acid, and put under blotting-paper; then the forgery is held close to the fire. After it has been smeared with a dirty cloth, even on close examination it seems exactly what it appears to be, for the ink has a rusted, faded look, the surface is tinted a fascinating brown, while the soiled cloth has left marks and smears which bear a very near resemblance to the stamp of time.

FIG. 1.—The Autograph Forger at Work.

Sometimes autographs are traced upon ordinary paper, carefully mottled to resemble the " foxed " paper found in ancient manuscripts and books; this is creased until almost threadbare, the folds and edges are damped, rubbed, and singed until a look of antiquity is imparted to the surface. This process gives an effect to the writing which appears incongruous to the experienced eye, for it tints the paper to a darker colour than time ever gives. Letters have been traced on tissue-paper and then smoothed over with size, and pasted to paper of suitable age: this process lends a parchment-like effect to the document.

Forgeries are also consummated by means of a sticky paint or sepia, which proves a good imitation of old ink. Another plan, perhaps, even more difficult to discover, is forgery by photography. In this way many spurious imitations are purchased by delighted collectors, who believe themselves extremely fortunate.

In order to discriminate between the genuine and false, the collector has several points to consider, the most important being ink, blotting-pad, paper, and water-marks.

(1) *Ink* was formerly a home-made fluid, and varied accordingly in colour and thickness. Some of these primitive concoctions assume peculiar shades of reds, browns, and yellows. A simple test, when doubtful of the integrity of a document, is to damp the writing with hot water. Should the letter be penned with modern manufactured ink the words will smudge, but if it is what it appears to be, the damping will leave no mark. A quicker experiment is to touch the writing with the tongue: a peculiar taste condemns it as spurious. In some cases, crystals of sulphate of iron can be discovered by examination with a lens.

(2) *Blotting-pad.*—Bearing in mind the ostensible date of the document shown him, the collector will have a valuable aid in remembering that the blotting-pad is of comparatively recent date. Quite a casual glance suffices to show whether ink has been allowed to dry or has been soaked by blotting-paper. Until the end of the eighteenth century sand was sprinkled over wet ink, and even now it is a curious and interesting fact that in many authentic documents of that and earlier times a magnifying glass will show fine grains adhering to slopes and curves of the penmanship.

Ordinary sand was used until the middle of the eighteenth century, when it became the fashion to colour it to resemble gold and silver ; so that the collector, keeping this fact in mind, may with the aid of his lens not only discover whether a document is authentic, but, also, form a pretty exact estimate as to the period to which it belongs.

(3) *Paper.*—Old paper is generally coarse and rough in texture, and unbleached. Chlorine was first used—as applied to writing-paper— in 1814. The paper of Tudor times was very fine and white. The differences between the primitive wire-frame and the later woven papers provide important clues in discovering the genuine qualities of an autograph.

(4) *Water-marks.*—The marking of letter-paper is in itself a most interesting study, and of valuable aid in testifying to the period and real worth of autographs. Even primitive papers had water-marks woven into their surface, and a knowledge of the gradual evolution of these, often affected by political circumstances, protects the collector from the cunning of the unscrupulous dealer.

FIG. 2.—The First Bull's-head Water-mark.

Upon linen paper, introduced in Europe at the beginning of the fourteenth century, the first water-mark of the bull's head is found, Fig. 2. Later, a star or flower was added and placed between the horns Fig. 2A. Other marks, such as the scales Fig. 3, the hawk, Fig. 4, the bell, Fig. 5, succeeded during the latter half of the fourteenth and middle of the fifteenth century.

In Caxton's time the ox-head and star, with many others, such as the trefoil and shield and crown, were used, the jug or pot in the sixteenth century, Fig. 6, the flagon crowned with crescent, seventeenth century, Fig. 7, post-horn, late seventeenth century, Fig. 8, the fool's-cap, Fig. 9— supposed to be an ironical witticism of Cromwell's, which took the place of the crown—the cardinal's hat, earlier seventeenth century, Fig. 10, the fleur-de-lys, middle seventeenth century, Fig. 11.

When machine-made paper was introduced in 1801, the appearance of the texture became smoother and finer in quality.

FIG. 3.—The Scales Water-mark.

FIG. 4.—The Hawk
Water-mark.

FIG. 5.—The Bell
Water-mark.

Paper laid over moulds of wire-frame shows marks of manufacture absent from woven material.

The size of paper has varied considerably in later times, and here,

FIG. 6.—The Flagon.

FIG. 7.—The Flagon and Crescent.

FIG. 8.—The Post-horn.

again, with a little study the collector becomes possessed of a nice discernment when considering the value of an autograph, and the forger will need all his cunning to impose on him some "doctored" autograph.

In considering the purchase of an autograph, the margin, water-

mark, style of writing, phraseology, and spelling are all of great account, and must harmonise. Even when a forgery is perfectly executed, the calm, judicious eye is almost sure to observe a certain hesitancy and weakness in the penmanship, which in a genuine specimen flows steadily with all the force of the

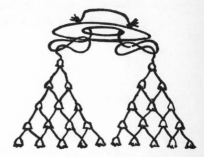

FIG. 9.—The Fool's-cap.

FIG. 10.—The Cardinal's Hat.

writer. Some forgeries, however, are so cleverly manipulated that occasionally even experienced collectors are deceived; therefore the novice cannot be too careful. Indeed, at the outset, his only means of protecting himself is to get the advice of an expert before purchasing specimens.

Abbreviations of technical terms in catalogues will at first puzzle the youthful collector, but he will soon come to understand them.

Many ancient and very rare autographs may be viewed in the British Museum, as well as cathedrals, old churches, and libraries, and these will help the novice to a familiarity with different periods and personalities of calligraphy.

FIG. 11.—The Fleur-de-lys.

THE TREATMENT OF AUTOGRAPHS

Autographs, provided they are protected from the damp and from destructive hands, give little trouble to the collector. The novice possessing the bump of neatness and not liking to see some of his treasures tattered at the edges may be tempted to trim them with scissors and paste them in an album. By so doing, it is as well to warn him that he is seriously injuring his specimens.

The great charm of autographs is to cherish them exactly as they

FIG. 12.—Glass Case for Specimens.　　FIG. 13.—Isaac D'Israeli's Signature.

are, worn at margins, thumb-marked, dilapidated, and blotched—no matter. An album is only used by the ignorant. The wisest plan is to keep the autographs unattached in a large folio of strong cartridge-paper, and on no account must notes or numbers, even in pencil, be written upon them. When the paper is badly tattered, pieces of thin tissue-paper and starch may be used for repairing.

FIG. 14.—Signature of Tom Hood.

A letter which has suffered very much from decay should be floated on starch, placed on a sheet of paper, and pressed down with weights over blotting-paper. This process is only possible when the letter is written on one side of the sheet, and the collector will need to exercise great caution in order to avoid moistening the ink. When both sides of a letter have been written upon, it is best to place it firmly between two sheets of thin glass and employ glazed calico to bind the edges of the glass, thus making a case for the preservation of the document, Fig. 12.

Autographs that become mouldy from a damp climate or sea air should be wrapped in woollen material, first dipped in quicklime and sulphate of soda and allowed to dry, or a solution of gum, resin, and alcohol may be brushed lightly over the surface of letters.

For the rest, the collector should be constantly reading histories and autobiographies until saturated with the circumstances and surroundings of the great men and women whose autographs he wishes to possess.

PECULIARITIES OF SIGNATURES

Some observation of facsimiles will help him to recognise the style and peculiarity which distinguished the signatures of different writers. Many of these have set somewhat eccentric flourishes beneath their names which should be carefully noted, as, for

FIG. 15.—Signature of George Cruikshank.

example, that of Henry Kirke White (poet), Cardinal Wiseman, Isaac D'Israeli (essayist), Fig. 13, Thomas Hood (poet), Fig. 14,

FIG. 16.—Signature of Charles Dickens in 1832.

B. R. Haydon (painter), George Cruikshank (artist), Fig. 15, Charles Dickens (novelist), Figs. 16 and 17, Louis Philippe (King of France), Charlotte, Princess of Wales, and many others. The remarkable alterations in some signatures penned by the same hand at different periods must also be considered.

John Baillie, the dramatic poet, began by writing his name in a rather thin, timid style, but at a later date confidence and sense of his own worth are noticeable in his penmanship, while the early and later writing of William Makepeace Thackeray can scarcely be credited as being those of the same individual.

Compare the complex letters of the illustrations

FIG. 17.—Signature of Charles Dickens in 1859.

of Charles Dickens' signature in 1832 with that of 1859; it would seem from these that the self-reliance imbued by a swiftly-rising fame is accountable for these extraordinary variations.

A similar difference may be observed in the signatures of the poet and essayist Charles Lamb, and indeed in many other writers—differ-ences which will doubtless confuse the collector until he has spent some time in learning to recognise the same individual beneath these disguises.

Different styles of English should be studied. Indeed, for this fascinating hobby considerable knowledge in all the branches briefly mentioned is absolutely essential, for it lends a nice distinction on discovering the genuine treasures the centuries have left us; for autographs are not only hand, but brain and heart-prints " on the sands of time."

CHAPTER XL

BIRDS' EGG COLLECTING

THE TREASURES OF THE HEDGEROWS

To the collector of birds' eggs Nature reveals her domestic economy in a very special way. Content to please the eyes of the casual and uninitiated wayfarer with a wealth of tree and hedgerow, field and heath, she conceals her most intimate affairs from all but those who can be trusted to reverence and respect her provisions for the protection of her little ones. So it is that of the myriads of nests in which every spring the birds bring up their young, many are so cunningly hidden that none but those in the secret know where to find them.

Almost every species of bird employs a different scheme of architecture for nest-building. From the mud-plastered home of the martin to the delicately-woven nests of some of the smaller birds, every imaginable device is used, whereby concealment, strength, or durability may be obtained as circumstances require. The art and scientific care devoted to these feathered homes can only be appreciated by those who have actually seen the nests in their original surroundings.

Before embarking upon a collection of birds' eggs, it would be as well to make a careful inquiry as to the local by-laws relative to the close season. From the 2nd of March to the 31st of July—both inclusive—it is illegal under the Wild Birds Protection Act to tamper with the nests of most birds. Local Councils have, however, authority to abolish or vary this close time in connection with any or all of the species so protected, and the collector must therefore make himself acquainted with the conditions prevailing in the district in which he lives.

To the sympathetic and conscientious collector, there is little need to address the following hint. Never empty a nest of all its eggs. Take one or two at most, but for pity's sake, if for no other reason, do not rob the mother of *all* her eggs. The rarer the bird, the more should this advice be considered, for ruthless collectors (if they can be called such) have done their utmost to exterminate many of our native species by taking entire broods.

No general instructions can be given as to finding nests. Birds of each species choose those sites which prove the most adapted to their particular habits. Nor is it necessary to give any detailed explanation of how to climb trees—that art being inherent in the average boy. A very strong warning must be given, however, against undertaking any foolhardy attempts to reach nests built upon high or fragile branches. There is not an egg in the world worth risking a limb for, so all experiments in the matter of climbing should be avoided, and unless the tree looks sound and the branches are accessible, the nest should be abandoned until a better opportunity offers.

How to Blow an Egg

The method of blowing an egg is very simple. A single hole should be bored in whichever side of the shell presents fewest and least

FIG. 1.—Glass Blow-pipe.

characteristic marks. A glass blow-pipe, Fig. 1, should then be held beneath the hole and directed in such a manner that the nozzle points sideways into the hole, as shown in Fig. 2. The current of air thus forced into the shell expels the contents very thoroughly. When the shell is quite

FIG. 2.—Blowing an Egg.

empty it should be carefully washed out with warm water.

Some British Eggs

Although it would manifestly be impossible to give a complete list of those British eggs which may be collected in an ordinary way, the following remarks will serve to guide the beginner in knowing where to seek and how to recognise the eggs of some of the principal birds that nest in this country.

BITTERN.—This bird, although once a frequenter of the Fen lands in East Anglia, is now but rarely seen. The Bittern builds its nest on the mud, constructing it of reed and rushes. The eggs, often pointed at both ends, are of a buff or grey colour, and very smooth and glossy in appearance.

BLACKBIRD.—No definite rule can be laid down for finding the nest of this bird, as hedges, shrubs, trees, stacks, holes in chalk or gravel pits, and other such out of the way places are chosen as suitable sites. The nest is large and cup-shaped, built of all sorts of twigs and stalks bound together with mud. Even the eggs vary to a remarkable degree; some are of a greenish-blue tint, others of an olive-grey, some are pale chalky-blue, and yet others sandy-brown; sometimes they are long and pointed in shape, at others short and broad. A fairly representative specimen is shown in A, Fig. 3.

BULLFINCH.—The best place in which to seek the bullfinch's nest is in the horizontal branches of a yew-tree, but these birds frequently build in low hawthorn bushes. The nests are neat and fragile, and frequently lined with hairs or root fibre. The egg, B, Fig. 3, is pale blue, spotted with blackish-brown marks at the larger end.

CHAFFINCH.—This bird usually builds its nest in a hawthorn hedge, using moss, hairs, and spiders' cocoons for the purpose. The eggs are

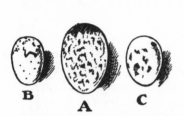

FIG. 3.—A, Blackbird's Egg; B, Bullfinch's
Egg; C, Chaffinch's Egg.

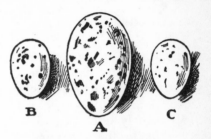

FIG. 4.—A, Chough's Egg;
B and C, Cuckoo's Eggs.

greenish or of a rose colour, marked with dark brown patches seen in C, Fig. 3.

CHOUGH.—Nests of this bird are found in Cornwall, Devon, and on the East coast, and are generally situated in some almost inaccessible hole or cranny in the face of the cliff, or upon the walls of deserted ruins. The nest is built of dry stems or heather, lined with dead grass, wool, or hair. The eggs, A, Fig. 4, are of a dull cream or greenish colour, streaked with brown and grey.

CUCKOO.—The cuckoo's habit of depositing her eggs in other birds' nests has become a byword. It is not, however, generally known that this bird actually lays her eggs on the ground and carries them in her bill to another bird's home—often unsuited in size and strength for the extra strain. The eggs of the cuckoo vary in colour and markings to an astonishing degree, as may be seen from a glance at B and C, Fig. 4.

GOLDFINCH.—The nests of these birds are usually to be found in orchards, often on the branches of an apple-tree. They are small and cup-shaped, and occasionally lined with thistledown. The eggs, A, Fig. 5, are greenish-white, the larger end being covered with purple-brown spots.

GREENFINCH.—Hawthorn hedges are very favourite places for the nests of these birds, who build their homes of straws, twigs, or any similar material that may be handy. The eggs are of a green or buff tint, and covered with irregular brown markings at the larger end, B, Fig. 5.

HEDGE-SPARROW.—The nest of the hedge-sparrow is never built more than three or four feet from the ground, and, as the name

FIG. 5.—A, Goldfinch's Egg; B, Green-finch's Egg; C, Hedge-sparrow's Egg.

FIG. 6.—Eggs of the House-sparrow.

implies, usually in hedges. The egg, C, Fig. 5, is well known, being of an exquisite turquoise blue and entirely unmarked. The eggs vary from an oval to a very distinct pear-shape.

HOUSE-SPARROW.—The common sparrow makes no attempt to build a shapely nest. Choosing some crevice in a wall or bank amongst the ivy or in the thatching, birds simply build rough cup-shaped nests in which the hens lay small eggs varying in colour and marking to an extraordinary extent, as the accompanying illustrations in Fig. 6 will show.

FIG. 7.—A, Jackdaw's Egg; B, Linnet's Egg; C, Pheasant's Egg.

JACKDAW.—Belfries and chimneys, castle walls and ruined towers, are the favourite resorts of jackdaws. A few sticks and scraps of straw are sufficient material for building the clumsy nests in which these birds lay their eggs. These latter are a delicate pale-blue colour, spotted with grey and sepia markings, A, Fig. 7.

JAY.—Jays build their nests fairly near the ground in hawthorn, sloe, or holly, as well as in fir and yew-trees. The eggs are pale blue, but very closely mottled with yellowish spots.

KINGFISHER.—These birds do not really build a nest, but dig passages some 18 in. long, terminating in a small chamber in which their pure white eggs are laid.

LINNET.—Built in plantations and orchards, the nest of the linnet can usually be found quite easily. The eggs, B, Fig. 7, are a pale green, and in most cases spotted with red or brown markings at the larger end.

MAGPIE.—The magpie frequently builds her nest, which is large and bulky, high up amongst the branches. It is covered with a lid of thorny twigs. The eggs are a pale green, dotted with olive-coloured spots, especially towards the large end.

NIGHTINGALE.—The nest of the nightingale is generally to be found in a hole on the ground, and is almost always built of rushes or broad-bladed grass. The eggs are brownish in appearance, the large end occasionally having a red or red-brown zone around it.

PARTRIDGE.—These birds lay their eggs in a hole scratched in the ground, and lined with grass. The eggs are yellowish-buff in colour. The gamekeeper's permission will have to be obtained before taking either partridge or pheasant eggs.

PHEASANT.—Like the partridge, this bird merely scrapes a hole for its nest. The eggs are greenish in colour, and rather pointed in shape, C, Fig. 7.

STARLING.—A hole in a tree or bank frequently furnishes this bird with a site for its nest, which is constructed of grass or straw. The eggs, which are unspotted, are sometimes a bluish-white, but more often a deep blue.

SWALLOW.—The swallow, as a rule, builds its nest beneath the eaves or against the walls of barns and cottages. The eggs vary very much in colour and markings, but are usually brownish-white with darker brown spots.

THE COLLECTION

Birds' eggs, when properly blown, should be kept in cabinets or cases, the drawers of which must be divided into compartments, and lined with cotton wool. Labels stating the name of the bird, place, and date of finding, and any further particulars of interest can be gummed to the egg or placed in the partition for reference.

Birds' egg cabinets are, undoubtedly, the best for those collections numbering many specimens, but as such cabinets are rather costly, 50s. being the least for which one can procure a cabinet of any use, some more economical method of housing the collection will be desirable. A large cardboard box, such as tailors and dressmakers use, will suit the purpose admirably. A number of matchbox drawers, lined with cotton wool, will serve for the smaller eggs— those in which Messrs Bryant & May sell their large matches being specially recommended. These, side by side, are even more convenient than the ordinary partitions in a cabinet drawer, as they can be removed bodily without disturbing the remainder of the eggs.

Drawers for larger eggs can be easily cut from cardboard after the manner shown in Fig. 8. Assuming that the required depth of

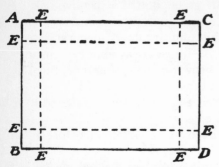

the box is one inch, mark off the points E that distance from ABCD respectively, and connect them with light pencil lines as depicted in the diagram. Cut out the squares thus formed at each corner. Then draw a sharp knife lightly down the pencilled lines in such a way that the card is half cut through. When this has been done, bend along each line, thus forming a tray. The corners may then be made secure by gumming strips of paper round them, and the whole tray finished up to appear as in Fig. 9. Trays of this description can be made to any size required.

FIG. 8.—How to make a Tray.

The practice of varnishing eggs was much resorted to in former days, but it cannot be recommended to any one who values his eggs from a natural point of view. The great object of Natural History collectors is to keep their specimens as like to nature as possible, and anything more artificial than a shining, varnished egg it would be difficult to imagine.

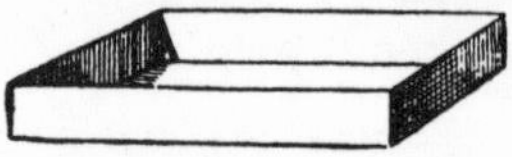

Place the egg in its compartment in such a way that the most prominent markings are uppermost and easily discernible, whilst where

FIG. 9.—The Tray complete.

there are several specimens of the same egg, they should be placed in adjoining compartments so that the different varieties are clearly exhibited.

As time goes on the collector will find opportunities of adding specimens, by means of exchange or purchase, which he could not possibly obtain personally, and these, together with what he finds for himself, will eventually render his collection representative and complete.

CHAPTER XLI

THE COLLECTING OF BUTTERFLIES AND MOTHS

A SCIENTIFIC COUNTRY HOBBY

MOST lovers of nature have, at some time or another, begun a collection of butterflies and moths, although comparatively few have had the patience and perseverance to make it a hobby—a work of love. This probably arises from a want of proper knowledge as to the way in which a collection should be started and maintained. The little details so essential for the beginner to know are usually passed over in silence by writers on the subject, or are described in such learned and technical terms that the uninitiated reader becomes hopelessly fogged after perusing a page or two of their instructions.

The following hints as to the formation of a collection will, it is hoped, put the whole subject in a very plain light.

WHERE TO FIND BUTTERFLIES

There are some sixty-eight species of British butterflies, some of which, such as Camberwell Beauties and Queen of Spain Fritillaries, are exceedingly rare. It will be a red-letter day for the entomologist when he is able to add a specimen of one of these varieties to his collection. These rarer specimens have probably immigrated from the Continent, but, since any butterfly caught in Britain is considered a British species, they will take their places in the collection with the rest. Other immigrants, such as the Painted Lady or the Clouded Yellow, are sometimes found in great abundance.

A considerable number of butterflies are distributed generally over the country, but there are many species whose peculiar fancies and tastes for some especial food confine them to certain localities.

Fritillaries and Hare-Streaks will be found in woods—especially large woods—whilst the chalk downs are the homes of some of the Blues and Skippers.

The grassy sides of lanes in any country district will often prove likely spots for captures. Visitors from the neighbouring woods and clover fields frequently wander to the roadside, and thus save the conscience of the collector, who might otherwise go trespassing in search of his victims.

To a certain extent these remarks apply to the collection of moths, the larger kinds only of which number over a thousand varieties. No special direction, however, can be given regarding their "habitats," as entomologists style their favourite haunts.

If the collector should have the good fortune to discover a spot where a rare or local species is found, he will do well to take but a few specimens for fear of exterminating the variety. If, however, there are sufficient to warrant his netting a number, he will find them prove very useful for exchange. To give an example of this : a collector some years ago found the Essex Skipper swarming in a country lane ; he accordingly made a "haul," netted some two hundred, leaving many more uncaught, and succeeded in exchanging these rare species for specimens of other local varieties from all parts of the country.

THE NET

A butterfly-net may either be purchased for about 3s. 6d. or made at home, and as the majority of entomologists prefer home-made nets, the beginner will probably wish to follow their example and make his apparatus according to the following method.

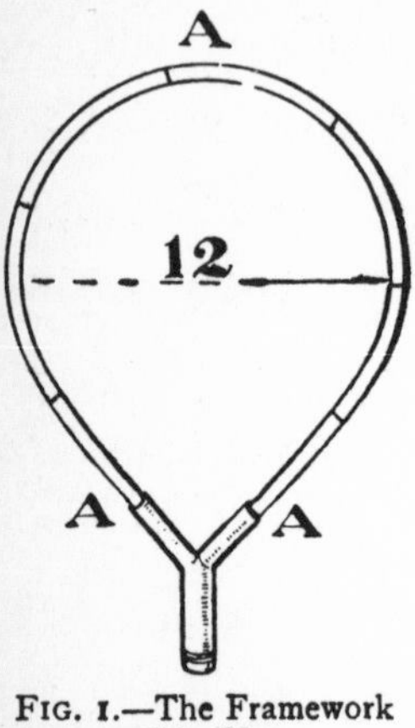

A folding framework, AAA, made of light bamboo, can be purchased from any dealer at a cost of about 2s. 6d. This framework, when fitted into the brass Y, Fig. 1, should measure 12 in. from side to side, as seen in the diagram.

The brass Y, costing about 6d., should hold the two ends of the cane when bent very securely in the arms AB, Fig. 2, whilst the end C of the stock should be large enough to receive the ferrule end of a walking-stick.

FIG. 1.—The Framework of the Net.

Unless care be taken to see that these all fit tightly, disaster will follow, for when the collector is about to catch the species he has been seeking for years, the net will probably collapse and trouble will ensue.

The net itself, which should be of white mosquito-netting or green muslin, must have the same circumference as the bamboo framework, and should be about 30 in. deep, as seen in Fig. 3. A cotton hem must be doubled

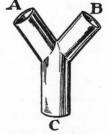

FIG. 2.—Brass for holding Frame.

over on the top for the frame to pass through, and a slit, E, made some 4 in. deep where the brass Y comes. This slit must be very strongly bound.

The finished butterfly-net will now appear as in Fig. 3, where the frame A is shown threaded through the hem in the net B, and fastened to the brass C, which in its turn is fitted on to the end of the walking-stick at D.

Before using the net it should be soaked in three or four waters, and, when dry, well rubbed to take out any stiffness and render it as soft as possible.

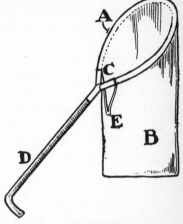

FIG. 3.—The Complete Net.

CATCHING MOTHS

Moths, being mostly night-fliers, are caught in a different manner. Some, such as the larger Hawk Moth and many of the Bombyces, can only be obtained by searching for and rearing the larvæ, *i.e.* caterpillars, or hunting for the pupæ, *i.e.* chrysalides. The Noctuæ must be obtained by "sugaring." All these processes are too complicated for brief description, and the collector should study the matter in more advanced works on the subject.

Many of the Geometers are caught by "mothing" of an evening, with a net along the hedge banks or in the depths of woods, where, again, many species may be found by examining flowers and shrubs by the light of a lantern.

Privet, heather, and, in the late autumn, ivy blossoms, are great favourites with moths, and yield species not found elsewhere.

THE NECESSARY OUTFIT

A collecting-box, which may also be used as a relaxing-box, can be purchased for about 1s., and should be made of zinc and cork-lined.

A good relaxing-box can be constructed of a biscuit-tin with two or three inches of damp sand at the bottom. Over this sand a few sheets of paper should be placed. When using this box the insects should be removed as soon as they have relaxed or lost all the stiffness of death, as otherwise there is a danger of their becoming mouldy.

A killing-bottle will also have to be purchased, and can only be obtained of dealers, the prices being from 2s. 6d.

A supply of chip boxes may be obtained for a few pence. A stock of pins will also be essential, and must be kept handy in a small pin-cushion, Fig. 4, made to fit the waistcoat pocket, the sides being made of cardboard or stiff material and the inside of flannel.

A linen satchel with a flap and button is useful for carrying chip boxes, whilst the true entomologist will see that his coat pockets are capacious enough to carry the boxes in which his prizes are confined.

FIG. 4.—Pin-cushion.

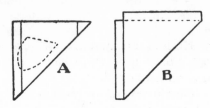

FIG. 5.—Entomological Envelope.

The entomological envelope shown in A, Fig. 5, is useful for carrying specimens, when the appliances for setting the insect are not at hand. A piece of paper measuring about 4 in. by $2\frac{1}{2}$ in. is folded as in B. The antennæ, or feelers of the insect, are folded between its wings, and as soon as possible the specimen must be relaxed and set.

KILLING

The larger butterflies can be killed by carefully pinching the thorax, the wings being folded and pinned at once. The smaller species of butterflies, however, should be taken home in the chip boxes and killed in the following manner :—

The lids of the boxes must be moved slightly to one side, and the boxes then piled upon one another beneath a medium-sized biscuit-tin, which may also contain the specimens from the collecting-box.

A small sponge or rag must now be soaked in the strongest ammonia (− 880) and placed in the tin, the lid of which should be closed immediately.

In about a half-hour's time all the captives will be dead and in perfect condition for pinning and setting.

PINNING

The successful setting of an insect depends a great deal upon how it has been pinned.

The pin should be inserted in the centre of the thorax and in a slightly diagonal manner, as shown in Fig. 6, so that the point emerges between the second and third pairs of legs.

It must be passed through just sufficiently to raise the specimen, when set, in such a manner that no part of it touches the bottom of the drawer or box in which the collection is kept.

FIG. 6.—Pinning an Insect.

SETTING

Nothing but practice will enable the collector to set his specimens well. Setting-boards, which are best made at home, can be very easily constructed as follows :—

Obtain several strips of soft deal 12 in. to 14 in. long, 1 in. thick, and from 1 to 6 in. in width. Make a groove AA, Fig. 7, from end

FIG. 7.—Setting-board.

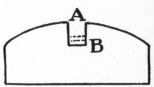

FIG. 8.—Section of Setting-board.

to end of each strip, varying the depth and width of the groove according to the size of the strip of deal.

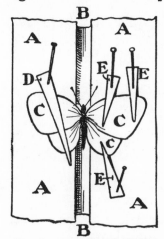

FIG. 9.—Setting a Specimen.

Plane and sand-paper the top of the board, so that in section it appears as in Fig. 8.

Having done this, cut strips of cork and glue them along the bottoms of the grooves, B, Fig. 8. Smooth white paper can now be pasted over the whole board, if desired, although this is not absolutely necessary.

A plentiful supply of braces, D and E, Fig. 9, should be cut from cardboard, and a number of strong pins about 1½ in. long prepared ready for use.

A setting-needle should also be made by mounting a stout darning-needle in a wooden penholder.

The butterfly may now be pinned into the groove in the board so that the body is straight and in a natural

position, as seen in Fig. 9.   The wings should be bent down temporarily with large cardboard braces, D, Fig. 8, and placed in proper
position by aid of the setting-needle.   They can then be fixed with

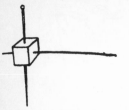

small and permanent braces, EEE, the larger
pieces of cardboard, D, being removed.
Other pins may occasionally be required for
fixing the antennæ.

Some entomologists prefer the setting-
bristle seen in Fig. 10 to the cardboard
braces just described.   This setting-bristle

FIG. 10.—Setting-bristle.   consists of a strong bristle fastened in a
cork cube through which a pin is driven, as illustrated in the diagram.

The setting-board should be kept in a dry, airy place secure from
dust, insects, or mice.   After about fourteen days, according to the
size of the insects and the state of the weather, whether damp or not,
the specimens may be taken from the setting-boards and the braces
and pins carefully removed.

THE COLLECTION

A proper cabinet is indispensable for the housing of a collection,
and can be purchased in any size at prices ranging from 20s. upwards.
Until this is obtained, however, the specimens may be kept in store
boxes, costing about 2s. 6d each, which must be as air-tight as possible.

The entomologist's worst enemies are mites, the ravages of which
can occasionally be prevented by pinning inside the box a piece of
muslin soaked in naphthaline.

Where mites have already made their appearance a drop of benzine
must be applied to the specimen at which they are working, and, if
these pests are numerous, the whole collection will have to be so
treated.

Owing to the explosive nature of benzine, *it should only be used in
the daytime,* and the bottle ought never to be opened when the gas or
candles are alight.

The collector should take an early opportunity of mastering all
the Latin and scientific names of the insects, and for this purpose
must consult some authority—South's " Butterflies and Moths of the
British Isles," for example.   With such a sound and reliable book of
reference at hand, the student will find his collection becoming of
greater interest day by day, his knowledge and love of the subject
increasing with every new specimen placed in his cabinet.

CHAPTER XLII

THE MAKING OF A BOTANICAL COLLECTION

THE INTEREST OF A PLANT DIARY

THE formation of a herbarium is one of the greatest pleasures in connection with botanical study. Apart from its great scientific utility, it is the diary of many a pleasant ramble, the record of many a delightful excursion. Each specimen recalls some incident, revives some impression, and tells its own tale to the collector. A herbarium is therefore a necessary luxury for every botanist, and the following instructions will enable the beginner to lay the foundations of a collection that will prove a source of life-long pleasure.

THE COLLECTION OF SPECIMENS

Specimens should be gathered in fine, dry weather, and, so far as possible, the flowers, leaves, stem, and root must be obtained.

In some of the smaller plants, however, it will be impossible to show more than the root, which should be washed and cleansed from soil. On the other hand, when the stem is too large, it is only necessary to take portions ; whilst a leaf may be folded to suit the size of the drying-paper. Where practicable the radical or root leaves must always be obtained, for, in most plants, these differ considerably from the stem and upper leaves. Several sheets are frequently necessary to exhibit a large plant satisfactorily.

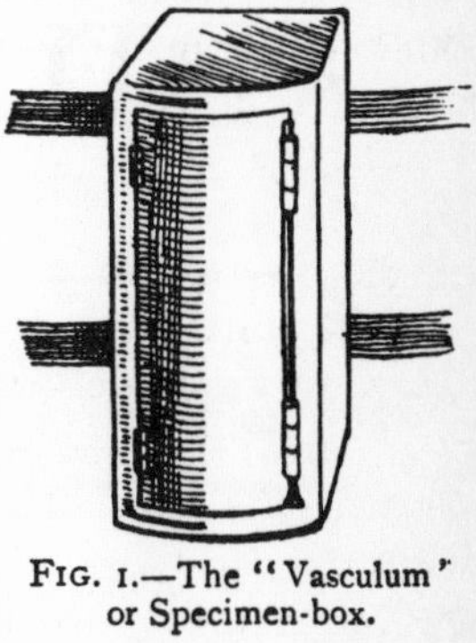

Flowers should, of course, be in full bloom. As the male and female flowers in some instances are on separate plants, a specimen of each must be mounted, whilst a third sheet should exhibit the seed-pods or capsules. It need scarcely be added that only the most perfect specimens should be gathered.

FIG. 1.—The "Vasculum" or Specimen-box.

A japanned tin box or "vasculum" is necessary for taking specimens home. It should be about 20 in. long, 10 in. wide, and 5 in. deep ; the lid, which will occupy the whole of one side, fastening with a pin and sheath, as shown in Fig. 1.

With the addition of straps to pass through loops at either end, the box can be slung over the shoulder or carried by hand.

In addition to this an ordinary pocket sandwich tin will prove very handy for carrying small plants, though many botanists prefer a portfolio for this purpose. This portfolio should contain a quantity of drying-paper, in which the plants must be neatly inserted as gathered, the case being secured by an ordinary rug-strap and handle. It is most useful for carrying plants with delicate leaves, water-plants, and flowers with fugacious or falling petals, such as poppies and veronicas.

A digger or trowel, seven or eight inches in length, will be necessary, and can be carried in a leather sheath attached to a strap around the waist. A long string fastened to the handle and tied to the sheath will prevent the trowel being lost. A pocket lens must never be forgotten, and will be handy at home as well as on an excursion.

Specimen Finding

It is impossible to give more than general instructions as to finding specimens. Every locality has its own peculiar species, but the mountainous and hilly districts of the north, both of England and of Scotland, are the most prolific sources for rare and local plants. The south and wild parts of the south-west have their own especial treasures, as do marshes, woods, and the seashore.

Nor must the roadsides and commons of the Midland and agricultural districts be neglected, for finds are often unexpectedly made in the most unlikely corners. Attention must be paid as carefully to common species as to the rarer varieties, and it is frequently interesting to take specimens of the same plant from different localities in order to observe the effect produced upon the growth by altitude. A pocket Flora is a useful and almost necessary companion for determining doubtful finds.

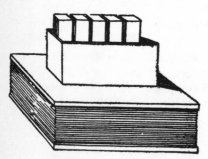

Fig. 2.—A Simple Press.

The Botanical Press

The botanist must now consider the method of pressing the specimens he has collected. One of the simplest presses can be made from two pieces of well-seasoned wood, each measuring 24 in. by 18 in., the ends being neatly finished. Drying-sheets are placed between these boards, and the necessary pressure obtained by placing a box containing five or six bricks upon the upper board, Fig. 2. This contrivance has the double advantage of being easily manipulated, and of exerting a pressure that adjusts itself to the shrinkage of the plants.

Such a simple press is only serviceable for home use, however, and a little further construction will be necessary if a portable press is to be made. Two boards as above described should be carefully chosen from $\frac{1}{2}$ in. or $\frac{5}{8}$ in. wood, and must measure a couple of inches longer than the drying-papers (the sizes of which are given in the next paragraph). A strip of thin iron must be let in along each end of these boards, those of the lower board having a square hole in the centre, those of the upper board a round hole.

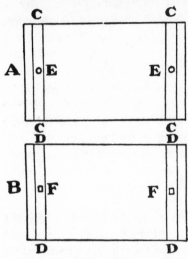

FIG. 3.—Boards for Portable Press.

FIG. 4.—Rack Screw.

This is clearly shown in Fig. 3, where A is the upper and B the lower board, the iron strips CC on the former being bored with round holes EE, whilst the strips DD in the lower board have square holes FF. Two rack screws with square bases, Fig. 4, must now be procured and so adjusted that, the bases fitting the square holes of the lower board, the screws pass freely through the round holes in the upper. A couple of thumbscrew nuts complete the apparatus, which, when filled with papers, should appear as in Fig. 5. A press like this can be conveniently carried as luggage or sent in advance, and may be provided with an oil-cloth covering for its travels, which should be removed as soon as practicable.

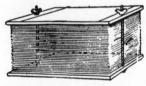

FIG. 5.—Portable Press complete.

DRYING PAPER

Botanical drying-paper is made in sizes varying from 16 in. by 10 in. to 20 in. by 16 in., and may be purchased from Messrs. West, Newman & Co., Hatton Garden, London, at prices ranging from 1s. 1d. to 2s. 2d. a quire, according to size. The second size, viz. 18 in. by 11 in., is very useful, and costs 1s. 4d. a quire. If the beginner cannot afford to purchase sufficient paper to fill the press, newspapers can be used as padding, and will successfully serve to eke out a few quires of the proper paper.

Special paper for mounting the dried specimens can also be procured. Ordinary cartridge paper is equally serviceable, however, and much cheaper. Specimens being mounted on single sheets, these in their turn are inserted between double sheets of brown paper containing all the specimens of a genus.

Pressing the Specimens

All the apparatus having been prepared, a few directions may now be given as to pressing and drying. In the cases of plants that are too large for the papers, a judicious selection must be made of those parts which display the best and most characteristic features. It may prove necessary to fold some of the stems, and small slips of paper, slit in the middle, should be prepared to secure these portions whilst drying. During the proceedings a pair of surgeon's forceps and a thin paper-knife must be kept handy.

Four or five sheets or newspaper pads must first be laid on the bottom board of the press. The plant should then be carefully placed on a sheet of drying-paper, the natural position being preserved as far as possible. Full-blown flowers may be gently pressed down to keep them open. Another sheet of paper must now be placed over the plant, and the whole affair put in the press. Four or five sheets of padding should be added before another layer of plant is inserted, and when nine or ten layers are in the press, a strong piece of mill-board can be placed in preparation for another set of layers. When all the specimens have been dealt with in this manner, the upper board can be placed in position and screwed down tightly.

The papers will be ready to be changed after twenty-four hours, and the plants must then be transferred to another sheet with the help of the paper-knife and forceps. At this point any leaves that have got out of position may be adjusted.

The sheets having been replaced, pressure should be applied for four or five days, after which the pads will be the better for changing, although, except in cases of succulent plants, the drying-papers need not be disturbed. After another five days the plants will be ready for mounting, and the drying sheets can be set in the sun to dry.

Drying

Special directions are necessary for the drying of certain specimens. Succulent plants, such as stone crops, should be plunged into boiling water for five minutes to prevent further growth, whilst heaths may be similarly immersed for a minute to prevent the leaves dropping off.

Some of the composite plants, which are apt to perfect their flower growth and appear as seed, can be treated in the same way. Plants with thin, membranous leaves, such as water-plants, should be arranged on a piece of thin Crown Tea paper between the drying-sheets, being very carefully removed when ready for mounting. Flowers with thin petals, such as poppies, may be treated in a similar way, the flower stalk being removed close to the stem and replaced when the remaining part of the plant is dry.

Thick flowers such as thistles may either be split or placed between papers and carefully crushed under foot, thus reducing the bulk before it is put under pressure. The same process serves with hard, prickly leaves like holly. Bulbs and tubers can be halved or divided in such a way as to show their natural form.

Plants such as grasses and sedges dry very quickly, whilst others require more time. On no account should a plant be removed from the papers before it is quite dry, although, to make room, the whole parcel of plants may be taken from the press after fifteen days and kept under weights.

A slip of paper should be placed in each sheet with the date and locality of collection.

Mounting the Specimens

Only the best specimens of dried plants should be selected and mounted on white paper. Some botanists like to fasten the plants with glue, but the best plan is to mount them with little bands of gummed paper, as shown in Fig. 6. These can be easily removed.

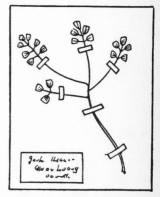

Two or three examples of small plants may be exhibited on a sheet, but, as a rule, a single specimen is sufficient. In many cases, indeed, when the radical leaves are large, several sheets for each plant will be required. Separate examples of a plant in seed should be obtained where possible, and mounted by themselves.

All the sheets must be labelled in the lower left-hand corner, with the scientific

Fig. 6.—Mounting the Specimens.

name, the English name, and the date and locality of finding.

When the plant has been obtained from another botanist, his name should also be shown in the proper place. The right-hand top corner of each sheet should bear a number, preferably that designated in the ninth edition of the London Catalogue. By means of these numbers a certain uniformity is maintained amongst collectors, and much ambiguity avoided.

The sheets of each species may now be placed in brown wrappers bearing the name of the genus on the outside cover. At this point a word of warning will be appropriate. When examining the sheets, the utmost care must always be taken to avoid turning them over. Let them be lifted from side to side, and there will be but little chance of the specimens being broken.

The further fate of the herbarium will now depend upon the will and pleasure of its owner. In a large collection such as a diligent student will soon form, a special cabinet with shelves as deep as the length of the papers, and four or five inches apart, will be necessary ; but until they are obtained the sheets of plants may be stored in portfolios or bundles, tied with tape and preserved in a dry cupboard.

Constant and careful inspection will be necessary to ascertain whether mites have made their appearance. There is no other remedy for these pests but painting the specimens with a solution of corrosive sublimate in camphorated spirits or naphtha (half-drachm to the ounce). Upon their first appearance strong measures must be instantly taken, and for this reason a systematic inspection of the herbarium is advisable.

CHAPTER XLIII

HOW TO FORM A HOME MUSEUM

A COLLECTION TO INTEREST EVERY ONE

THE making of a museum is a most interesting and valuable hobby, and only needs direction and control to ensure an immense deal of pleasure to any person who undertakes the task. Unfortunately it is seldom made the subject of a regular pastime—people buy this,

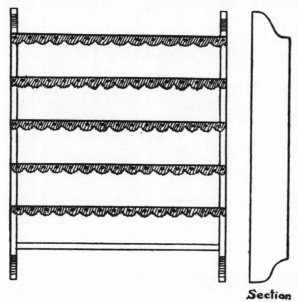

FIG. 1.—Shelves for the Museum.

that, and the other without any definite object—buy as the fit seizes them, and never think of properly housing their treasures. To remedy this start your own home museum—you will find it an altogether fascinating hobby.

HOW TO BEGIN

If you have a "den" all to yourself the question of housing the collection is very much simplified. Otherwise, a fair-sized corner of any room can be fitted for your treasure house. A recess will do splendidly, and can be easily adapted. Put shelves of $\frac{1}{2}$ in. board, Fig. 1, about a foot apart, from floor to ceiling, nailing them to proper supports in the wall. Close these shelves in with a glazed door if the recess be narrow, or a pair of doors, Fig. 2, if it is wide. Any boy of a mechanical turn of mind will be able to make and put in the glass for such doors after examining how an ordinary glazed window-frame

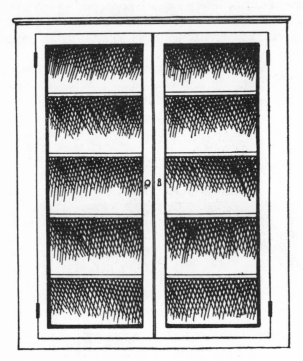

FIG. 2.—A Glass-doored Cupboard.

is made. Should you desire to have the museum open—which, of course, admits the inevitable dust—procure and nail along each shelf a neat piece of fancy edging, and colour all the wood with walnut or some such stain.

WHAT TO COLLECT

This will depend on your own taste. Some things are sure to exert a greater fascination than others, but the most interesting home museum as a rule is one that contains the most diverse curios gathered from the widest sources. "Something of everything" is not at all a bad motto in this connection. Of course, where you can secure a number of different specimens in one line all the better.

Natural History objects are among the easiest and most interesting to collect ; stuffed birds, fishes, and small animals always have a charm for the collector.

One of the chief things to strive for in your museum is rarity.   It is a mistake to load the shelves with preserved creatures, unless you intend having a collection illustrative of a particular species in its entirety.   Some of our ordinary English song-birds, such as the goldfinch and the bullfinch, are very pretty indeed when stuffed and mounted, but are too familiar to excite more than a passing interest.   It is possible, at a moderate cost, to secure good specimens of South

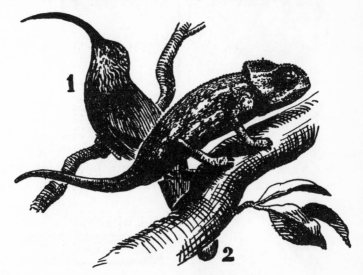

Fig. 3.—Brazilian Sickle-bird and Chameleon.

American and Eastern birds, which are vivid and strange in colouring, and very striking in form.   So with regard to mammals and other creatures ; few people care to examine a stuffed dog, but their interest will be at once stirred by a jerboa, an armadillo, or a chameleon, Fig. 3.

There are quite a number of weird denizens of the deep—the sun fish, Fig. 4, angler, &c., that always draw attention, their strange shapes evoking a hundred questions when being shown to friends. Some of the skeletons, too, are very remarkable when properly preserved, and prove a fascinating study to the young naturalist.

It will be as well to have a separate section for marine objects. Let them be properly arranged ; nothing looks worse in a collection than for the various objects to be kept in disorder, so that when you wish to exhibit a certain curio you have to make a general hunt for it, disarranging specimens and giving yourself annoyance.

A collection of shells will form a really beautiful section of the museum. Never keep them loose in a box, but affix them to white cards according to the species and size, writing the names neatly upon each card. Some very beautiful shells, Fig. 5, can be procured for a

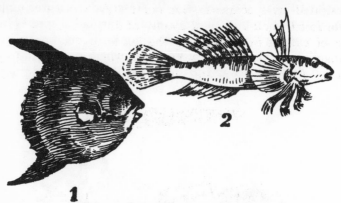

FIG. 4.—Sunfish and Japanese Dragonet.

few pence each, or, while you are at the seaside, you can often come upon some good specimens if you search along the beach. Indeed, you will find, when once the museum is started, that both at the seaside and in the country there are scores of splendid natural history

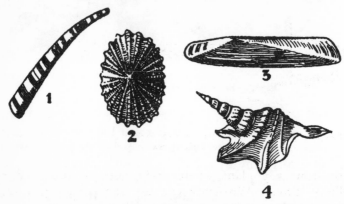

FIG. 5.—(1) Elephant's-tusk Shell; (2) Horse-limpet Shell; (3) Paper-razor Shell; (4) Pelican's-foot Shell.

curios which can be obtained without any cost, if you are on the alert with eyes always open for treasures to add to your collection.

Butterflies, moths, and insects will also demand a place in your museum. These should be carefully kept under glass, as constant handling is sure to cause damage at some time or another. They should also be named on small slips, and a standard book on entomology consulted whenever there is any doubt as to the name and habitat of your specimen.

It is worth while to devote a section to fossils of all kinds; the life of the remote past is always of living interest when properly explained and illustrated by specimens. Do not fill the shelves with huge examples of fossil wood and great chunks of dull quartz. A nice perfect example of extinct flora, showing the leaves and veins clearly, is far better than an indistinct mass of stone-like substance without any character. A number of specimens can be secured in your own

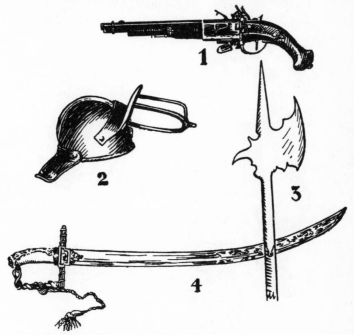

FIG. 6.—(1) Eighteenth-century Revolver; (2) Helmet of 1680; (3) Halberd of 1550; (4) Naval Officer's Sword of 1800.

district or from any place where earth borings are made, such as near colliery towns. Whenever you see excavations, be on the alert to secure something of interest for your museum. Moreover, when you are on holiday or visiting a mining centre, look out for the various fossils which are constantly brought to the surface in these places.

MILITARY CURIOS

In contrast with your natural history section will be a collection of curios relating to military life. At the present time a good many war implements are being discarded, and there are favourable opportunities of securing some capital things. Old swords, Fig. 6, bayonets, pistols, and guns can be secured for a trifle. Daggers, knives, tomahawks, and spears are also to be had for a shilling or two. Interesting additions to these are the metal crests of the various regiments of British and foreign armies—some of them works of art. Belt buckles and soldiers' buttons are also worth securing. War medals are somewhat expensive, but repay collecting.

Personal ornaments and small articles of dress worn by half-civilised peoples and savage tribes are of peculiar interest. If you

FIG. 7.—(1) A Buddhist Goddess ; and (2) a Roman Cameo.

happen to have any relatives or friends in distant lands write to them and ask for something quaint of native manufacture. Some of the most interesting things in my own museum have come from friends in far-off countries. From South Africa can be obtained bead ornaments which are worn by both men and women, whilst one of my friends from India presented me with a number of small bronze gods, Fig. 7 —Vishnu, Brahma, &c. Yet another tourist around the world sent me several most ingenious mechanical toys which he procured in Japan, in which, by turning a small handle, or winding up a cylinder, the strangest possible figures appear and perform remarkable evolutions and acrobatic feats. From China I have received various beautiful carvings, whilst from various quarters I have obtained some of the most curious figures in coloured pottery, Fig. 8. I mention these items to show what very uncommon things may be obtained for a collection in an easy and inexpensive way.

From time to time various articles are issued as souvenirs of great events, and a selection of those can be the nucleus of a historical section. The commonest forms are the mug and goblet. On different occasions while out collecting I have bought for very small sums a number of mugs and goblets relating to our English history—one bears the portrait of Nelson, another that of John Wesley, whilst several Victorian mugs were made during her long reign. These bear her portrait or coat-of-arms, with an inscription giving an account of the

FIG. 8.—(1) Staffordshire and (2) Peruvian Pottery.

event which the article commemorates. Busts in pottery or metal are other forms taken by the historical souvenir. Our colleges of Oxford and Cambridge have characteristic souvenirs of distinction which are full of interest. As an example I possess a copy in China ware of the historic nose which formed for several centuries the knocker of Brazenose College, Oxford.

In connection with these historical souvenirs there are many models in miniature of famous buildings and structures which are of never-failing interest. You can obtain for a few pence excellent models of St. Paul's Cathedral, Westminster Abbey, Shakespeare's house, Anne Hathaway's cottage, Robert Burns's birthplace, Cleopatra's Needle, old Irish crosses, the Tower Bridge, Nelson's Column, and many other similar objects of local or foreign interest. It would be necessary, of course, to look up the histories of all these things and write out a brief account to accompany the specimens.

THE BOTANICAL SECTION

Botany also deserves a corner in your museum. Some naturalists devote their researches to trees, and among their treasures are splendid collections of woods. These can be obtained from various wood-yards, and each specimen should be about six inches square and half an inch thick. The wood must be smoothly planed, and will then show clearly the colour and texture of the particular tree from which it was taken. Sandalwood, teak, spruce, oak, fir, and a great number of woods from trees that grow in all parts of the world can be obtained and brought together, a short description of the tree and its characteristics being appended to each specimen.

But it is easy to go beyond this and have specimens of an enormous number of plants and flowers preserved in your museum. Any garden will furnish many beautiful examples. Cut off the single leaves of the oak, chestnut, maple, plane, and other trees, place them between sheets of blotting-paper, and press them until they are perfectly dry. This can be done with all the flowers growing in the garden or in the open fields, and, indeed, the herbarium described in Chapter XLII. will be a useful adjunct to the museum.

MECHANICAL EXHIBITS

Even if possessed of but slight skill in mechanics yourself, a corner devoted to model mechanical inventions will have great fascination for many of your visitors. Nowadays small working models of many ingenious contrivances are obtainable at moderate cost. Aeroplanes, locomotives, steam dredgers, horizontal engines, boilers, printing machines, telegraph and telephone instruments, are a few of those now on the market. Some of them can be obtained for only a few pence, although a highly finished and complicated engine costs a large sum. Numbers of cheaper models are available, and although simple in construction they afford unbounded delight if the ingenious way in which they work be properly explained. A visit should be paid to the South Kensington Patent Museum—that marvellous storehouse of inventive genius which the greatest mechanicians of the day constantly consult. There such inventions as the miners' lamp can be traced from the earliest stages up to the latest patterns, whilst miniatures of the greatest engineering triumphs are open to inspection. Many a good hint can be gleaned in this way for the home museum.

OLD PRINTS

A museum that is to give pleasure both to yourself and friends should embrace objects to suit all tastes. The British Museum—a worthy model for the amateur—has its print room, and there is no reason why you should not have a section of this description. Make a large portfolio about two feet square in which the prints can be kept flat. It will be better to devote your attention to historical subjects at first. At different bookstalls and picture-dealers' shops you can always meet with hundreds of small engravings of notable places and persons, obtainable sometimes for a single penny.

Even from an architectural point of view these prints are worth keeping. Quaint bits of our older cities, especially of London, are daily becoming rarer and more valuable, whilst pictures of cathedrals and palaces in Europe are always interesting to have.

In addition to these are the steel engravings of worthies of all countries, men and women who have made history, the kings and queens of literature and art, great warriors and famous statesmen. A short visit to the barrows and stalls which are to be found in most towns on market day will often repay the collector handsomely.

MISCELLANEOUS CURIOS

As you go about collecting for your museum you will meet many things, domestic and personal, which are well worth procuring. Pipes, Fig. 9, may be cited as examples. It is astonishing what a number of pipes of various patterns and designs are in existence, from the handsome German and Swiss pipes with long curved wooden stems and bowls made of beautiful pictured china, to the Turkish hookahs and the quaintly ornamented pipes used by Indian tribesmen—from the long Cavalier pipes to the modern clays adorned with the heads of well-known national heroes.

When the news has got abroad that a museum has been started, friends usually empty their curio drawers and send a varied assortment of old coins, tokens, silhouettes, and other miscellanies which are all welcome to the museum maker. Nothing really interesting or out of the way should be refused, although when it comes to buying, a considerable amount of discretion which is, alas, only to be acquired by experience, must be exercised. It must never be forgotten that antiquities bought on the spot are not invariably antique. Hundreds of scarabs and little figures sold by the natives on historic sites in

Egypt have first seen the light in some of our Midland manufacturing towns, whilst the supply of genuine Roman bronzes keeps many an English factory busy.

There is, however, no golden rule whereby the genuineness of an antique can be tested, and therefore, until experience has taught the collector to discriminate between what is worth and what is not worth buying, he had better go slowly and refer to books whenever in a quandary.

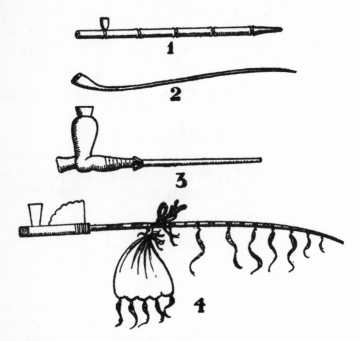

FIG. 9.—(1) A Chinese Pipe ; (2) A Cavalier Pipe ; (3) A South Sea Pipe ;
(4) A Patagonian Pipe.

PART IV

OUTDOOR HOBBIES

CHAPTER XLIV

SCOUTING

THE IDEAL OUTDOOR HOBBY

SCOUTING may be said to combine in itself every hobby that the ordinary healthy out-of-doors boy would be likely to pursue. Whether it be upon the asphalt pavements of a large town, or amidst the moving shadows of the pine woods, the Scout can carry on his duty with equal skill and application. Scout-craft embraces so many branches of knowledge, that in whatever direction a boy's fancies may lie, he will have ample opportunity of developing his particular bent, being able to bring to his assistance all those other qualities of observation and diligence which the Scout training teaches.

How to Become a Boy Scout

Any boy over ten years of age can become a Scout, and although some patrols show little anxiety for such young recruits, the best Scouts are those whose training was begun at an early age.

The first step to take is to make an application to the secretary or Scoutmaster of some local patrol, showing him the written authority of your parents consenting to your becoming enrolled. The person to whom you have applied will introduce you as a "tenderfoot" to some experienced Scout, who will tell you exactly what you must know before you can be admitted into a patrol.

Before the Scout's Oath can be taken, he must know—

(1) The Scout's laws, signs and salutes.

(2) What the Union Jack means, and how it should be flown.

(3) How to tie four out of the following knots: Reef, sheet bend, clove hitch, bowline, middleman's, fisherman's, sheepshank.

Signs and Salutes

The half salute is made by raising the hand as high as the shoulder, with the palm turned outwards.

The secret sign, usually given at the same time as the salute, is made by holding the hand with the palm to the front, the thumb resting on the tip of the little finger, which is bent down as in Fig. 1.

FIG. 1.—Half Salute and Secret Sign.   FIG. 2.—The Full Salute.

The full salute is made by raising the hand to the forehead, Fig. 2, and is used to all superior officers, and at the hoisting of the colours.

THE UNIQN JACK

The Union Jack is a combination of the three crosses, of St. George, St. Andrew, and St. Patrick. It should always be flown as seen in

FIG. 3.—The Union Jack.

Fig. 3, with the broad white band on the diagonal arms in the left-hand corner uppermost.

KNOTS

The "tenderfoot" must be able to make any four of the knots shown in Figs. 4 and 5, namely:—

A, The Reef Knot.

B, Sheet Bend.

C, Clove hitch.

D. Bowline.

E, Middleman's Knot.

F, Fisherman's Knot.

G, ⎫
GA,⎭ Sheepshank.

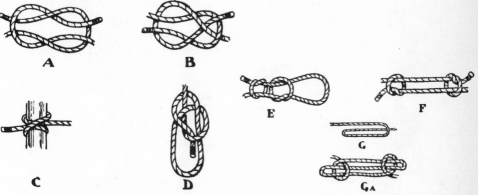

FIG. 4.—Knots which a Scout must know.   FIG. 5.—Some more Knots.

THE SCOUT'S OATH

After a month's service as a "tenderfoot," the time comes for taking the Scout's Oath, which binds you, on your honour, to carry out the following pledges :—

To do your duty to God and the King.

To help other people at all times.

To obey the Scout Law.

When these promises have been solemnly made in the presence of the troop, you will be formally enrolled as a Scout and drafted to one of the patrols.

UNIFORMS

The complete uniform of a Scout, shown in Fig. 6, is composed of the following items :—

Hat.—Flat brim and khaki-coloured, with a chin-strap and strap round the crown.

Shirt.—Blue, khaki, grey, or green, with two buttoned patch pockets and shoulder-straps.

Knickers.—Blue or khaki. They should only reach to just above the knees.

Neckerchief.—This must be of the colour belonging to the troop. The neckerchief is worn loosely knotted at the throat.

Belt.—This should be of brown leather, and may carry swivels, a pouch, and an axe. The metal part must be coloured in some dull tint.

Stockings.—Khaki or any dark colour. They may have coloured tops, and should be worn turned down below the knee.

Shoes and Boots.—Brown or black leather.

Haversacks.—Worn over the back like a satchel.

Shoulder Knots.—These must be 6 in. in length.

Whistle and Knife.—Carried on lanyards.

THE SCOUT LAW

The Scout Law sums up in a few words all that a Scout must do, and points out the clear path of his duty.

A Scout's honour is always to be trusted; he must never be untruthful or evade the performance of his duty.

FIG. 6.—A Scout's Uniform.

A Scout is loyal to his King and country; he is loyal not only to his officers, but to his parents and friends, never talking about them behind their backs, always sticking up for them through thick and thin, and serving them to the utmost of his power.

The Scout is a friend to every one, rich or poor, man or woman. One most important part of his duty is to do a good turn every day. He must be polite to people of all classes, neither sneering at those who have not had his advantages of education nor being envious of others who have had better chances in life than himself.

A Scout is kind to all animals, for, if he helps men and women who should be able to take care of themselves, how much kinder should he be to dumb creatures!

A Scout always obeys orders, whether from his parents or from his patrol leader, and he does this because he knows that a boy who will not obey can never become a man to command.

A Scout is always cheerful, no matter how hard his task may be, no matter how dull a portion of the daily routine falls to his lot. He never shows impatience in the most exasperating circumstances, but smiles and whistles until better times come.

A Scout is always thrifty, not spending money on silly things, but using all that he has sparingly and sensibly.

Such are the Scout laws, and it is not difficult to see that they are rules which every honest boy will gladly take to guide him through life. There is nothing weak or "goody" about them, they are just common-sense, plain maxims, such as were observed by our forefathers, and helped to make them the men whom the world learned to reverence.

THE SCOUT'S GOOD TURN

One of the most exacting of a Scout's duties is to do a good turn to somebody once a day at least, and to ensure his not forgetting this, he should make a knot in his tie or handkerchief and keep it there until the good turn has been done.

A good turn need be but a small thing, a little deed of charity, helping a child across the road, or giving up a seat in the tram-car to an older person. But until he has done this, the Scout's duty for the day is unfulfilled.

PATROLS

A Scout Patrol consists of a number of Scouts who form a band and have their own colours, call, and badge. Each patrol is named after some bird or beast, and naturally the patrol call is some

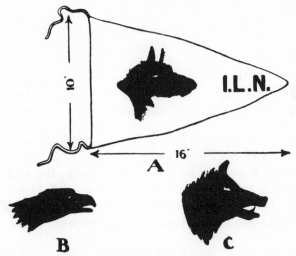

FIG. 7.—A few Patrol Badges.

attempt at an imitation of this creature's cry. The patrol badges shown in Fig. 7 will serve to illustrate how this is put into practice :—

A, The Wolf. The call is "How-ooooo" and resembles the howl of that beast. The colours are yellow and black.

B, The Eagle. The call is "Kreeeeee" uttered very shrilly. The colours for the patrol are green and black.

C, The Wild Boar. The call is "Broof-broof" uttered in a piggish grunt. The colours are grey and pink.

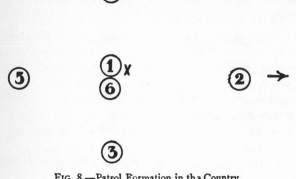

FIG. 8.—Patrol Formation in the Country.

When working across country a patrol goes in the open order depicted in Fig. 8, but when passing down a street or along a country road, the formation is similar to that shown in Fig. 9. It will be noticed that in each of these formations the patrol leader, marked (x), occupies a position in the centre of his corps.

Each patrol leader has a corporal to assist in the management

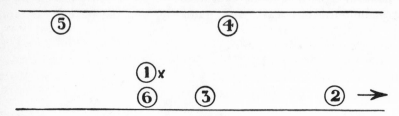

FIG. 9.—Patrol Formation on a Road.

and training of his men. The corporal is distinguished by a piece of white braid above his left elbow.

Three or more patrols form a Troop under the command of a Scoutmaster, who has charge of all the Scouts in his town or district. The Scoutmaster has the training of his men and superintends all the movements of the patrols under his command.

WOODCRAFT

By woodcraft Scouts do not mean any particular knowledge of botany, although a Scout should certainly make himself acquainted with the practical side of that science, but it means the power of closely observing everything he may meet in the course of a walk, whether through town or country. The Scout learns to track animals by their footprints, to watch Nature in her endless guises, to take stock of the clothing of the people he meets, to note their faces, and to read the stories that are so often written thereon.

TRACKING

Tracking is one of the most interesting and important branches of Scouting. But, like everything else, it must be done methodically, proper charts of tracks being constructed and exact measurements taken where human footprints are concerned.

The method of measuring a man's footprint is shown in Fig. 10, which represents the track made by a hob-nailed boot. The width of the broadest part must be carefully noted, as also the length from toe to heel. Missing nails can be indicated by an X. The length of the stride, measuring from the toe of one foot to the heel of the other, as well as the exact length

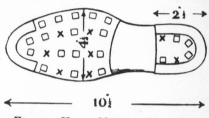

FIG. 10.—How to Measure a Boot-print.

of the heel, must be carefully noted, as these form very accurate means of identification.

In dealing with the prints of bare feet, which at first glance appear to resemble one another amazingly, a line should be drawn from the tip of the big toe to the tip of the little toe, and the relative positions of the other toes carefully noted. It will be found on comparison that no two tracks are exactly alike in this respect.

The pace at which a horse has traversed the ground can always be

FIG. 11.—The Hoof-prints of a Walking Horse.

ascertained by a careful study of his hoof-prints. In Fig. 11 are depicted the tracks left by a walking horse. You will notice that the off hind and the off fore-prints are quite close together, whilst the

FIG. 12.—Tracks of a Trotting Horse.

distance between the off hind-hoof and the near fore-hoof is about two feet eight inches. The distance is greater when the horse has been trotting, as in Fig. 12. The pace is further indicated by the splays of dust or mud in front of each hoof-print.

A cantering horse leaves tracks similar to those shown in Fig. 13, whilst a galloping horse makes the very distinctive trail shown in

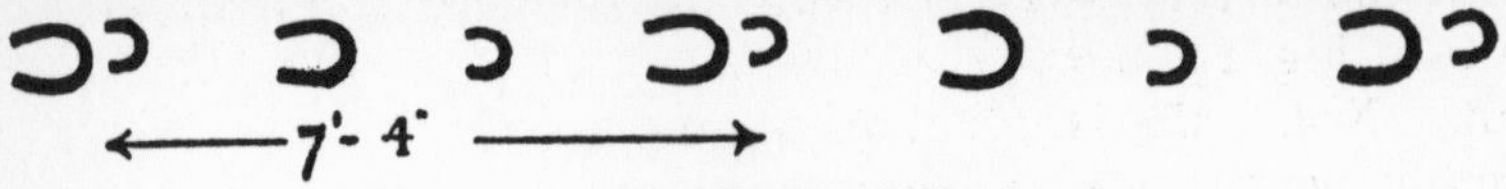

←——7'-4"——→

FIG. 13.—A cantering Horse's Hoof-marks.

Fig. 14 (O. F. and O. H., &c., meaning Off fore and Off hind, &c.). It will be noticed that the distances are very irregular, whilst the same splay of dust or mud is made as when the horse trots.

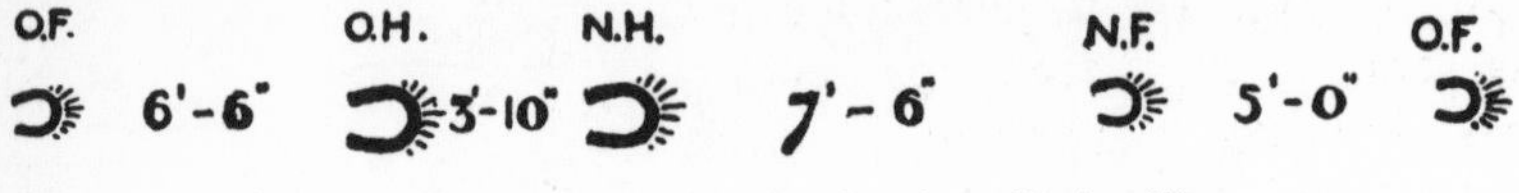

O.F. O.H. N.H.   N.F.   O.F.

6'-6" 3'-10" 7'-6"   5'-0"

FIG. 14.—The unmistakable Tracks of a galloping Horse.

NIGHT SCOUTING

In the darkness, when his sense of sight can be of less use, a Scout must employ all his other faculties to the best of his power, and naturally the sense of hearing becomes of first importance. It is a well-known fact that the earth is one of the best conductors of sound, and the thud of a horse's hoofs may often be heard very far away by placing the ear to the ground and listening to the vibration of the hoofs upon the distant road. A penknife with both blades opened should be stuck into the earth, the free blade being held between the teeth. The quivering steel, intensifying every vibration of the ground, will render the slightest noises distinctly audible.

SIGNALLING

Every Scout must know how to signal, and he should be very proficient in all the different types of signals that he may possibly have occasion to use.

Smoke and Flare Signals.—When green leaves are heaped upon a fire, dense volumes of smoke are formed which, on a fairly quiet day, form an excellent means of signalling. A wet blanket should be held over the smouldering leaves, and only removed in order to allow puffs of smoke to escape, the number and regularity of the puffs constituting the code. Some of the most important messages are—

Three big puffs in succession : GO ON, ADVANCE.

A number of small puffs : RALLY—COME HERE.

Alternate small and big puffs : DANGER.

At night this code can be applied to flares, a roaring fire being made and a blanket held before it, which is only removed to make a long or short flare as required.

The Morse Code.—A knowledge of the Morse dot-and-dash code, shown in Fig. 15, is essential to every Scout. Not only is practically all telegraph work done with this code, but it forms the basis of most of the other systems of signalling, whether flashlight or semaphore.

The semaphore signalling code shown in Fig. 16 is performed by arms, and is invaluable for talking across country. The first seven letters, it will be noticed, are done

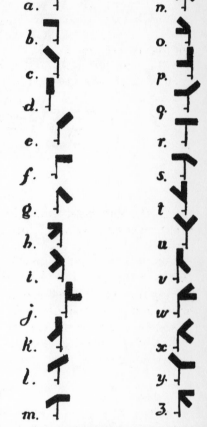

A	· —	N	— ·
B	— · · ·	O	— — —
C	— · — ·	P	· — — ·
D	— · ·	Q	— — · —
E	·	R	· — ·
F	· · — ·	S	· · ·
G	— — ·	T	—
H	· · · ·	U	· · —
I	· ·	V	· · · —
J	· — — —	W	· — —
K	— · —	X	— · · —
L	· — · ·	Y	— · — —
M	— —	Z	— — · ·

FIG. 15.—The Morse Code.   FIG. 16.—Semaphore Signal Code.

with one arm only, whilst the remainder require the use of both arms, turned often to one side of the upright.

PATROL LEADER'S WHISTLES

The patrol leader signals to his corps with his whistle, the most important signals being:—

One long blast: SILENCE—ALERT.   EXPECT SIGNAL.
A number of long low blasts: EXTEND—SCATTER.
A series of short blasts: RALLY—COME TOGETHER.

HUT-BUILDING

Where a camp is pitched for any length of time, it is often as well to build huts for bivouac and night shelter. The simplest hut

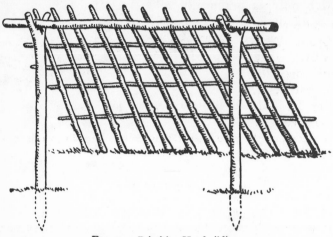

FIG. 17.—Primitive Hut-building.

to make is shown in Fig. 17. Two forks of wood are driven deep into the ground, and a cross-bar stretched between them as a ridge pole against which other bars may be leaned as seen in the diagram.

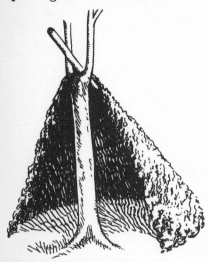

FIG. 18.—A temporary Shelter.

This hut can be thatched with grass or bracken, and should prove comfortable and afford a sound shelter.

Another easily made hut is shown in Fig. 18, and consists of nothing but a branch placed against the fork in a tree and heaped over with bracken or branches. This shelter is very easily blown down and disturbed, however, and a good Scout will only erect such a hut when he is pressed for time or is not remaining long enough in the same spot to warrant the trouble of building a more substantial shelter.

If the heat of the sun makes the interior of a hut too warm for comfort, a layer of blankets placed upon the roof will serve to keep the heat out, and obviate the stifling atmosphere engendered by the confined space.

The Camp Bed

The best way to make a proper camp bed is illustrated in Fig. 19. Take a couple of poles 7 ft. long and two other poles 3 ft. long, and lay them on the ground in the form of a parallelogram. Then drive in stakes 2 ft. long at each corner to keep the poles in place. The interior of this space can be filled with

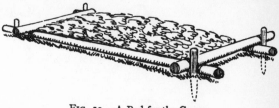

FIG. 19.—A Bed for the Camp.

fir branches, hay, or bracken as depicted in the figure, and covered with blankets.

Camping Out

One of the most prominent features in Scouting is camping out, and it is here that the Scout's general handiness comes to the fore. The camp may either consist of tents or huts, and in either case only the most essential articles must be included in the outfit. Apart from clothing, which should contain a change of garments, sleeping-suit, and an extra pair of boots, the following articles will be essential :—

Corkscrew.

Scissors.

Tin-opener.

Axe (for chopping wood).

Mallet (for driving in tent-pegs).

Spade.

Towels.

Housewife (including needles, thread, buttons, &c.).

One of the secrets of keeping warm when sleeping in the open is to make sure that there are as many blankets under you as there are covering you.

The Camp Fire

Before lighting a camp fire, clear away all heather and bracken that might accidentally be set alight. Great damage is often caused by the bushes around catching fire, and the utmost caution must be exercised to prevent this happening.

Begin laying the fire with some dry bark, placing upon this a few dry twigs or dead branches. A layer of pine needles will help the fire to blaze up, and, when it burns brightly, one or two logs can be added.

A fire laid in the manner shown in Fig. 20 will last with very

little attention for a long time. Large logs are placed with their ends together, and as these ends are consumed, the logs must be thrust in towards the centre of the fire, thus presenting a fresh piece of wood to the flames.

FIG. 20.—A Camp Fire.

KEEPING THE CLOTHES DRY

It is very important after a day in the rain to get the clothes dry as soon as possible.   When camp is reached, build a little tripod over a red ash fire and hang the clothes upon it, wrapping yourself in a blanket the meanwhile if you do not possess a change of garments in camp.

CAMP COOKING

It is quite a mistaken idea that camping means "roughing" in the matter of meals.   Good, wholesome and tasty food may be prepared in a camp as well as in a kitchen.

Water can be boiled in the billy which every Scout should take with him to camp, and, unless it be otherwise used, the vegetables or even meat can be cooked in the same utensil.

Meat may be broiled by sticking it on a sharp point over a good fire, or it may be wrapped in damp paper and thrust into the embers of a wood fire.   Some Scouts wrap the meat or birds they intend for dinner in a coating of clay, and put the lump thus formed into the fire.   When thoroughly baked, the clay will break off and reveal a tasty piece of roast within.

Boil the billy either upon logs or, better still, upon a triangle of three green poles tied into a tripod.

HUNTER'S STEW

A good standing dish for a camp is hunter's stew, which is made thus :—Cut the meat into small squares about an inch and a half in size, chop up any kind of vegetable, and place the pieces in the billy, which must then be half-filled with clean water.   Rub the meat in flour, salt, and pepper, and then place the pieces in the billy, which must be stood in the embers and allowed to simmer for about an hour and a quarter.

The camp way of making bread is not one that would commend

itself to many bakers, yet very good bannocks or buns can be made, and no Scout is an epicure.

The first thing to be done is to spread a coat or piece of cloth on the ground, and in the centre make a pile of flour, scooping out a portion into which the water may be poured. A little salt must now be added and the whole mess kneaded and rolled into a lump of dough. Small buns or loaves should then be shaped out of the dough, placed on a gridiron, and allowed to bake.

PATH-FINDING

It need scarcely be said that a Scout should never lose his way, even in entirely new country. Indeed, there is no reason why any person need get lost if he keep a good look-out and carefully note each landmark as it is passed.

When starting out, always notice which way the wind is blowing, as this will generally prove of use in ascertaining the direction in which home lies. All landmarks, such as church spires, chimneys, or other prominent features, should be carefully noted.

It is absolutely necessary that a Scout should not only know the points of the compass, but that he should be able to find the north by means of the sun or stars. Accordingly the following points should be memorised, as they will be found of great service :—

At six o'clock the sun is due east.

At nine o'clock it is south-east.

At noon it is due south.

At three o'clock it is south-west.

At six in the evening it is due west.

To find the south by means of the sun, the following method must be employed. Place your watch, face uppermost, with the hour hand pointing to the sun, and measure half-way between the hand and the figure XII. The point thus obtained will be due south. At night the north can be easily discovered by the stars. The pointers of the Great Bear, shown in Fig. 21, a constellation always visible in the northern

FIG. 21.—How to find the Pole Star.

hemisphere, are in a direct line with the Pole or North Star, which itself is the last star in the tail of the Little Bear. As the Pole Star lies due north, when once it has been found, the points of the compass can be easily and accurately ascertained.

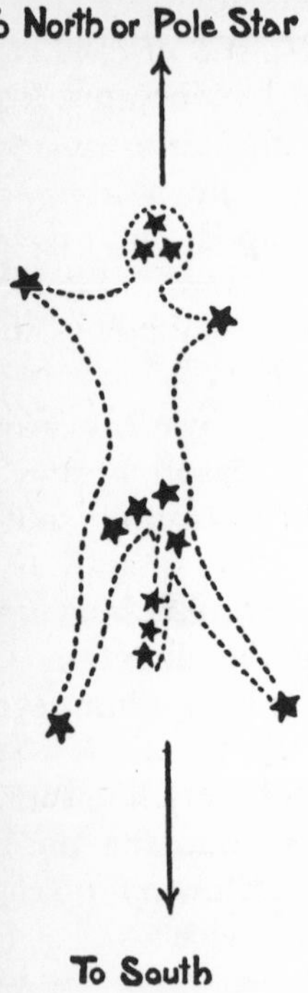

To North or Pole Star

The constellation called Orion, shown in Fig. 22, is another guide to the north. A line drawn through the centre star of the head and the centre star of the belt points due north and south as depicted in the illustration.

FIRST AID

One of the most important things to know in connection with accidents is the proper way to carry an insensible person. The patient should be laid on his face, then propped into a kneeling posture whilst you crawl under in such a manner that his stomach rests upon your right shoulder. Then pass your right arm between his legs and grip his right thigh, draw his right hand under your left arm, and rise carefully, as shown in Fig. 23.

To South

FIG. 22.—The Constellation of Orion.

Many a person who has been dragged from the water while drowning has subsequently expired through the ignorance of those who saved him, as animation must be restored in a methodical and drastic manner.

Lay the patient on his stomach, the arms extended and the face slightly to one side. Then kneel by him, or squat across his body, and place the hands in the small of his back — the thumbs together and the fingers reaching to his lowest ribs.

Now bend forward and press the patient steadily against the ground, thus causing an even pressure

FIG. 23.—How to carry an Insensible Person.

against his stomach, and expelling the air from his chest. Count three very slowly, and swing back, relieving the pressure, but still retaining the grip on his body. These movements should be continued until the patient starts breathing in a natural manner, when his wet clothes can be removed and hot bottles or warm flannels placed between his legs and beneath the armpits. Under this comfortable warmth he will fall into a gentle sleep.

Broken limbs, although not in themselves of any very great danger, are liable to bring about serious complications if they are not dealt with properly from the outset. As soon as there is the least sign of a limb being broken, it must be straightened out and bound to something stiff, such as a wooden baton, or even a tightly rolled newspaper. This piece of wood or paper is called a splint, and should be long enough to project beyond the joint above and below the break. If possible a splint should be placed each side of the bone and the limb bound firmly from end to end with strips of linen or handkerchiefs. Medical aid should then be sought immediately.

A broken or wounded arm should be placed in a sling. Make a large three-cornered bandage, the two sides of which should measure at least a yard each. Tie the two ends together and hang the bandage round the neck, resting the arm in the sling thus made. Bring the third point of the bandage round the elbow and pin it in place as shown in the figure.

It is through the kindness of Messrs. C. Arthur Pearson, Ltd., the proprietors of the official organ of the Boy Scouts, that I have been able to give these particulars concerning the organisation of the movement.

CHAPTER XLV

SIMPLE SURVEYING

A HOBBY FOR SCOUTS

"Boys will be boys." That truism is established to-day as ever, and the sooner idealists recognise its endurance, the better for their reflections. Youth will play kick-can, throw stones at flower-pots as improvised targets, or, with the aid of bull's-eye lanterns, convert the city pavements to railway tracks, and only, if such tricks can in any way be organised, will the occurrence of mishaps be minimised. To this end, seemingly, the Boy Scout movement is primarily valuable, inasmuch as its parties of quasi-pioneers find wholesome recreation in vaulting hedges, practising woodcraft, and spying out the land. Now the subsequent paragraphs purpose to show that it is not a league step from the last pursuit to simple surveying, and a few explanations will be given such as, it is hoped, scouts and, equally, those readers who favour more solitary rambles may follow with interest.

FIG. 1.—Stand for Theodolite.

By simple surveying is meant essentially the determination of heights and distances which cannot be actually tape-measured. One crude instrument—it would be presumption to call it a theodolite—is necessary for the purpose, but this can be readily made at home, with slight expense.

A HOME-MADE THEODOLITE

A broomstick is whittled down at one end to a tapering point and toughened by placing in the embers of a dying fire. At the other end two holes, AB, are bored, $\frac{1}{2}$ in. diameter—either with brace and bit or red-hot poker—as shown in Fig. 1. The next business is to buy or make a 9-in. length of cardboard tube about $\frac{3}{4}$ in.

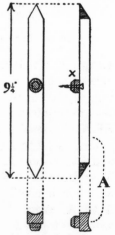

FIG. 2.—Wooden Cradle and Boss.

diameter (made by pasting brown paper round a $\frac{3}{4}$ in. wood rod and drawing off when dry) and glue it in position

366

on a wooden support of the design shown in Fig. 2. The circular boss "*x*" is a disc of wood—*e.g.* a draughtsman cut to a cone shape on one side and then glued in place.

It must be noticed that the bar of wood is pointed evenly at both ends and that its extreme length is 9¼ in.—somewhat above that of the cardboard tube—to form a cradle for which, moreover, it is grooved on the side opposite to the wooden boss. Before the tube is glued in the groove, A, Fig. 2, a 2-in. wood screw is driven through the bar at the centre of the wood boss, with its head countersunk from the grooved side—so that it may not interfere with the snug repose of the tube. If the screw is wetted, it will rust in position. Three or four washers, or a couple of glass beads, such as will thread easily on this

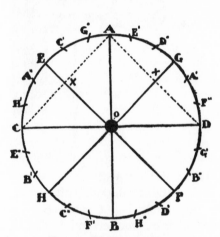

FIG. 3.—Dividing the Circle.

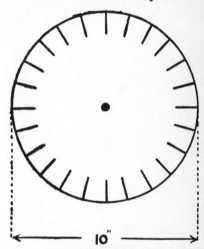

FIG. 4.—Preparation of Disc.

screw, are needed, and also a 10-in. circle of stiff Bristol board, with hole of similar size at its exact centre. This is divided up as shown in Fig. 3, the plan adopted being to pencil AB, CD, straight through O—the centre of the disc—at right angles to one another; then EF, GH—also at right angles and drawn so that they divide the lines joining AC and AD at their middle points (*x*). In other words, EF and GH halve the right angles which AB, CD, make with each other. Now from each A, G, D, F, &c., in turn, the points, A', A'', G', G'', &c., are marked on the circle's edge at distances of 5 in.; *i.e.* from A to A', A to A'', G to G', G to G'', &c., measure exactly 5 inches, which is the radius of the cardboard circle. In this way—provided the spacing has been carefully done—the disc will be divided into twenty-four equal parts, and the lines AB, EF, DC, GH, &c., may be ruled in ink—preferably not right across the disc, but each drawn from the circumference inwards for a distance of 2 in., Fig. 4.

The equal spaces so obtained are again divided by eye judgment into three equal parts, and the new lines ruled about $\frac{1}{2}$ in. long, whilst the divisions are numbered as in Fig. 5. The pencil spacing marks

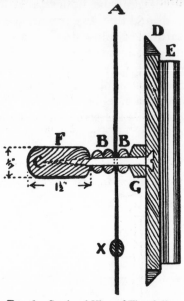

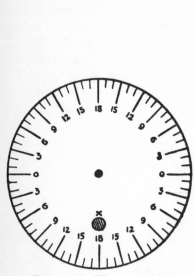

FIG. 5.—The Disc completed.

FIG. 6.—Sectional View of Theodolite.

being rubbed out, the card disc A is assembled with the beads or washers BB upon the screw C attached to the cardboard tube cradle D and E, the whole being screwed to a $1\frac{1}{2}$ in. length of $\frac{1}{2}$ in. wooden rod F, Fig. 6. By means of the last arrangement, G being the wooden boss, the paraphernalia can be mounted on either of the holes A and B, Fig. 1, in the broomstick, the appearances being respectively those of Figs. 7 and 8. One last refinement is essential, viz. the

FIG. 7.—The Disc mounted horizontally.

FIG. 8.—The Disc in a perpendicular Position.

riveting of a leaden "bob" through the card disc in the position "x," Figs. 5 and 6, heavy enough to cause it always to set with the weight downwards when in a vertical position.

The description of this instrument thus ends. Prolonged though it may seem, the construction and character are proportionately simple, and its usage not a whit abstruse.

MEASURING HEIGHTS

By reference to Fig. 9, it will be clear that if a certain observer, A, first regards a tree, TB, 50 feet high, and then a chimney stack, SC,

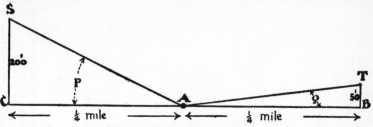

FIG. 9.—Study of Relative Angles.

200 feet high, both a quarter of a mile distant, the angles P and Q must differ in some way according to the object's height.

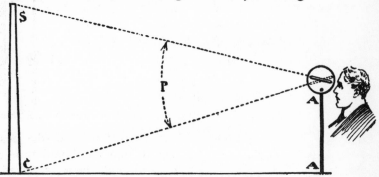

FIG. 10.—The Theodolite in Use.

Now suppose the reader is the observer, and, having fitted the cardboard disc arrangement into the hole B, Fig. 1, in the broomstick, he sets up the latter, AA, Fig. 10, vertically at a known distance from a certain chimney. The tube points towards this, and the observer peering through, turns it about until the base of the chimney is visible. The position which the tube's cradle indicates on the card—*i.e.* the numbers of the lines pointed to—is noted, and the tube is then carefully turned upwards until the stack's summit is observed. The card disc, owing to its plumb bob weight, should now revolve and the tube's new position can be noted. Fig. 10 illustrates these operations, and Fig. 11

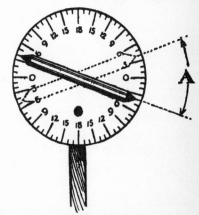

FIG. 11 —Two Readings on Disc.

represents the two readings noted on the disc, their difference being eight divisions, A, Fig. 11.

Now the angle through which the tube has to revolve from its position of viewing the chimney's base to that of seeing the summit, is the angle P, Fig. 10, and in the table below is given the number corresponding to any particular angle which must be used to multiply the distance AC in order to know the height of the chimney. For example, suppose the distance from the observer to the chimney (AC) = 100 paces ; and that the angle P is 8 units, upon referring to the table it is found that 100 paces has to be multiplied by 84 and divided by 100.

$$\frac{84 \times 100}{100} = \frac{8400}{100} = 84 \text{ paces.}$$

The chimney therefore—reckoning $2\frac{1}{2}$ feet to a pace—is roughly (84 by $2\frac{1}{2}$) 200 feet high.

TABLE OF ANGLES AND FACTORS

Angle	Multiply AC by	and divide by
1 unit	9	100
2	18	,,
3	27	,,
4	36	,,
5	47	,,
6	58	,,
7	70	,,
8	84	,,
9	100 (AC is the same size as object)	,,
10	12	10
11	14	,,
12	17	,,
13	21	,,
14	27	,,
15	37	,,
16	57	,,
17	11	,,
18	If this angle were measured, the observer would be standing at the base of the object.	

TO DETERMINE THE BREADTH OF A RIVER

A similar principle to that just detailed is employed in determining any inaccessible distance, *e.g.* the breadth of a river. Suppose its banks are represented in Fig. 12 by the wavy lines AB, CD, on the latter of which the observer O is situated, and that he wishes to know the approximate distance to the other bank. He must first select a certain landmark, *e.g.* tree, house, or telegraph pole, P, on that further bank, and then walk to a place on his own side as directly opposite as can be judged, this position being distinctly marked, *e.g.* by a walking-stick placed in the ground.   Then let him continue along the river

bank as far as he can keep the walking-stick and landmark in view, taking note of the paces taken, and there, R, erect the broomstick, the cardboard disc being fixed in the hole A, Fig. 1, and, therefore, horizontal.   By keeping this in one position and sighting through the cardboard tube first the walking-stick

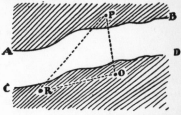

FIG. 12.—Measuring Width of a River.

and then the landmark, the angle PRO, Fig. 12, can be measured.

Suppose it happens to be 9 units, then, from the table given earlier, it is seen that the width of the river, PO, is the same as the distance OR, which has been walked, and the length of which in paces is known, *e.g.* 200 = 500 feet roughly.   Similarly, if the angle were 6 units, the distance, OR, would have to be multiplied by 58 and divided by 100 to give the river's width.

$$\frac{500 \times 58}{100} = 290 \text{ feet.}$$

CHAPTER XLVI

WALKING

PLEASURES OF THE ROAD

WALKING bears the same relation to cycling as that pastime does to its sister, or rather daughter, pursuit, motor cycling. For the wheelman, tramping lacks attraction, inasmuch as there exists no exhilaration of speed, and it is therefore pre-eminently a pleasure which needs cultivation. Nevertheless a walker's enjoyment is very real indeed and endures hardily, for it lingers long after the pleasure's actual existence.

The appreciable length of a journey depends but slightly upon its actual mileage. Strange though this may seem, the tale of the two pilgrim monks who had to undertake a penance with peas in their shoes and one of whom took the precaution to boil his first, will forcibly suggest that a journey is impressive rather according to the wealth of pains or pleasures accruing to it, than in relation to its length. So a five-mile stroll amid country lanes, noting old stocks and whipping-posts and similar relics of bygone times, or through city byways, with their notable meeting-houses and fragmentary remains of fortified walls and boundary stones, may impress the traveller as being far longer than a London to Edinburgh railroad spin.

However, this does not necessitate despising trains or bicycles. Potterers on the pneumatic-shod horse derive immense pleasure from their hobby, and—as more concerns the present notes—that vehicle and the railway may both be of inestimable service in annihilating the distance between the tramper and his fields of exploration. Ardent pedestrians will not easily forgo Saturday afternoons, be they ever so short, and very often excursion trains to some outlying place are available. Popular football matches and race meetings account for many such facilities, and, of course, there is no reason why one should not attend the particular attraction.

The pedestrian's garb boasts no distinctive features. Provided with the nether garments which our civilised state exacts, he need don little more than a shirt—a respectable cut by preference—in order to wear the clothes of a happy man. At all events, the sparsely and moderately clothed plodder will usually be more at ease than his fashionably attired brother, and the writer must confess to a preference for trousers tucked up at the bottoms, barge style, rather than for knickers and tight-fitting hose. Boots, of course, are indispensable, and stout, thick-shod ones at that—no weak-ankled shoes with ball-room soles, or the delusion that country roads and pathways are dancing-floors may be painfully dispelled.

STEP, STRIDE AND POSITION

Strange to say, very few people know how to walk well. The step, the stride and the position of a good walker are things that one rarely meets on the highroad, but nevertheless it is essential for any one who desires to make a good pedestrian to study with considerable care the proper form to be observed.

The correct attitude is very simply acquired :—Stand at attention, the shoulders thrown well back, the head up, and the arms extended by the side, Fig. 1.

Now take a stride forward with the right leg, the heel of the foot striking the ground first ; then another stride bringing the left foot into a direct line with the right, as shown in the tracks of the footprints, Fig. 2. The footprints illustrated in Fig. 3 are characteristic of the stride of an indifferent pedestrian.

There is no reason at all why a trained walker should make large strides. Step out naturally, and adopt whatever stride comes the easiest, whether it be short or long, for it must ever be remembered that, walking being a natural exercise, Nature will dictate the best means of performing it successfully.

FIG. 1.—Attention !

At all cost avoid the habit of stooping, shown in Fig. 4. Not

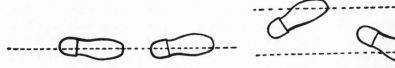

FIG. 2.—Footprints of a good Walker.   FIG. 3.—A bad Stride.

only is it bad for the figure, but it prevents that free action of the arms, so essential to a pedestrian. The right arm should be swung back with the motion of the left leg and, as the stride is completed, this arm should be brought back smartly across the chest as in Fig. 5, a similar action being performed by the left arm in unison with the right leg.

Woollen socks should always be worn when walking. Any other kind of sock will cause blisters and the pedestrian has no greater enemy to fear. When the blisters are very small they may frequently be cured by bathing the feet in hot water into which a little boracic

powder has been dissolved, but when they are large and close to the surface, the best plan is to pierce the skin with a needle and allow the water to escape. On no account should the skin of a blister be removed ; it will peel away in its own time, when a new skin has been formed beneath.

SUMMER HOLIDAY TOURS

When the walking hobby is to provide pleasure for the summer holidays, the question of clothing has to be more seriously approached. Every pound of baggage carried means additional insurance against enjoyment.

FIG. 4.—An ugly Stoop.

FIG. 5.—The proper Attitude for Walking.

Generally speaking, a complete change in the shape of a light flannel suit, slippers, and socks should be carried in case of rain. Possibly one will be out of shelter at the time of a deluge, and if this prove persistent, the best plan will be to " dig " in for the night at the first promising quarters, even if the latter part of the day be so spent. Mine host and hostess of country inns are nothing if not considerate towards travellers, and to sit reading, or writing letters home, clothed in dry garments, whilst the others are steaming before the fire, is a pleasure only second to that of tramping itself.

Another problem is that of securing changes, at intervals of a few days, of handkerchiefs, socks, and possibly shirts. The solution which is most feasible is that of mapping out the journey before starting and arranging for parcels to be forwarded at stated times either by railway or addressed " post restante " to particular towns *en route.*

Walking being at the same time the natural and the most reliable mode of locomotion, as much certainty as is possible among human beings may be felt as to reaching destinations at pre-arranged times. The way may seem long, as with the two Americans who, becoming anxious, inquired of a native the distance to their goal and were told two miles. Further along, however, the same answer was vouchsafed by a passer-by, and yet again after more plodding. Then the remark passed, "Waal! say, friend, I guess we're real glad to be holding our own." However, they were not quite discouraged, and, provided they kept their eyes on the sign-posts, they doubtless reached their destination in due course.

At any country town not only may the walker's kit be replenished, but soiled linen be "dropped"—*i.e.* packed, addressed, and forwarded home—together with packs of exposed film if he be a photographer.

TRAMPERS' HOBBIES

Two convenient hobbies for trampers are sketching—a kindred pastime to photography — and brass-rubbing at rural churches. Neither of these call for cumbrous outfits—a drawing-paper, block, and a pencil for the former, and some black lead with thin tough paper for the latter, being the only requisites.

The walking-stick is the pedestrian's sceptre, offering, as it does, support, and engendering a certain indefinable feeling of independence. With it he may probe fox-holes, mole-hills, and suspicious hollows in trees or hook down a branch from above for closer scrutiny. Not a less valuable accessory, though a rarer, is a pair of field-glasses. The old refrain held that—

> "With a pair of opera-glasses,
> One could see 'cross Hackney marshes
> If it wasn't for the houses in between!"

and the walker should not fear stepping out several miles of rising ground to a vantage point, whence there need be no "houses in between." Therefrom in all directions the pronounced colours of the immediate landscape merge tardily into the grey mist of the horizon. The devious path which has been trodden may be unravelled by locating here a church and there a mill, or may possibly follow for some way the course of a river, and in the middle distance the town's smoky mantle will be discerned, which cloaks so many struggles for a livelihood. On the other hand, divers routes will stretch ahead awaiting the glasses' scrutiny and their owner's choice. The bent of his interest will decide whether his road shall link up the lives of the human race, or, shunning them as evil blots, hug the hedgerows of the countryside.

CHAPTER XLVII

ASTRONOMY

THE STUDY OF THE HEAVENS

ONE of our great English writers has somewhere spoken of "the stately march of the spheres," and it would be hard to find a happier description of that marvellous system whereby the stars and planets pursue an endless course. As a hobby, the study of astronomy presents many fascinating points of interest, for, without entering into the details of all the mathematical laws which so nicely regulate the motions of celestial bodies, intense pleasure can be derived from the most cursory searching of the skies.

The use of a telescope greatly enhances the pleasure to be drawn from a study of the stars. The stronger the telescope the more fascinating is this pleasure ; although even a pair of good field-glasses suffices to reveal much that is hidden to the naked eye.

How to Make a Telescope

A simple astronomical telescope, strong enough for ordinary work, can be made at very little expense according to the following instructions.

The tube, which will be 39 in. long, is the first thing to be constructed, and should be made of brown paper, and prepared in the following manner. Obtain a length of wood 39 in. in length and 2 in. in diameter—a piece of curtain pole will serve the purpose admirably—and rub it over thoroughly with dry chalk. Now take a large sheet of dry brown paper, roll it tightly round the curtain pole, and glue the edges together. The tube thus made will need to be stiffened, and this can be done by soaking several sheets of brown paper, smearing them over liberally with glue and binding them closely around the roll, where they should be left to harden. When the wooden pole is removed the tube will be found strong and perfect.

A short piece of brass tubing, procurable at any ironmonger for a few pence, about 4 in. long and large enough to contain the larger lenses, of which more hereafter, must now be obtained.

The lenses can be procured from a reliable optician, and are three in number—a 2-in. "forty-inch" focus object-glass double convex, costing 1s. 6d.; a 1-in. and a 2-in. focus plano-convex lens costing 3s. 6d. or 4s. the pair.

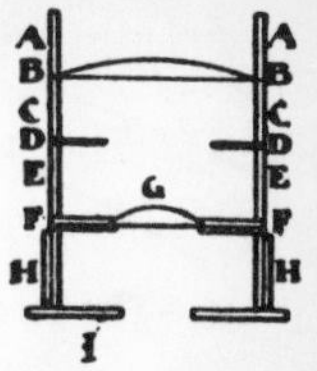

FIG. 1.—Section of
the Eye-piece.

A strip of cardboard, A, Fig. 1, must be cut of just sufficient length to be bent into a ring to fit the interior of the tube tightly at 2 in. from the end. From the other end lower the larger of the two lenses, B, technically known as the field-lens, rounded side outwards, on to the little cardboard shelf thus formed. Then make a similar strip of cardboard, C, ¾ in. in width, and push

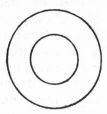

FIG. 2.—Cardboard Disc.

it down after the glass, thus serving to keep it firmly in place. A disc of cardboard, Fig. 2, containing a circular hole ½ in. in diameter, must then be sunk down upon this ledge, D, Fig. 1, and a 1-in strip of cardboard, E, should be inserted above this.

Other discs of cardboard, similar in design to Fig. 2, but so arranged as at F, Fig. 1, to hold the remaining lens, G, in position, will now require to be inserted and kept in place by a further piece of cardboard, H. Thus arranged, the lenses should be separated by exactly 1¾ in. from edge to edge. A cap, I, can be made by any tinman for 6d., and when in position will complete the lower end of the telescope.

FIG. 3.—The Telescope.

The object-glass should be fastened in position at the other end of the tubing by strips of cardboard in a similar fashion, the strips being glued in position securely.

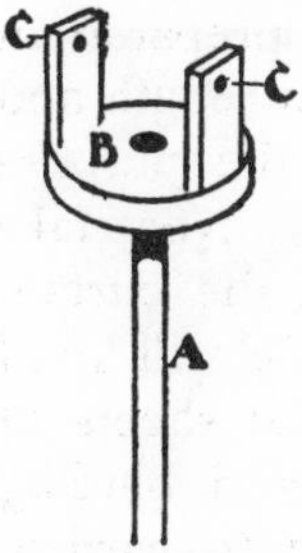

In order to make the eye-piece adjustable, a portion of the block upon which the tubing was rolled must be cut off, a hole large enough to contain the tube bored in it, and the wood glued into position in the paper tube. If the tubing fit too loosely, a lining of velvet or felt may be inserted.

FIG. 4.—Swivel
for the Cradle.

A couple of discs made of some hard wood will now be required, and should be cut 5 in. in diameter and 1 in. thick, each disc being bored in the centre with a hole 1 in. in diameter. To one of these discs hinge three wooden legs 4 ft. 6 in. long, as shown in Fig. 3.

In the hole bored through the centre of the other disc fasten a wooden rod 2 ft. 6 in. long, A, Fig. 4, gluing it flush into the top as at

B. The two uprights, C C, should be 4½ in. high, and must be dove-tailed or housed into the disc as shown in the diagram.

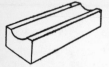

FIG. 5.—The Cradle.

A wooden cradle 8 in. long and 3½ in. wide, Fig. 5, should be cut and grooved, and into this the telescope can be glued, as shown in the finished diagram, Fig. 3. This cradle must be suspended between the two supports on the upper disc.

Nothing now remains but to take some measures to steady the telescope, so that when levelled at any definite object it will not move. In the first place, when the rod, A, Fig. 3, has been inserted through the circular hole in the disc B, to which legs are attached, a heavy leaden weight, C, should be fastened to the lower end, this serving to steady the whole stand. A piece of stout whipcord, fastened round the telescope at the eye-piece and twisted round a screw or nail driven into one of the legs, will secure the telescope at whatever angle it may be tilted, as shown in the diagram.

Thus equipped the student may begin a systematic study of the heavens.

THE SOLAR SYSTEM

The first interest in astronomy very naturally centres around those objects which can be easiest seen from the Earth. As our Earth forms a part of the solar system, the first investigations will be directed to the Sun and his planets.

THE SUN

The Sun, from which we get our life and light, is the centre around which the whole system of planets, of which this Earth is part, revolves. The Sun is not a dense body like the Earth, but is really a huge sphere of gaseous matter—so huge, indeed, that it is nearly 100,000 times greater in diameter than the Earth. With a very small telescope a great deal of interest can be obtained by looking at the Sun (it need scarcely be remarked that a darkened glass is essential for the purpose). Although at first sight nothing appears but a disc of a yellowish-white colour, closer examination will reveal the

FIG. 6.—A Sun-spot.

fact that there are several blackish spots or patches on its surface. These, which are usually called sun-spots, are supposed to be rifts in the gaseous envelope which corresponds, in a way, to the atmosphere of our Earth. A closer inspection of these spots reveals the fact that they are somewhat similar to that shown in Fig. 6. The black portion in the centre is known as the "nucleus"; the surrounding part is the "umbra," whilst the shaded fringe which surrounds the whole is called the "penumbra."

A slight idea of the exceeding strength of the Sun's rays can be gathered from the fact that our Earth receives only a 2300 millionth part of the whole. It has been said that 5563 wax candles concentrated at a distance of one foot from the observer (were such a thing possible), would equal the illuminating power of the Sun ; or again, 500,000 full moons shining at the same time would yet scarcely represent the enormous volume of light shed by the god of day.

THE PLANETS

Our Earth is only one, and a very small one, of the number of bodies which revolve around the Sun. Taken in the order of their nearness to that luminary, the planets are Mercury, Venus, the Earth,

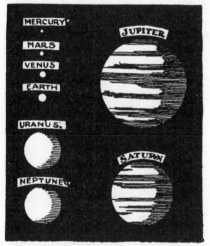

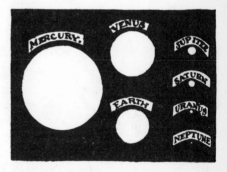

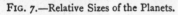

FIG. 7.—Relative Sizes of the Planets.   FIG. 8.—The Sun as seen from the Planets.

Mars, Jupiter, Saturn, Uranus and Neptune. In addition to these there is a belt of minor planets revolving between Mars and Jupiter.

The relative sizes of these planets are shown in Fig. 7, from which it will be noticed how very insignificant is our little Earth compared with such giants as Saturn or Jupiter. It need scarcely be said that to those planets situated near the centre of the system, the Sun appears larger than to those more remotely placed. This is very clearly shown in Fig. 8, which depicts the comparative size of the sun as seen from various planets.

Even to the naked eye most of the planets are easily distinguishable from the stars. Besides appearing very much brighter, they do not, as a rule, scintillate or twinkle, but shine steadily and clearly. Recourse must be had to some reliable almanac, such as Whitaker's, for information as to the exact locality in which to look for the various planets, whilst the same authority will give valuable hints as to such phenomena as eclipses of the satellites.

So far as we know, Mercury is the nearest planet to the Sun, and for this reason it can only be observed during the glow of sunrise or sunset. Many astronomers hold that Mercury only revolves on its axis once during its orbit. As the planet only takes 88 days to go round the Sun, this would mean that in the whole year there is only one night and one day.

Venus, like Mercury, is never seen far from the Sun. It has been almost conclusively ascertained that this planet possesses an atmosphere, and some observers have stated their conviction that snow is observable at its poles. A year on Venus is equal in length to 224½ of our days.

The next planet in the system is our Earth, which is situated about 93,000,000 miles from the Sun. It revolves in 365 days and a fraction, which, as is generally known, is rectified in our calendars by the addition of one day in every four years.

THE MOON

The Moon, which is a satellite of the Earth, has been supposed by

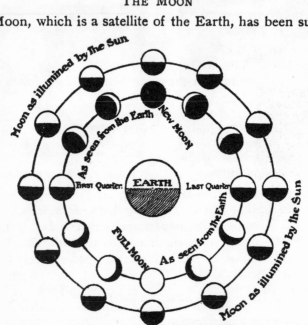

FIG. 9.—The Phases of the Moon.

some astronomers to have been thrown off from the Earth's surface many millions of years ago. Whatever life she once possessed is now dead, and the light that she sheds upon this Earth is simply reflected from the Sun as though she were a mirror.

The phases of the Moon are easily explained by glancing at Fig. 9. This shows not only how the Moon receives the Sun's rays, but also how she appears to us. Unlike the Earth, the Moon does not revolve rapidly upon her own axis. She always presents the same face to us, and therefore only makes one complete revolution every time she encircles the Earth, *i.e.* every 28 days.

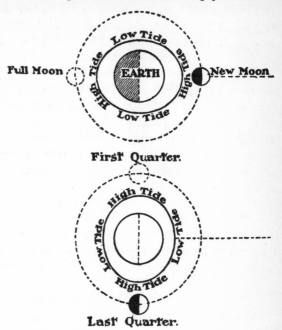

FIG. 10.—The Action of the Moon and Tide.

One of the most remarkable effects of the Moon's presence is the action of the tides. The Moon is like a huge magnet, drawing towards her all the water on the face of the Earth, as shown in Fig. 10. As the Moon varies so do the tides ; in fact, it may be roughly said that the water follows the Moon over the face of the Earth.

FIG. 11.—Lunar Craters.

Every one has heard of the mountains in the Moon, and a very moderate-sized telescope will reveal these quite plainly Many of them present the appearance of craters, Fig. 11, and the various ranges of mountains and plains have been named by astronomers in much the same way as the physical features upon our own Earth.

IS MARS INHABITED ?

Mars is the next planet to the Earth, and of late years has been the object of much interest and conjecture. Observations have centred very largely upon the "canals," as the thin network of lines shown in

Fig. 12 is called. Some scientists hold that these are artificial, being the work of creatures upon that planet corresponding to mankind upon this Earth. There certainly seem to be some

grounds for such conjectures, as constant observation has revealed the fact that these canals radiate from certain centres and circulate over practically the entire area of the planet. At each pole of Mars a large white patch has been observed, and during the period when the Martian summer is at its height, these patches grow markedly smaller and the lines or " canals " increase proportionately in size. The conclusions drawn from these phenomena point to the fact that the white patches at the poles are

FIG. 12.—The Canals on Mars.

formed of snow, which, melting under the heat of the Sun, is conveyed in the shape of water through the various canals and thus dispersed over the face of the planet. This has been taken as being the work of intelligences equal to, if not greater than our own!

Mars, which is 140,000,000 miles from the Sun, revolves once in 686 days; the Martian year is therefore almost twice as long as our own.

THE KING OF THE PLANETS

The next planet in the solar system is Jupiter—the greatest of all the bodies revolving round the Sun. Large telescopes reveal the fact that the surface of this planet is covered with streaks and belts similar to that shown in Fig. 13, which are supposed to be caused by an atmosphere very similar to that of our Earth.

Jupiter has five moons, all of which can be seen with quite a small telescope. Many an interesting hour may be spent watching the eclipses of these moons. As, on an average, they revolve round the planet in a little over a day, this is not so rare an occurrence as with our own Moon ; but more interesting still is it to watch what is known as the transit

FIG. 13.—Jupiter.

of one of these moons. This means the passage of the Moon across the face of the planet, and one can very often see the black shadow thrown by the Moon on Jupiter's surface. Jupiter revolves round the Sun in twelve years at a distance of about 483,000,000 miles.

Beyond Jupiter is the planet Saturn, the phenomenal rings, Fig. 14, of which can be seen through a medium-sized telescope. Science has failed to explain what these rings really are, many astronomers stating their belief that they are small particles of matter, whilst others imagine them to be what one might describe as a huge ring of meteors. Saturn has eight moons, some of which can be seen with a small telescope, and their constant motions, together with the phases of the rings, will prove an unending source of interest to the observer. A year in Saturn corresponds with 29½ years on the Earth, and the enormous distance

of 886,000,000 miles makes the planet receive but one-hundredth part of the light which we get on our Earth. This is, however, made up by the eight moons and the brilliant rings which surround it.

Uranus and Neptune are the two farthest planets from the Sun, and are of comparatively recent discovery. Attended by his eight satellites, Uranus revolves round the Sun in a period of eighty-four years. Neptune, owing to its immense distance from us, cannot be carefully observed, for it takes 164½ years to revolve round the Sun at a distance of 2,791,000,000 miles. As a matter of fact, from Neptune the Sun appears no larger than a star.

COMETS

Last year the appearance of Halley's Comet recalled the fact that comets are not mere wanderers in the sky, but revolve in their orbits around the Sun with as much precision as do the larger planets. Halley's Comet was an old friend, as it revisits the Earth about every seventy

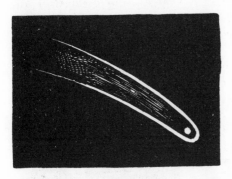

FIG. 15.—The Comet of 1811.

years. On the last occasion, however, it was disappointingly small, and did not spread a flaming tail across the sky as magnificently as did the great comet of 1858. Some comets have long tails similar to that shown in Fig. 15, while others appear more as a blurr of light, Fig. 16.

Although Halley's and some dozen other comets revolve around the Sun in so small an orbit that they reappear at stated intervals, there are others whose course is so vast that centuries elapse between their visits. Other comets, again, suddenly appear and disappear, having no apparent connection with the solar system.

FIG. 16.—Comet of 1892.

As to what a comet is made of, and why it has a tail, scientists differ, but it is generally supposed that it is formed of some gaseous matter which is cast off as it whirls through space.

ECLIPSES

Before taking leave of the Solar System, it will be as well to explain what an eclipse is.

An eclipse of the Sun takes place when the Moon comes between the Earth and the Sun. A total eclipse, as the name implies, is when

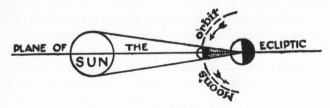

FIG. 17.—An Eclipse of the Sun.

the entire body of the Moon interposes and obliterates the Sun, whilst a partial eclipse is when only a portion of the Sun's surface is concealed. Fig. 17 explains how this happens.

Eclipses of the Moon, Fig. 18, are caused by the interposition of

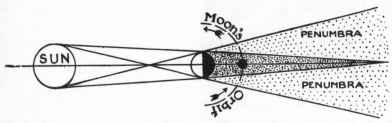

FIG. 18.—An Eclipse of the Moon.

the Earth between the Moon and the Sun's rays, and the effect of the great shadow cast by our globe as it slowly steals across its satellite's face is most interesting to watch.

THE STARS

In our Northern hemisphere about 3000 stars are visible to the naked eye, and the most casual observer must have noticed that they appear disposed in certain "patterns," as one might say, which are always clearly recognisable. These regular dispositions of the stars are known as constellations, and one of the first lessons to be learned by the astronomer is to recognise the different stars and the constellations to which they belong. It must first be noted, however, that the same motion of the Earth which produces the alternation of night and day, taking the form of the apparent rising and setting of the Sun, is observable in connection with the stars which in like manner appear to rise and set. There are some constellations, however, in the North, which, although changing their positions the whole night through, never set, but are always visible.

THE CONSTELLATIONS

The constellations in which the stars are grouped are named, for the most part, from imaginary resemblances to objects, mythological and otherwise, and consequently bear Greek and Roman names. To become acquainted with the stars and constellations thoroughly, a systematic study of the sky is indispensable, more especially since every star rises above the horizon four minutes earlier each day, thus bringing into view different stars as the year wears on.

Although most of the large stars have been given names, astronomers make a practice of distinguishing the different stars in a constellation by the letters of the Greek alphabet, which the student must commit to memory.

The most conspicuous constellation in our Northern sky is the Great Bear, Fig. 19. In olden days this was known as King Charles's Wain,

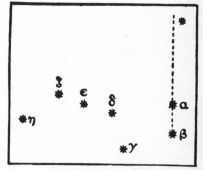

FIG. 19.—The Constellation of Ursa Major.

or The Plough, although the scientific name is *Ursa Major*. The back stars or pointers are in direct line with the North or Pole Star, and this constellation therefore makes a good starting-point from which to commence surveying the skies.

Continuing the line of the pointers through and beyond the Pole Star, the constellation of Cassiopeia, resembling a large W, or at certain times of the year an M, is seen. This constellation is situated in the Milky Way—that broad band of stars that seems to stretch across the sky.

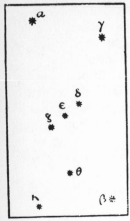

FIG. 20.—Constellation of Orion.

Descending the Milky Way we reach Perseus, in which the large star Algol shines very clearly. Still in the Milky Way, but in the opposite direction, is Vega, the largest star in the constellation of Lyra.

An imaginary line carried through the upper stars of the Great Bear points to Aldebaran, which is the lower star in the end of the V, which appears lying on its side. At right angles are the Pleiades, and near by Orion, Fig. 20, one of the most conspicuous and easily recognisable constellations in the firmament.

A straight line carried through the three stars forming the belt of Orion points to Sirius, the Dog Star, which was once supposed to be the nearest star to this earth.

A full and systematic survey of the heavens should, however, be made with a proper map of the stars, with the assistance of which every body in the heavens can be easily recognised.

THE DISTANCES OF THE STARS

The stars are classed into "magnitudes," or sizes, according to the brilliance they exhibit to observers on the Earth. The largest and brightest stars are ranked in the first magnitude ; others are placed in the second, third, &c., down to the sixth magnitude, which comprises the smallest stars visible to the naked eye, although telescopes of great strength reveal stars so small as those of the fifteenth magnitude. There are some twenty-one stars of the first magnitude, of which Sirius is the brightest. It is, however, very difficult to determine where the line can be drawn between the different magnitudes.

Figures seem wholly inadequate when dealing with the distances of the stars. Astronomers, indeed, reckon the stellar distance units by the distance travelled by light in a year—light travelling at the rate of 185,000 miles a second. Observation has shown that the light from the nearest star, a Centauri, takes four and a half years to reach us ; that star can therefore be reckoned as 24,750,000,000,000 miles away. Truly our system of numeration is unable to cope with such figures !

The Number of the Stars

During the course of the year an observer situated in some place on the equator would see all the stars visible in both hemispheres, but in our country no more than some 3200 stars can be observed with the naked eye. Yet this gives no idea of the enormous number of the stars. Indeed, to modern science the stars cannot be counted, for the larger the telescope the more stars can be discerned, and the number is therefore only limited by the means of observation. The great astronomer, Herschel, who occupied himself very largely with this branch of astronomy, is supposed to have observed only $\frac{1}{260}$ part of the sky, yet he reckoned that on one occasion 258,000 stars passed before his telescope in forty-one minutes. As a result of his and his son's observations, they estimated that an 18-inch reflector telescope showed no fewer than twenty million stars.

Coloured Stars

It needs but little observation to notice that, as the stars vary in brightness, so they likewise vary in colour. Aldebaran, for instance, is most distinctly orange, whilst Sirius is unmistakably blue. Although the question of these colours and how they are formed occupies a considerable position in higher astronomy, the beginner will be unable to do more than watch and admire the varied colours of those distant suns.

Nebulæ

In different parts of the sky are certain clusters, whether of stars or of gaseous matter has not yet been discovered, which are known

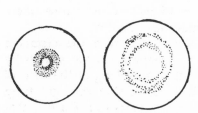

Fig. 21.—Ring Nebulæ.

Fig. 22.—Spiral Nebula.

by the name of *nebulæ*. These nebulæ are sometimes in the form of rings, as in Fig. 21, and sometimes spiral, Fig. 22, whilst others again assume strange forms, an example of which is the Owl Nebula, Fig. 23, in Ursa Major.   Perhaps one of the most conspicuous nebulæ is that situated in the belt of Orion, and although the most powerful telescopes have failed to reveal of what it is composed, every astronomer takes a great interest in observing this phenomenon.

FIG. 23.—The Owl Nebula.

THE MILKY WAY

The Milky Way, which is so plainly seen stretching across the sky, is composed of innumerable stars of small magnitude which are relatively near one another, although removed a vast distance from us.   Herschel considered that our sun is one of the stars in the Milky Way, but since his time astronomers have thrown doubt on this theory. For over two thousand years men have been wondering about the construction of this celestial road, but even with the powerful telescopes and the knowledge of the heavens by which they are now aided, no satisfactory results have been obtained.   Among the various names given to the Galaxy, as it is properly called, are "Jacob's Ladder," "The Way to St. James," and "The Watling Street."

For a further study of the stars the student must have recourse to handbooks which, advancing in difficulty as he proceeds, will gradually lead to a better and more intimate knowledge of those worlds which are nightly spread in the firmament above.

CHAPTER XLVIII

OUT AND ABOUT WITH A GEOLOGICAL HAMMER

THE HISTORY OF THE EARTH WRITTEN IN STONE

SHAKESPEARE has told us that the thinking man can find sermons in stones. It is equally true to say that a store of delight may be found in rocks, flints, and similar substances. We live in a world of wonder; the very crust of the earth is full of fascinating mystery, and very pleasant it is to read this attractive stone book and unlock its secrets.

FIG. 1.—A Geological Hammer.

No more delightful hobby for the open air can be desired than geology, while for quiet hours indoors the collection of minerals is absorbingly interesting.

Two articles are all that are required to help you outdoors. One is a geological hammer, Fig. 1, and the other a strong bag, Fig. 2, to hold the specimens as they are secured.

FIG. 2.—The Leather Collecting-bag.

THE CRUST OF THE EARTH

The crust of the earth is a wonderful envelope to our globe. The rocks and minerals of which it is composed are as diverse as can be imagined. On the first blow of the hammer you will find some substances so hard and compact that they can scarcely be broken, whilst others are so soft that they crumble away at the slightest touch. Think of the differences between granite and chalk, coal and clay, marble and sand; then remember how widely they are distributed. Go north to Scotland where you can get specimens of granite, to our Southern coast-line and see the great cliffs of chalk, or to the Eastern counties where soft clays can be met with in abundance. In a word, the crust of the earth consists of stratum on stratum, or a series of strata, in which our hammer can reveal the most serviceable materials, as well as some of the most precious gems worthy to adorn a monarch's crown.

Before starting on an expedition with a geological hammer it is well to know something of the position and composition of the strata we shall be likely to meet with. If we search deeply near a river-bed we shall find the layers quite even; but if our search is in the neighbourhood of a quarry, we shall come across quite a different arrangement of the various materials—some parts will be horizontal, and other parts inclined. In hilly districts we get bent and contorted strata—one kind of material will be bent over into another kind, altogether unlike it; some of the terms for these irregularities being slip, fault, and dyke. All hills and mountains are the irregular breaking up of the earth's surface.

ROCKS

Should we come upon rocks, it will be useful to know the names used to describe their internal structure. A rock is granular when it consists of particles like granite; porous, when full of holes, like pumice; fibrous when it looks like asbestos; vesicular, like larva; saccharoid, as if consisting of grains of sugar; acicular, when it is shaped like a lot of needles.

Commencing our investigation by the side of a river, it will be noticed that the first layer is ordinary mud, which consists of very fine particles worn away by the water, carried along and deposited in the bed. Below it is sand—hard grains derived from rocks amongst which are quartz grains and tiny pieces of shells, and still lower you see shingle—quite large fragments.

As a contrast to this a stroll should be taken along the chalk cutting of a railway. Chalk is composed of carbonate of lime, is very light, and breaks with an earthy fracture. The mass we now look at is white, but chalk is sometimes grey and yellow. It forms a large portion of the secondary rocks of England. Use your hammer if you cannot break it off with your fingers, and try to find a piece with something in it, for it frequently contains the remains of both marine and land animals. In any case take a piece home, put it under the microscope, and examine the countless shell-like remains, which the naked eye could never discover.

ON THE CLIFFS

When next you are at the seaside, do not fail to go for a good search about the cliffs, hammer in hand. Wherever you see something irregular, or different from the surrounding mass, examine it closely and secure a portion of it. It may contain fossil plants and remains of creatures altogether distinct from those living in our own times.

When you come across a cutting do not omit to examine

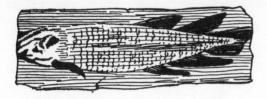

FIG. 3.—Fossil Fish.

FIG. 4.—A Fossil Sea Urchin.

it carefully. Not only does it afford a fine example of stratification, but on looking into it something of an extremely interesting character may be found.

FIG. 6.—Outline Fern.

In the same way many a delightful hour can be spent in an old disused quarry. In Devonshire, for instance, pay a visit to the old red sandstone quarries, in which are

FIG. 5.—Fossil Nautilus.

to be found abundant remains of ancient fishes as well as the scales of extinct marine creatures, and traces of vegetable forms. In the lower group are reptiles, mollusca and fishes, Fig. 3, sea urchins, Fig. 4, shells, Fig. 5, and numerous beautiful outlines of extinct plants, Fig. 6. Use your hammer freely when searching for speci. mens.

Some of the fishes are remarkable in appearance. There is the Buckler-head, with a head like a shield ; the Wing fish, with strange appendages attached to its body ; the Berry Bone, having its bony place dotted over with knobs like berries ; and the All Wrinkle fish, whose enamel scales are wrinkled up grotesquely.

COAL

Nor must you miss exploring, hammer in hand, the various coalfields of England, when an opportunity offers. As you may know, the coalfields are huge mineralised forests of the carboniferous period. The vegetable growths of this far-off time were enormous. In the coal measures can be found pines, huge reeds, tree ferns, palms, mosses, and many other plants perfectly fossilised ; perhaps the most interesting of all your specimens will be found in these coal measures. In the shales are the remains of the tongue leaf fern, the wedge leaf, the nerve leaf, the comb leaf, the hair leaf, and numerous others.

Do not despise the commonest things in your geological walks. Even a pebble has its beauties. Get small specimens of the various kinds of gravel, Portland stone, pudding stone, marbles, and rocks. Along the Cornish coast are specimens of variegated rocks which should be secured when possible.

THE COLLECTION

While pleasantly engaged during the bright weather in collecting the commoner geological specimens outdoors, you must remember

the spare hours indoors when your treasures must be classified and formed into a collection. As you come across your specimens, you will, of course, first ask people in the district, especially master workmen, the name of each piece, and then check it by showing it to a friend who knows about the subject, or else consult a geological text-book. This will induce you to include in your collection minerals of all kinds.

A fair-sized cabinet, Fig. 7, filled with deep shelves partitioned off, will be necessary to house the specimens, and can be made of thin boarding, measured up to the dimensions of 18 in. wide, 12 in. deep, and 30 in. high. The compartments in each tray would be 2 in. wide by 2 in. long.

FIG. 7.—The Cabinet.

Many collectors of minerals aim at a certain distinctive property in the specimens they acquire. Colour is the chief of these—brilliant scarlet, green, blue, and orange are all to be met with even in ordinary quartz. These colours occur in very diverse substances.

As a rule the name and quality of any material must be learned from personal inspection ; no mere description on paper will convey the true idea. But there are several characteristics in all minerals which should be borne in mind. They are—external form, structure, fracture, hardness, transparency, lustre, colour, flexibility, and refraction.

As to form, only a few minerals have precise external form, because of being broken off from a surrounding mass. The form of the crystal is the most common. A crystal may be defined as a symmetrical solid, having several plane faces or sides. Examine a piece of chrysolite or soda crystal, and either will give you a good example of this.

Lustre is a very interesting quality in many minerals. It is of several kinds, and the same lustre which you see in a mineral internally, you will find to differ externally in crystallised substances. Metallic lustre is peculiar to metals in their pure state. It is seen in plumbago, specular iron, and grey copper. If you get a piece of bronzite and hold it up to the light, in a particular way, only then will its lustre be revealed. Adamantine lustre exists in the diamond, some varieties of corundum, and sulphate of lime. Only such minerals as have a great degree of transparency or power of reflecting light have this intense lustre.

METALS

Specimens of the metals in their native state are very interesting. Native iron is a pale steel grey in colour, native volcanic iron is found in lava, and native meteoric iron is extremely heavy. Specimens of iron pyrites can be obtained in Cornwall, white iron pyrites imbedded in fluorspar is to be met with in Derbyshire, and red iron ore in Lancashire.

Pure silver is found with an admixture of copper, arsenic, antimony, and iron. In colour it is pure white, with shining metallic lustre, tarnished outside to a greyish black owing to sulphur. It generally occurs in veins of spar or quartz.

Gold in its native state is in the form of regular cubes, of an orange red, or reddish yellow colour. It sometimes occurs on the surface of rocks, as gold dust in the beds of rivers, and in quartz, derived from primary rocks, principally granite.

FIG. 8.—Crystals of Sulphide of Lead.

Copper is brownish red when seen in its native ore. Lead, Fig. 8, is of a bluish white colour, and occurs in masses of regular sexhedrons.

But besides these fine metallic specimens there are scores of other minerals which are worth possessing. Malachite is a lovely green mineral of attractive appearance, the crystallised variety being extremely rare. Amber is always interesting to examine. The experiments of Sir David Brewster on the optical properties of amber prove that it is derived from a vegetable substance. If possible, secure a specimen in which a fly or other insect has been imbedded and can be clearly seen.

The varieties of felspar are all attractive, glassy felspar and Iceland spar affording remarkable instances of refraction, and showing many reflections of articles put near them.

As your collection proceeds you will find numberless minerals with wonderful qualities, from the pretty specimens of quartz at 3d. to the costliest precious stones, such as diamonds, emeralds, &c.

Be careful in the arrangement of your collection, and see that each specimen is correctly named and labelled. Handle your treasures with care, and keep them free from dust and disorder. Learn all you can about the simplest things, and make the showing of your collection a real pleasure to all your friends.

CHAPTER XLIX

CAMPING

A NOVEL FORM OF HOLIDAY

CAMPING was formerly a mode of living wont to be followed only by nomads and expeditions as a matter of necessity, but of recent years it has reached the dignity of a pastime. Civilisation brings in its train complications as well as comforts, so that the desire for simplicity, which is to some degree innate in every man, is intensified by civilised conditions, and brief spells occur of longing to reject life's humdrum trammels, although only at holiday times can these be indulged.

During the last decade the rise of two organisations — the Association of Cycle Campers, and the Boy Scouts—have given successive impulses to the pastime, although doubtless their operations differ widely, and possibly neither would acknowledge the other. Whereas the former cater rather for small parties, and thus devote all their attention to the lightening of impedimenta, the latter pursue more military schemes, and, since the numbers of the parties are seldom limited, aim at completeness rather than lightness of baggage. However, inasmuch as the Boy Scout movement may induce parents just for once to hazard their charges "catching cold" by sleeping in the open—a most remote mishap—whilst the Cycle Campers' Association encourages the pastime among people of mature age, they are both helpful fellowships, and equally militate against the too widespread fear of fresh air.

AN IDEAL SHELTER

For any extended camp a military bell tent, which can be obtained second-hand and in excellent serviceable condition for about 30s., is probably the best shelter. At least one downpour of rain may be expected, when the comfort of a roomy tent will be appreciated ; but they are cumbersome and heavy and in nowise adapted for brief week-end picnics, when a minimum of preparation and a maximum of pleasure are to be sought. For this purpose, a linen tent, C, supported on poles, AA, Fig. 1, of triangular cross section and about 6 ft. long—for comfortably sleeping at full stretch—and provided with a flysheet, B, to intercept the worst of any rain, is the ideal shelter, and can be smartly erected well within ten minutes —*i.e.* provided it is folded correctly, and the cords twisted with

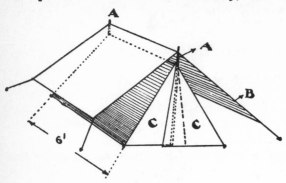

FIG. 1.—The Tent.

their respective pegs in orthodox fashion, as per the Cycle Campers' handbooks.

A snug tent having been settled upon and the weird outdoor night thus far anticipated, sleep may probably have to be still further wooed by providing bedding, seeing that absolutely nothing is harder than Mother Earth about three o'clock in the morning, if the camper couched thereon be so unfortunate as to wake. Of course, to pass the daylight hours actively and arduously is the best insurance, although even then, amidst strange surroundings, sleep often stands aloof, thus causing an absence of enjoyment.

Frequently, if the camp be pitched in wooded grounds, leaves may be gathered in a sack sling, and piled up to form mattresses, over which waterproof ground sheets are spread before the bed rugs go down. In a few districts again heather fit for pallets grows to perfection.

But the most responsive couches are hammocks, which on a fine night and for nomads willing to sleep in the open, may be suspended from convenient trees. Care, however, should be taken that this is stoutly effected, or the recumbent one may alight suddenly on the earth in the small hours, as did one friend of the writer, and, with the moonbeams for candles, be compelled to devote his unwilling attentions to re-erecting the treacherous bed.

HAMMOCK-SLINGING

A practical method of slinging the hammock inside a tent is shown in Figs. 2 and 3, where AA are light frames of crossed bamboos—with rope ties and wooden cross-bars at the top—which raise the head about 21 in. from the ground and the feet about 15 in., whilst hemp ropes, passed through tough running hooks, B and round a peg or tree, CD, without the sides of the tent, EE, stretch the hammock, F, so that,

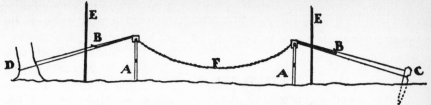

FIG. 2.—A practical Method of slinging a Hammock.

when occupied, its lowest part dips to within about 4 in. of the

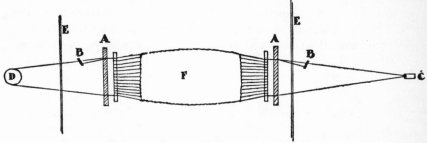

FIG. 3.—The Hammock viewed from above.

earth. The bamboo cross-pieces, Figs. 4 and 5, are bound together

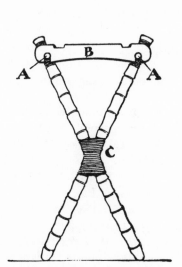

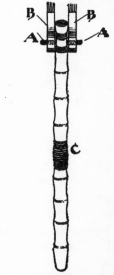

FIG. 4.—Crosspiece for Hammock.   FIG. 5.—Sectional View of Crosspiece.

with twine at C, and have two pegs, AA, to support the wooden
cross-bars, BB.

Certainly, to sleep in a hammock inside a tent is cosy enough, whereas slumbering in the open is a more eerie experience than might be imagined, and not a little disconcerting if the sleeper is awakened by the patter of raindrops or screeching of owls in the early night-hours.

PREPARATION OF MEALS

During daytime, probably the most absorbing duty will be the preparation of meals. A serviceable stove can be made by digging an L-shaped trench, about 6 in. deep and with limbs, AB, 2 ft. and 1 ft. 6 in. long, Fig. 6.

A long inverted baking or biscuit-tin, C, some 3 in. deep and having a 2-in. circular hole cut at one corner, E, is placed lengthways over the longer limb near the bend, and above the hole are stood several milk

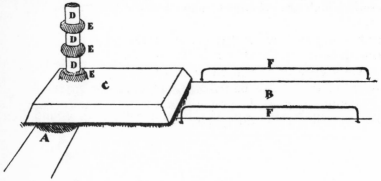

FIG. 6.—A Camp Stove.

tins, DDD, to a height of 18 in., the ends being removed, and the joints secured with wet clay as at E.

This crude arrangement constitutes a chimney, which will make the wood fuel, *e.g.* sticks or touchwood, burn rapidly, and thus render the improvised hob fairly hot. Round flat cakes may be baked direct, or another tin superimposed to form an oven.

Extending along each side of the trench, two longer U-shaped pieces of iron rod, FF, are stuck in the ground, Fig. 6, serving to take kettles, saucepans, frying-pans, and what not. They are also available for toasting slices of bread and grilling the tasty kipper.

Fuel is fed beneath the oven from the shorter trench, and, the chief requirement being a plentiful supply, a more satisfying mode of collection than that of gathering by armfuls should be employed. If two persons make expeditions in company, and carry a hammock slung between them, piles of fuel can be easily collected and carried.

The problem of obtaining drinking-water is best solved by camping near a pump, or, if on private ground, arranging with the owners for a supply. Very frequently, produce like eggs and butter can be purchased at the same emporium. Alternately—and, after all, it is best to pitch near a stream whenever possible—the clear running water may be safely boiled for such beverages as tea and cocoa, in which, moreover, any insipid flavour will be unnoticeable. As to personal cleanliness, doubtless soap will be carried for the periodical ablutions, but if, as is likely, this be mislaid, it is useful to remember that wet clay—paradoxical though the statement sounds— is an efficient dirt-remover.

Pots and pans may be scoured by means of dry leaves, sand, and water, so that conceivably the camping outfit may be reduced almost indefinitely, provided the available "dodges" are known. The only makeshift which seems almost nauseous is the drinking of hot tea from tins.

Sufficient has been written to indicate that a camping holiday presents some novel features, and at least tends towards self-dependence. Only experience will show to what extent and in what details the weight of the kit can be reduced, but if, in starting the first camp, major attention is given to preparation for the night accommodation, the pioneer will not err widely from the path of good management.

CHAPTER L

CARAVANNING

THE PLEASURES OF A LAND CRUISE

THERE are few pleasanter ways of spending a country holiday than in a caravan, which, in its neatness and compact construction, makes a very comfortable wheeled home for a week or more. The aimless independence, the absolute freedom from the annoyances of time-tables and other troubles incidental to the more usual forms of travel, and the perfect lack of restraint, under the blue vault of heaven —all these things go to make a caravan holiday one of the most pleasurable things in the world.

To the healthy lover of the open there is little need to enlarge on the pleasures of drifting across the country, passing down the quiet lanes, and after the day's toil, camping beneath the shelter of the cool trees on some delightful meadow, by whose side a noisy little stream pursues its varied course. Small need is there, either, to dilate on the fragrance of the fresh morning air, when, awakened by the birds, the caravanner steps down the little ladder from his travelling home to find the world all freshened with dew and glistening in the glory of another summer day.

THE CARAVAN

Caravans are built in various styles, and the cost of hiring naturally depends upon the type of vehicle. From the gay and ornamental gipsy cart to the huge and unwieldy motor van, there are numberless grades and qualities—hardly any two caravans being built exactly alike.

One of the best ways to hire a caravan is to insert an advertisement in some good paper which deals with out-of-door pursuits, such as *The Bazaar, Country Life* or *The Field*. Possessors of caravans are often glad to let their vehicles when not in use, and the van thus obtained is more likely to be fitted up in a suitable and comfortable fashion than a vehicle hired from a travelling showman.

During the height of the season, in July and August, a fully

400

equipped caravan should be obtainable for about £20 a month, or five guineas a week, this sum including all requisites in the way of bedding, crockery, and cooking utensils. To this amount must be added the cost of hire for the horse, which, if the animal be taken for the whole period, will work out at about 30s. a week. If a man be taken to look after the horse, the inclusive cost will be from 45s. a week, the man finding himself in food.

Where there is any intention, however, of camping for some length of time in one place, the better plan is to hire a horse for the journey alone, the cost of this usually working out at sixpence per mile, this sum including the services of a man. Horses for this purpose can often be procured from the farmer upon whose land the camp has been pitched, and he will generally be very glad to let out his beasts when there is no other work doing.

The rent of the van is almost invariably payable in advance, and all breakages and damage must be repaired by the hirers. The owners usually stipulate that the van shall not be "slung" on a railway truck or be transported in any other fashion than by road.

Professional showmen are often glad to let their vans during a portion of the

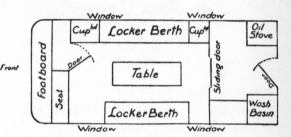

FIG. 1.—Plan of Caravan with an End Door.

summer months, but advertising is of little use in this case, the only way to obtain the vehicle being to make a personal tour of inspection amongst the vans which are usually put up during the winter in the vicinity of large towns. The owners of these vans are, as a general rule, remarkably hard-working and honest men, and there is little fear of being cheated. On the other hand, they are looking out for business, and will naturally ask as much for their "cart" as they think the prospective hirer will be likely to pay. It is difficult to obtain a satisfactory van for less than £5 a week, and it will be found advisable to take one's own bedding and crockery, simply requiring the proprietor to have his van thoroughly cleaned before handing over possession.

Caravans usually have the door at the end, although in some cases the entrance is made in the side of the vehicle. An example of a van with an end door is shown in Fig. 1, the exterior of the same van being illustrated in Fig. 2. It will be noticed that this caravan contains a dining-saloon, but in many smaller vans this apartment is dispensed with, meals being taken in the open air, where a table is rigged up and the cooking done under the lee of the van.

Not an inch of space in the caravan is wasted. Every available

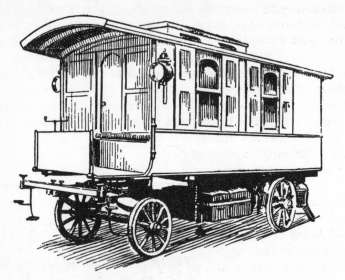

FIG. 2.—A Caravan with an End Door.

corner is used for cupboards or lockers, and it need scarcely be said that the greatest method and tidiness are necessary to ensure so many things being packed in such limited space.

The lighting arrangements of a van should be good, for the caravanner must be prepared for wet or chilly evenings, which will have to be spent indoors with a book. Acetylene-lamps and oil-lamps are often recommended, but a good yacht candle-lamp, similar to that shown in Fig. 3, will prove the safest and most certain means of illumination.

THE OUTFIT

FIG. 3.—Candle-lamp.

Having chosen the van, the question of fitting it out naturally arises. The bedding, which plays so important a part in the comfort of a tour, must be sound and suitable. Spring mattresses are always preferable, both on account of the extra comfort they afford and of their cleanliness. The blankets should be "all-wool," as, wrapped up in them, the sleeper need have no fear of the night damp which so often arises near the sea or in the vicinity of any stretch of water. A bed-spread to match the other upholstering of the van will also be necessary to cover the beds and keep out dust in the day-time. All cushions should be tied or strapped to their respective lockers or seats to prevent their falling about whilst the van is in motion.

Curtains can be made of some material that will not catch the dust, whilst dark blinds will be essential to those accustomed to sleeping in dark rooms. The floor of the van should be covered with some plain linoleum, and one or two good strong door-mats must be provided for use after tramping along muddy roads or over miry fields.

So far as the crockery, glass, and table linen are concerned, these can usually be taken from home. It is quite a mistaken idea that caravanning must be so rough and primitive that meals will have to be par-taken from earthenware mugs and with any make-shift appliances that may

FIG. 4.—A Caravan Bookcase.

prove handy. The utmost comfort can be combined with an out-door life ; and, indeed, a point should be made of having everything as nice as possible, for nothing gives a greater distaste for the caravan holiday than the rough and ready, "anything will do" spirit which so many people think characteristic of what seems to them nothing but a prolonged picnic. If the plates and glasses be carefully packed in sheets of baize they can be carried without fear of accidents ; and no one will deny that water tastes sweeter from a glass than from a tin mug.

Cooking utensils should be of aluminium, a material which is not only lighter to carry, but can be cleaned much quicker than any other. A methylated spirit stove for making the early morning tea, heating shaving-water, and boiling eggs, is also a useful adjunct.

It is always advisable to take a certain number of books wherewith to while away the evenings or such rainy days as the caravanner may be unfortunate enough to encounter. These books should be stored in bookshelves which are so arranged that a cord or line can be run along the backs of the books, Fig. 4, to retain them in position when the van is in motion. Without this precaution the volumes will be scattered about the vehicle.

A certain amount of provisions in the nature of biscuits, flour, and condiments must also be stored in the caravan. The larder will, of course, be replenished every day, but it is always as well to carry a substantial tongue or ham to fall back upon in case of emergency.

ON THE ROAD

Thus far instructions have been given solely about the preparation for the trip. When all is complete, the caravan may set forth early some sunny morning, and embark upon its land cruise. With the horse jogging on between the shafts and the hedgerows passing in procession upon either side, the caravanner's heart will grow lighter and lighter as each mile removes him farther from the smoke and bricks of civilisation.

The first thing to strike a novice will be the almost deafening rattle and clatter which accompanies his progress. This can be easily remedied, however, as it is only caused by loose window-bolts and odd articles which jostle and jingle against one another with the motion of the van. A few moments' attention will soon set this to rights, and with careful supervision the caravan should continue its journey as smoothly and silently as a saloon railway coach or an elegant brougham. Vessels containing liquid must not be too full, or they will slop over and drench all in their immediate neighbourhood.

When proceeding uphill the roller must be applied and watched to see that it does not slip aside, whilst, when descending, the brakes must be put on, the shoe placed in position where necessary, and the wheels tied when the hill is very steep.

Although some caravanners prefer to wander aimlessly about the country, the best plan is to make a rough itinerary of the intended route, and procure ordnance maps and contour books for the district. High roads, being better repaired and in more frequent use, are usually better adapted for progress than side lanes, although it must be confessed that these latter provide far more interesting changes of prospect. Where the country is inclined to be hilly, the by-ways should be avoided, as they are likely to prove exceptionally heavy and loose.

Camping

Unfortunately the brave days when it was allowable to draw up the van by any roadside or common have passed away for ever, leaving the caravanner under the sad necessity of asking permission from the local authorities to make his camp. There are still certain spots, however, where camps may be pitched for not longer than twenty-four hours, but as these localities are naturally frequented by itinerant hawkers and gipsies, whose company is not calculated to enhance the pleasure of the night's pitch, it is in every case advisable to seek permission from some farmer to draw the van into one of his fields. Although he may not make any charge, his acquiescence will not be entirely disinterested, as he will naturally expect that such provisions as eggs, milk, poultry, and butter will be purchased from him. Of course, for a lengthened stay, a definite arrangement will have to be made.

The All-important Question

The continual fresh air and healthy exercise attendant upon caravanning make the question of feeding of most vital importance, and it is in the commissariat department that the really useful caravanner makes himself beloved of all. The office of cook should be undertaken by the members of the party in turn, the spirit of rivalry goading cook to display his prowess and eclipse the attempts of his predecessor. It may be casually remarked that the same spirit of emulation will seldom be noticed when the time comes for " washing-up."

The day should be commenced with a hearty breakfast, consisting of eggs and bacon, omelette, or fish, if some member of the party has been fortunate enough to catch any in a neighbouring stream.

Lunch should always be cold and of a fairly light nature, the cook's *tour de force* being reserved for the preparation of the evening meal, which, partaken after the toil and travel of the day, will be eagerly looked forward to by all the members of the party.

Soups are easily made of dessicated soup tablets, whilst the cookery book which every well-appointed van should carry will supply endless hints as to other dishes that may be concocted. Where the van contains an indoor stove and cooking apparatus there is no limit to the number and quality of dishes that may be prepared, but where an outdoor fire is necessary, the general pot will be found the most invaluable article of the cooking appointments. Scraps of meat, remnants of poultry, a rabbit or even a hedgehog—a tasty dish the townsman knows nothing of—old pieces of bread, cooked potatoes, vegetables of any sort (onions most essential), and a seasoning of Worcester sauce or ketchup — all these thrown indiscriminately into the pot help to form the delicious dish known as " pepper pot."

To a very large extent the old adage, "the more the merrier," is very true of caravanning, but the party should nevertheless be selected with some care. Every one must be prepared to work hard—there must be no " deadheads " on the tour. All friction should be sedulously avoided, and the utmost cheerfulness exhibited even under the trying conditions of a pouring day with a steady head wind. If every member of the party is prepared to be a Mark Tapley, to take things as they come, and to feel his spirits rising when the rain is descending, then the caravan tour will prove an unqualified success and be the forerunner of many pleasant holidays spent in similar fashion.

CHAPTER LI

GRASS AND SNOW TOBOGGANS

A SPORT FOR THE HILLS

IN this snug little island of ours we are not granted a very long acquaintance with the Snow Queen. Very few of us, therefore, know the pleasures of tobogganing—the delights of flashing down a steep hill on a small wooden sled, with the air whizzing past our ears as the pace grows faster and faster, until—a bend in the track—we take it too sharply, and—thud!—our sled has overturned, gracelessly depositing us upon the cruel, hard ground.

But tobogganing may be indulged in even when snow does not cloak the hillside. In summer, when the rays of the sun have baked the grass to a brown, slippery stubble, the tobogganist may still toboggan to his heart's content, for the sun-baked grass will form as excellent a "track" as the firmest of snow. Here, therefore, are instructions for making both a grass and a snow toboggan, and they will be found not only extremely simple to construct, but quite inexpensive as well.

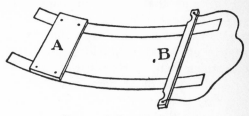

FIG. 1.—A Grass Toboggan.

For the grass toboggan we shall first require two staves from a fairly large barrel. These may be taken from an empty flour or sugar barrel— which fourpence and a little persuasion will readily entice from the local grocer.

Lay the two staves upon the floor about 4 in. apart. Connect them together near one end by securely nailing across a piece of board A, Fig. 1, 8 in. wide, $\frac{1}{4}$ in. thick, and just long enough to reach to the outer edge of each stave.

Now nail a second piece of wood, B, 2 in. wide and $\frac{1}{2}$ in. thick, across the staves towards the other end, letting it project about 4 in. on each side. This is to act as a foot-rest. At each extremity of this foot-rest holes should be bored by means of a red-hot poker or a gimlet, and a loop of rope knotted through them. This loop may be termed "the reins," and by its aid the tobogganist is able to retain his seat upon the sled when it is in motion. On each side between the hole and the stave, gouge out a hollow for the reception of the foot.

The toboggan is now finished, and a suitable "track" must next be made.

Take the toboggan to the top of a steep hill, covered with dry grass, and get a friend, brother, cousin, or uncle—the heavier he is the better—and ask him to take a seat upon it. Then proceed to make your "track" by pulling him down the hill three or four times. After the grass has been "polished" by this performance, the toboggan will take its passenger down the decline by its own weight. Moreover, as the runners and the "track" get more polished, the faster will the pace become, and the merrier the fun.

THE SNOW SLED

For the snow sled we shall require four more staves from the sugar-barrel to act as runners. If the barrel be at all large, the staves may prove a trifle too long for our purpose, and in this case they must be shortened an inch or two at each end.

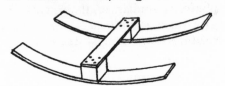

FIG. 2.—Runner for Snow Sled.

Having cut the runners to a suitable length, a block of wood must be nailed or screwed to the centre of each, as shown at A, Fig. 2. Now select two of the runners and connect them together by nailing a strip of wood 8 in. long and $\frac{1}{2}$ in. thick to these blocks, Fig. 3. The other pair of runners must be similarly treated; the only difference being that the strip of wood must be 16 in. instead of 8 in. long,

FIG. 3.—Back Runners.

thus making a projection of 4 in. at each side, Fig. 4. These projections should be roughly rounded with a knife, and finished off with coarse sand-paper, to furnish grips for the hands.

Having, for the time being, dispensed with the runners, we will turn our attention to the platform, or body of the sled. This merely consists of a piece of board 12 in.

FIG. 4.—Front Runners.

wide, $\frac{1}{2}$ in. thick, and about 3 ft. long, the front being roughly shaped as shown in Fig. 5, by having the two corners sawn off.

Now take the back runners—those without the projecting hand-grips—and securely nail them to the underside of the platform. This done, a hole, C, Fig. 4, must be bored in the centre of the remaining pair of runners. A red-hot poker is the simplest instrument with which this may be accomplished. A cor-responding hole must also be bored in the front of the platform, C, Fig. 5.

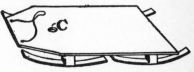

FIG. 5.—Snow Sled completed.

From a neighbouring iron-monger's purchase an iron bolt—costing about two-pence—and loosely bolt the front runners to the platform. A washer should be placed between the platform and the bar of the runners to act as a kind of swivel upon which the latter can turn.

Now for a trial trip on our snow sled.

The tobogganist lies full length upon the platform, gripping the projecting handles of the front runners. He then starts the sled by giving a slight "push off" with his feet upon the ground. If he wishes to change the direction in which the toboggan is travelling, he simply pulls at one of the handles. The angle of the front runners will thus be altered, and round will swerve the toboggan—sometimes capsizing in the act.

It is advisable to have a loop of rope attached to the front of the platform, similar to the "reins" of the grass sled, so that the tobog-ganist can easily trail his "snow carriage" to the top of the "track" in readiness for the next descent.

CHAPTER LII

CYCLING AND CYCLE REPAIRS

MODERN KNIGHTS OF THE ROAD

MAN had learnt to balance himself on two wheels in the old hobby-horse days, yet the innovation of the "ordinary" bicycle in 1863 did not meet with extensive favour. Not only was considerable daring required to master the steed, but an opportune brick wall was almost essential to ready mounting, whilst—even this accomplished—a perch separated from the earth by five feet of spokes and rubber was soon found to be none of the most reassuring. Doubtless then, as now, the exhilaration of speed exercised some charm over human nature, but not until this was enjoyable with a maximum of security and comfort on the "safety" machine, did cycling as a hobby storm the civilised world.

Probably no recreation has ever influenced the conventions of humanity so considerably. Devotees of the new pastime found that scattered friends could be brought within hail, or nooks hitherto undreamed of searched out in the country-side on Saturday afternoons —the week-end habit took birth. All classes of wage-earners realised that a long tramp became one-third the journey on two wheels, and they settled their homesteads accordingly; the congestion of population ceased to threaten so menacingly. These changes in large part, though no one may say entirely, owe their growth to the advent of cycling.

A CYCLE TOUR

A cycle tour can well claim to constitute one of the most refreshing holidays imaginable. The writer's wishes took this bent recently, and although he had some misgivings as to enjoying travel and seeking nightly "diggings" without the moral support of a chum, these fears vanished utterly as the days flew past, whilst the entertainment proved limitless.

A little forethought demands the curtailment of the baggage to a minimum, and experience shows that its weight must be distributed about the machine, with the slightly larger share over the back wheel.

A mackintosh, with a pair of slippers and flannel suit, for a change in case of drenching rain, are conducive to comfort, whilst for those spells of travel which are blessed by the smiles of old Sol, knickers with jersey and undervest, will prove a desirable —because easy—attire.

A coat and hat lend somewhat of an air of respectability, but they hinder the wind's cooling embrace, which gives life on a sultry day, and without which long spins are ordeals, rather than continuous surveys of delightful panorama. If carried at all, they should be donned as a matter of diplomacy, when prospecting for the night's quarters at wayside inns.

If the districts to be explored are at all hilly, a coaster brake, supplemented by front and back rim brakes for emergencies, will engender some sense of security, which in itself is delightful. A variable

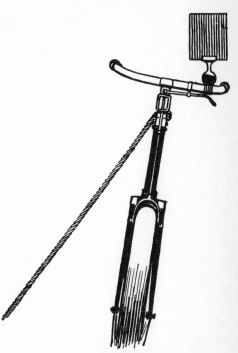

FIG. 1.—Ball and Socket Camera-stand for a Bicycle.

gear, moreover, is a valuable luxury, but the normal should scarcely exceed 70 in., whilst the low gear may be well in the neighbourhood of 45 in.

Touring over strange country has not for its object to speed along like the wind, regardless of obstacles—to which end alone a high gear tends—but rather to coast unconcernedly downhill, to climb the rising gradients steadily, and, above all, to halt or walk where fancy prompts. These are the essential features of a pleasure ramble.

CYCLING AND PHOTOGRAPHY

Cyclists who are also addicted to photography as a companion hobby doubtless regard the tripod as a necessary nuisance. Not only is it heavy and inconvenient to carry, but many a minute slips away in unfolding or repacking. It is, however, almost superfluous, for its

duties are efficiently performed by the bicycle itself. Supported after the manner shown in Fig. 1, a ball and socket camera-stand is a fixture on the handle-bars, and if placed to the side away from the peg and cord, Fig. 2, ample room is afforded for the operator to conduct his focussing arrangements.

A minor trouble, but yet an unmitigated nuisance to the wheelman, is the denting of the cotter pins which fix the cranks to the bracket axle. It has seemed to prevail during recent years, and, being due to a lack of temper in the pins, is probably one of the penalties of modern rapid manufacture.

FIG. 2.—Peg for Bicycle.

Fig. 3 depicts the trouble aggravated, so that it may be judged how the dent, A, allows of play between the crank and axle, causing a jar to the foot every pedal revolution.

An excellent method of prevention is to file the flat on the cotter

FIG. 3.—Damaged Cotter Pin.

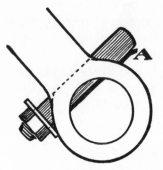

FIG. 4.—Preventing Cotter Pin being damaged.

slightly more than would be necessary for a good fit, and then insert a short length of steel clock spring, A, Fig. 4, before tightening up the nut. The steel service takes the wear, and denting is entirely obviated.

CARE OF TYRES

Tyres constitute the heaviest expense to the cyclist, provided that he has no accidents, and takes reasonable care of his mount. Even supposing that they fulfil their estimated career, until the tread wears smooth, the cost of replacement occurs too soon ; moreover, such equal wear is only possible to a rider of light build.

A burst usually occurs somewhere round the circumference, and unless it can be properly repaired, an otherwise serviceable cover has to be discarded. It may just be noted here that probably no repair will prove successful unless the clearance between tyre and forks is about 4 in. on either side. The usual method adopted is to solution a repair band, C, to the weak part, B, of the cover, A, allowing it to dry for twenty-four hours in a concave position, Fig. 5, so that when in place on

FIG. 5.—Temporary Repair for Tyre.

FIG. 6.—Another Way of repairing temporarily.

the wheel rim and inflated, the repair band constricts the tyre to approximately its normal width. This plan is widely known and serves well —without the necessity for solutioning—as a temporary repair on the road, but the chief disadvantage lies in its short life, owing to the thickening of the tyre and consequent undue wear on the slender band.

A different device was recently noticed, which would appear to be quite novel. It is certainly neat and durable on all but very muddy roads, under which conditions the dirt gradually works in and forms an unsightly lump. The damaged cover is cut away round the burst to the least possible extent, so as to form a square aperture, Fig. 6, and the canvas inside is solutioned for a distance of 6 in. The next step is to cut a sound 6-in. length, A, Fig. 7, from some discarded tyre and, after drawing the wires or tearing off the bead, to carve away all the thread possible with a sharp knife or razor—not the tonsorial implement daily used by some elder relation—until a projecting square of rubber, B,

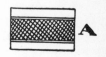

FIG. 7.—Using a Length of old Tyre for repairs.

remains, corresponding to the hole in the damaged cover. Fig. 7 illustrates these operations. There is nothing further to be done than to solution this piece of tyre where the rubber has been cut away, and, after allowing it several hours in which to dry off, to place it in position within the tyre with the raised rubber square and hole coinciding. A liberal dusting with French chalk, followed by inflation, will put the finishing touches to a durable repair.

INNER TUBES

Frequently, after several years' use of an inner tube, the inexplicable leakage occurs which defies detection even beneath water. This may usually be attributed to a weakened valve seating, in which case a remedy is found by changing the latter. The nut, A, Figs. 8 and 9, is unscrewed—whilst holding the flattened sides of C with pincers or a small vice—and removed together with the plate B. Three or four inches along the inner tube a slight incision is made, and through this the valve neck C is pushed from inside, the thick rubber washer D having been previously renewed if, as is probable, it seems misshapen. The inner tube E, Fig. 9, is solutioned some little way round the valve tube and a 2 in. by 4 in. piece of canvas, with rounded corners D, Fig. 8, and a hole in the centre, fixed in position, Figs. 8 and 9. The

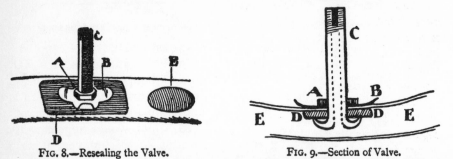

FIG. 8.—Resealing the Valve.   FIG. 9.—Section of Valve.

plate B is then replaced, and the nut A screwed down tightly, after which the old valve hole is mended with rubber solution and a patch, E, Fig. 8, as any ordinary puncture would be treated.

Paraffin oil is justly held in high esteem as an illuminant and as a cleaning agent. Its power to expel grit from bearings and wearing parts is patent knowledge to every wheelman, but care should be taken to prevent its reaching the crevices between wheel and tyre, because it is directly and indirectly harmful to the rubber—indirectly, seeing that it rusts the metal if the rim be of plated steel.

Vaseline—a paraffin preparation—is indispensable for temporarily keeping ball bearings in position whilst the component parts are being assembled.

Only recently have bicycle lamps been devised for the consumption of paraffin oil, although they have the incontrovertible advantage of being replenishable in nearly every district—in hamlets where colza oil, or carbide would be unknown to the populace. It is possible, however, to burn paraffin in an ordinary cycle lamp, by sewing the lower end of the wick to a three-yard length of surgical bandage, AA, Fig. 10, which latter is coiled round and round—ship's hawser style—into the reservoir, until only a small well about as large as a shilling is left in the centre, C. Oil is poured in until the packing becomes thoroughly soaked, the liquid just covering the reservoir bottom, and then the wick,

B, is tucked in and the burner replaced. Fig. 10 shows the arrangement in detail, whence it will be seen that the wick is trimmed hollow, so that the flame is as square as possible and the tendency of paraffin to smoke is discounted.

The foregoing are the more particular notes which the writer has to jot down about cycles. But before the pen runs dry, he would like to add a general adjuration to bicycle owners, that they learn something of their mounts, the ailments to which they are prone, and the remedies available.

Let fastidious cyclists especially note that dirt outside a machine matters not one iota compared with grit among the bearings, and that the latter may be dispelled by judicious dosing with paraffin.

FIG. 10.—Burning Paraffin in Lamp.

Let every wheelman realise that inner tubes and patches are best cleaned—previous to solutioning for repair—with mineral naphtha, and that solution may mostly be allowed to dry for a full hour if a durable patch over a burst is desired.

Holes with an area of several square inches may be safely mended in this fashion ; and if the gash has occurred near the valve, this should be moved and seated in a sound part of the tube.

All such schemes are worth consideration to the economist, especially with the recent tight markets in rubber. Finally, a last injunction—do not playfully squash distended bags on the highway, or a brick may peradventure be discovered with attendant buckling of forks and precipitation over an adjacent hedge. As the Irishman observed to the bystanders, who pressed forward after he had come hurtling down from a sky-scraper, "Faith and 'twasn't the going, but the suddent stoppin', as done it."

CHAPTER LIII

MOTOR CYCLING

HINTS ON SELECTING AND MANAGING A MACHINE

THERE is a feeling of independence experienced by the possessor of a motor cycle—he is not bound by railway time-tables—he starts when he likes, takes whichever route he prefers, selects his own pace, and, instead of sitting cramped in a stuffy railway carriage, he enjoys the fresh air and open country. A few years ago the motor cyclist was never sure of reaching his destination, but with a modern machine one can state within a reasonable limit the time of arrival at a destination even a hundred miles distant, that is, of course, barring accidents, which are liable to occur in any vehicle whatsoever.

A great many people do not take up motor cycling because they are afraid that they would never be able to understand or manage the machinery connected therewith. It is with a view to helping all such possible and prospective riders that the following instructions have been written.

THE CYLINDERS

The method of propelling the motor cycle is by either the four-stroke or the two-stroke internal combustion engine. The former is the more widely adopted, and will therefore be described in greater detail.

Four stroke (two cycle) means that the cycle of operations is completed during the four strokes of the piston or two revolutions of the fly-wheels. Of these four strokes, one downward stroke provides the power—the engine being provided with heavy fly-wheels, the momentum of which carries the piston over the other three strokes.

The four strokes are as follows :—

1. Induction stroke (downwards) } First revolution.
2. Compression stroke (upwards) }
3. Power stroke (downwards) } Second revolution.
4. Exhaust stroke (upwards) }

During the induction stroke a charge of gas, *i.e.* vaporised petrol mixed with air, is drawn into the cylinder through the inlet valve. This charge is then compressed by the upward motion of the piston,

A, Figs. 1 and 2. When the charge is in this compressed condition it is fired by an electric spark at the sparking plug, F. The combustion of the small atoms of gas, which are in very close contact through the compression, causes considerable and rapid expansion of the charge, and thence the power is derived. All the used or burnt charge is expelled from the cylinder by the upward travel of the piston, the gases going out through the valve, J, and the exhaust pipe, I, into the silencer.

In two-stroke engines the power is derived in the same way as in the four stroke, *i.e.* by the expansion of petrol gas; but instead of one power stroke in four, they have one in two. These engines are very

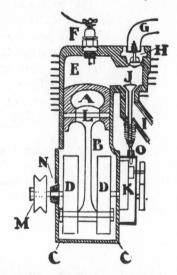

FIG. 1.—Side View of Cylinder.

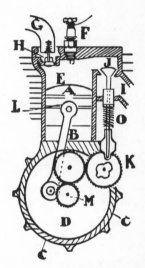

FIG. 2.—Front View of Cylinder.

often called valveless engines, having no valves or timing gear. The charge is firstly drawn into the crank case, and on the downward stroke of the piston it is forced into the cylinder through a pipe, the inrush of fresh gas, together with the peculiarly shaped piston, discharging the burnt gases.

The following explanation will give a key to Figs. 1 and 2.

A. Piston.
B. Connecting rod.
C. Crank case.
D. Fly-wheels.
E. Combustion head.
F. Sparking plug.
G. Inlet pipe.
H. Inlet valve.

I. Exhaust pipe.

J. Exhaust valve.

K. Timing gear.   (Two to one.)

L. Gudgeon pin.

M. Pulley.

N. Bush for main shaft.

O. Exhaust valve spring.

CARBURETTOR

In the petrol motor the first operation is to turn the liquid petrol into gas and mix it with air.   This is done by the carburettor.   Modern pattern carburettors consist of two chambers, the float chamber, and the spray chamber.

The petrol first enters the float chamber.   This contains a hollow brass float which governs a small needle valve, thus keeping a regular amount of petrol in the carburettor.   In the second chamber is a small jet connected to the supply in the float.   The petrol is drawn through this jet by the suction of the engine, and as the small column of petrol comes in contact with the air, it vaporises and mixes with it, making the explosive mixture, which is then drawn into the engine, compressed, fired, &c.

THE SPARKING

The spark is created by an electrical current which is either supplied by a magneto driven off the engine, or by a battery and induction coil as shown in Fig. 3. This current is made and broken at the correct period for firing the engine.   With regard to the magneto, the timing gear is practically built in the machine, therefore no attention will be paid to it in this article, for the amateur should not try taking a magneto to pieces, but, if anything goes wrong, should send it to the makers.

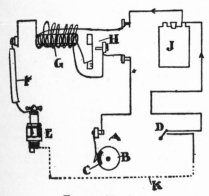

FIG. 3.—The Coil.

The lettering in Fig. 3, which shows an ordinary accumulator, coil, and diagram of wiring, may be thus explained.

A. Wipe contact.

B. Cam, or 2 to 1 gear.

C. Brass segment.
D. Handle-bar switch.
E. Sparking plug.
F. High-tension wire.
G. Coil.
H. Trembler.
J. Accumulator.
K. Frame of machine.

On accumulator or dry-cell machines, however, separate timing gear is provided. There are two patterns, namely, the Make and Break Contact, Fig. 4, and the Wipe Contact (with trembler coil), Fig. 5.

In both cases the cams are driven off the 2 to 1 gear, *i.e.* a gear revolving half the speed of the engine, thus making and breaking contact on every fourth stroke (second revolution).

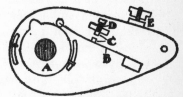

FIG. 4.—Make and Break Contact Timing Gear.

In the first case the cam, A, consists of a steel disc with either a bump or an indentation in the circumference. On this a contact blade, B, presses, and, as it comes to the bump or indentation, as the case may be, the low-tension circuit is suddenly made by the pressure of the two platinum points, CC, against each other. The current comes through the terminal, E, Fig. 4, and the adjusting screw, D ; accordingly, so soon as the contact blade has regained its normal position on the circumference of the cam, a separation of the two points, CC, breaks the contact, and the spark is broken between the points of the sparking plug.

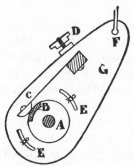

FIG. 5.—Wipe Contact Timing Gear.

The principle of the wipe contact is very similar. A, Fig. 5, is a fibre cam, in the circumference of which is the brass segment, B. Against this cam the contact blade, C, presses evenly, and is itself connected with the terminal, D. The two slits, EE, in the fibre base, G, allow the spark advance, whilst F is the control lever.

ACCUMULATORS

Accumulators are fitted in nearly all the non-magneto machines. These can, of course, be charged when they have run down, and may usually be reckoned to carry about 600 miles on a charge. A good dry battery, either a Hellesen, or a Siemens Obach, will certainly take a single-cylinder machine with an economical coil for a distance of 1500 miles, and after a rest several hundred more.

The great advantage of these batteries is that they can be carried at any angle—there is no acid to spill and corrode the terminals as in an accumulator, and there are no lead plates to crack.

OIL

The fly-wheels of the petrol motor are enclosed in an aluminium crank case, which is partially filled with a very thick lubricating oil, supplied from a small tank through a pump. The normal amount of oil required is a pumpful every ten or twelve miles, or better still, a half pumpful every five or six miles. This oil splashes up from the fly-wheels to the walls of the cylinder on to the gudgeon pin and crank pin, also working into the main bearings of the crank case.

If this supply of oil were cut off the bearings and piston would dry up, and the engine would "seize," *i.e.* the piston would bind into the cylinder, which, of course, would mean serious trouble.

VALVES

The valves on modern machines are mechanically operated, but on earlier patterns the inlet valves were automatic. Those of the former type are lifted off their seatings by cams driven on the 2 to 1 gear, and pulled back by strong springs, J, O, Figs. 1 and 2.

Automatic inlet valves are kept closed by a weak spring and opened by the suction of the engine on the induction stroke. If well adjusted, that is with the correct amount of opening, and well balanced, these valves give very good results ; but on slow speed and very high speeds they are inclined to stick, and in many instances the ignited charge gets blown back through the inlet pipe into the carburettor, setting light to the petrol. If this should happen, shut off the petrol supply from the tank, also the air to the carburettor, and open the throttle wide.

CONTROL OVER THE ENGINE

On most engines the rider has three or four controls, which may be briefly enumerated thus :—

(1) The Main Switch, which completely breaks the low-tension circuit, thus stopping any explosion in the engine. With a magneto the current is not broken, but "shorted" and as this is not con-

sidered good for the magneto, a switch is very often omitted altogether.

(2) The Air Lever which controls the amount of air to be mixed with the petrol gas in the spray chamber. On a wet day very little air can be used, whereas with a warm clear atmosphere the engine will run with the air port open to the full.

(3) The Throttle or Mixture Lever which controls the amount of mixture (petrol and air) to be admitted to the cylinder. For starting this will have to be wide open, being gradually closed as the machine gets warm and increases in speed.

(4) The Spark Advance Lever by which the timing of the spark can be controlled within a certain range.

Theoretically the explosive mixture should be ignited just as the piston is about to begin its downward stroke, and the gas is highly compressed, all the particles of petrol mixture being in close contact.

In slow speeds this is obtained by breaking the contact just as the piston is in position, but for higher speeds the time (although infinitesimal) taken for the current to be made or broken and to complete the circuit must be allowed for. It is obvious that with an engine revolving at about 1200 r.p.m., the smallest fraction of a minute is appreciable, and it is for this purpose that the spark advance lever is provided. If, however, the engine were started with the spark advanced, back-fire would occur, *i.e.* the mixture would be exploded before the piston reached the top of its stroke and would drive it backwards, whilst the momentum of the fly-wheels, trying to push it in the other direction, would cause an opposition of forces.

A powerful back-fire may quite easily cause a bent connecting rod, or damage the timing gears, &c. At slow speeds, advancing the spark too much will cause a very undesirable knocking, whilst a too far retarded spark, although not in itself serious, will make the engine suffer considerable loss of power—the charge being expelled before full use has been made of its expanding properties.

Owing to the construction of the magneto the spark has to be slightly advanced for starting, but it can be retarded when the engine is well in motion.

SELECTION OF A MACHINE

Having grasped the principle of the petrol motor, the next thing is to select a suitable machine.

It is advisable to get a good second-hand one. There are many reliable machines on the market, at prices ranging from £10 to £20, but great care should be exercised in choosing a mount, and, if possible, expert advice should be obtained. This being unavailable, the following points should be carefully looked to :—

(1) The make.—It should be of a well-known and recent make, so that spare parts may be easily obtained.

(2) Condition of the engine.—The compression can be tested by standing on the pedal with the back wheel jacked up. The compression should hold one's weight for a few seconds at least. Where pedalling gear is not provided the machine should be run a few steps along the road; if the compression is at all good the back wheel should skid.

(3) The main bearings should be tested by taking hold of a pulley and seeing whether there is any vertical play.

(4) The condition of the tyres and belt must certainly be looked into, as they are very expensive items.

(5) The frame.—The bicycle parts require careful examination, as does also the state of the enamel. Spring forks are preferable.

(6) The ignition-magneto, of course, should be chosen where possible, for accumulators, although they answer their purpose, are not to be compared for cleanliness, reliability, or economy with magnetos. However, it must be remembered that dry cells may always be substituted for the storage battery, and that those of a modern type are possibly cheaper in the end than the magneto.

Having purchased a suitable machine, it is best to go carefully over all the parts, making necessary adjustments.

In the case of accumulator ignition, have the accumulator well charged, and all the terminals thoroughly cleaned with sand-paper. Empty any stale lubricating oil out of the crank case by taking out the screw provided in the bottom for the purpose.

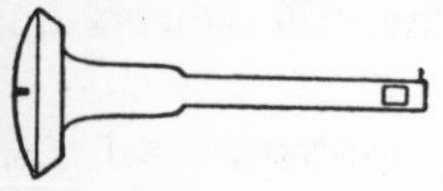

FIG. 6.—Mechanically operated Valve.

Having replaced this screw, inject five pumpfuls of fresh oil from the tank. Take out the valves and carefully examine their faces.

With the mechanical valves raise the cotter and spring, extract the key, and then release the cotter; the valve can then be lifted out. If the faces of the valves are at all pitted, they must be ground in—this process, although very easy, requiring considerable care. First make a mixture of emery powder and oil, then stuff plenty

FIG. 7.—Inlet Valve and Seating.

of waste round the valve seating and any recesses in the cylinder, smear the paste evenly over the valve seating and also on the face of the valve. A mechanically operated valve is shown in Fig. 6, whilst Fig. 7 depicts an inlet valve and seating. A is the slit for the screwdriver used in grinding in the valve, B is the valve itself, the faces, CC, of which require to be ground. D is the spring which operates on the valve and is attached thereto by the washer and split pin at E.

Replace the valve and rotate it with a screwdriver, putting fresh paste very frequently on the faces. This operation must be continued until all the pits on the face of the valve and seating have been removed. Clear away any remaining paste or emery powder from the cylinder, as this would soon work its way into the bore and be fatal to compression. Replace the valve and repeat the operation with the inlet. In the case of an automatic inlet valve, the seating and valve is taken out of the combustion head complete.

In some machines the combustion head is separate from the cylinder. With this type it would be as well to take it off, and, if there is any carbon deposit on the piston or in the combustion head, it must be scraped off and then thoroughly cleansed with petrol. If there are any signs of oil having blown out at the joint, a new copper-asbestos washer must be fitted. When replacing the combustion head, first screw down the four nuts with the fingers, and then carefully tighten up all round with a spanner.

If the exhaust valve spring is at all weak it should be replaced, as this cften makes a great improvement in the running of the engine.

The belt should be made as tight as possible by taking off one half of the fastener, cutting off a piece of the belt with a sharp knife, and joining up again. If a leather belt is provided, all grit should be scraped from it, and a dressing of Collan oil applied. All the bicycle parts should also be carefully adjusted, such as wheels, steering pillar, chain, free-wheel, &c.

Being satisfied that the machine is in good order, the next thing is a trial run on the road.

THE FIRST SPIN

First turn on the petrol and flood the carburettor by agitating the tickler. Shut off the air supply, and open the throttle wide, retard the spark and switch on the current, then with the exhaust valve lifted, run a few yards (pedalling, of course, if gear is provided). On dropping the valve the engine should fire and the rider may settle down into the saddle.

When the engine has got under " weigh," advance the spark a notch or two, and gradually open the air valve. Directly the engine shows any sign of misfiring, close the air valve slightly, and then gradually shut off the throttle in the same way. By this means the most economic and explosive mixture is obtained, and the beginner will soon be able to feel the exact amount of air and mixture that the engine will take.

If the engine is at all inclined to knock, shut off some air and retard the spark a little ; this knocking may be caused either by play in the bearings, or by carbon deposit on the piston and combustion head.

On coming to a steep hill, get up a good speed by advancing the spark and rush up the hill as far as possible ; directly the engine begins to slacken, retard the spark, slowly cut off the air supply, and open the throttle. Having done all this, as a last resource open the air valve slightly.

BREAKDOWNS

If the machine breaks down on the road, there are several things to be inspected. In many cases the ignition (especially on accumulator machines) is a source of trouble. A faulty sparking plug is very common, soot forming on the two points. This can be easily tested by taking out the sparking plug, Fig. 8, still attached to the high-tension wire, and lodging it on the top of the combustion head. Now revolve the back wheel, and if the plug be in good condition, sparks will jump across the points.

FIG. 8.—Sparking Plug.

Look at all the other connections and see that the terminals are screwed down tightly. Test the accumulator with a glow-lamp if one is carried.

If a trembler coil is used, clean any grit from between the blades with a clean rag, although if the coil already buzzes when the back wheel is revolved this is not necessary. Carefully clean the contact-breaker, cam, and contact, and also clean the platinum points.

Explosions in the silencer before stopping are generally due to stoppage of petrol, and if the engine starts up again after a rest of a minute or two, it shows that it is only a partial stoppage, most probably in the petrol pipe.

A complete failure of compression is generally due to one of two causes. Either the split pin of the automatic inlet valve has broken and let the valve fall, or grit has worked its way under the face of the exhaust valve, thus holding it off its seating.

On a second-hand mount it is especially important to carry a good supply of tools and spare parts, the most useful being :—

(1) Spare inlet and exhaust valves with springs.

(2) Two spare sparking plugs with copper-asbestos washers.

(3) A good selection of nuts, washers, terminals, split pins, &c.

(4) Spare lengths of high and low-tension insulated wire.

(5) A small test-lamp for accumulator.

(6) A good puncture outfit.

(7) An adjustable spanner—any spanner with the machine, an old file, a piece of glass paper (for cleaning terminals), and a screwdriver.

(8) A spare belt-fastener and a small piece of belt.

With these spares and a fairly modern mount, of whose idiosyncrasies some slight knowledge has been obtained, the rider need have little apprehension of trouble, and will be certain to have many hours of unalloyed pleasure with his trusty steed.

CHAPTER LIV

WHAT EVERY BOY SHOULD KNOW ABOUT RAILWAYS

INTERESTING FACTS ABOUT TRAINS AND HOW THEY ARE RUN

ALTHOUGH a knowledge of railway matters can scarcely be considered as a Hobby, so many boys have their own model railways, more or less complete, that it may well prove interesting to learn something about the actual working of the system. Railways have become such an all-important factor of every-day life that no boy should be without some idea at least of how they are worked. One of the best ways of acquiring such knowledge is to construct a model, making it as complete as possible in every detail ; yet even in the most perfect replica of an up-to-date railway, there are various points that cannot be reproduced, and it is with the idea of supplying some information concerning these that the present chapter has been written.

The system of controlling the vast network of lines that radiate through the country in every direction is very complicated, and when it is remembered that hundreds of thousands of lives are daily committed to the care of the railways, the skill and wisdom with which the roads are worked seem almost incredible.

THE PERMANENT WAY

The condition of the permanent way, as the actual course of the rails is called, demands the greatest care and attention on the part of the Railway Company. With huge engines, weighing many tons, constantly dashing over the rails at express speed, it stands to reason that the utmost vigilance must be exercised to see that the lines are maintained in such perfect condition that they are able to bear the heavy strain put upon them. Rails are made of Bessemer

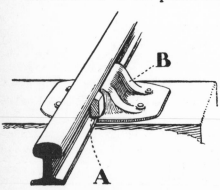

FIG. 1.—Chain and Wedge for fixing Rails.

steel, and are gripped securely into chairs with a wooden wedge, A, Fig. 1. These chairs, B, are in their turn bolted to sleepers laid about thirty inches apart on beds of ballast.

POINTS

Trains are transferred from one line to another by means of points, shown in Fig. 2. The two tongues A and B are moved by the switch-rod C, and, as the flanges of the wheels run inside, when the points are set as shown in the

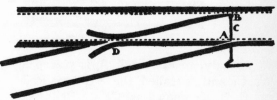

FIG. 2.—Simple Points.

diagram, the wheels pass over A, miss B, and so across the "frog" D, in the direction shown by the dotted lines.

SWITCH-BOLT FOR POINTS

Terrible accidents might happen if, by any chance, the signalman should alter the points whilst a train were crossing them. Accordingly, where there is any possibility of this occurring, a device known as a Switch-bolt, shown in Fig. 3, is employed.

An iron bar A, of sufficient length to stretch over the longest gaps between the wheels of the train, is placed against the inside of the

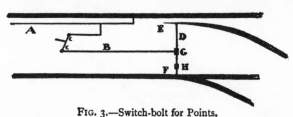

FIG. 3.—Switch-bolt for Points.

rails, and is connected by means of the lever CC to a long bolt, B, which, in its turn, passes through the transverse bar D, lying between the tongues E and F.

In this bar D are two holes, G and H, so arranged that, whichever position the tongues occupy, one of the holes is opposite the end of the bolt B.

When a train traverses the points, the wheels depress A, and keep it down whilst the train passes over. The pressure on A shoots the bolt B into that hole in D which happens to be opposite, thus locking the rod during the passage of the train, and making it impossible for the signalman to alter the points.

CROSS-OVER ROAD

The line connecting two parallel sets of rails as shown in Fig. 4, is known as a Cross-over Road. In order to keep the wheels per-

FIG. 4.—A Cross-over Road.

fectly steady, an extra rail, A, is placed against the line opposite the frog C, and is called the "Guard Rail." The ends of the other rails B, B, are known as "Wing Rails."

FIG. 5.—The Check Rail.

A similar device for retaining the flanges in position whilst passing a curve in the line is the check rail seen in Fig. 5.

CATCH POINTS

The Catch Points illustrated in Fig. 6 are intended to derail any

FIG. 6.—Catch Points.

vehicle which may attempt to travel over them in a wrong direction. They are especially used on inclines, where, if a carriage in the rear of a train were to break loose and roll backwards, it would be derailed before any serious harm could be done.

COMPENSATING LEVERS

Where the rods for working the points cover a considerable distance, experience has proved that some provision must be made for the expansion or contraction of the metal caused by the weather. Accordingly, the Compensating Lever, seen in Fig. 7, was devised, and has proved a perfect success.

The rod A comes from the signal-box, and is attached by the

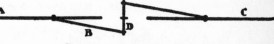

FIG. 7.—Compensating Lever.

smaller rod B to the lower end of the lever D. A similar connection joins the upper end of D to the rod C, which eventually works the points. The result of this arrangement is, that A and C, both expanding to a similar degree, work in opposite directions upon the lever D, with the result that each counteracts the expansion or contraction of the other.

LEVELS

It is the ambition of every railway engineer to make his line level. But the natural face of the country renders it impossible to obtain a continuous level, and, as the great weight of the train makes a very appreciable difference to the engine when travelling uphill, the gradients are marked by the side of the line in order that the driver may know exactly how steep an incline he has to negotiate. The gradient post illustrated in A, Fig. 8, shows that on the right there is a rise of 1 foot in

FIG. 8.—Gradient and Mile Posts.

145, whilst in the other direction there is a drop of 1 foot in 160.

The mile post, B, Fig. 8, depicts a very useful method of gauging the speed of the train. The miles are numbered from the London terminus of the Railway, whilst intermediate posts mark every quarter of a mile.

A ready way of ascertaining the speed of the train is to count

the number of seconds taken in passing from one quarter-mile post to another, and to divide 900 by the sum thus obtained, the result giving the speed per hour at which the train is travelling

SIGNALS

Nothing goes further to make the reputation of a railway than its system of signalling. Not only are there less accidents likely to occur, but the general speed and punctuality of the trains are more reliable where the signalling is carried out according to an efficient method.

Amongst British Railways, the Great Western is probably the best managed in this respect, and to this may in great part be attributed the speed and safety with which their express trains traverse the country.

Fixed signals are almost invariably constructed with semaphore arms that indicate safety or danger according to their position.

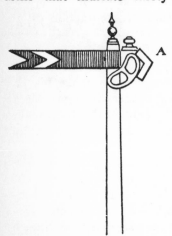

FIG. 9.—A Distant Signal.

Looking ahead, the engine-driver usually finds his signals to the left of the line and on the left of the signal-post, as in Fig. 9. The front of the signal arm facing him is painted red with a white stripe a quarter of the distance from the end. The other side of the arm is white and has a black stripe. Drivers, of course, ignore all white signal arms, since these only apply to trains travelling in the opposite direction.

Unless a train be expected the signal arm is horizontal and in that position means "Danger." To allow a train to pass, the arm is lowered to an angle of 55°, this indicating "Line Clear."

As the arm cannot be seen at night, however, coloured glasses fitted in a frame known as "spectacles," are attached in such a manner that when the arm is down a green light shows the driver that the line is clear, whilst at other times a red light betokens "Danger." The white angle light, seen at A, Fig. 9, distinguishes a distant signal, and this angle light does not move with the spectacles, but shows the same whether the signal be up or down.

SIGNAL ARMS

A glance at Fig. 10 will show the various types of semaphore arms used on signal-posts, which may be briefly described thus :—

A, The Distant signal.

B, Home or Starting signal.

C, Home and Distant placed on same post.

D, Starting and Shunt signal.

E, Bracket signals placed before a point where two lines branch.

F, Backing signals to control the placing of trains on a siding.

G, Siding signals, to run a train from a siding to the main line.

H, Signal not be heeded.

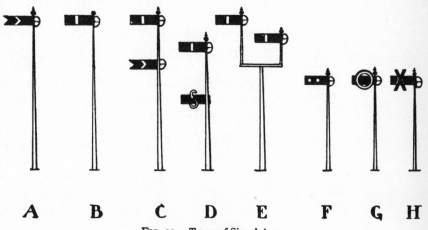

A   B   C   D   E   F   G   H

FIG. 10.—Types of Signal Arms.

DISTANT AND HOME SIGNALS

For purposes of signalling, the whole length of the line is divided into sections, each section being controlled by a signal-box. The first signal a driver meets when entering a section is the Distant signal, which is always distinguishable by its notched arm, A, Fig. 10. If the signal be down the driver proceeds at full speed, but if the signal be against him, showing Danger, he diminishes his speed but does not actually stop, for the Distant signal is only intended as a warning that the next signal may be against him, and that in consequence he will then have to pull up the train.

The caution thus given by the Distant signal is very necessary for fast trains which could not possibly draw up in a few yards, but which can easily be slowed between the Distant and Home signals.

Having passed the Distant, the engine next reaches the Home signal, which is near the signal-box, and, if that be at a station, guards the entrance to the platform, as seen in Fig. 11. The Home signal is known as a Stop signal, for, unlike the Distant, it obliges the driver to stop dead until it is lowered to show that the line is clear.

STARTING SIGNALS

After the Distant and Home signals, the driver next encounters the Starting signal, which, at a station, is at the far end of the platform. Like the Home signal, it is a Stop signal, and allows the train to proceed into the next section. In some cases, however, an Advanced Starting signal is used, and then this latter passes the train on to the next signalman.

Taking the plan of lines at a station similar to that shown in

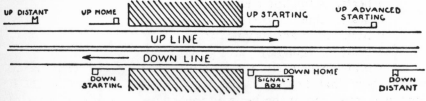

FIG. 11.—Signals at a Station.

Fig. 11, a through down train would find the down Distant, Home, and Starting signals all lowered if the line were clear. But, if the signalman wished to stop the train at the station, he would leave all the signals at Danger, and the driver, as soon as he saw the Distant against him, would slacken speed and be prepared to stop. As he approached, the Home signal would be lowered and the train drawn up and stopped by the Starting signal, which would not be changed until the signalman was ready to pass the train along the line.

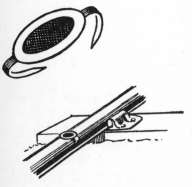

FIG. 12.—Fog Signals.

FOG SIGNALS

When the signal arms are concealed by fog, detonators or Fog Signals, consisting of percussion caps fastened to the rail by lead clasps, as shown in Fig. 12, are placed on the outer rail by men acting under the instructions of the signalman. When the signal is at Danger, the man places two caps on the line about five yards apart, and, as soon as the signal is lowered, one of these is removed.

The driver, hearing the report of the explosion, is thus made aware of the state of the line ahead.

INSIDE THE SIGNAL-BOX

Signalmen communicate with one another by means of telegraphs and bells. There are usually telephones in the box as well, but very stringent rules are enforced against the use of these for any but strictly official conversations.

The Bell Code, by means of which trains are " given " by one signal-box to another, contains some forty or fifty messages, of which the most important are the following :—

    1 beat calls attention at the other end.

    2 beats, Train entering section.

    3 beats (given irregularly thus, 1-1—1), Train has left section.

    4 beats, Is the line clear for an express ?

    6 beats, Line obstructed.

    7 beats, Stop and examine train.

    8 beats (irregularly, 3 and 5), Cancel signal.

    11 beats (irregularly, 1-5-5), Shunt train for another to pass.

To show that he has received and understood a message, the signalman must repeat the beats to the box whence the message was sent, nor may the sender be content until he knows for certain that his message has been correctly received.

An Express train is allowed to pass any slower trains that may be on the line, and the signalman must arrange to shunt these slower trains to sidings or hurry them on to places where this can be done.

As a train passes his box, whether by day or by night, the signalman must see that the last carriage bears the tail-lamps, as only by this means can he be sure that no vehicle has become detached during the journey from the last box. If he cannot see the lamps he rings nine consecutive beats to the preceding box, where the man tells the next engine-driver passing in that direction to look out for any loose carriages on the line.

The signalman is also obliged to look closely at every train that passes, and, if he

FIG. 13.—Electric Signal-repeater.

sees anything wrong, he must send a bell message to the next box and have the train stopped.

If by some accident, such as the damage caused by a snow-storm, all the telegraphic communication between two boxes be broken, the engine-drivers are warned to proceed with caution, and immediate steps are taken to set everything right again.

Where signals are concealed from the box by a curve in the line, an electric repeater, shown in Fig. 13, informs the man whether the signal has worked properly, as the little arm duplicates the exact position of the actual semaphore.

PICKING UP WATER

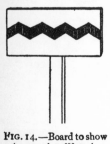

FIG. 14.—Board to show Approach to Watering-trough.

Great delay would be entailed by stopping fast trains in order to replenish the boilers. On main lines, therefore, long troughs of water are placed between the rails, and, as the engine passes over them, a suction pump draws the water up through a hose and thus refills the tanks.

A board marked with a zigzag line, as seen in Fig. 14, warns the driver of his approach to one of these troughs, giving him time to slacken speed if it is his intention to take up water.

THE TRAIN

COLOURS OF ENGINES

In the United Kingdom practically every railway has its engines painted in distinctive colours. Amongst the principal English railways using different colours may be mentioned the following :—

Great Western (G.W.R.).   Green picked out in Black.
Great Northern (G.N.R.).   Plain Green.
Midland Rly. (M.R.).   Chocolate Crimson.
North Eastern (N.E.R.).   Green.
Great Eastern (G.E.R.).   Blue (Goods engines, Black).
Lancashire and Yorkshire.   Black picked out in Red and White.
South Eastern and Chatham (S.E. & C.R.).   Dark Green.
London and North Western (L. & N.W.R.).   Black picked out in White.
London and South Western (L. & S.W.R.).   Green picked out in Chocolate and Black.
London, Brighton and South Coast (L.B. & S.C.R.).   Brownish Yellow.

HEAD-LIGHTS

At night it is very important that signalmen and station officials should know the nature of trains travelling over the lines. Standard arrangements of Head-lights have therefore been instituted, which, with a few local exceptions in the neighbourhood of London, obtain throughout the country. Attached to the engines, these lights serve to indicate the exact nature of the train.

Express Passenger trains carry a lamp over each corner above the buffer, as shown in A, Fig. 15.

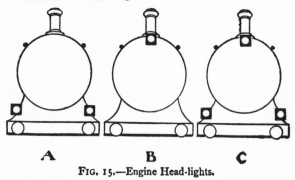

A   B   C

FIG. 15.—Engine Head-lights.

Slow Passenger trains carry one lamp under the funnel as in B.

Empty Passenger trains have one lamp over each buffer and one under the funnel, C.

Express Goods trains carry one lamp under the funnel and one immediately below it, as in A, Fig. 16.

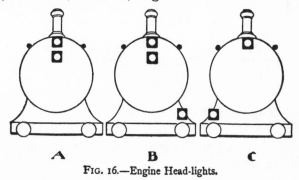

A   B   C

FIG. 16.—Engine Head-lights.

Slow Goods trains carry the same lamps as the Express, with the addition of a lamp over the left-hand buffer B, Fig. 16.

Fish, Meat, and Cattle trains carry one lamp under the funnel and one over the right-hand buffer C.

Fruit and Vegetable trains carry a lamp under the funnel and one over the left buffer, as in A, Fig. 17.

Through Mineral trains carry three lamps in a row B, Fig. 17.

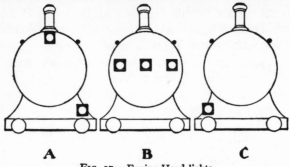

A B C

FIG. 17.—Engine Head-lights.

Light engines carry one lamp over the right buffer C, Fig. 17.

Green lamps are sometimes used in local services near large stations, but the code described above is in general use throughout the British Isles.

TAIL-LAMPS

In the same way that engines carry Head-lights to show their identity, the last vehicle of a train bears Tail-lamps to inform any driver that may be following in the same direction whether the train ahead is on the line upon which he is travelling, or whether it is upon

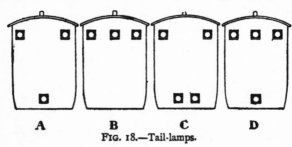

A B C D

FIG. 18.—Tail-lamps.

a side line. The following, shown in Fig. 18, are those most generally used:—

A, Three lamps in a triangle show that the train is on the passenger line.

B, Three lamps in a row show the train to be on a goods line.

C, Four lamps in a kind of triangle indicate that a special passenger train will follow.

D, Three lamps in a row with one beneath show that a goods special will follow.

TAIL NOTICES

Occasionally it happens that a horse van or a goods truck is attached to the last vehicle of a passenger train, and in such cases a board with the letters L.V. (Last Vehicle) is placed on the tail, as in A, Fig. 19.

In times of great pressure the regular trains often fail to provide accommodation for the public, and other trains have to be run. Accord-

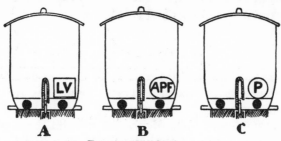

A　　　　　**B**　　　　　**C**

FIG. 19.—Tail Notices.

ingly a board is attached to the last carriage of the ordinary train with the letters A.P.F. (Another Portion Follows), illustrated in B, Fig. 19.

Again, when a station-master learns that a special train will be run, he affixes a red board with the letter P to the last carriage of the train immediately preceding the special, as seen in C, thus apprising every railway servant of the fact.

COMMUNICATION BETWEEN PASSENGERS AND GUARD

The Board of Trade has very wisely made it compulsory that there should be some means of communi-cation between the passengers and the engine-driver and guard, so that in the event of any emergency the train may be stopped and the neces-sary assistance rendered. This com-munication, of course, may only be used in cases of really urgent need, and a penalty of £5 is attached to any improper use of the alarm.

A chain runs the whole length of every coach, passes through each compartment within easy reach of the passengers, and terminates in an iron rod, AA, Fig. 20. To both ends of this rod are fixed discs, BB,

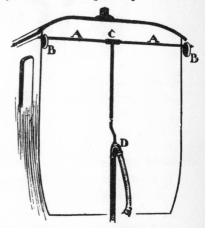

FIG. 20.—Communication between Passenger and Guard.

which fall to a downward position when the chain is pulled, thereby showing the guard from which coach the alarm has been given.

The centre of this rod works a valve, C, in a little pipe which admits a small quantity of air into the main vacuum pipe at D, thus automatically applying the brake. As soon as he perceives that the brake has been applied, the driver stops the train, whilst the guard hastens to the coach and ascertains what is amiss.

Some old types of railway carriages still retain the electric bell apparatus, but most of the large lines have adopted the chain system and have proved it to be the most efficacious.

The Brake

The question of brakes has always been considered of the most vital importance, and the Board of Trade regulations are very exacting with regard to what must be effected.

There are two descriptions of brake that fulfil the demands of the Board of Trade—namely, the Westinghouse, and the Automatic Vacuum Brake.

In the Westinghouse Automatic Brake compressed air supplies the necessary force, and is stored in a large reservoir on the engine, whence the driver can admit it to the main pipes and brakes throughout the train.

The Automatic Vacuum Brake is the reverse of the Westinghouse, being worked, as the name implies, by means of a vacuum. Beneath the floor of every vehicle in the train is an iron pipe, connected with the piping D of the adjoining carriage by the flexible tube shown in Fig. 21. At the end of the tube, B, is a coupling head, A, constructed to fit the companion coupling head on C belonging to the next carriage, and when all the coaches are coupled together throughout the train, there is a continuous pipe running from the engine to the last vehicle.

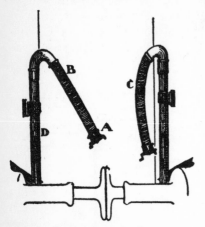

FIG. 21.—Vacuum Brake Connection.

The air is exhausted throughout this continuous pipe by means of a tap in the engine, and when the vacuum is thus established the brake is off. By the admission of air into the pipe, piston rods in each carriage work the brakes, and therefore any accident, such as the breakage of the couplings, would immediately wrench the tube apart and automatically apply the brakes in every part of the train.

LIGHTING OF CARRIAGES

In olden days railway carriages were illumined by oil-lamps, which were frequently extinguished by the motion of the train. It was not long, however, before these were replaced by gas, stored in tanks beneath the carriage floors, and lit from the roof by hand.

Electricity has now almost superseded gas, and all the newer coaches are lighted by electric bulbs, the current being generated in a dynamo driven by the axles of the wheels as they revolve when the train is in motion.

SLIP CARRIAGES

To avoid the delay occasioned by stopping express trains at stations where several passengers are to be set down but there are none to be picked up, slip carriages are attached to the rear of the train and slipped at the required station.

By the very simple device shown in Fig. 22, the guard in charge of the slip carriage can disconnect the coupling and allow the main portion of the train to proceed on its way, leaving him at the station. The coupling link from the last carriage, B, of the main portion of the train is held in the hook D of the slip carriage A. This hook is made with a joint, so that when the bolt C is withdrawn by means of the lever F, the upper portion of the hook falls down to the position shown by the dotted lines and allows the link to fall free.

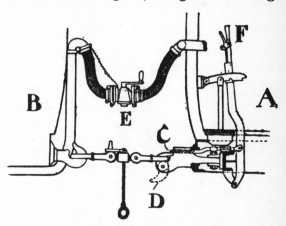

FIG. 22.—Slip Carriage Connections.

It is, of course, important that the vacuum tube arrangement should not be disturbed in any way by slipping, accordingly the guard, before disconnecting the coupling, leans out of the window in front of his carriage and turns the slip-cock E, by this means sealing the vacuum in the pipe.

Just before slipping, the guard applies his hand-brake, so that as soon as the coupling has been disconnected, his part of the train slows down. He then sounds the whistle as he enters the station.

Trains carrying a slip portion bear red and white lamps side by side, as tail-lamps.

The Whistle Code

The engine-driver has no other, and indeed could have no better, means of communicating with the signalman than by using his whistle. Every large station has its own special code which the local engine-drivers must know by heart, but on the line itself there is a universal or standard code, some of the signals of which may be explained thus :—

Express trains only are allowed to give one long whistle when passing a station.

Two short blasts mean that an engine on a down main line wants to reach the down siding.

Three short blasts mean that an engine on the up main line wishes to reach the up siding.

Four short blasts show that a main line engine wishes to be switched to another main line.

A short blast followed by a kind of shriek or crow informs the signalman that a train has been taken right on to a siding and is clear of the main line.

Upon entering a tunnel the driver gives one blast to warn any one that may be on the line that his train is approaching.

Shunters' Signals

The shunting of goods trucks from one line to another requires the presence of a trained shunter, who, by moving his arms, can indi-

Fig. 23.—Shunters' Signals.

cate to the engine-driver what he must do. The more common signals are shown in Fig. 23.

A shows the sign for Stop.

B „   „   Advance slowly.

C „   „   Return to former place.

D „   „   Right away.

THE BREAK-DOWN GANG

Although accidents are, happily, rarely attended by any fatality, they invariably cause great inconvenience. Sometimes the derailing of a single goods truck will upset the entire working of the main line, causing annoyance and expense to hundreds of people. It therefore behoves the railway companies to be prepared for such emergencies, and to have the means at hand to enable them to clear the lines with the utmost expedition.

At certain large stations break-down trains are kept in constant readiness. As soon as an accident occurs the nearest signalman telegraphs for assistance, his message, marked D.M. (Danger Message), interrupting any other despatch that may be in course of transmission.

The break-down train, with its staff of men, immediately proceeds to the scene of the accident with the utmost speed, being signalled throughout as an express passenger train, to make room for which every other train must be side-tracked.

The composition of the break-down train varies, to a certain extent, according to the nature of the accident to be dealt with. As a rule, a large travelling crane is coupled next to the engine, and is followed by the break-down van, the interior of which is fitted with shelves containing over five hundred implements of all kinds, sorted and ready for immediate use, so that every possible contingency can be coped with at the shortest notice. After the van follows a carriage for the officials and staff, who are all trained men, fully competent to overcome whatever obstacles may lie in their way.

Two of the most interesting and important appliances carried by the break-down gang are the hydraulic and the traversing jacks. The hydraulic jack, shown in Fig. 24, is a very simple affair in appearance, and can be manipulated by a little child. By working the handle up and down, the ram is raised with such force that it will lift a large engine with ease.

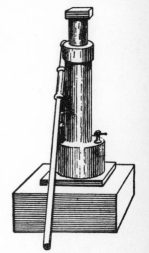

FIG. 24.—The Hydraulic Jack.

The traversing jack, Fig. 25, combines the action of the hydraulic jack with a traverse motion, so that a vehicle can be raised in the ordinary way and then carried a short distance transversely. This jack is especially useful for replacing engines that have slipped a short way off the lines.

The ramps shown in Fig. 26 are useful for replacing empty trucks and coaches on the line when they have been derailed.   The

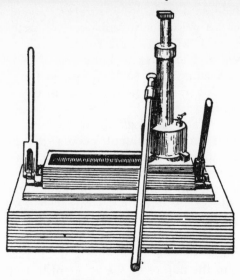

FIG. 25.—Traversing Jack.

ramps are put before the front wheels of the vehicle, which is then

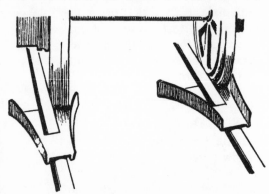

FIG. 26.—Ramps for Carriage Wheels.

drawn slowly forward until the ramps have guided the wheels on to the line again.

THE SNOW-PLOUGH

In the northern parts of Scotland it occasionally happens that a heavy fall of snow buries the permanent way to such an extent that no train could possibly advance through the drift.   An enormous plough, therefore, shown in Fig. 27, with a share which has a cutting edge just clear of the rails, is run over the line, and tosses the snow upon either side, forging a passage through the drift wide enough to admit of the passage of a train.

The snow - plough is usually placed on the front of a heavy engine to which two or three other engines are frequently coupled behind, and the whole party charges into the snow at full speed. The result is marvellous ! A mighty cloud of white arises on either hand, and a road is ploughed through glistering walls which often tower high above the tops of the coaches.

FIG. 27.—The Snow-plough.

MAIL COACHES

Special sorting coaches are carried on nearly all the fast mail trains that speed from London to different quarters of the kingdom. A trained staff of sorters travels up and down in these vans, deftly carrying on their work, wholly unconcerned at the swaying and jolting of the train.

The interior of the sorting coach is lined with hundreds of pigeon-holes, each hole referring to a district or village. No sooner has the last sack of letters been placed in the coach by the General Post Office carriers, than the sorters start their work and place the letters in their proper pigeon-holes.

In one corner of the coach is a stove upon which the sealing-wax is heated for sealing the sacks when they have been filled with the letters belonging to the district, and as soon as they are ready for delivery, these sacks of letters are stored in the order in which they will be required for distribution.

There is no need, however, to stop the train in order to collect or deliver the mail bags at wayside stations. When a mail train has to collect a sack in the course of its journey, the local postman places this sack upon an arm attached to a post by the side of the rail, illustrated in Fig. 28, and, as the train passes, a net hung out from the sorting coach catches the bag off the arm. The net is then drawn into the coach and the contents of the bag sorted. The process is reversed for the delivery of mail bags, although in some cases the sacks are merely dropped from the sorting coach as the train passes the station.

A plain white board, depicted in Fig. 28A, warns the

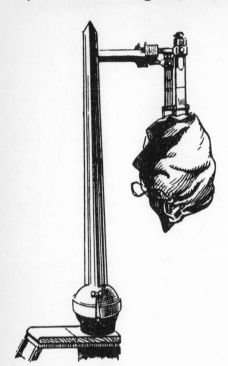

FIG. 28.—Arm for Collecting Mail Bag.

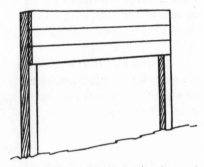

FIG. 28A.—Notice Board showing Approach to Mail-bag Collector.

sorters that they are approaching a mail post, and gives them an opportunity of having everything in readiness to receive or distribute the bag, as the case may be.

THE TWO BEST TRAINS IN ENGLAND

Foremost amongst the splendid trains of which our country is so proud must be mentioned the Cornish Riviera Express, with its great non-stop run to Plymouth. The Great Western Railway holds the record for the fastest trains in the United Kingdom, and spares neither pains nor expense to maintain their reputation, and even increase it by the luxurious accommodation afforded to their passengers.

The Cornish Riviera Express, running every week-day from Paddington to Penzance, whirls down to Plymouth, a distance of 226 miles, without a stop, although the various slip-coaches dropped *en route* serve most of the large towns through which it runs. Dining-cars and splendid saloons render the journey a delightful experience, and form a remarkable contrast to the discomfort with which such a long journey would have been attended in the old days of stuffy compartments.

But the greatest non-stop run is accomplished by the "Ocean Specials," belonging to the same company, and conveying passengers to Fishguard, a distance of 260 miles, without a stop. The great coaches, seventy feet long, are the most comfortable and the largest in England, and each train carries over a dozen attendants to assist the passengers. Hot water and milk are provided for the children, and a skilled female attendant sees to the comfort of ladies and invalids travelling by the train.

At the terminus of one of these large restaurant trains is a building where all the food is stored and provided for the use of the cooks. Before starting on a journey, the *chef* takes what he considers necessary to supply the *menu*, which is different every day, and before the train steams out of the station he and his staff have set to work with their cooking.

On long journeys, such as those to Scotland, the attendants travel up one day and return with the train the next, for the staff are always attached to one train or vehicle, and follow its fortunes wherever it may take them.

THE KING'S TRAIN

In no country in the world does Royalty travel with such comfort as in England. Every large railway company has its own luxuriously equipped Royal train, the interior of which, fitted sumptuously and upholstered in the daintiest of styles, is more like what one would expect to find in a palace than in a railway coach.

The train is usually made up of a brake van, a special saloon, the Royal saloon, another special saloon, and a rear brake van. In the King's saloon are a bedroom about 15 feet in length, a smoking-room, a private room, and a compartment for his personal attendants. Indeed every possible arrangement is made to ensure the Royal passenger arriving at his destination unfatigued.

A special time-table is constructed for the Royal train as soon as a railway company learns that it is to be honoured with His Majesty's patronage, and every individual on the line, from the station-master down to the platelayer, is advised of the fact and required to sign a paper showing that he has received due notice.

A reliable man is placed at every facing point along the line of the Royal train half-an-hour before the train is due, and has orders to lock every gate giving access to the line. All the fog-signalling staff is called out an hour before the train is due to pass ; in short, no precaution is neglected to ensure the safety of the Royal travellers.

The whole line is kept clear for the train ; shunting on side lines must be stopped half-an-hour before its arrival, and all drivers near the line must see that their engines are neither smoking nor whistling whilst the special passes.

The arrangements for signalling the Royal train cannot be much more stringent than those for an ordinary train, as the utmost care of the lives entrusted to them is exercised by the railway companies in any case ; but all telegraphists are obliged to be in attendance whilst the train is on the lines ; and, of course, every one does his best to protect the Sovereign from accident.

It must not be imagined, however, that the King travels as a guest on the railways in his country. A charge is made for his train, and, paying first-class fares for every passenger in addition to the charge for the special train, His Majesty spends exactly the same amount as would any other passenger travelling under similar conditions.

WHAT SOME OF THE RAILWAYMEN DO

The Station-master.—The responsibilities attached to the position of station-master seem almost overwhelming at first sight. In the larger stations, of course, he has a staff of skilled subordinates to whom he relegates much of his work, but even then he is, to a large extent, responsible for the proper carrying out of his orders.

The whole section of the line affected by his station is under his entire control. The station-master has to supervise the running of the trains and ensure their punctuality ; he is personally responsible for the condition of the permanent way ; he must see that his station is in good order, and that all the men are performing their duties properly.

Not the least of the station-master's duties is to inspect the signal-boxes, and see that all the regulations are being carried out correctly. He must keep himself informed of the state of the lamps on the signal-posts, and be sure that they are properly lighted and kept well trimmed. In addition to all this, he has to control the clerical work connected with the booking and goods, which in large stations is very considerable.

The Engine-driver.—The actual safety of the passengers is almost entirely confided to the engine-driver, upon whose vigilance and care the running of the train depends. The career of an engine-driver is, on most railways, arranged on the following plan :—

At about seventeen years of age he enters the works as a cleaner, and learns all about the construction and manipulating of the machinery. Three years are spent at this work, and the ability the lad shows during this period is taken into consideration when his turn comes for promotion.

It is as the fireman on a "shunter" that the budding driver first makes acquaintance with the actual handling of an engine. The "shunter" is an engine employed solely in shunting trucks on a goods siding, and, although the work is not of great interest, it provides an excellent training for the young engineer.

As the eyesight is an important thing with an engine-driver, who must be able to distinguish coloured lights and signals from afar, the tests through which he has to pass are very stiff. When he has satisfactorily proved that his sight is good, the "shunter" fireman is promoted to be fireman on a goods train; thence he is transferred to a passenger train, and, if he proves to be efficient, after a time he is given charge of a goods engine. Having undergone further tests, he is promoted to the rank of a third-class driver, working a slow passenger train.

Promotion from a slow train to one of the large engines depends entirely upon a man's record and the ability he has shown during the course of his career.

The engine-driver must, of course, know the line perfectly by day or night. Nothing but experience can teach a man to tell where he is by the sound of the engine, whether it is crossing a bridge or passing through a cutting; and it is only after many years in the cabin of a small engine that a driver can attain the summit of his career and work an express.

The Fireman.—The fireman, as his name suggests, has to keep the furnace burning evenly and clearly during the journey. It is also his duty to assist the driver in keeping a look-out, and naturally the greater part of the cleaning falls to his lot. He must know what to do in emergencies, and be able to draw up the train if the driver should be suddenly taken ill at his post. In fact, the fireman must make himself generally useful, and show himself competent to take charge of an engine when his time comes.

The Guard.—The guard has the actual control of the train. He is given a list of the carriages, and estimates the weight of the train, communicating the result of his calculations to the driver. The guard is obliged to see that all the couplings are secure, that the tail-lamps are correctly placed, and that the passengers are properly accommodated.

He is responsible for the punctual starting of his train, and for this purpose carries a special watch regulated weekly at the works. Until the guard gives the signal, not even the station-master can authorise the departure. He must watch the speed at which he is travelling, and if he finds it is going too quickly, it is his duty to apply the brake, and, if necessary, bring the train to a standstill.

In the event of an accident, the guard must run back and warn any approaching train to slow down, and for this purpose he carries a few detonators in his brake van which he can place on the line and thus attract the driver's attention.

THE RAILOPHONE

The application of wireless telephony to railway traffic bids fair to revolutionise several points of engineering. An electrician at Birmingham, in the course of his experiments, discovered that by installing two larger coils of wire on a travelling vehicle, direct electric

FIG. 29.—The Railophone.

communication could be established with a wire lying upon the track as shown in Fig. 29. This wire A is connected to the signal-boxes C along the line, and when telephone receivers and transmitters B and D are attached to each, the signalman can talk with ease to any person standing at the receiver on the moving train.

Passengers will find it as easy to call up their friends in London as if they were in the office, and the pleasure of whiling away the tedious hours of travelling by conversing with friends cannot fail to gain unreserved appreciation.

But the marvels of the invention do not end here. Two drivers, dashing along the lines, will be able to converse with one another, or give warning of their proximity, and many a disastrous accident will thus be avoided. The benefits of this will be especially noticed in fogs, and at times when from some reason or another the signals are invisible or fail to work.

By a further ingenious application of this principle, a signalman by pressing a lever will be able to apply the brake to any train along the line, whilst the same power will lie with every engine-driver. Thus the driver of a light engine, hearing an express train dashing up behind him, will not only have it in his power to warn the approaching driver, but he will be able to pull up the overtaking train ere it has dashed upon him and caused a terrible disaster.

Underground Railways

The construction of tubes is the latest development of any importance in the railway world, and the numerous lines that worm their way beneath the London streets give ample proof of the success of the idea.

The first step in the construction of a tube is to sink a vertical well or shaft to the required depth, about 60 or 70 feet, and from there bore a circular tunnel to another shaft sunk where it is intended to have the next station. The work has to be done in compressed air, and as a rule only about fifteen feet can be removed in the twenty-four hours, although this, of course, depends upon the soil through which the men are boring.

Iron rings prevent the walls or roof of the cylindrical tubes from falling in, and the trains are built in such a way that the carriages almost fill the tube. At first it was thought that the moving train would thus renew the air supply during its passage, but although this proved true to a certain extent, it has been found necessary to supplement the supply of air by other arrangements.

The signalling for the underground service is practically the same as for the ordinary railroads, although the fact that the lines rarely cross renders the system simpler. As the length of the trains at the busy time of day is frequently such that there is no room for the motor-man to pull up with his engine at the platform, a special board marked with a larger 7, referring to the number of coaches in the train, is affixed to the signal-post, as seen in Fig. 30, and indicates where he must stop.

FIG. 30.—Underground Railway Signal.

SOME REMARKS ABOUT PASSENGERS

There are several other points in connection with railway travelling which are well worth knowing.

Tickets.—Many passengers imagine that if they are unable to produce their tickets when called upon to do so, they must pay the fare over again. This is not the case. If he has lost his ticket, it is quite sufficient for the passenger to give his name and address and settle the matter upon his return home. More than this cannot be legally demanded, and whether it be a season-ticket holder or an ordinary traveller, the railway officials cannot insist upon immediate repayment.

Luggage.—Railway companies are not responsible for luggage left lying upon the platform, and if the owner does not place his property in the cloak-room, the fault is his if it be lost.

If a passenger gives his bag to a porter who deposits it upon the seat in a carriage, the company is responsible for the safety of the article. They are equally responsible for trunks which the guard turns out on the platform upon arrival, but as soon as the property has been claimed by the owner, their responsibility ceases.

CHAPTER LV

WHAT EVERY BOY SHOULD KNOW ABOUT THE SEA

THE BRITISH BOY'S HERITAGE

STANDING upon the beach during those glorious summer holidays when school is exchanged for boating and bathing, every land boy must often look out to sea wistfully and wish he knew a little more about the ships and steamers that pass silently on their way, outward or homeward bound. The call of the sea is a very real thing to the greater number of British boys and men—indeed to many boys the sea and all connected therewith is the sole hobby that can offer any interest, and this is surely what should be amongst the sons of a nation that has earned the distinction of being called "The Mistress of the Seas."

TYPES OF SAILING BOATS

Almost the first question that arises in the landsman's mind concerns the different sailing ships and skiffs that race along before the wind or pass slowly and sedately across the far distant horizon.

FIG. 1.—Types of Sailing Boats.

Although there are many kinds of sailing boats, the types most commonly seen are those shown in the accompanying illustrations.

The cutter yacht, A, Fig. 1, is mostly used for pleasure, although some of the East Coast fishing smacks are built on very similar lines.

451

Topsail barges, B, are often to be seen around the coast carrying coal and miscellaneous cargoes from one port to another.

The brigantine, C, the brig and the full-rigged ship, A and B, Fig. 2, are gradually being replaced by steamers, and before many

B   **A**

Fig. 2.—A Brig and a Full-rigged Ship.

Fig. 3.—Register Number on a Small Boat.

years have passed away may possibly have disappeared from the high seas for ever.

The owners of all fishing smacks are, by law, obliged to register their craft at some port near to their homes, and the sails, as well as the boats themselves, must bear the initials formed by the first and last letters of the name of the port of registration, followed by the registered number. The boat shown in Fig. 3, for example, bears the initials IH, indicating that the port of registration is Ipswich, whilst the number 73 shows her number in the port books.

STEAMERS AND THEIR FUNNELS

By looking at the funnel of a steamer it is generally possible to tell whether she belongs to one of the large lines. The different

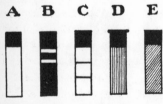

Fig. 4.—Some Steamer Funnels.

colours of the funnels, and the flags flying from the mast-head, are certain means of identification. In this limited space it would be impossible to give a description of the funnels belonging to boats of all the main lines that voyage to every quarter of the globe, but Fig. 4 shows the distinctive markings of some of the principal English lines.

A, Bibby Line; yellow funnel with a black top.

B, British India; black funnel with two white bands.

C, Cunard Line; red funnel with black band and two black lines underneath.

D, Union Castle Line ; red funnel with black top.

E, White Star Line ; buff funnel with black top.

BUOYS

At every harbour along the coast a certain number of buoys can be seen, and it is of the utmost importance that every sailor should know what they mean. The conical buoy, A, Fig. 5, must always be kept on the starboard, or right-hand side of boats entering the harbour, whilst the can buoy, B, should be kept on the port, or left-hand side.

When the can buoy is painted with vertical stripes, as in A, Fig. 6,

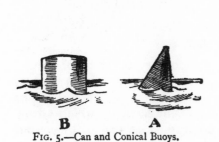

FIG. 5.—Can and Conical Buoys.　　　　FIG. 6.—Types of Buoys.

it indicates the mid-channel, and all boats must keep near it if they wish to avoid running aground.

The wreck buoy, B, Fig. 6, is always painted green, and is placed over submerged wrecks which are sufficiently near the surface to form a danger to ships sailing over them. The mooring buoy, C, is flat, and lies low in the water. Being strongly anchored to the bottom, ships may moor to it with perfect safety.

HARBOUR SIGNALS

At the entrance to a harbour there is usually a mast with a cross-yard, similar to that depicted in Fig. 7. Canvas balls are hung from this yard and show by their various positions how much water there is in the harbour. When the balls are hung as at A, it indicates that there is no water ; when as at B, that there are fifteen feet clear, whilst the position shown at C gives notice that there is the full depth of water in the harbour, and any boat may enter in safety.

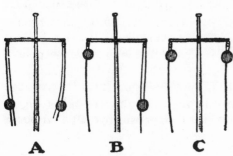

FIG. 7.—Harbour Signals.

COMPASS BEACONS

Compass beacons are placed at different dangerous parts along

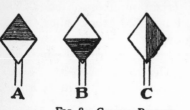

the coast, and indicate the course vessels must follow. The beacon seen at A, Fig. 8, shows that ships must pass to the north of that spot. B, C, and D show that the correct course would be south, east, and west respectively.

FIG. 8.—Compass Beacons.

LIGHTHOUSES

Lighthouses are erected at every promontory or point of danger on civilised coasts, and by their distinctive flashes the passing mariner is able to identify each. The lamps, which are usually either gas or electric, throw their light on to reflectors, in front of which strong lenses are placed, the combination thus formed serving to throw out very powerful beams which are visible for a far greater distance than were those from the old-fashioned reflector. A revolving hood, in which white or coloured lights are placed, serves to send the flashes out in periods determined by the speed at which the hood revolves. When these flashes appear and disappear suddenly, the light is known as "occulting," but when the beam slowly increases to its full power and then decreases, it is known as "revolving."

From the following few examples of the lights along the Kentish coast, it will be seen that sailors can easily ascertain their exact position by recognising the flashes of the lighthouses they pass :—

North Foreland : White light with a red sector, disappearing for 5 seconds every half minute.

South Foreland : White flash every $2\frac{1}{2}$ seconds.

Dover, Admiralty Pier : A white fixed light, and a flashing light every $7\frac{1}{2}$ seconds.

Dungeness : One white flash every 10 seconds.

These flashes are generally visible for about twelve miles on an average, and thus form a sure series of signposts for all that know how to read them.

STORM SIGNALS

At all coastguard stations storm signals are hoisted, according to the meteorological reports of the weather to be expected. The

South Cone, A, Fig. 9, shows that rough weather is expected from the south, whilst the North Cone, B, indicates the reverse. At night these cones are rendered visible by small lamps placed at each corner.

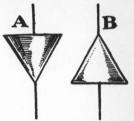

LIFEBOAT STATIONS

There is no need to expatiate on the services rendered to humanity by lifeboats. But splendid as are the inventions which have enabled these boats to be put to sea in the roughest weather, they would be of little use were it not for the noble men form-

FIG. 9.—Storm Signals.

ing their crews, who, taking their lives into their hands, fearlessly launch into the jaws of the storm to rescue others at their own peril.

The lifeboat is an open boat, fitted with air-chambers fore and aft, and keeled in such a fashion that she will float upright in the most raging sea without any fear of sinking. At the first signal for help, usually made by the firing of a rocket, the crew of the lifeboat are gathered together at the summons of a mortar, and in a few minutes have donned their life-belts and thrust out into the waves. An efficient crew will leave their work, reach the shore, prepare the boat, run her down the beach, and push off in less than ten minutes of the signal being given. Assisted by sails and oars, the boat proceeds to the ship in distress, takes the im-perilled crew aboard, and either tows the wreck to a point of safety or leaves her to founder in the storm.

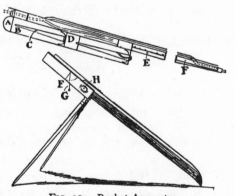

FIG. 10.—Rocket Apparatus.

The rocket apparatus shown in Fig. 10 is often used from the shore, when boats have driven in and run on the rocks. The rope, which passes up through the tin rocket stick, EF, is fastened to the wooden head, A, which is projected forward by the explosion of the powder, B, packed round the lead rod, C. This is exploded by means of the quick-firing powder packed in D. When this rocket is placed in the stand, F, it is aimed by means of the plumb line, G, and the quick-firing powder is ignited through the hole, H. The rope is then carried out with the wooden cap to the ship, whose crew seize the line and draw it in, hauling out a stouter cable, which they fasten to the mast. A pulley carrying a life-belt or breeches buoy runs freely along this rope, and is worked from the shore, thus serving to bear the shipwrecked crew from their place of danger to the dry land.

WRECKS AND DERELICTS AT SEA

It is the duty of every captain to go at once to the assistance of any ship that may be sighted flying signals of distress. If unable to render help himself, owing to the state of the weather or to the stranded vessel being in shallow water, he must "stand by" until other help arrives. If possible, he sends his boats across to the wreck and rescues any of the crew that can be saved. Should the boat be on fire, he must stand by her at a safe distance until she sinks.

Ships that have been abandoned and left to float about the high seas are called derelicts, and form one of the greatest perils of the ocean. Unmanageable, or with none to manage them, they drift aimlessly, the sport of every breeze and current, falling foul of any boat that comes in their path and working especial havoc in the darkness of the night. It is the duty of a captain who sights one of these derelicts to blow her up, or take any other steps that may be in his power to rid the ocean of this floating danger. These boats often drift for years, and not until their timbers rot and the hulls fall to pieces do they cease to menace the traffic of the ocean.

A MODERN STEAMER

It will probably prove the most interesting way of learning something about the management of a modern steamer, to follow her from the time the cargo is taken aboard until her arrival in port. Selecting for the purpose a boat belonging to the best line plying between London and the Continent, namely, the General Steam Navigation Co., whose excellent services have secured them the exclusive traffic to Bordeaux and the Biscay ports, and whose boats carry much of the commerce of the Mediterranean, let us follow her fortunes from the moment of taking the first load of cargo aboard at the docks near Tower Bridge. This line is all the more interesting in that it is the oldest steamship line in the world, its first boat having been launched just ninety years ago, on the 31st March 1821.

Before the cargo is touched, the boat must be coaled, and for several hours every object on board is covered with the thick black grime arising from the coal-shoots. Great cranes, capable of carrying a truck-load at a time, pour their black freight into the coal-bunks, and, whilst the operation lasts, not a clean spot is to be found throughout the boat.

Down below, the trimmers stack the coal away, with due regard to economy of room, working like veritable miners down in the bunkers of the ship.

LOADING

As soon as the coaling is finished, the holds are swept and the boat is cleaned. Then strips of wood, known as "dunnage wood," are placed across the bottom of the holds, forming a kind of grating, which prevents any possibility of damp attacking the cargo.

Winches and cranes heave the cargo over the side, and, with the help of slings, lower the packages into the hold, where men stack them away in systematic fashion, heavy goods at the bottom and lighter goods at the top, thus making sure that none of the cargo runs the risk of being damaged. But experience has taught shipmasters that too much weight at the bottom of a vessel makes her roll terribly in rough weather. Accordingly, a certain amount of the heavy cargo is stored away between decks, thus helping to steady the ship.

A   B

FIG. 11.—Loading and Plimsoll Marks.

All the loading is done by stevedores, and it is not until the night before departure that the crew, who have been signed on by the captain, make their appearance.

The amount of water a boat draws is always shown by the Roman numerals painted at her bow, A, Fig. 11. These figures are marked upwards from the keel, thus showing the vessel's depth in the water at a glance. The Plimsoll mark, B, shows the loading limit, and when the cargo has sunk a boat to the level of the Plimsoll mark, not another stick is allowed to be placed upon her before she puts out to sea.

THE CABINS

Most steamers have three decks appropriated to the use of the passengers, viz. the main deck, the promenade deck, and the boat deck. On a moderate-sized passenger boat the two first-mentioned decks will contain about fifty cabins each. The dining saloon is usually placed on the lowest of the three decks, whilst the music and smoking saloons are more conveniently built on the promenade deck.

The cabins to be found on the General Steam Navigation Co.'s boats are very different from those in which passengers travelled some forty or fifty years ago. The old hard wooden bunks are now replaced by comfortable spring-mattressed berths, whilst the spaciousness and airiness of the cabins render them as comfortable as ordinary bedrooms. Naturally, there are no inside cabins on such small boats and this makes the accommodation still more desirable, as, even on the best-constructed vessels, inside cabins are always liable to become stuffy and unhealthy.

THE BLUE PETER

As soon as the morning breaks on the day of sailing, the Blue Peter, Fig. 12, which is the letter P in the signal code, is hoisted to

FIG. 12.—The Blue Peter.

the foremast-head, thus signifying to all concerned that the ship will sail in the course of the day. The surveyor comes aboard, the captain receives a last report that all is well, and, as the hour of departure approaches, the telegraph bell begins to ring, whilst volumes of smoke pour out of the funnel. At last the pilot ascends the bridge, the first officer goes for'ard to superintend the anchor, whilst the second mate proceeds aft to see that the screw blades are clear of any ropes that may be trailing in the water. Then, amidst much sounding of whistles, the vessel is warped out into the stream.

With its complicated turns and twists, its ever-varying shoals and banks, the Thames is much too dangerous a river for any but a trained pilot to navigate, and, as a rule, this individual is taken as far as Gravesend, or even on to Deal. Whilst he is on board, the pilot takes absolute charge of the navigation of the vessel and is solely responsible for her safe passage.

LIGHTS AT SEA

All sailing ships and steamers carry a red light on the port side and a green light on the starboard side. These are known as side lights. Sailing vessels have no other lights, but steamers are also obliged to carry a white light at the foremast, and usually have an additional light on the aftermast-head.

When one steamer is towing another boat, she is obliged to carry two mast lights, one above the other, and an extra light for every additional boat she may have in tow.

A ship out of control carries two red lights on the foremast, whether she be a steamer or sailing craft.

By means of these lights approaching boats are able to tell on

which side they will pass one another, and the rule of the road **can**
be easily observed.   As the sea rhyme says :—

"Meeting steamers do not dread
When you see three lights ahead.
Port your helm and show your red."

THE RULE OF THE ROAD

It is just as important to observe the rule of the road at **sea as it**
is upon land, and Admiralty Courts have no pity on the mariner
whose carelessness causes a disaster.

When two boats meet in a straight line, each ports her helm, *i.e.*
keeps to the right, passing the other boat on her left.   Sailing vessels,
however, with a fair wind, will keep out of the way of others beating up
against the breeze, whilst steamers are always expected to steer out of the
path of sailing ships.

SIGNALLING

To enable ships to communicate with one another or with the
shore, there are several systems
of signals, all of which are
international, or, in other
words, are equally intelligible
to sailors of any country.

The International Flag

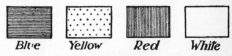

Blue   Yellow   Red   White

FIG. 13.—How the Colours in the Flags
are represented.

Code is shown in Figs. 13–16 in which the colours are dis-

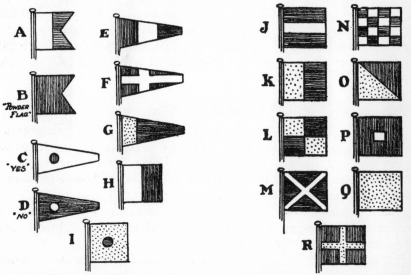

FIG. 14.—First Portion of Flag Alphabet.   FIG. 15.—Second Portion of Alphabet.

tinguished by the direction of the lines.   When a ship wishes to signal, she hoists the ensign with the Code flag beneath it, and, as soon as this has been acknowledged by the other ship, the Code flag is lowered, and she proceeds with her message. Each signal is kept flying until the answering pennant has been hoisted by the other ship.

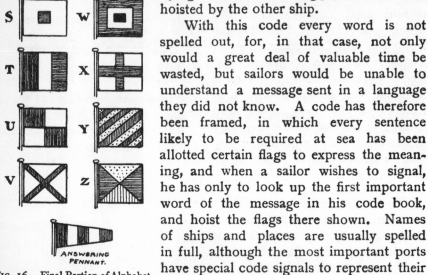

FIG. 16.—Final Portion of Alphabet.

With this code every word is not spelled out, for, in that case, not only would a great deal of valuable time be wasted, but sailors would be unable to understand a message sent in a language they did not know. A code has therefore been framed, in which every sentence likely to be required at sea has been allotted certain flags to express the meaning, and when a sailor wishes to signal, he has only to look up the first important word of the message in his code book, and hoist the flags there shown. Names of ships and places are usually spelled in full, although the most important ports have special code signals to represent their names.

When the weather is hazy, or when boats are too far apart to distinguish the colours of the flags, a system known as the "Ball, Pennant, Flag" is employed, as shown in Fig. 17. These signals

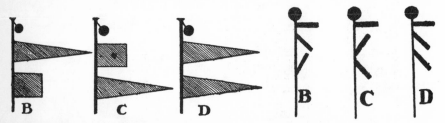

FIG. 17.—Ball, Pennant, and Flag Signals.   FIG. 18.—Semaphore Signals.

can be worked with a semaphore, the arm when horizontal representing the ball, when pointing upward the flag, and when downward the pennant. An example of this is shown in Fig. 18.

For flashlights and fog signals the Morse Code is adapted, a long flash or blast representing the dash, whilst a short flash or blast is used for the dot.

THE ENSIGN

Although the Union Jack is the British flag, ships carry different ensigns, according to their nature. The White Ensign, A, Fig. 19,
is only used by naval craft, the ordinary merchant and private flag being the Red Ensign seen at B, which is flown from a staff at the stern. The Blue Ensign, which is identical with the last-mentioned, except that the field of the flag is blue instead of red, is worn by all merchant ships commanded by

FIG. 19.—White and Red Ensigns.

officers of the Royal Naval Reserve or by ships employed by any public office.

DISTRESS SIGNALS

When a vessel in distress requires assistance from the shore or from a passing ship, the following signals should be displayed, either together or separately :—

A gun fired at intervals of a minute.

The International Code Signal N C, Fig. 20.

The Inverted Ensign B, Fig. 20.

The Distant Signal, Fig. 21.

Continuous blasts on the fog-horn.

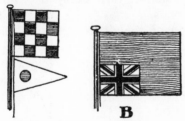

FIG. 20.—Distress Signals.

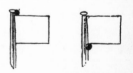

FIG. 21.—Distant Distress Signal.

Since the advent of wireless, another and a famous distress message has been added to the above list. "S.O.S." flashed through the air will appeal for help for miles around, and bring steamers hastening to the scene of disaster with all the speed they can muster.

THE COMPASS

Unlike the majority of compasses one sees ashore, which contain a movable needle, the mariner's compass consists of a large card marked with the cardinal points, Fig. 22, which swings bodily and points to the north. Within the compass-box is a black mark, known as the "Lubber's" line, which is in direct alignment with the ship, and shows exactly how she is heading.

THE WATCHES

In order that there should always be a certain number of men on duty, at the outset of a voyage the officers divide the crew into

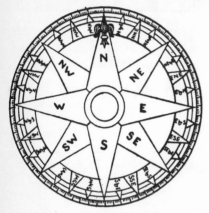

FIG. 22.—Mariner's Compass.

FIG. 23.—Arrangement of Watches.

watches, who serve their turns, according to the plan shown in Fig. 23. It will be noticed that by the division of the afternoon watch into two dog-watches the men have a different turn every day, and get an eight hours' night at regular intervals.

Each watch, with the exception of the dog-watches, is divided into eight parts, which are marked by the ringing of a bell. Half-an-hour after noon, for example, is one bell, one o'clock is two bells, and so on up to four o'clock, which is eight bells and the end of the watch.

THE LOG

The log-line is used to ascertain the speed at which a ship is travelling. When thrown into the water, the motion of the vessel causes a small screw to revolve in the log, this revolution being recorded on a dial in very much the same manner as the speed indicator on a cycle.

The old-fashioned log-line was a very simple contrivance, being

FIG. 24.—The Old-style Log

a piece of wood shaped in the form shown in Fig. 24 and weighted on the rounded side. When this is thrown into the water, it floats upright but remains stationary, whilst, as the ship travels on, the line is paid out, the time being measured by a sand-glass.

PART V

THE KEEPING OF PETS

CHAPTER LVI

HOW TO MAKE AN AVIARY

A HOME FOR FEATHERED PETS

THERE is a certain amount of gaiety attached to an aviary that makes the keeping of foreign birds a source of constant pleasure. The flashing plumages, the unceasing bustle, and ofttimes melodious songs prove so fascinating to all who take up the hobby, that it may fairly

FIG. 1.—An Aviary.

be said, once an aviarist always an aviarist. To the true lover of birds, an aviary, like the sea, is ever changing, and no one can have anything to do with that busy little feathered world without taking its affairs and interests to heart.

An ordinary sunny greenhouse may be considered one of the best positions for the aviary. Artificial heat is necessary for several kinds of foreign birds, but so many varieties can stand our English winter in the climate of a conservatory that, as a general rule, the question of stoves may be ignored.

Very little need be done to convert one end of the greenhouse into a large cage. Wire netting of a fairly close texture must be stretched from the roof to the ground, leaving an interior space about 36 in. in depth. If the end of the conservatory has been adapted, it is probable that there will be a window, and this will prove very pleasant and convenient.

A door should be made in the network, as shown in Fig. 1, as this enables the cage to be entered and thoroughly cleaned, whilst at the same time it provides the means to enter and catch the birds when necessary.

The floor of the aviary should be covered with very fine gravel, one corner, however, being turfed. Where it is possible to do so, a small tree may be planted, as the branches form a natural and unceasing pleasure to the captives.

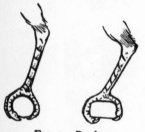

The walls and back of the cage can be covered with virgin cork, the many holes and crevices of which provide excellent sites for nests.

Attention may here be called to the necessity of exercising care in the selection of perches, whether for cages or for aviaries.

FIG. 2.—Perches.

Perches should be oval in shape—never round. A glance at Fig. 2 will explain the reason. If the perch be round, the strain upon the muscles of the bird's legs is so great that in many cases a kind of paralysis is caused, whereas oval perches enable the bird to stand with the muscles in a natural and easy state of tension.

The number and variety of the birds will naturally depend upon the size of the aviary and the taste and purse of the buyer. A very practical rule is to allow two birds to every foot of frontage; for instance, an aviary three feet in length should contain not more than six birds, who would not be overcrowded, but would live together in peace and harmony.

FEEDING

The majority of birds may be fed upon a diet made up of equal portions of hemp, charlock, millet, and canary seed. A second dish composed of bread crumbs, whole-meal, and a little finely-chopped fat may be given as a treat on special occasions. Apples, watercress, and a few nut kernels can also be used as a second course, and will be greatly appreciated by the birds.

The old-fashioned plan of putting a rusty nail in the water-pan cannot be improved upon as the means of administering the necessary quantity of iron.

In winter, when the birds are apt to feel the cold, it is most essential that they should be kept well supplied with food. As soon as evening sets in, place a lantern near the seed-pans so that the light falls upon the food and enables the birds to come and eat as often as they wish during the night. An ordinary "bull's-eye" will be found to serve the purpose admirably.

Fresh-filled baths must be placed in the aviary every day, as birds are very clean in their habits, and will soon feel the want of their daily "tub." Ordinary earthenware pans, holding at least a couple of inches of water, will make excellent baths, and should be placed on the floor where a little splashing can do no harm.

BIRD AILMENTS

As a rule, well-tended aviaries are liable to have but few invalids. There are certain ailments, however, that appear quite unexpectedly and which no amount of care can avert. Amongst these may be mentioned the following :—

Egg-Binding.—Foreign birds are very liable to this illness, for which every bird fancier has his own remedy. It can be ascribed in most cases to change of temperature, to a sudden shock of fright, or even to unnecessarily close confinement.

Egg-binding may often be prevented by adding soaked millet and canary seed to the daily diet, and administering a little finely-chopped suet. If preventives have failed, however, a cure of a rather delicate nature must be very carefully performed.

Administer a little oil at the vent, then fill a large jug with boiling water, wrap the bird in a fairly thick cloth, and hold her over the steam for about twenty minutes as

FIG. 3.—The Vapour Bath.

illustrated in Fig. 3. She must then be placed in a warm cage and given some slightly-heated water to drink.

Pneumonia.—In most cases this is a fatal illness, and it is very exceptional for any remedy to prove effective. A few drops of "liquor ammoniæ acetatis" are sometimes beneficial, however, and should always be given a fair trial.

Convulsions.—These are usually due to constipation, and may be cured by increasing the allowance of green food.

Pay great attention to the claws of caged birds, cutting them carefully when they grow too long.

STOCKING THE AVIARY

Foreign aviary birds are so numerous that it is impossible to do more than mention a few of the more popular varieties. Specimens of every kind of bird can be obtained through the agency of *The Bazaar*—the Friday issue of that paper containing advertisements concerning birds of all kinds.

Budgerigars.—These little birds, shown in A, Fig. 4, are very

A   B

FIG. 4.—Budgerigar and Cockatiel.

beautiful members of the parrot family. Their colour is a delicate grass green, with a primrose forehead and sky-blue cere, *i.e.* thin skin about the nostrils. These birds usually moult in June or July and begin to breed about August. They are very hardy and are general favourites.

Cockatiels.—These birds, illustrated in B, Fig. 4, are members of the parakeet family, and are grey, with a white bar on the wings, and have a fine long tail. The face of the male is of a delicate yellow hue, whilst both sexes are adorned with a small red spot on either cheek. Beginning in May, the hen lays four broods, and frequently a new family appears upon the scene before the last one has left the nest.

Cardinals.—These birds owe their name to the fact that they are of a bright scarlet colour, with very plain markings. Some fanciers have thought them too vicious to be included in an aviary containing smaller birds, but they are only quarrelsome during the mating season, which extends from May to August.

The Red-crested Cardinal shown at A, Fig. 5, is somewhat of an

FIG. 5.—Crested Cardinal and Virginian Nightingale.

exception to the rest of the family, being a delicate grey, with face, chin, head, and crest of a glorious red.

Virginian Nightingale.—As the name would suggest, these birds have a song which, though nothing near as sweet as that of our own nightingale, is full of a peculiar beauty of its own. The markings of these birds are very plain, as can be seen in B, Fig. 5, the male being scarlet, with a black throat, whilst his lady is a deep red brown.

Avadavats.—These birds, A, Fig. 6, are amongst the smallest inmates of the aviary. The female is uniformly of an ash-colour, but her partner changes his plumage with the seasons, his finest costume being of bronze and gold.

Java Sparrows.—These belong to the great tribe of finches, and are illustrated in B, Fig. 6. There are two varieties, one a leaden blue, the other a dull white. Being easily bred and reared, they are very good captives, and are to be found in most aviaries.

FIG. 6.—Avadavat and Java Sparrow.

Canaries.—The subject of canaries is large, and has been dealt with at length by numberless writers and fanciers, who have succeeded in creating a science of the breeding and rearing of these very noisy little birds. The subject is more fully treated in Chapter LIX., p. 485.

A perusal of the foregoing remarks will have given some idea as to starting an aviary. The constant attention that the well-being and happiness of the birds demands will soon add experience, and, as there is no golden rule for aviarists, the bird fancier will discover methods of his own for dealing with whatever may turn up in connection with the birds.

CHAPTER LVII

HOW TO MAKE A FRESH-WATER AQUARIUM

A STUDY OF POND LIFE

THE size and extent of a home-made aquarium must naturally be determined to a very large degree by circumstances, much depending upon the position. The tank should be placed against a wall, the light, which must not be very strong, coming from above, and not entirely from one side, as would be the case if it were situated directly under a window. Taking these conditions into consideration a conservatory will be found to offer the best position for the aquarium.

As a general rule, the length of an aquarium should be greater than its depth ; the following instructions will enable the beginner to construct a receptacle of a convenient and average size, having the back and sides opaque and the front transparent.

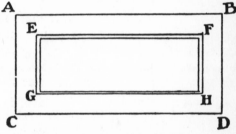

FIG. I.—The Base of the Aquarium.

Make a base ABCD of thick, seasoned wood, measuring 30 in. by 15 in. and in this cut four grooves as shown in Fig. 1. The grooves EG, EF, and FH should be ¼ in. deep and ⅜ in. wide. EF will be 24 in. in length and EG and FH must each measure 12 in. The remaining groove GH will, of course, be 24 in. long, but, whilst ¼ in. deep, it must only be ⅛ in. wide.

The sides and back of the aquarium should now be cut from ½ in. wood. Cut pieces 12 in. wide and of sufficient length to fit flush against the outer edges of the grooves EF, EG, and FH in such a way that the spare ⅛ in. of the groove is left inside. The back and sides must be securely glued and screwed at E and F.

Four pieces of glass must now be cut, 12 in. wide and of proper lengths to allow three of them to fit into the remaining portions of the grooves within the sides and back of the aquarium. The fourth piece of glass, exactly 24 in. in length, will fit into the narrow groove

473

GH. The fabric of the aquarium will now be entirely glass-lined and appear as in Fig. 2.

The next point to be considered is how to make the tank water-tight. Make a mixture consisting of three parts pitch and one part

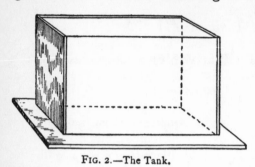

FIG. 2.—The Tank.

gutta-percha, melt it well, and smear liberally over all the joints and places where the water may possibly escape. The floor of the aquarium can also be coated with this mixture. When everything has hardened, let the aquarium be filled with ordinary tap-water and allowed to stand for twenty-four hours in some dry place. If, at the end of that period, there has been no leakage, the tank may be considered as perfect, and can be emptied and prepared for its inmates.

ARTIFICIAL ROCKS

Make some artificial rocks and crevices by placing suitably shaped clinkers against the back and in the corners of the tank. One or two of these rocks should reach above the water-level in order to provide dry land for such of the inhabitants as may desire it. The floor of the tank can then be covered with fine gravel to represent the bed of a stream.

Tap-water is of no use whatever for filling the aquarium ; water

FIG. 3.—The Syphon for emptying the Tank.

must be obtained from a stream or pond, as it contains thousands of algæ, or minute water-plants, which could never be obtained in tap-water, and these in themselves form no unimportant part of the stock.

In a general way the water of an aquarium should never be changed, but if, for any particular reason, it should be necessary to empty the tank, this can be done by means of a simple syphon, as shown in Fig. 3. The bent pipe must be filled with water, and the ends stopped with corks or the tips of the fingers. One end should then be inserted in the tank, and the other placed over a receptacle. When the corks or finger-tips are removed, the syphon thus formed will empty the tank into the lower vessel.

The plants with which the aquarium is to be stocked should be inserted ten days or more before the fish are introduced. One or two plants may be selected from the following kinds, all of which are suitable for a small tank :—

> Water Starwort.
> Water Crowfoot, Fig. 4.
> Frogbit.
> Soldier plant.

Water Crowfoot is exceptionally good for a small aquarium on account of its large leaves, which afford shelter and shade for the fish.

The selection of fish for the aquarium depends very much upon individual taste and circumstances. A good beginning may be made with carp and tench, whilst minnows and sticklebacks are easily obtained for the "small fry." Golden carp are handsome fellows, and prove an ornamental addition to the tank.

Little silver eels, no thicker than a pencil, are well worthy a place in the aquarium, whilst newts, despite their evil reputation, will be found distinctly interesting and per-fectly harmless members of society.

FIG. 4.—Water Crowfoot.

In addition to the natural food obtained from the water, small worms and "ants' eggs" make good articles of diet, and can be pur-chased at most seed-shops.

THE LANDING-NET

A small landing-net, similar to the little nets given to children at the seaside, should be used for removing the fish. By the same means any dead body must be immediately taken away, for a decaying fish will prove most injurious to the live inmates of the tank.

Muslin should be stretched across the top of the tank, as fish occasionally leap out of the water, and unless some such precaution be taken, severe losses may occur.

A shiny coat sometimes appears on gold-fish and other denizens of the aquarium. This can be easily removed by transferring the patient to a pail and then casting some fine silver sand upon his scales. This has the effect of cleansing them and restores the fish to a proper condition.

It is impossible to describe all the improvements that time and money can produce in an aquarium. Experience is a valuable asset towards the successful management of a tank, and it can only be gained by close and careful observation. Yet the experience connected with even a small receptacle such as above described will prove of the greatest service in training the learner to construct and maintain a much larger aquarium with rarer specimens of aquatic life.

CHAPTER LVIII

BEE-KEEPING

A COUNTRY HOBBY

ALTHOUGH the idea of any hobby being pursued for the purpose of making it pay is invariably and rightly deprecated, the successful apiarist finds himself practically confronted with the necessity of turning his hobby to lucrative account. The better managed the hives, the happier and healthier will be the bees; and the healthier the bees the more honey will they produce, for the disposal of which recourse must be had to the market.

Bee-keeping, it need scarcely be remarked, is a country hobby, nor is every one adapted to its pursuit. Nervousness is a fatal deterrent. Bees know at once if their keeper fears them—they weigh him up, and if he is found wanting he will discover in them a host of small enemies. If a bee means to sting you, he will do so, and no attempts of yours to avoid his wrath will avail. On the other hand, bees are neither spiteful nor malicious, and it may be taken as a general rule that if you do not worry them they will not molest you.

So far as a hobby is concerned, the keeping of bees may be the source of hours of enjoyment. The intelligence and skill exhibited by the army of workers, the unerring instinct which teaches them how to build, and the science they exhibit in all their constructions, make the study most fascinating. Mathematicians have discovered that the hexagonal cells constructed by bees form the most economical manner of utilising the wax of which they are built. More hexagonal cells can be built to the square foot than square cells of similar area.

VARIETIES OF BEES

Among the bees usually found in the British Isles the following are those most common :—

FIG. I.—The Black Bee.

The Black Bee, usually known as the English bee, has earned a high place in the opinions of all apiarists on account of its hardiness and industry. The original form of this bee, Fig. I, is unfortunately altering by reason of constant cross-breeding with other varieties.

The Ligurian or Italian Alp Bee is also widely distributed in this country. These bees are handsome and good workers, but offer great opposition and resistance to any one who attempts to interfere with the nest.

The Carnolian, sometimes called "The Ladies' Bees," are difficult to distinguish from their black kindred. They are not satisfactory to keep, and should be avoided by the beginner.

The Cyprian and the Syrian are very similar to the Italian bee in colour, but although they are good honey-gatherers, extreme irritability of temper renders them rather a nuisance than otherwise.

The Inhabitants of the Hive

In every hive during the swarming season there are three kinds of bees. Firstly, there is the queen, or mother bee; secondly, the drone, or male; whilst thirdly, there are the workers, or undeveloped females. In winter, autumn, and spring the drones are expelled and killed, as, in bee economy, every one must work, and since the males have neither wish nor power to do their share of the labour, they are killed.

The Queen Bee

The queen bee, Fig. 2, is the only lady in the hive. She is much longer and larger than the other bees, her jaws are weaker,

FIG. 2.—The Queen Bee.

and her tongue shorter. Although she has a sting, she very rarely uses it, and when taken up in the fingers she is usually quite friendly. Her business in life is to lay eggs, and this she does at the rate of from two to three thousand per day. The queen bee is the centre around which the whole hive revolves. She is the mother of every bee within its walls, and consequently the hive take care to see that the queen is young and vigorous, for as soon as she grows old the hive will dwindle and deteriorate. If a queen is removed from her hive, all the remaining bees will go out anxiously and search for her.

The Drone

The drones, Fig. 3, are large and somewhat cumbersome individuals. They make a great deal of

FIG. 3.—The Drone.

noise, but have no sting, and as soon as the queen has made her choice of one of them for her husband, they are driven out to perish.

THE WORKER

The worker is an undeveloped female, and is chiefly distinguished by an uncommon strength of jaw, by which it is enabled to chew paper and even cut rags when occasion demands. It is the worker that one usually sees gathering honey in field or garden. About half an inch in length, it swells to five-eighths of an inch when loaded with honey. All the work connected with the hive is performed by these bees. No sooner has the worker bee emerged from her cell in the first prime of youth, than she works incessantly and untiringly until the day when, with torn wings and worn-out body, she is thrown from the hive as useless and done for.

WHAT THE BEES MAKE

Every one knows that bees make honey, and this in its crude state is taken from flowers in the form of nectar. When carried to the hive this honey is placed in the cells and sealed over, being taken therefrom as required to feed the larvæ.

The cells are made of wax, which is a fatty material produced from the wax pockets in the abdomen of bees. When building the cells the scales of wax are exuded and built in thin sheets, which are then fashioned into hexagonal cells. Bees feed on pollen, which is gathered from the stamens of flowers.

FIG. 4.—Honey Cells.

COMBS

Combs vary in size according to the uses to which they will be put. As already mentioned, they are constructed of long hexagonal cells, as shown in Fig. 4. The workers' cells are usually about a fifth of an inch in diameter. When cells are occupied by worker larvæ they are sealed up with a certain amount of wax, and are thus left until the bees are ready to come forth.

The cells in which drones are kept are considerably larger, measuring, as a rule, a quarter of an inch in diameter.

The queen's cells, again, are quite different from those already described. A glance at Fig. 5 will illustrate this fact. They are usually built on the edge of the comb and hang down in a sort of

FIG. 5.—A Queen's Cell.

cup, and until the exit of the queen they are kept sealed. Drone and worker cells are both used for storing honey, in these cases the cells being sealed with wax and thus rendered perfectly air-tight.

HIVES

There is a regular Association Standard size for bee-hives, and all

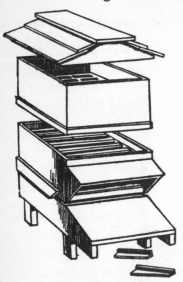

the appliances connected therewith should be arranged accordingly. An example of a bar-frame hive is shown in Fig. 6, from which it will be seen that the floor and stand are supported by short legs; upon these are placed the body, the sides of which are double-walled, the space being filled with sawdust or similar substance. A glance at Fig. 7 will show the adjustment of this box with the frame inside. It may be remarked the bee-hive should be purchased, as so much depends upon the exact construction and easy fitting of the parts that amateur work is better avoided.

A standard frame similar to that shown in Fig. 8 is the best for all purposes. The dimensions indicated

FIG. 6.—A Bar-frame Hive.

in the diagram, if used for all frames, will make it possible to transpose

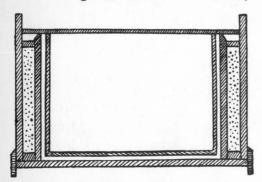

FIG. 7.—Box and Frame.

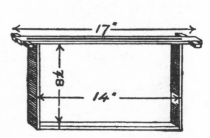

FIG. 8.—Standard Frame.

or use them indiscriminately. These frames are hung in the boxes at even distances apart.

TAMING THE BEES

It would be useless to attempt to handle bees unless they were first given to understand who is the master. This can only be done

by frightening them with smoke by means of a smoker, Fig. 9, consisting of a tin cylinder attached to a pair of bellows in such a manner

that when the cylinder is filled
with smouldering paper or
cotton, the bellows force the
air out of the nozzle in big puffs.
Of course, great care must be
taken to see that a refill is made
quickly, as otherwise the bees get
enraged and attack the keeper.

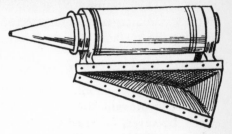

Various substitutes for fumi-
gation have been placed upon

the market, but they possess few advantages over that already described.

EXTRACTING WAX AND HONEY

To extract the honey from the cones without spoiling these latter
for further use, various appliances, somewhat similar to that shown in
Fig. 10, have been invented. They are generally arranged according to
the following plan. After the cell coverings have been removed, the

frames are fitted on to a central rod
which is revolved rapidly by means of a
handle at the top, this revolution causing
the honey to be thrown out. It is then
collected at the bottom of the tin and

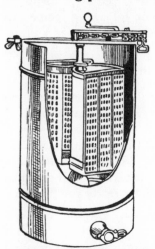

FIG. 10.—Honey-extractor.

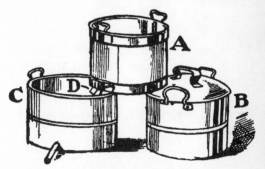

FIG. 11.—A Wax-extractor.

drawn away by a tap. A good extractor, and only a good one should
be bought, will cost about 35s.

Wax-extractors are used for separating the wax from the dross in
the cones. A very good one is shown in Fig. 11. In the upper perforated basket, A, are placed the pieces of cone which it is desired to
melt. The receptacle, B, is filled with boiling water, the steam of
which passes into A, where it melts the wax, which pours out of the

tube, D, into the vessel, C. The cost of this extractor will be about 3s. Various makeshift appliances for the purpose of extracting wax can be made at home; or the wax may be tied in bags of coarse calico and submerged in hot water. As this water cools, the wax will ascend to the surface, whence it can be removed.

VEILS AND GLOVES

All bee-keepers should wear veils arranged with wire fronts, which will serve to prevent the material flapping against the face. A black net veil, however, fastened tightly over the brim of the hat and tucked in beneath the coat will answer very well for the purpose.

As a general rule it may be taken that gloves should never be worn, a sufficient precaution being to tie the sleeves very tightly round the wrists to prevent bees crawling up the arm. In any case, kid or leather gloves are of little use, as they hamper the hands. For ladies, a thin muslin bag with two holes for the feet will have to be drawn up over the skirt.

FOOD

At certain times of the year artificial food is required for bees, and syrup is very useful for the purpose. The following recipe can be made with advantage: To every pound of loaf sugar add three-quarters of a pint of water, put the whole upon the fire and stir. This should not boil but simply be kept on long enough for the sugar to dissolve.

A special kind of candy composed of granulated sugar (about ten pounds), to which is added a teaspoonful of cream of tartar and $1\frac{3}{4}$ pint of water, is very commonly given as food. This mixture is put over a brisk fire and allowed to boil. After three minutes the receptacle containing the mixture should be plunged into cold water, and the contents stirred until it assumes a porridge-like texture. It can then be poured into dishes, and as soon as cool will be ready for the bees' consumption.

SWARMING

When the bees in a hive increase considerably in numbers, instinct leads them to swarm, i.e. send out a colony to form a new home. This usually takes place during June or July. Strange as it may appear, the party which sets forth in search of a new home is not composed of the young bees, who, in the course of nature would make a colony of their own, but is composed of the original occupants of the hive, who leave their old home to the rising generation and themselves undertake the task of founding a new hive.

As not infrequently the swarm flies far away from the original hive, serious loss will happen to the bee-keeper if he does not take some active measures to keep them at home. Of course a new hive must be prepared in the first place. Next the nozzle of the fumigator should be placed in the entrance of the hive and four or five big puffs of smoke blown in. As soon as the nozzle is removed the entrance to the hive must be carefully blocked up. One or two sharp raps are then given to the walls of the hive, the stopper is withdrawn, a little more smoke puffed in, and when the bees have been thoroughly subjugated a number of the combs are removed to the new hive, where the bees will follow.

As soon as the swarm has taken up its quarters in its new home it should be fed plentifully with the syrup already described. When they have been nine or ten days in the hive, the feeding may cease, and frames be inserted in which the bees can build their combs.

How to Manage Bees

Considerable tact is required to handle bees successfully. Like human beings they are apt to be indolent in the heat of the day, and can then be tackled in comparative safety. Towards evening, however, their tempers become sharper, and they can rarely be approached without causing great commotion. At all times, however, bees know their master, and, like all creatures, are instinctively aware of any person who feels frightened or nervous. It is extremely unwise to tackle a hive of excited bees, and their keeper should leave them to a more opportune moment. Always approach them with a veil, and do your utmost to handle them quickly and decisively, as any bungling is liable to irritate them beyond all measure.

As bees naturally take very careful note of their surroundings, it is easy to understand that very great confusion will be caused if the hives are moved whilst the inmates are out foraging for honey. It is therefore most inadvisable to move any hives unless absolutely compelled to do so. Winter time is the best period for doing this, or if really necessary to do so in the summer time, the work being done in the evening.

Honey

Upon removing the honeycombs in their frame, a special cupping knife similar to that shown in Fig. 12, should be taken and set in hot water. With this knife the caps or sealed-up ends of the cells should be carefully removed in a sheet. Repeat this process upon the caps on the other side, and place the combs in the honey-ex-

Fig. 12.—A Cupping Knife.

tractor shown in Fig. 10. As already mentioned, several rapid turns will cause the liquid to flow out of the cells and drop to the bottom of the receptacle.

From this receptacle the honey should be strained into vessels and left to stand until the bubbles and odd particles have risen to the top.   This matter can then be skimmed off and the clear honey poured into bottles or jars in which it can be sealed and stored.

If the honey be neatly sealed in glass jars with an attractive label, local shopkeepers can often be induced to sell it, whilst, after a time, the ambitious apiarist will find himself in a position to send his produce to some of the larger cities where there is always an open and profitable market.

CHAPTER LIX

CANARIES

HOW TO KEEP AND BREED THEM

AMONGST bird pets there are probably few more popular than the little songsters whose piercing trills and irrepressible joyousness have won a golden place in the hearts of thousands. Canaries, to use a well-worn phrase, are to be found alike in cottage and palace, but whether the prison be a little cage or a spacious aviary, the captive is just as happy, so long as a ray of sunlight can beam through the bars.

Although originally of one type, canaries have now developed into

FIG. 1.—A, The Wild Canary; B, The Norwich Canary.

various different shapes and colours through long and careful breeding. The wild canary, A, Fig. 1, is a native of the Madeira Islands, but for some three hundred years the birds have been domesticated in this country. This bird, whose Latin name is *Serinus canarius*, is only about four inches in length, but breeding and selection have now produced tame canaries almost double that size, with many varieties of colour and shape.

One of the richest coloured birds is the Norwich canary, B, Fig. 1, although the Cinnamon, A, Fig. 2, possesses a lovely plumage almost equal to that of the Norwich.   The Yorkshire, B, Fig. 2, is exceedingly

FIG. 2.—A, The Cinnamon ; B, The Yorkshire Canary.

slim and neat in appearance, a compliment which can scarcely be paid to either the Scotch or the Belgian Fancies, Fig. 3, whose almost

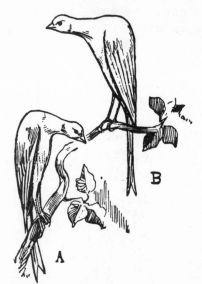

FIG. 3.—A, The Scotch Fancy ; B, The Belgian Fancy.

humpbacked forms are more peculiar than beautiful.   The London Fancy, Fig. 4, is a pretty little bird, yellow or buff in colour, with black wings and tail. The Lizard canary, seen in the same picture, is so named from its speckled appearance. Birds with tufts or crests are known as "coppies," a good specimen of which is the Lancashire Coppy, C, Fig. 5, whose crest is much admired by many fanciers.

FIG. 4.—The London Fancy and the Lizard Canary.   FIG. 5.—The Lancashire Coppy.

Without doubt, the most interesting feature in keeping canaries as pets lies in breeding them, and it is with the idea of starting beginners on this most fascinating hobby that the following hints have been written.

CAGES

A very useful single compartment breeding-cage, Fig. 6, can be purchased for a few shillings from any large ironmonger or bird fancier, the usual size being about 20 in. long, 16 in. high, and 10 in. wide. The seed hopper should have a glass cover to preserve the seed from dirt, as well as to prevent the birds from scattering their food outside the cage, whilst the water trough should be placed at the other side of the cage, as seen in the illustra-

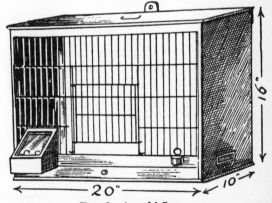

FIG. 6.—A useful Cage.

tion. A long perch, stretching from end to end of the cage and placed at a convenient height, will enable the birds to feed and drink in comfort.   Two other perches should be placed across the cage, one at each side of the door.

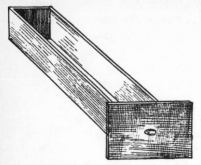

FIG. 7.—An Egg-drawer.

A breeding-cage with four compartments would measure about 3 ft. square and be some 10 in. wide.   Such cages are frequently made with doors communicating from one compartment to the other, and this proves a very convenient arrangement for separating the cock when he shows signs of becoming troublesome. Seed hoppers and water troughs are placed in each cage as usual.

Where no provision has been made for troughs in which to place the egg food, a long narrow drawer, similar to that shown in Fig. 7, can be easily inserted between two bars bent aside for the purpose. These egg troughs can be purchased in tin or zinc for about sixpence each, or more expensive ones made of porcelain can be procured if desired.

BREEDING

The cage being in readiness, nothing remains but to purchase as many cocks and hens as are wanted.   The prices of canaries depend entirely upon the merits and pedigrees of the birds concerned, and may vary from three or four shillings to as many pounds.   The birds should be bought of a good reliable fancier, whose honesty and judgment are above suspicion.

Until the breeding-cages are ready, the cocks and hens must be kept apart, preferably in different rooms ; for if they are able to see each other, it often happens that a cock takes a fancy to some particular hen, and if he be not mated with her, shows his discontent by ill-treating the wife that Providence, in the shape of his master, may allot him.

In January the hens may be placed in the breeding-cages, and the cocks with which they are to be mated should be put near by, so that the hens may make their acquaintance.   This is very essential, as, if it be neglected, the hens are apt to quarrel with partners whom they have never seen before.

The birds may be put together about the middle of March, and as soon as this has been accomplished they will require a good liberal diet of hard-boiled egg chopped up very fine or grated with an equal quantity of bread. About two teaspoonfuls of this should be given to each pair every day, whilst a little hemp seed or some millet may be given every second day.

FIG. 9.—Felt Lining for the Nest.

Three or four days after the birds have been together they should be provided with a nest. The best nests for canaries are made of tin similar to that shown in Fig. 8, and lined with felt, a piece of which, cut in the form depicted in Fig. 9, will fit into the concavity and can be sewn to the tin through holes perforated in the bottom. The nest should then be hung on a screw driven into the wall of the cage.

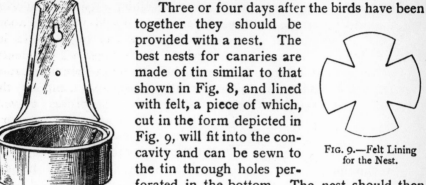

FIG. 8.—The Nest.

TREATMENT OF THE HEN

When a hen begins laying, her eggs should be removed one by one until she has laid three, a nest-egg being substituted for her real progeny until this number is completed. These nest-eggs are made of wood or bone, and can be purchased for a few pence from any fancier. When she has laid three eggs, the hen should begin to sit, and after fourteen days she will hatch her brood.

As a general rule, the cock may be left with his mate when she is sitting, but sometimes he begins to annoy her and break the eggs, and he must then be removed at once. It is not an uncommon thing for a cock to turn cannibal and eat his own offspring. If he takes to breaking and eating the eggs, he should be allowed to try one or two stale eggs that have been unsuccessfully sat on for over a fortnight—his vice will soon be cured.

When a hen is going to hatch her brood, she must be given a supply of egg, bread, and green food, with a little hemp seed, and this diet must be continued until the little fledglings are about six weeks old, at which age they will begin to feed themselves.

Occasionally it happens that a hen refuses to feed her young, or does not give them sufficient food to keep them healthy. Matters will be greatly simplified if there is another hen who can take up the duties of foster-mother ; but if this plan should not be feasible, the little birds may be fed by hand, their meals being placed in their beaks by means of a goose-quill nib. For the first six or seven days they should be fed thus every hour, with food composed of ground-up arrowroot biscuit and hard-boiled egg, mixed into a thick paste with warm water.

When the young birds have been taken away from their parents they should be given egg and green food until they are at least seven weeks old. The amount of egg may then be slowly diminished until they are able to crack seed for themselves.

Breeding should cease before August, for the birds will then begin to moult, and serious ailments will ensue if care be not taken to prevent them having further families.

MOULTING

The moulting season usually begins in July and lasts until November, and it is a critical time for all concerned. Help can often be given to the older birds by pulling out one or two of the tail feathers, this giving the bird an encouragement, so to speak, to continue the good work.

Young birds start moulting at the age of eight or nine weeks although some of the first brood will often take longer in beginning.

Whilst they are moulting, canaries should be fed liberally with a plain diet, such luxuries as egg or hemp seed being administered very sparingly. They ought not to have green food during this period, but may be allowed a few slices of boiled carrot once or twice a week.

Listlessness is the first sign usually given by a canary that it is about to moult, and the bird will often appear to wander aimlessly about the cage in apparent dejection. A few loose feathers will next be observable, and when this sign appears every precaution must be taken to keep the birds from any draught or undue cold. A little magnesia may be added to the drinking water, or resort may be had to the old-fashioned plan of placing a rusty nail in the trough.

On no account allow a moulting bird to be kept in a damp place or a room where gas is extensively used, for neglect of this point may mean the entire loss of the bird's voice for singing.

SINGING

Young male canaries begin to sing soon after they have reached the age of one month, but their songs do not attain any fulness or richness until they are five or six months old. At this early age it is possible to detect the sex of the bird by its attempts at song. The young male breaks out into a strong, if inharmonious song, whilst the female bird will only utter short and disjointed notes in a feeble and twittering fashion.

Canaries can usually be made to sing by exciting them to emulate some continuous noise, such as the grinding of a coffee mill or the sharpening of a knife on a grindstone. One authority on birds states that they like nothing better than the sound of frying—the delicate sizzling of a piece of bacon over a brisk fire exciting the birds to a gala performance of their songs. It must be confessed, however, that none of these artifices can be relied upon with any security.

Occasionally birds are too nervous to sing in the presence of other birds, and for this shyness there is no cure. On the other hand, it is no uncommon thing for a canary to learn the song of some other bird, whilst, if taught young, they occasionally learn to copy a flute or some similar musical instrument.

CHAPTER LX

DOGS

AND HOW TO KEEP THEM

IT is no exaggeration to say that the dog stands first favourite amongst pets. His companionship, fun, fidelity, and other good qualities make him pre-eminent, and there is scarcely a boy who would not like to possess such a desirable friend. Some practical information on the matter will therefore prove useful.

Whatever kind of dog you intend to have it is first necessary to consider how it is to be housed. All the talk about dogs being a nuisance is generally owing to their being badly accommodated, so make up your mind to give your pet a house such as he deserves. A very rudimentary knowledge of carpentry will enable you to make a good weather-proof kennel, but in any case, a ready-made house can be purchased at little cost.

If it be decided to keep a toy dog which will live indoors, all that is required is a simple box, about one foot high, and large enough for him to lie down in comfortably. A few pieces of boarding neatly nailed together will make a good receptacle.

THE KENNEL AND RUN

A larger dog should live outside the house, and will require a kennel made of $\frac{1}{2}$ in. boarding with a width of 18 in., a depth of

FIG. 1.—A simple Kennel.

30 in., and a height of 24 in.—such a house should prove comfortable for a medium-sized dog. Let it rest above ground on two pieces of wood to keep out the damp, Fig. 1. Make the roof overlapping and sloping to carry off rain, and cut a hole about one foot wide in the front or side to admit the animal. It is well, also,

to have a covered run to your dog's house. Put together a stout frame, so as to enclose the house in a width of at least three or four feet. Fasten to it a strong iron wire-netting, Fig. 2, covered in with a sloping wood roof and containing a door. Before starting to make this kennel choose a dry, sheltered spot, and measure off exactly the space you intend to devote to it, and

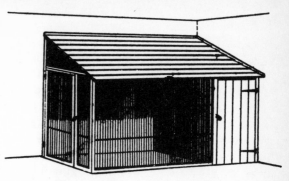

FIG. 2.—A Run attached to the Kennel.

keep to these measurements when cutting materials for the run. Several coats of paint should be given to preserve the woodwork.

BEDDING

For the bed of the small dog kept indoors a strong piece of warm carpet, placed at the bottom of the box, will be sufficient, although he may have another piece of carpet to arrange as he likes and scratch up at his pleasure.

A good supply of clean straw, changed as often as possible, forms the best bedding for the dog kept outdoors ; there is nothing like cleanliness in the treatment of a pet. I would advise the use of a disinfectant, especially during the summer, to keep everything sound and sweet.

EXERCISE ESSENTIAL

Dogs need plenty of exercise. Only a watch-dog should be chained ; the ordinary dog ought to have plenty of freedom. Of course, some kinds require more than others, and there is no difficulty in seeing when your pet has had too much. The morning is a good time for a dog to have his necessary exercise, in the form of a run ; he will then enjoy a spell of freedom to the full. Late in the evening, before sleep, he will keep fit if he has the benefit of more exercise. Directly after a meal let your dog rest ; it is altogether unwise to make him exercise on a full stomach.

FEEDING

Some owners of dogs are very careless in the matter of feeding their canine friends. One day they will give them a too copious meal, and the next day or so the poor creatures will have scarcely anything to eat. To feed a dog irregularly is most reprehensible, for the discomfort needlessly inflicted is very keen. Two meals a day is the usual practice, although many dogs thrive excellently on only one.

In the morning give him a breakfast of some dog biscuits. The next meal should be in the evening, when he can have some more biscuit, over which gravy has been poured, or a portion of bread and meat. To keep him healthy, he should be given every other day a supply of greens cooked and chopped up.

The leavings from the dinner-table can all be given to your dog, but a word of caution is necessary. Such scraps usually consist of fat, and too much greasy matter is not advisable. Nor should you put into your dog's feeding-dish any fish-bones or small bones from game that are easily swallowed, or are likely to stick in his throat. A big bone is a delight to most dogs; they can gnaw it to their heart's content, exercise their teeth, and enjoy themselves with huge delight in their own way. On no account pamper your dog by giving it all through the day every tiny scrap that is left over from the meals. Such treatment will take all the brightness and nimbleness out of him ; he will only be able to waddle about awkwardly, and will be liable to various complaints.

Naturally, large dogs that live in the open air are big feeders, and must be provided for, not only copiously but with some variety. Their food should have a good proportion of meat—sheep's haunches, bullocks' heads, shins of beef, hound meal, and oatmeal. Sometimes a dog is a lax feeder, and requires encouragement ; on the other hand, some dogs are too voracious, and need allowancing with their food.

As a contrast to the giants of the kennel you will find the toy dogs very dainty feeders. Pieces of dog biscuit or stale bread well soaked in gravy are suitable for them as a first meal, whilst at noon they want a little underdone meat, well minced, and a third meal at night. But no hard and fast rule can be given on the question of feeding ; you must judge from the condition of your own particular animal.

CLEANLINESS

To enjoy the companionship of your dog, he must be kept scrupulously clean. His coat should be bright and glossy, his eyes sparkling, and his muzzle and paws without a dirty stain. Every one who keeps a dog should take a personal interest in its condition. Use the brush and comb well; when the hair is long, it must be groomed every day. Some fanciers, after the dog is brushed, rub him down with a soft wash-leather, or even a silk handkerchief, to heighten the gloss.

Most short-haired dogs need a bath every fortnight at least to keep them thoroughly healthy. Get an old zinc bath, and fill it with warm water, and, with the aid of proper dog soap and a brush, administer a good scrubbing, taking care to dry him well after the operation. Should the dog be of the long-haired variety, use the brush more than the bath, as washing has a bad effect upon the coat.

BREEDS OF DOGS

Popular favour awards the palm to the FOX TERRIER, Fig. 3. He has many good points that commend him strongly; in fact, he is an ideal dog for a young master. Bright, intelligent, alert, with an excellent temper, natty in size, he can scarcely be eclipsed. A great deal of attention has been given of late to a variety of this breed—the wire-haired fox terrier. The only difference is in the coat, which is wiry and close.

FIG. 3.—Fox Terrier.

The COLLIE is a splendid playfellow. His form is too well known to make a description necessary. He is a good protector, but is liable to fits of temper, and needs to be treated firmly and kept obedient.

The courage of the BULLDOG, Fig. 4, is proverbial. Some boys are not enamoured of his appearance, but he is a fine animal, and will protect his master right loyally. There are many "points" to be studied about a pure-bred bulldog. He should have a square head, broad in front, the frontal bones high and broad, the neck short, the upper lip thick, chest deep and wide, legs short, teeth strong and regular, small ears, straight apart, and the back short and curved to the tail.

FIG. 4.—Bulldog.

The IRISH TERRIER, Fig. 5, is a delightful pet. He is full of affection for his master, and has plenty of courage, his endurance being wonderful. With a wiry and hard coat, black nose, long head, back and legs strong and straight, his colour wheaten, bright red, and tawny, the Irish terrier is a handsome fellow.

The RETRIEVER is a noble-looking dog, and, as its name implies, was

FIG. 5.—Irish Terrier.

FIG. 6.—Schipperke.

originally used for bringing in game.   Through careful breeding this dog possesses a fine character.

Indeed, the variety of dogs, from which a companion can be selected is extremely large. The SKYE TERRIER, the SCHIPPERKE, Fig. 6, the BLACK and TAN TERRIERS, the POODLE, SPANIELS,

FIG. 7.—Chow.

FIG. 8.—Borzoi.

CHOWS, Fig. 7, BORZOI, Fig. 8, and many others have their own claims, either on the score of appearance or character.

Opinions vary exceedingly in regard to the PUG.   A great favourite with ladies, he possesses but few of those canine qualities which appeal to the masculine mind.   He is, however, an affectionate pet, and when well kept, makes quite a respectable addition to the household.

Before deciding, however, it would be as well to examine the varieties at a good dog show, where the various breeds can be seen to perfection, and where observation will exhibit the characteristics of each particular dog.

PUPPIES

The breeding of dogs is a difficult affair, and is best left to experts. Your dog may, however, at some time or another, present you with a litter of puppies. Provision should be made for the mother, giving her a sheltered corner with a piece of carpet. When the pups arrive she must have quiet, and be given a nourishing diet of warm milk, broth, or bread and milk, but only a mere scrap of meat. After five weeks the puppies will be able to feed themselves, and may be given a little bread and milk in a low dish. Puppy biscuits, broken up and made moist with the addition of milk, are also good for them. Owing to rapid growth, puppies need meals four times a day. They should also have a fair amount of exercise. With the aid of nippers, take off what are called the dew-claws soon after they are born.

DISTEMPER

Dogs are subject to various complaints, and in most cases the safest plan is to consult a veterinary surgeon. Distemper—one of the worst enemies—shows itself by fits of shivering and heat, violent attacks of sneezing, with nose hot and dry. The clogging of the nose causes the dog to "sniff" in a peculiar way, and this is almost invariably a sign of the disease.

CHAPTER LXI

GUINEA-PIGS, OR DOMESTIC CAVIES

THE PETS OF THE ANCIENT PERUVIANS

THE guinea-pig, or, as it is sometimes termed, the domestic cavy, is a mild, gentle little creature of which few civilised people knew anything until it was introduced into Europe by the Dutch in the early part of the sixteenth century.

When Francisco Pizarro conquered Peru in 1531 the guinea-pig, or, as the Spaniards termed it, *cochinillo das Indias*, was as wild and plentiful as the llama and alpaca, and occupied the same position in the Peruvian market that the rabbit does in England.

The word "cavy" is a corruption of "coni" or "cony," the name given by an ancient Indian tribe who inhabited Peru previous to the coming of the Spaniards.

Many early travellers to South America have left testimony in their writings that in most Brazilian and Peruvian households the cavy was sufficiently domesticated to run about the house as freely as poultry, and that the cat amiably shared her place of honour at the hearth with this bright-eyed creature, which was, indeed, her bosom friend.

The squaw, or Indian housewife, when called upon suddenly to provide a meal for unexpected visitors, was frequently known to resort to the cavy, a dish much appreciated by her guests, and even more dainty and nutritious than the rabbit.

In England and many other countries the guinea-pig is regarded as uninteresting and stupid, whereas it is really of a very intelligent and even affectionate disposition.

There are three different tones in its voice—the shrill pipe, denoting fear, hunger, or thirst; the lower-pitched squeak, signifying placid content and welcome; and the grunt, expressing displeasure.

The cavy soon knows and becomes attached to its feeder, and will whisk forward at his approach with every sign of recognition and delight that a dumb animal can show.

It is quite an inexpensive pet, and, provided the hutch be kept clean, dry, and warm, it will thrive and multiply abundantly.

Homesteads are quite easy of manipulation, and a pair of cavies need very little space. When, however, there are more than two, it is better to have sufficient room to allow them exercise.

The guinea-pig revels in the sunlight, yet is extremely fond of snow. In severe winter weather it will devour a pan of snow with relish, and at those times needs nothing else to quench its thirst, Fig. 1.

FIG. 1.—The Guinea-pig.

The home of a couple of cavies may be an old cask or a candle-box, where they will be perfectly happy, provided everything is kept sweet and clean.

Damp and cold are fatal, and those who wish to keep their pets from disease and death must shelter them carefully during the winter months.

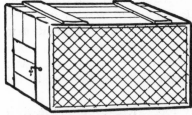

FIG. 2.—Hutch for Guinea-pigs.

A packing-case makes a handsome domicile. Fine-netted wire should be nailed over the front, and a small wooden door fixed at one end for the purpose of feeding and cleansing. When possible, the wood should be lined with zinc, as this keeps the interior from absorbing the damp. The box, Fig. 2, should always be painted, so that it does not warp or rot.

The most convenient way of keeping the cage sanitary is to fit in a zinc or wooden tray, Fig. 3. This should frequently be sprinkled with a mixture of clean sawdust and dry sand, and removed as often as necessary, scalded and left in the air for a few hours.

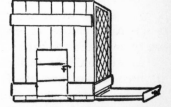

FIG. 3.—Cage with Moveable Tray.

Cavies need constant feeding, but it is not wise to provide the whole day's supply in the morning, for the cavy is very apt to lie on its food, thus rendering it dirty and unwholesome. This is injurious to its health, whilst the fur becomes clotted and discoloured.

Although the cavy loves to bask in the sunlight, it needs shelter, so that during the summer months, when the light is too dazzling, it may retire at pleasure to the shade. In Fig. 4 is shown another type of hutch.

A plank fixed across one end of the box, and not too high for the cavy to reach, is very necessary, for this provides exercise and a resting-

FIG. 4.—A Type of Hutch.

place after feeding. There should also be a supply of shelters for breeding purposes, as well as clean water in well-washed pans, which will not overturn and wet the cage when the cavy drinks. A partitioned trough, to hold his bran and drink, with a high back pierced for nails, to keep it from overturning, is the best article, Fig. 5. Saucers are easily upset, and not only wet the flooring, but deprive the cavies of that supply of water which they constantly need.

When Mr. and Mrs. Cavy have babies to look after, great care must be taken to prevent the parents from unintentionally trampling upon their young. Should it happen that there are several couples and families of varying ages, it would be well to remove the little ones with their mother to a nursery until they are strong enough to hold their own against larger relations.

Growing boars are apt to give themselves airs as they near maturity, and often cause constant breaches in the happiness of the home life. Papa Cavy makes a vain attempt to retain his authority and importance, but, alas! he is frequently one against many, and for this reason a large family should be divided into different homes.

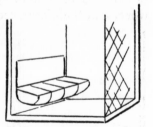

FIG. 5.—Trough for Hutch.

Sometimes a deadly vendetta occurs between two cavies, who feel that the world is too small to contain them both. At such times the bigger boar naturally has matters all his own way, and will pursue his enemy with remorseless enmity, biting him so severely that before long the foe's head and back are covered with bleeding wounds. Before matters become so serious, the keeper must, of course, remove one of them to another hutch if he wishes to avoid the expense of a funeral.

The cavy's foe is the rat, whom, strange to say, he does not in the least fear. This young gentleman, a very fox in cunning, will use all his strength and might to force his way into Mrs. Cavy's cottage. Wood is as digestible to him as sponge-cake to a baby; he gnaws and scratches until he has entered and committed a cowardly crime upon his defenceless prey.

Zinc or small-meshed wire, Fig. 6, surrounding the cage at a sufficient height from the ground is the only means of baulking this treacherous foe of his prey. Traps may, of course, be set ; but prevention is always better than cure.

The larder of the cavy household is quite economically supplied. Cabbage leaves, groundsel, brock, carrot-tops, and other kinds of green meat will be very much appreciated.

Some guinea-pigs turn up their small noses at turnip-tops, and will only eat them when nothing else is forthcoming, yet they may be trained to eat most things in season.

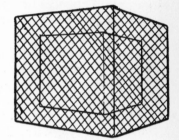

Fig. 6.—Wire-netting as a Protection against Rats.

Green refuse from the kitchen or garden, providing it is fresh, is very welcome, and the cavies' trough should always contain a supply of bran mixed with water. When Mother Cavy is weaning her young, which sometimes occurs before they are three weeks old, they must be removed and supplied with milk and special fare until this stage is over. Babies need a slanted floor, Fig. 7, so that they are not crushed beneath the feet of their parents and relations.

The cavy that sulks in a corner, refuses his food, and shows signs of extreme unsociability, is not a hermit or genius planning some great work, and therefore preferring solitude—he is ill. A sluggish liver or the beginnings of dropsy may be troubling him, caused either by indiscreet feeding or damp. At the first symptoms he should be isolated and treated to light and dainty fare, with only a little food at a time. Warm milk and care will soon restore him to his normal condition.

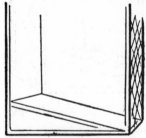

Fig. 7.—Slanting Floor for Hutch.

Vermin are even more deadly than the rat, and attack the poor little creatures when they have been overcrowded or neglected. Vermin spread fast, and means must at once be taken to stop the invasion. Keating's powder, change of diet, and the removal of those infected are the only means of restoring the cavies to a wholesome condition.

Cavies love grass, and it is a good plan to have a bottomless box always at hand, and from time to time give them a chance of feeding on the lawn.

When a cavy has suffered from the enmity of his fellows, his wounds should be cleansed in lukewarm water and soothed with a mixture of oil and sulphur.

BREEDING

Those who pay especial attention to breeding, and desire to maintain a certain type of cavy, or exhibit animals at shows, must take care to prevent all chances of inter-breeding.

Sows and boars of pure pedigree should, of course, be kept separate from their fellows.

There are three kinds of fancy breeds, Fig. 8—the Smooth cavy, the Abyssinian, and the Peruvian. The variety of colours usual to the Smooth cavy are six in number, the Abyssinian has ten, and the Peruvian five.

Of the Smooth kind, the pure white red-eyed cavies are the best subjects for experiments in transmission, although some of the spotted tribe show promise of reproducing their colours.

The Abyssinian differs very much from the Smooth cavy, and

FIG. 8.—Abyssinian, Peruvian, and Smooth Guinea-pigs.

cannot be mistaken. Its head is crested with fur, which grows in clumps and makes it somewhat resemble a long-haired spaniel. Its face is plentifully whiskered, its nose broad and distinct, and the ears are more crinkled than those of the Smooth cavy.

The Peruvian is the most delicate and the rarest species. It has long, thick hair, which reaches below its feet in a heavy fringe, and bears a plentiful crest on its head. Care should be taken to keep the coat glossy and free from tangles and mats.

Occasional bathing with a damp sponge and gentle combings would reward the owner who wishes to exhibit his pets in the show pen.

It is a mistaken policy to have too many boars in a cage, for each has a masterful spirit which is apt to destroy the harmony of the home and lead to fierce civil warfare. Some hostile fathers have been known to destroy their young, perhaps with an eye to their future incursions. Concord is established when one boar shares his home with several sows. The latter are usually friendly, and often, when two of them litter at the same time, will share their duties in nourishing their young.

CHAPTER LXII

PIGEONS

PETS FOR A SUBURBAN GARDEN

ALTHOUGH scarcely coming under the denomination of pets, pigeons are exceedingly interesting birds to keep, and those who devote their attention to the matter find a pigeonry a most fascinating hobby. Each variety of bird has its own especial peculiarity, and in the selection of his pigeons the fancier will be able to suit his individual taste.

THE LOFT

There is no doubt that the best possible place in which to keep pigeons is an attic, which, on account of its size and finish, is likely to prove more healthy and damp-proof than an outdoor loft; but local restrictions and clauses in leases, however, frequently render this impossible. It will therefore be as well either to buy or make a proper house for your pets.

A good loft can be built in a back yard or garden, and may measure about 16 ft. by 10 ft., this giving accommodation for about one dozen pairs. A loft thus built can be divided into three, the centre compartment serving as a storehouse, whilst the two end divisions accommodate the birds. This loft should be built of 1-in. timber, and can be constructed according to instructions given in the Chapter on Carpentry, p. 26.

FIG. 1.—A Pigeon Loft.

The roof can be of corrugated iron or felt, and the sides may be similarly covered with advantage to the occupants. A cheaper loft is shown in Fig. 1. This being large enough to accommodate three or four pairs of birds will probably prove more suitable for the beginner.

The pole-locker, Fig. 2, is either square or hexagonal in shape, and is usually placed on a pole some 5 or 6 ft. high. Pole-lockers are constructed as simple boxes having doorways of sufficient size to allow the birds free access to the loft.   Some bright colour should be painted on the lofts, as this serves to attract pigeons and show them their homes.

The best perches are bracket-shaped, and must be purchased from an ironmonger.   A useful perch is the V-perch, which is made by nailing two short pieces of wood in the shape of an inverted V.

The floor of the loft must be covered with fine sand or sawdust, which should be renewed three or four times a week.   A grit box, filled with equal parts of crushed flint, oyster shell, red sand, old mortar, and salt, well mixed together, is essential, as grit serves to keep the birds in health.

FIG. 2.—A Pole Locker.

Nest-boxes measuring about 18 in. deep and 2 ft. 6 in. long, should be arranged on the sides of the loft in such a way that the birds can use them conveniently.   Portable nest-boxes made from soap-boxes are often used, and may be purchased for a few pence from any grocer.

VARIETIES OF PIGEONS

One of the most popular of pigeons is the TUMBLER, so named from its habit of turning somersaults in the air.   As seen in A, Fig. 3, the Tumbler is a short-legged bird, with a rounded head and squat appearance.   Tumblers are of various colours, blue, silver black, red, and white, being the most usual.   The reason for the bird's acrobatic feats in mid-air is unknown, but it may be assumed that these evolutions are performed from the mere joy of living. A certain amount of care and attention are necessary in training these birds when young.   They must not be left entirely free, as if this be done, they will acquire the habit of sitting on the

FIG. 3.—A, Tumbler ; B, Pouter.

roof instead of mounting into the sky.   They should be flown in the morning, and kept in confinement for the remainder of the day.

The POUTER, B, Fig. 3, is one of the most marked examples of what can be done by judicious breeding.   The enormous crop or pouch which distinguishes this bird is considered by most fanciers a point of elegance. Opinions, however, differ on this point, and many keepers of pigeons eschew a variety which appears to savour of an abortion. The Pouter is either blue, black, red, or white, and bears a large white crescent on its pouch.

The CARRIER is a large bird measuring some 17 or 18 in. in length, with the legs close into the body, the neck long and thin, and a large beak-wattle more than 4 in. in circumference, A, Fig. 4. The best Carriers are either black or blue, whilst the iris of the eye is of a fiery red.

The HOMER. — These are very favourite birds on account of the unerring instinct which induces them to return to their homes no matter at what distance therefrom they

FIG. 4.—A, Carrier Pigeon ; B, Homer.

may be liberated. There are cases where these birds have been known to fly over four hundred miles across country with which they were unacquainted, guided solely by this marvellous instinct. The Homer, B, Fig. 4, is generally blue or red-chequered in colour, and is somewhat larger than the Tumbler.

The RUNT is a huge common pigeon, individuals frequently weighing as much as $2\frac{1}{2}$ lbs. Black, red, and yellow Runts are common, but the birds are difficult to rear, and can scarcely be recommended to the amateur.

FIG. 5.—The Archangel.

The ARCHANGEL.—This bird, so named from the metallic lustre on its wings, has a copper-coloured body, with black wings, Fig. 5. The birds are hardy and breed prolifically, and for this reason are frequently kept by fanciers.

The JACOBIN.—This bird is so called from the ruff round its neck, which is supposed to resemble a monk's hood, A, Fig. 6. This ruff centres in a rose upon each side of the neck, and should come forward as far as the eyes. These birds are usually red, yellow, black, or white, and are occasionally splashed or mottled with lighter colours.

The FANTAIL.—This is probably the greatest favourite amongst pigeons. The feathers of the tail are, as the name implies, spread out like a fan, B, Fig. 6. The head should be thrown back until it rests

against the tail and is below the level of the chest. A good bird is unable to walk forward when its body and tail are thrown out, and is obliged to move backwards, Epimetheus fashion. The perfect tail should form at least three - quarters of a circle and be absolutely perpendicular, whilst the wings should lie

FIG. 6.—A, The Jacobin ; B, The Fantail.

close to the body. Fantails are usually of a pure white colour, and markings of any kind are considered to detract from its beauty.

SELECTING PIGEONS

In purchasing pigeons it is well to bear the following hints in mind, as it is not desirable to procure old birds when beginning. The eyes of younger pigeons are smaller, fainter, and not so prominent as are those of older birds. The neck of older pigeons are very strong and hard, whereas in the younger birds they are weak and soft, whilst the bill is sharp and not worn by picking up food. Again, the feet of old pigeons are much harder than those of younger birds, whose feet are soft and red.

Attention should be paid to the feathers in the tail and wings. Every wing should have three long feathers at the end called the flight feathers, after which are six feathers gradually diminishing in length, then eight smaller feathers. The tail should consist of twelve feathers in most birds, although fantails have thirty-six.

TREATMENT OF PIGEONS

Pigeons will eat any kind of grain food. They may also occasionally be allowed such green food as lettuce and cabbage. A special mixture for pigeons can be bought from any corn-dealer, but care should be taken to remove extra large seeds. Hemp seed, which tends to make the birds lazy, should be used very sparingly. A lump of common rock salt, which corrects acidity, should always be kept in the house ; whilst a supply of fresh water must be provided daily in fountain bottles.

BREEDING

Pigeons commence to breed at the age of nine months, and continue laying every month thereafter, so that with ordinary care a pair of birds could produce nine or ten pairs annually for at least three or four years. No pigeons lay more than two eggs at a time, and the cock and hen take turns in sitting on the eggs. After the young have been hatched about a fortnight, the cock will often begin to prepare another nest whilst the mother will be thinking about enlarging her family.

So soon as the breeding is finished for the year, the old nests should be burned, new ones substituted, and the houses well scraped—indeed, they may be washed at intervals of about three months throughout the year. It need scarcely be added that the utmost precaution must be taken to ensure the house being perfectly dry before the birds are put back.

MOULTING AND AILMENTS

If pigeons fail to moult at the proper period it is a certain sign that they are in bad health. In such cases the birds should be removed to a warm place, where a gentle hint may be administered by pulling out their tails. Hemp seed added to their food, and clary or saffron mixed with the water will prove very beneficial at this period. It is not an unusual thing for pigeons to be attacked with vermin. In such cases the most efficacious remedy is tobacco smoke, which should be puffed in large volumes over the bird. Tobacco dust sprinkled over the birds as well as into the nest is very effective when young pigeons are attacked by black or pigeon fleas.

Wet roup is a cough to which these birds are susceptible, and the best cure consists in placing three or four peppercorns in their nest once in three days. Dry roup is a husky cough, usually only apparent during moulting, and three or four cloves of garlic once a day will, as a rule, completely cure this ailment.

Pigeons suffer from vertigo, or the megrims, which causes the bird to flutter and finally fall to the ground. There is no cure for this, and it is better to kill the bird thus afflicted.

Pouter pigeons are very liable to become gorged when feeding the young ones, and for this reason it is better to obtain foster mothers to feed the pouter babies. When gorged, that is when the crop becomes loaded and hangs down, the pouter is liable to die from starvation. The old cure was effected by hanging the bird upside down until the food passed naturally into the stomach; but it is equally effective to place the bird in a long narrow box in such a way that the crop can rest upon a pad of straw. After a day or two of this confinement the ailment will be cured.

CHAPTER LXIII

POULTRY KEEPING AND REARING

FOR PLEASURE AND PROFIT

WITHOUT doubt, poultry-keeping can be followed by any intelligent boy, not only with immense pleasure but with some amount of monetary profit. There is a real delight in possessing a good collection of well-selected fowls—their handsome plumage, interesting habits, and the pretty ways of a young brood are continual sources of interest; while far more than the actual outlay is returned in eggs and poultry. Then there is the delightful feeling of kinship engendered between your birds and yourself—they seem to strike up a friendship with you as their provider and protector, crowding round you at feeding-time, when tit-bits are about, and showing unbounded delight at your presence among them.

HOUSING THE BIRDS

The first thing to think of before purchasing a single bird is the place in which you intend to keep your pets. It is a great mistake to imagine that any hole or corner will do for fowls. To enjoy your hobby and to obtain the best results from it you should have a proper "run," as it is called, where the birds can be comfortably housed, and where you can go at any time to admire them in proper surroundings and give them that attention which they deserve.

Of course, accommodation is bound to differ with circumstances. Boys living in towns cannot get the room which those in the country usually possess.

You should endeavour to secure as much space as possible. Chickens thrive best with plenty of exercise. To coup up a number of them in a confined corner is unwise in several respects.

Choose a south or south-west aspect for their home, if you can possibly do so ; avoid a spot where keen winds are liable to weaken the birds ; and provide as much shelter as you can from inclement weather or the hot sun. Should you have a nice plot of grass-land or a good field, the fowls will be all the healthier and better for having it placed at their disposal. To prevent them from roaming or to save them from vicious animals and other enemies, it is quite easy to procure a quantity of wire-netting with which to make an enclosure.

Keep a keen eye on the dangers which surround your pets. A friend of mine lost several valuable birds owing to their wandering across a railway line which ran close to his home ; while another fancier, greatly puzzled at repeatedly missing his chickens, set a watch, and discovered that a vicious dog belonging to a neighbour had developed the habit of lying in wait for the younger fowls, chasing them down, and then killing and carrying them off.

Provided you are at all skilful with a few tools, it is comparatively easy to build your own chicken-house. The materials required are few and inexpensive, and the mere making of it will afford a great deal of pleasure. Remember that fowls to be healthy must be kept in a structure free from draughts, rain, and damp.

Choose a blank wall for one side of the house, and erect the structure against it. First decide on the measurements of the

FIG. I.—A good Poultry Shed.

house. Convenient dimensions would be, height 6 feet, length 6 feet, and width 4 feet. The lean-to roof should be made to slope considerably, so as to carry off the rain and moisture. Any wood merchant will supply you with a sufficient quantity of match-boarding to answer your purpose.

The roof-boards must be nailed together, each one over-lapping and the last one projecting. The boards forming the front and sides must be nailed to stout wooden vertical supports inside. Almost in the centre make a ventilator; near the ground form a sliding door, and a little distance from it, at the end, another door, to open and shut, and fitted with a lock. Where the shed has a run, the sliding door should be in the position indicated by the dotted lines in Fig. I. Inside provide a nest-box, also a strong perch for the birds.

If the wood be rough, plane it smooth. When finished, give the house a good coat of dark-green paint to preserve it against the ravages of the weather.

Should there be no wall against which to build your poultry-house you will want a structure somewhat similar to that shown in Fig. 2, the roof of which should be double. The door will be placed at the centre of one end, and the sliding shutter be arranged near it.

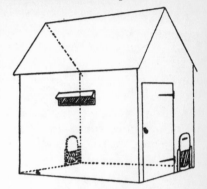

Should your fowls be hampered for room, you must make a "run" for them. This should be attached to the house, the sliding shutter giving access to it. Measure off the ground you can allot for the purpose, taking care that the earth is nice and firm—not boggy or sloppy. First give it a good flooring of cinder ashes or similar dry earth.

FIG. 2.—A Lean-to Shed.

Now procure some stout boarding to form a frame to extend the whole length of the run, and nail to it, both top and bottom, a length of wire-netting, Fig. 3. Make a door

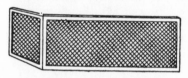

FIG 3.—A Wire Run.

at one end to open and shut, if you desire it, although this is not essential.

While engaged in making your poultry-house, it would be as well to fashion a chicken-coop. This is simply a box-like structure, made of match boarding big enough to accommodate a brooding hen. The front should be open, with four or five pieces of wood to form a partition, to enable the chicks to leave the mother and pick up their food outside, whilst the roof should lift up and slope a little, in order to carry off the rain. Fuller instructions with regard to detail work, particularly in the making of a lean-to shed, will be found in the chapter on Carpentry.

VARIETIES OF FOWLS

One of the charms of poultry-keeping as a hobby is the great variety of breeds from which selection may be made. Tastes differ, so that there will always be preferences for one or another kind of bird. Some people like large birds, others prefer small ones ; some are attracted by beautiful and brilliant plumage, while others favour subdued colours. Again, nothing appeals so much to some fanciers as strange and curious birds or rarities. No matter what your taste may be, it can be satisfied when making a selection.

Perhaps the most popular of all breeds is the DORKING—a fine fowl brought to England by the Romans. They are large, solidly-built birds, with full feathers and white legs. Professor James Long, an authority on the subject, considered them to be the best sitters and mothers. There are four varieties of Dorkings—the Silver-grey, Fig. 4,

FIG. 4.—Silver-grey Dorking.

Coloured or dark, Fig. 5, the Cuckoo, and the White. As a rule, the Coloured or dark Dorking is the largest of the group. In addition to these there are the Indian Game Dorking and the Dorking Brahma.

The Dorking, which is in great request for the table, lays well, the eggs being large and quite white. The birds need a grass run, and ought not to be kept in damp places or confined to close quarters. It is a striking fact that the chickens mature quicker than those of other breeds. In selecting these birds, all individuals possessing the malformation known as bumble foot—a peculiar enlargement of the feet and toes—should be carefully avoided, as this deformity is hereditary.

COCHIN-CHINA fowls, which are large birds and massively handsome, came originally from the Far East, and were extremely popular when first introduced, though they have since been found unserviceable for general use. A distinguishing feature of the Cochin is its much-feathered legs. As the introduction of the tulip into England caused a sort of mania for that flower, so the introduction of the Cochin caused a rage for poultry here some time ago.

Among the varieties of Cochin may be named the black Cochin, the white Cochin, the buff Cochin, and the

FIG. 5.—Coloured or Dark Dorking.

partridge Cochin. They are suitable for keeping in towns as, being very heavy birds, they remain well in bounds, and require a comparatively small run—even a 3-foot fence will prevent them from escaping. They are very tame and lay well, the eggs being brown in colour.

Many poultry fanciers consider HAMBURGHS to be the finest of all fowls, and those who prefer beauty to profit make a hobby of keeping this variety. There are many differences in colour among them—silver and golden pencilled, silver and golden spangled, and the Black variety, Fig. 6. Hamburghs are noted for the great number of eggs they lay ; but these are small, and the birds do not make good sitters. The Black variety lays the largest eggs, but, although hardy birds, they do not always prove a success when in confinement.

The BRAHMAS are said to have come from India, and they are fine birds, which look well on any run. There are two varieties—the light

FIG. 6.—Black Hamburghs.   FIG. 7.—Dark Brahmas.

and the dark, Fig. 7. In the light kind, the ideal colouring of the feathers is a fine white, without any yellow tinge. There should also be a proper amount of black markings in the hackle, *i.e.* the glossy feathers on the neck. Brahmas are healthy and lay throughout the winter, and whether the run be small or large they will soon adapt themselves to circumstances.

THE GAMECOCK

The ENGLISH GAMECOCK is a bird that few lads can look at without a feeling of admiration ; the carriage of the bird is so proud and confident, the colouring is so splendid, whilst his courage is proverbial. Like other pets, it has been the subject of many experiments, and now we have the old English gamecock and the modern gamecock. There are other classes to be met with at the principal shows, such as brown-red, black-red, pile, spangle, and duck-wing. At the present time many breeders are going back to the old English variety.

FIG. 8.—Anconas.

ANCONAS, Fig. 8, are pretty, active birds, that are winning the good opinion of many patrons of poultry-keeping.   They are light, smart fowls, with a character for wildness, though somewhat shy.   Anconas lay all the year round, but must be kept in houses with plenty of fresh air.   The eggs are small, but this is compensated for by the fact that the birds lay prolifically.   If you should select this bird as a pet, make sure your run is covered in with wire, for the Ancona can fly well, so that you are likely to suffer losses if this precaution be not taken. Anconas are pretty in appearance ; the plumage is black, each feather being tipped with white.

Experts agree that the first large Asiatic fowl brought to our country was the MALAY.   It is not a particularly attractive bird, as its

striking eyebrows, white or yellow eyes, long beak and head, and extended legs and neck give it a somewhat repellent aspect.   However, some fanciers like to possess pets out of the usual run of conventional beauty.   When fully matured, the Malay reaches a height of 2 feet 6 inches.   If you are anxious to procure eggs, you must not select this variety of bird, as the hens are not prolific.

FIG. 9.—Plymouth Rocks.

PLYMOUTH ROCKS, Fig. 9, as the name indicates, came from America. Although useful birds, it is doubtful whether they should be kept for breeding purposes.   Fanciers are of the opinion that this fowl was produced by the mating of the black Java, the Brahma, and the Dominique.   It should be noted that the Barred Rock variety has cuckoo-coloured plumage.   These birds are usually very good for-agers, and delight to spend their time hunting about for food wherever they find themselves.   They are both hardy and tame, and their eggs are fairly large and brown-coloured.   Besides the Barred Rocks there are the Buff and White Rocks.   When the chicks show black or red and white feathers, this is an indication of their Java ancestry.

ORPINGTONS

ORPINGTONS have lately established themselves in much favour. They are the result of experienced cross-breeding, the Lang Shan being the chief bird used to produce this variety.   Probably the first Orpingtons to be shown were of the black variety.   In tracing their history, it is interesting to note that black Minorca cocks were mated with black Plymouth Rocks. Afterwards the Lang Shan relations gave a distinctive mark to the black Orpington, which resembles the short-legged, neat Lang Shan.

Another variety is the Buff Orpington, Fig. 10, the origin of which is doubtful, some fanciers attributing it to the Buff Cochin, Hamburgh, and Dorking, while other experts contend for the Lincolnshire Buff. It is a good sitter, but in hot weather must not be allowed to indulge in this. Mention must also be made of other varieties of this popular fowl, such as the white, the black and buff, and the spangled. Jubilee Orpingtons are distinguished by their

FIG. 10.—Buff Orpingtons.

mahogany colour. Black touched with white indicates the spangled kind. These birds must not be overfed, or they will lay soft-shelled eggs.

SPANISH FOWLS

SPANISH FOWLS were at one time in very great request, and although their popularity has been eclipsed by some of the other breeds already mentioned, they are fine-looking birds. In-breeding is largely responsible for the decline in favour of Spanish fowls, for their white faces make them extremely delicate.

Allied to the Spanish are the MINORCAS. Should you be in any doubt as to which kind of fowl to patronise when starting, I would recommend this one. Minorcas can be easily kept in such small spaces as the majority of town-dwellers are forced to accept. At the same time, these fowls are quite at home on a big run. In their favour, it should be mentioned that they produce eggs abundantly, they are good in appearance and eat moderately; whilst, if the house be well sheltered, they will be found to lay during the winter. Such a favourite has this breed become that in some quarters it has quite eclipsed the Spanish.

WYANDOTTES

WYANDOTTES hail from America. They have become very popular in Great Britain as well as in Australia, one reason being that they present such variety in plumage that almost every fancy can be satisfied. The birds are handsome, hardy, and good egg-layers.

Some of the colours are white, Fig. 11, golden, buff, silver-pencilled, blue-laced, silver, and black.   Probably the silver and the golden are the greatest favourites.   At egg-laying competitions they are wonderfully successful, and their admirers declare them to be the hardiest of all poultry.

FIG. 11.—Wyandottes.

LEGHORNS are favourites with all who wish to make money.   Upwards of two hundred eggs a year are sometimes laid by a single fowl, and this through all the severities of rainy, hot, or frosty weather.   The white Leghorn, Fig. 12, makes a good second for productive power and hardihood ; but, unfortunately, Leghorns are not good sitters.

HOUDANS are a French variety, related to the Dorkings, as is evident from the five toes they possess. They are not bred for fancy's sake, but because they are useful. They are big birds, with strong bodies and short legs ; the plumage is mottled all over in black and white. The crest of the Houdan cock often becomes so large that it has to be cut in order to permit the bird to see properly.

The breed known as the LANG SHAN was introduced into this country from North China. Some fanciers declare it to be a variety of the Cochin-China, although in the principal shows it is allotted a distinct class. Black, blue, and white are the colours of the different kinds.

FIG. 12.—White Leghorns.

BANTAMS

There is a number of other breeds of poultry that are sought after by the enthusiastic fancier. From those varieties already described it will be easy to select one or more kinds to start with. But mention must be made of the BANTAMS—those miniature, smart little fowls that are so captivating to most people. Naturally, the Game Bantam is the most sought after. There are many different kinds from which to select, most of them diminutive editions of the principal breeds already mentioned. The Japanese variety, with an immense tail, to which the head is thrown back until it nearly touches, with short legs of a yellow colour, white or black speckled plumage, and a generally smart appearance, is very popular.

How to keep your Poultry

Having provided yourself with a house and made a selection of poultry, due attention must be paid to looking after the birds carefully. It need scarcely be said that you should take a real personal interest in your feathered friends. Look upon them as lovable pets, and treat them accordingly. Make their feeding, the condition of their quarters, and their general comfort and health your personal care, and only when compelled to do so delegate these pleasant duties to others.

Keep the house scrupulously clean inside and out; above all, never allow dampness to enter, and never let the run become unhealthily sloppy.

Allow the birds to have plenty of exercise; they should not be confined any longer than is absolutely necessary.

Feeding

Feeding is the chief thing to be considered in the well-being of poultry. Each morning they must have a good meal of grain, in the form of crushed oats or, as a change, of barley meal and sharps, *i.e.* those hard grains of wheat which require a second grinding. Let these be mixed with hot water until they are of a pasty consistency. Do not make the food so wet that it is sloppy, but, if you have added too much water, thicken the meal with some bran or pollard.

Fowls are early risers, and, as a rule, by midday need a second meal. But it must not be too abundant—a little should go a long way; and it ought to be scattered about, thus giving the birds plenty of exercise in searching for it. Should you be so fortunate as to have a field in which they can roam at large, this midday meal will be found unnecessary, as fowls are always in search of food for themselves. A good sprinkling of sound corn may be given just before they go to roost.

While it is foolish to expect fowls to find all, or nearly all, their own food, it is, on the other hand, unwise to overfeed them. If you are extravagant, dealing the corn out in such a way that much of it lies about neglected, the birds become lethargic for want of due exercise.

Remember, moreover, that your pets will not keep in good condition unless provided with a plentiful supply of coarse grit or well-crushed oyster shell. Not only does this aid digestion—it also serves to make them lay eggs with good strong shells.

Fowls need more food in winter than in hot weather. By increasing the quantity in the cold months of the year, they will be induced to continue laying longer than could otherwise be expected.

Breeding and Rearing Chickens

Early in December select the birds from which you wish to breed, and in January start them hatching. The number of eggs to be placed under a hen will vary according to her size—ten or a dozen being the usual number. The sooner a hen begins to be broody, she should be taken from the other fowls, and put, quite by herself, in a nest-box about fifteen inches square, her bed being made of fine straw or hay.

To accustom the hen to the nest, two eggs should be placed in the nest as an encouragement. In two or three days she will be fit to have the proper number of eggs placed under her, this being done at dusk. Attention must be paid to the hen while she is sitting. Every morning she should leave the nest to feed and exercise herself, and should she refuse to do this, she must be gently lifted off the eggs. It is well to provide a dust bath so that she can keep herself clean and healthy. Wheat maize, barley in plenty, and a copious supply of clean water will furnish an excellent diet during this period, which lasts for twenty-one days.

Chickens

The chicks require no food for the first twenty-four hours. The hen should be placed in the coup already mentioned with her chickens, and, should the weather be cold, the coup must be set under shelter ; if fine, let it face the warm south.

Opinions differ as to feeding the chickens. Some give bread and milk with hard-boiled eggs chopped fine at various times during the day. Water is not necessary when their food is soft and moist. A little coarse oatmeal mixed with stale bread crumbs likewise forms an excellent diet. In a day or two millet, canary seed, and crushed wheat form a proper diet, whilst boiled rice rolled in oatmeal can be strongly recommended.

Lettuce leaves, grass, chopped-up cabbage leaves, and garden produce are all suitable food-stuffs. Be sure to feed the young ones regularly—the first thing in the morning, at mid-day, and before they go to roost.

Well-kept poultry in clean coups with a healthy run will be practically immune from disease, and will yield enough pleasure and profit to repay amply whatever time and trouble their owner cares to devote to their welfare

CHAPTER LXIv

RABBITS

POPULAR OUTDOOR PETS

Few outdoor pets have attained more popularity than rabbits. The expression "outdoor" is used advisedly, since, no matter how scrupulously clean the hutches be kept, the presence of these pets in the house can never be other than objectionable.

It must not be imagined, however, that any vacant spot in the garden or yard will be a suitable site for the hutches. If it be remembered how snugly rabbits dwell in their burrows, usually made in a warm, sandy soil, it will be clear that their hutches should be similarly placed in some sheltered position, hidden from the cold winds, and, what is even more important, protected from the damp. The captive rabbit has no worse enemy than the damp.

A good position having been secured, the hutches may be ranged in tiers against the walls, the lowest tier being about one foot from the ground. Where different-sized hutches are used, the smaller ones should naturally be placed at the top.

As a general rule, it may be taken that hutches should measure 20 in. in height, 24 in. in depth, and be about 4 ft. 6 in. long. The floor must be constructed with a slant, making the back about 2 in. lower than the front. As this sloping floor serves to drain the hutch, a zinc gutter about $\frac{1}{2}$ in. wide must be placed along the back to carry off whatever may drain down to it.

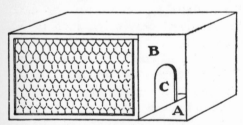

FIG. 1.—Hutch and Sleeping Compartment.

The larger rabbits will require a sleeping compartment in their hutches, as shown in Fig. 1. The space A, measuring about 18 in., must be shut off with a sliding partition B, in which is an arched entrance C, the edges of which have been very carefully rounded and smoothed, in order to avoid injuring the coats of the inhabitants.

The cleanliness so essential to the welfare of rabbits can be ensured by fitting the hutches with false bottoms made of interlaced laths, beneath which zinc-lined drawers are placed so arranged that they can be pulled out and cleaned daily. The position of this drawer can be clearly seen in the stack of hutches depicted in Fig. 2.

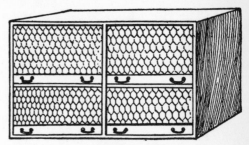

FIG. 2.—Hutches in Tiers.

The interior of the hutches can be kept clean and fresh with whitewash, which must be allowed to dry very thoroughly before the inmates are permitted to return to their homes. Before the approach of winter the hutches should be thoroughly overhauled and repaired wherever necessary.

Provided that it be dry, there is no especial rule to be observed regarding the bedding. Dried grass, hay, bracken, and similar litter are excellent for the purpose, and, being easily obtainable, can be renewed frequently.

Considerable care must be exercised to maintain an even temperature in those sheds where fancy breeds of rabbits are kept. The thermometer should never be allowed to fall below 60°, and may be kept well above that figure. Whatever the heat may be, it must be constant, as sudden variations in climate are very likely to prove fatal to foreign rabbits.

FANCY BREEDS

Fancy breeds thrive excellently with regular feeding and a steady temperature. Before selecting the inmates for the hutches, however, it will be as well to consider the points of beauty by which rabbits are judged.

The value of some breeds depends upon the dew-lap, or pouch beneath the throat. This should be full and well shaped. The length, shape, and position of the ears are important points in all varieties, whilst the texture of the fur and general build of the animal are matters of much consideration with fanciers.

FIG. 3.—The Full Lop.

Amongst the fancy breeds of English rabbits may be mentioned :—

(1) The Full Lop, shown in Fig. 3, whose ears should measure not less than twenty inches from tip to tip.

(2) The Oar Lop, thus named because the ears stand out like a pair of oars.

(3) The Horn Lop, whose slanting ears appear curiously contorted like a pair of horns.

(4) The Flat Lop, with ears touching the ground.

FOREIGN BREEDS

In addition to these there are various breeds of foreign rabbits, many of which are extremely popular and pretty pets.

ANGORAS.—The long coats of these rabbits, shown at A, Fig. 4, require careful attention, and should be thoroughly combed, especially

FIG. 4.—Angora and Belgian Hare.

at the time when they are changing their fur. The most valuable Angoras are pure white, and have an exceedingly soft coat, whilst their ears are short.

BELGIAN HARES.—Like English hares, these rabbits are of a sandy colour; and have erect ears about five inches in length, B, Fig. 4. The underneath is more or less white, but there should not be a single white hair on the back or sides.

CHINESE OR HIMALAYANS.—The coat of this variety is white, the ears are tipped with black and are upright. The eyes have a strange pink light shining in them; but none of these characteristics are developed until the rabbit is six or seven months old.

The DUTCH is the smallest breed of rabbit, specimens being sometimes found weighing less than 2 lbs. A white band encircles the neck, a white line runs down the face, and the feet are white, Fig. 5.

FLEMISH GIANT.—As the name implies, this breed is the largest of the rabbit family, the average weight of individuals being from 12 lbs. to 14 lbs. The coat is grey, and the ears, which are erect, should measure about six inches.

FIG. 5.—The Dutch Rabbit.

PATAGONIANS. — These rabbits have a deep grey fur, with white or sandy bellies. The head is large, and the ears measure about seven inches, but are not so erect as the ears of the Belgian breed, having a tendency to hang over at the tips.

POLISH RABBITS.—It is rather difficult for the amateur to distinguish between this breed and the ordinary type of rabbit. The Poles, however, are smaller and more delicately formed. The colour is white, and the ears short and upright.

SILVER-BROWNS.—The coat of this breed is brown with a beautiful silver tinge. The ears are short, and the tail appears of a dark silver blue colour.

FIG. 6.—The Silver-Grey.

SILVER-CREAMS.—The fur is of a faint yellow colour, often tending to red, and flecked with light fawn hairs, whilst the forefeet are delicately silvered. The ears measure about four inches. There is a dark red tint in the eyes.

SILVER-GREYS.—This rabbit, shown in Fig. 6, should be of a silvery grey colour from head to tail, the underneath being a light steel blue. When young, however, the fur is black. The ears of the Silver-Greys are short and erect.

BREEDING

Good, healthy parents are necessary for breeding purposes, the buck being about a year old and the doe a couple of months younger. Although wild rabbits have four litters a year, it is advisable to allow fancy rabbits no more than three, and then the doe must only be allowed to suckle four little ones at a time.

The utmost care must be taken to prevent the doe being disturbed for some time after she has had her family, as, if frightened, she will mutilate her offspring or abandon them altogether.

A plentiful supply of milk and water should be at hand for the doe when the time comes for her to litter, and she must be fed up for the seven weeks she is nursing the young.

The little ones should be weaned one at a time, and kept apart from the bucks, who are frequently very cruel to the babies. At the age of six months the sexes must be entirely separated.

FEEDING

Apples, peas, swedes, carrots, oats, turnips, boiled potatoes, meal, oil cake, &c., are all suitable for a rabbit's diet. Green stuff such as lettuce, cabbage leaves, and clover will supply the necessary moist food.

Once a week the rabbits should be given two tablespoonfuls of water to drink.

A warm mash of potatoes, peas, and meal can be given in cold weather, but care must be taken to see that the mixture is only warm —not hot.

Two meals a day are quite sufficient as a rule, and only enough for each meal should be put in the hutches.

DISEASES

At the first sign of any ailment a sick rabbit must be taken from the others and put in a separate hutch. Many diseases are catching, and unless this precaution be taken dire results will follow.

Diarrhœa.—This is caused by too much green food. An acorn should be crushed into a mixture of arrowroot and bread crumbs and administered to the sick rabbit. Green stuff must not be given again until some time after the patient's recovery.

Canker of the Ear.—This complaint shows itself by a thick yellow discharge, and is accompanied by loss of appetite. The sore ear must be thoroughly washed with warm water and anointed with olive oil.

Red Water.—This is a kidney disease which may prove fatal. The invalid must be transferred to a warm hutch and dieted with milk food, whilst a few drops of sweet spirit of nitre should be administered as medicine.

Snuffles.—A damp hutch is usually the cause of this throat affection. The patient must be fed with warm mashes of barley meal and milk, into which doses of three grains of sulphate of copper should be mixed.

Parasites.—This trouble is usually caused by damp and dirty hutches, and frequently affects the roots of the ears. The hair must be cut short, and the place sprinkled with Keating's powder or sulphur.

With ordinary care none of these ailments ought to appear in the hutches, and if cleanliness and good feeding are thoroughly attended to, there is no reason why rabbits should not be happy and healthy and the source of very great pleasure to their owner.

CHAPTER LXV

SILKWORMS

A HOBBY ENTAILING NEITHER TROUBLE NOR EXPENSE

IT is difficult to realise that the rich silken fabrics of which robes are made for kings and queens, are the simple products of humble caterpillars. The empress in all her grandeur owes the magnificence of her stately costume to the instinctive labours of an insignificant insect.

No hobby can give less trouble than the keeping of silkworms, and the expense entailed is practically *nil*. The worms can be purchased from seedsmen or fanciers at a cost of 4d. a dozen, and the price of the mulberry leaves on which they feed is only about 5d. per quarter-pound.

It is usual, however, to start the hobby by obtaining a quantity of eggs, which may be purchased for a very few pence. These should be placed in paper trays or boxes—collar-boxes will prove admirable for the purpose—and kept in a fairly cool place, where they are perfectly dry and can hatch in quiet.

Meanwhile, a store of fresh mulberry leaves must be obtained so that the worms may begin feeding as soon as they emerge from the egg. Some fanciers give them lettuce leaves, but these cannot be advised, for silkworms are apt to gorge themselves with this succulent food, and frequently die from the effects of their surfeit.

Like all their tribe, silkworms moult, or slough their skins several times before attaining maturity. At first the worms are of a dark colour, but with each successive change they become lighter until finally they are almost white in hue.

The main business of a caterpillar is to eat, and in consequence a fresh supply of mulberry leaves must always be at hand. These leaves should be carefully dried, and no remains from one meal allowed to stand over until the next, as it is most important that the diet should be perfectly fresh.

It is characteristic of silkworms that they never attempt to stray away. Placed in a paper tray or collar-box, they can be kept in a drawer or even out in the room without any fear of their wandering. Being perfectly clean, the most fastidious of parents can raise no objection to their presence in the bedroom or study.

MOULTING

A week after hatching, silkworms undergo their first moult, and prepare for this by a day's fasting. The old skin is sloughed in the same fashion as that of a snake, every portion, down to the very jaws, being cast aside. The new skin being soft, they grow rapidly, until, at the end of another week, the second moult takes place. It is not until these changes have occurred four times that the silkworms attain their full size. At each change of skin they grow considerably, until at maturity they measure about three inches in length, and appear as illustrated in Fig. 1.

FIG. 1.—The Silkworm in maturity.

Ten days or so after its final moult, the silkworm will begin to grow uneasy, and will wander about the tray or box seeking to find some spot in the corner in which to spin the cocoon. It is always possible to tell when this stage has been reached, from the transparent appearance the worm presents, this being caused by the silky substance or fluid collected in its body. On exposure to the air this fluid hardens into tiny threads as the caterpillar emits them from its mouth.

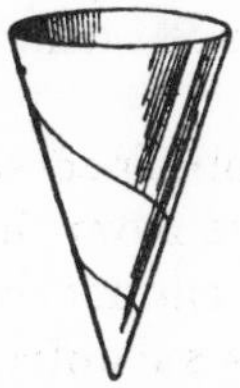

It will now be time to move the silkworms from the tray in which their existence has up to the present been passed, and place them in the small conical paper bags shown in Fig. 2, which are very similar to those used in sweetshops or by grocers.

FIG. 2.—Cocoon Bag.

At this point it may be remarked that it is always advisable to avoid moving the worms with the finger. When small they can be picked up with a fine camel's-hair brush, and when large, they should be coaxed on to a piece of paper upon which they can be moved.

SPINNING

When once the worms have been placed, each in a little paper cone, they set to work spinning their silken cocoons, and after ten days the silk will be quite ready for unwinding. Before unfastening the cone, however, it should be shaken ; if the caterpillar, which has now become a chrysalis, is heard to rattle within, it may be taken as a sign that the cone can be undone.

The cocoon, when extracted from the paper cone, is about the size of a pigeon's egg, and appears as in Fig. 3. This ball is composed

of one continuous thread of silk, often 1100 ft. in length, which is wound round and round with indescribable skill.

FIG. 3.—The Cocoon.

The cocoon must be placed in a hot oven or in boiling water, in order to kill the chrysalis inside, since if this were left alive, it would eat its way up through the silk and entirely spoil it. The hot water also serves to soften the gummy outer covering and loosen the strands of silk within. Several cocoons should be done at the same time, so that when the ends of the strands have been found they may be placed together, and wound on a reel.

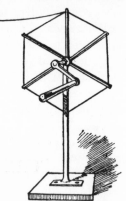

Wooden winders, similar to that shown in Fig. 4, can be purchased for a few pence, and will serve to wind the silk as it is unwrapped from the cocoon. Of course, the silk is raw, and must undergo several processes before it can be woven or adapted to any use, but the beautiful glossy threads, pressed between the leaves of a book, will last for years.

FIG. 4.—A Silk-winder.

It is often interesting to preserve some of the cocoons and allow the course of nature to take its way. These cocoons should be placed on a cloth in a dark room of which the temperature must never vary much from 72°. In a week

or two the moths, Fig. 5, will appear, and they should be immediately placed in a paper-lined box, as they will set to work laying eggs almost at once. It is one of the peculiarities of the silkworm tribe that they never attempt to escape, and the moths will quite contentedly fulfil their avocation

FIG. 5.—The Moth.

in the confinement of the box, without evincing any inclination to explore the outer world.

And so with their four stages of egg, caterpillar, chrysalis and moth, these little workers pass their existence, giving employment to thousands, and, unwittingly, helping to adorn the wealthiest and greatest of mankind, or rather womankind.

PART VI

THE PLEASURES OF RADIO

THE PLEASURES OF RADIO

HOW TO BUILD A CRYSTAL RECEIVER THAT WILL RECEIVE TELEPHONY AND MORSE SIGNALS

BY ELLISON HAWKS,
AUTHOR OF "THE ROMANCE AND REALITY OF RADIO," ETC.

ONE of the most interesting of all indoor hobbies is Wireless, or "Radio," as it is now called. Since broadcasting stations have been established in this country many types of receiving sets have been introduced, and these are sold at prices ranging from 10s. 6d. to £100, or even more. Those who are fortunate may be able to buy one or other of these sets, but those who prefer to make their own may do so at a reduced cost. With a receiving set, music and speech and telegraphic signals in the Morse Code may be received distinctly at distances that vary according to the type of receiving set used. Naturally, the more expensive sets will receive from greater distances than low-priced sets.

To enable us to better understand exactly how to derive the greatest amount of pleasure from Radio, we must first learn something about its theory, and how it is made to "work" a receiver.

WONDERFUL ELECTRIC-WAVES

Radio is made possible by the transmission of electric-waves through a mysterious medium, called the ether. This permeates everywhere. The stones, bricks, and timbers that form our houses, the atmosphere, and even space itself is filled with ether—which, by the way, must not be confused with the ether of the chemist. It is by causing electric-waves in the ether that the transmission of radio signals is made possible.

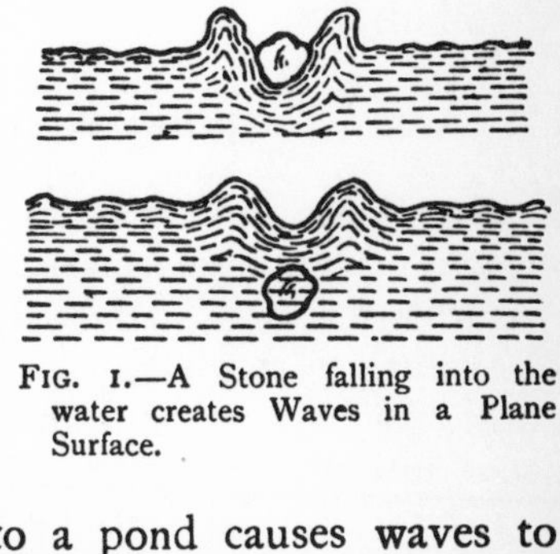

FIG. 1.—A Stone falling into the water creates Waves in a Plane Surface.

Ether is not the only medium in existence, for both water and air are also conducting media. A stone thrown into a pond causes waves to spread outwards from the point at which the stone entered the water (Fig. 1). Here the water is the medium through which the waves pass. Another illustration, in which air is the medium, is furnished by the manner in which the human voice causes sound-waves in the air. Sounds are caused by disturbances in the air, giving rise to waves that spread upwards in ever-widening spheres (Fig. 2).

There is one great difference between waves in a pond and sound-waves, however, and this is that the waves in the pond travel along the surface of the water, but sound-waves travel in all directions. They resemble, indeed, a vast number of soap-bubbles placed one within the other, and constantly expanding. Waves in a pond

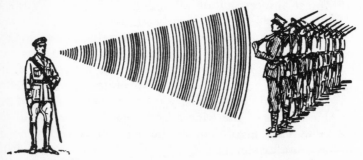

FIG. 2.—Sound Waves are a succession of spheres of compression and relaxation.

are known as waves on a plane surface, but waves in the air are known as spherical vibrations.

When an officer shouts to his men his vocal cords vibrate, and cause sound-waves to leave his mouth. Travelling through the air in the form of expanding spheres of compression, these waves fall upon the listeners' ears and cause their drums to vibrate. By means of nerves and brain, the vibrations are converted into the sensation of sound.

How Messages are sent by Radio

In Radio, transmission and reception depend on very similar principles, for signals are sent and received by means of electrical disturbances in the ether, which spread outwards or radiate from the transmitting station. Instead of the vocal cords, a transmitting apparatus is used, and this changes the sound-waves of speech or music into electric-waves, which are then sent out by a suspended wire, called the "aerial," at the transmitting station. These waves travel through the ether in the form of expanding spheres of compression, and fall upon the aerial at the receiving station (Fig. 3). By means of suitable apparatus the electric-waves are converted into sound-waves, that may be either the "dot-and-dash" signals of the Morse Code, or music and speech, according to what is being transmitted.

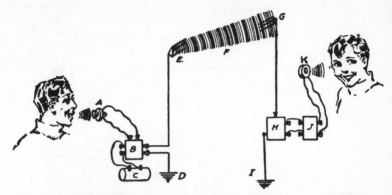

FIG. 3.—A radio-telephone is exactly similar in principle to an ordinary line-telephone. A, Transmitter; B, Modulator; C, Oscillation generator; D, Earth; E, Aerial; F, Radio waves; G, Aerial of receiving station; H, Tuning apparatus; I, Earth; J, Detector; K, Telephone receiver.

Radio-telephony is based on a modification of the principles of radio-telegraphy, and it is carried out in a similar manner to line-telephony. In the ordinary line-telephone we speak into a transmitter, and our voice strikes a diaphragm. This consists of a metal plate behind which carbon granules are packed (Fig. 4). Carbon possesses the useful properties of passing very little current when it is loosely packed, and when subjected to pressure allowing a comparatively large amount of current to flow. In the telephone transmitter variations in the resistance of the carbon are caused by sound-waves impinging on the diaphragm. As the carbon is connected in the telephone circuit, it is clear that these sound-waves will in turn cause variations of current in the circuit, and a corresponding variation in the receiver. Here, by means of another diaphragm, the original sound-waves are exactly reproduced, and so the listener is able to hear what is being said by the speaker (Fig. 5).

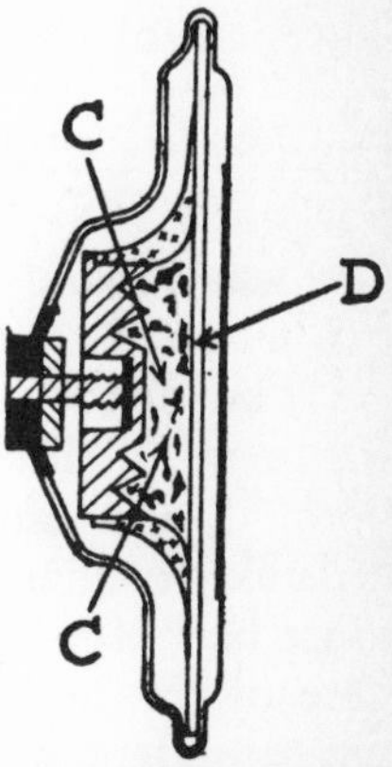

FIG. 4.—Telephone Microphone. C, Carbon granules; D, Diaphragm.

The variations in current used in line-telephony are not suitable for use in radio-telephony. Instead, a "carrier wave" is employed. This consists of a very large number of steady, continuous waves that are all of uniform amplitude.   These are sent out by the transmitter, and the " carrier wave " is modulated, or altered in a certain manner, by the action of the voice upon a diaphragm included in the trans-

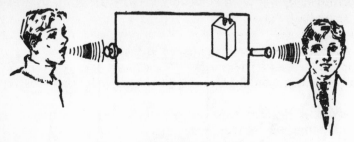

FIG. 5.—A simple Telephone Circuit.

mitting circuit.   At the receiving station these variations are received in exactly the same form as that in which they left the transmitting station, and here they are converted into sound-waves in the ear-piece of the listener-in.

AN ACCIDENTAL DISCOVERY

The existence of the electric-waves that have made Radio possible was predicted in 1863 by a famous mathematician, Professor J. Clerk Maxwell, of Cambridge.   The waves were not discovered until some years later, when Professor D. E. Hughes accidentally discovered them.   He did not announce his discovery, however, and it was not until 1888 that Professor Hertz demonstrated the existence of the waves, and thus established the truth of Maxwell's brilliant prediction.

The disturbances caused in the ether at a transmitting station travel in all directions.   Wherever an aerial is erected they impinge upon it, and cause in it minute currents of electricity.   Before it is possible to change these currents back again into sound-waves they must be " rectified," or passed through what is known as a " detector." One of the best known of rectifiers is the crystal detector.   Let us try to understand the principle on which a detector is based.

THE PURPOSE OF A RECTIFIER

The minute currents induced in the aerial are of that type of current known as alternating—that is to say, the current changes its direction at a very rapid rate, flowing first in one direction and then in an opposite direction, alternating many thousands of times in a second. The usual method for converting electric-waves into sound-waves is to employ a telephone ear-piece. In this case, however, the currents received in the aerial are of too great a frequency to be of service, for in this condition they act on a telephone ear-piece as though they were giving it a very rapid succession of "pushes and pulls" alternately. As a matter of fact the diaphragm of the telephone receiver is subjected to many hundreds of thousands of these pushes and pulls each second. If the currents were not rectified, nothing would be heard, for each push would negative each pull.

In effect a rectifier cuts out all the pushes but leaves in all the pulls, with the result that every time a current is induced in the aerial there is one strong pull given to the telephone ear-piece, made up of a large number of small pulls, the pushes being eliminated by the rectifier (Figs. 6 and 6 a).

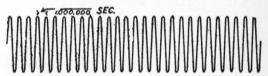

FIG. 6.—Rectified High-frequency Currents of a Continuous Wave. (Compare Fig. 6a.)

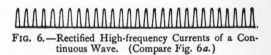

FIG. 6a.—Continuous Wave. In this example the interval between each successive oscillation is one-millionth of a second.

Sounds are made up of a number of vibrations, and when these vibrations are very numerous, the effect is that of a note with a high pitch. Low-pitched notes are made up of sounds with few vibrations per second, and between the lowest and the highest audible notes there is a very wide range. It is not difficult to understand, therefore, that if the number of pulls to which the telephone ear-piece is subjected be varied, the sounds in the ear-piece will also change. As the electric-waves generated at the transmitting station are controlled by the human voice, when speech is being transmitted, it follows that the vibrations received in the ear-piece at the receiving station will correspond to the vibrations of the voice that speaks into the transmitter. Thus we are able to hear speech and music exactly as it occurs at the transmitting station.

An Opportunity for Inventors

There is one drawback in radio-telephony, and that is that "duplex working," or speaking and hearing at the same time, is not yet practicable. In the line-telephone we can both listen and speak simultaneously, but in Radio it is necessary to speak and then to listen for the reply. This is accomplished by throwing over a switch that cuts out the transmitter, and switches in the receiving part of the apparatus.

Radio has another disadvantage in that it is not possible to call up a station by ringing a bell, as in the case of the line-telephone. Therefore, stations must communicate one with another at predetermined times. Because of this it is necessary on board ship that an operator should always be listening for his call signal, and it is a rule that a continuous " watch " shall be kept by the wireless operators, turn and turn about. These two difficulties will, no doubt, be overcome in time, and they present a splendid opportunity for any inventor. A solution of the problems would not only result in pecuniary gain, but would be of great service to mankind, and this, after all, is the greatest consideration.

*   *   *   *   *   *

Having seen something of the theoretical aspect of Radio, let us now turn to its practical side and learn how easily messages may be received, and how delightful it is to possess a receiving set with which to entertain our friends.

A few years ago the owner of a receiving set could hear only Morse signals from ships at sea and various stations throughout Europe and farther afield. Nowadays, however, there is a great deal more to be heard, and consequently, interest in the subject has largely increased. Ships at sea may still be heard, but what is more interesting is the music and concerts sent out broadcast at prearranged times from several stations in this country.

Broadcasting was first commenced in America in November 1920, and two years later it was introduced in London by the British Broadcasting Company, formed by the leading Radio manufacturers. Broadcasting stations have been established at London, Birmingham, Manchester, Newcastle, Cardiff, Glasgow, Bournemouth, and Aberdeen. From these stations musical numbers, orchestral items, lectures, news reports, and weather forecasts are sent out every evening from 6 to 10.30 p.m., and also at special times during the day. Full particulars are usually to be found in the daily papers.

How to Obtain a Licence

Before installing a receiving set it is necessary to obtain a licence from the Postmaster-General. At present there are two types of licence, either of which costs 10s. The first type, the broadcasting licence, may be obtained immediately on application at any Post Office. The second type, known as the experimenter's licence, is granted only to those who are qualified to experiment in wireless telegraphy or telephony. For an experimenter's licence application must be made for a form to the Secretary, General Post Office, London. There is generally a delay of some weeks before an experimenter's licence is granted, assuming the applicant's qualifications be approved. Neither type of licence is issued to any one under 21 years of age, but if you are under age this difficulty may easily be overcome by persuading your father or elder brother to take out a licence for you. To instal a transmitting set a transmitting licence is necessary, and these are granted only to applicants with special qualifications. Application in this instance also must be made to the General Post Office, London.

A broadcasting licence permits only of the use of receiving apparatus that bears the stamp "B.B.C.," signifying that the particular type of apparatus has been approved for use by the Postmaster-General. The types of B.B.C. apparatus cover a very wide range, however, and the requirements of most listeners-in will be met by one or other of these instruments. Those who wish to make their own receiving sets cannot do so unless they possess an experimenter's licence. At the time this article is being written, a special Parliamentary Committee is sitting to investigate the whole broadcasting position, and it is expected that a third form of receiving licence will later be issued, under which the listener-in may construct his own set without having to obtain a special experimental licence to enable him to do so.

Erecting the Aerial

In order to receive messages and signals it is necessary to have (1) an aerial, (2) a detector, (3) a device for tuning the aerial, and (4) a telephone headphone.

Aerials differ considerably in design, and the type used depends largely upon your situation and local conveniences for its erection. The main thing

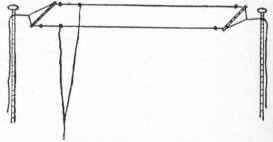

Fig. 7.—Inverted L-aerial.

to bear in mind is to have the aerial as high up and as long as possible.

Two types of aerials are usually employed by amateurs. One is known as the inverted "L" type, because of its resemblance to the letter "L" (Fig. 7), and the other is known as the "T" type, because of its resemblance to the letter " T " (Fig. 8). Either of these types may be slung from poles that are attached to the house chimneys (Fig. 9) ; or one end of

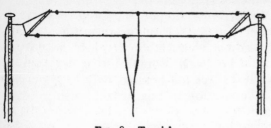

FIG. 8.—T-aerial.

the aerial may be attached to a pole fixed to the chimney, whilst the other end is taken to a tall pole in the garden, or even to the branches of a high tree.

If the receiver is situated up to, say, ten miles from a broadcasting station, good results may be obtained by attaching one end of the aerial to the frame of an upper window,

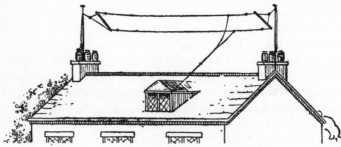

FIG. 9.—Inverted L-aerial on House-top.

and the other end to the garden fence, or to a clothes-post at the bottom of the garden. Remember always to obtain as high a posi-

FIG. 10.—Single-wire Aerial between Houses.

tion as possible, and bear in mind that an aerial stretched between two upper windows (Fig. 10) will be much more efficient than an aerial that is taken from a window to a garden fence. Obviously an aerial 40 ft. in length at a height of 40 ft. will give better results than an aerial 50 ft. in length that is 20 ft. in height at one end, and 6 ft. in height at the other.

The main wire of the aerial, called the antenna, may be composed of two or even three wires, or may be a single wire only. If more than one wire is used, the wires may be separated by a spreader, consisting of a piece of light wood or bamboo. Bare copper wire, 16 gauge, is satisfactory for the antenna, but stranded copper wire, 7/22's, is even better.

Soldered or clipped to the antenna is another wire descending into the room in which the receiver is located. This is the lead-in wire, which must be very carefully insulated at the point where it enters the house. It should not be allowed to touch or approach too near the wall, and may be passed through a porcelain or fibre tube inserted in a hole in the woodwork of the window frame.

Whatever type of aerial is used, it is of great importance that the antennæ should be perfectly insulated from the supporting poles or buildings. They must not come into contact with any "earth," or the Radio waves will not reach the receiver. Insulation is obtained by means of porcelain insulators placed between the antenna and the supporting ropes, and two or more insulators at the end of each wire are recommended. It is advisable to occasionally lower the antenna and clean the insulators. Especially is this true if situated near a large manufacturing town, where the soot or dirt in the atmosphere collects on the insulators and forms a conducting surface, resulting in the escape of energy, and causing results that are not so good as would be possible with a perfectly insulated aerial.

The combined height and length of the aerial permitted by the Postmaster-General is 100 ft. This includes the length of the span, plus the height of the lead-in wire, measured vertically from the leading-in point. Any number of wires may be included in the span or in the lead-in. If the distance between the two points of suspension exceeds, say, 80 ft. (thus leaving 20 ft. for the lead-in wire), the distance may be bridged by stringing the insulators with rope at either end.

Although these many details may sound complicated, and although some of them may present difficulties, the ingenious amateur will not be prevented from receiving signals because of any difficulty in contriving or erecting an aerial.

Connecting to "Earth"

In addition to the aerial, the receiving set will require to be connected to "earth" by means of a copper wire. It is very important to have a good earth connection, and a long lead to earth should be avoided if possible.

A very satisfactory earth connection may often be obtained by soldering, or clipping, the earth-wire to a water pipe. Care should be taken to use the cold-water pipe, for the hot-water pipe may lead only to the cistern. It is necessary that the pipe should be scraped clean from dirt and paint before the contact is made. The wire may then be wrapped around the pipe, and bound to it very tightly with wire, or fixed with a clip. A Meccano strip, bolted around the pipe, will give a firm and permanent connection.

Earth connections should not be made to gas pipes, as very often the conductivity of the gas pipe is interrupted by the red-lead used in the joints.

Every precaution should be taken to obtain the fullest benefits, for a good aerial and a good earth will enable signals to be well received that, with only an indifferent aerial or earth, cannot be heard. Wherever possible connections should be made by soldering, or by means of clips. Loose joints are similar to draughty windows or doors, for whilst they may not entirely prohibit the passage of the Radio waves, they admit of leakage, and leakage means loss of power that can be ill afforded.

The Receiving Apparatus

Assuming a satisfactory aerial to have been erected, the next consideration is the receiving apparatus. In this article we have not space to deal with the various types of receivers, and we must confine our remarks to the most simple form of receiving set, that known as the Crystal Receiver.* This consists, in the first place, of a device that will tune the aerial to respond to the vibrations sent out by the aerial of the transmitting station. Perhaps several stations are sending at the same time, and to pick up all the messages simultaneously would result in a confused jumble. It is therefore necessary to select those particular messages we wish to receive, and this is done by the tuning apparatus.

* Full particulars of valve-receiving sets, and further information on the subject generally, will be found in *The Romance and Reality of Radio*, by Ellison Hawks (T. C. and E. C. Jack, Ltd., 3s. 6d. net).

The simplest form of tuner for the reception of broadcast is an inductance coil, composed of about 40 yards of enamel-covered copper wire, gauge 22 (cost about 6d.), wound around a cardboard tube, of about 4 in. in diameter, for a distance of about 5 in.

Mounted on a rod alongside the tube is a metal pointer, called the "slider," which may be moved along a straight line to any part of the length of the wire-covered tube. At the point where the slider touches the wire, the enamel on the latter is scraped away, thus exposing the bare wire, and enabling the slider to make electrical contact. By moving the slider along the coil, more or less wire is brought into the circuit, according to the direction of the movement.

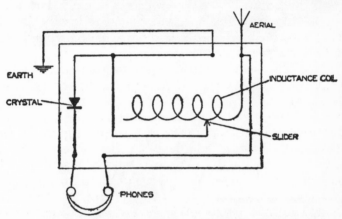

FIG. 11.—Simple Circuit for Crystal Receiver.

Thus the inductance of the aerial is increased at will, for the wire is connected directly to the aerial, and the circuit is completed through the slider, as will be seen from the wiring diagram, Fig. 11.

The detector is a piece of lead sulphide, galena, or one of the many specially selected crystals, such as Hertzite or Radiocite (cost from 6d. to 2s.). The set is completed by a single telephone earpiece, costing 7s. 6d., or if a double head-phone is used the cost will be increased to 15s. or £1. Fig. 12 shows a simple crystal receiver of the type described, and Fig. 11 is a wiring diagram of same.

BUILDING A CRYSTAL RECEIVER WITH MECCANO PARTS

Meccano boys will be able to make a complete and very efficient Crystal Receiving Set from Meccano parts, if they carry out the following instructions.

The parts necessary to construct this set are on the market complete, or those who already possess some of the necessary

FIG. 12.—A Simple Crystal Receiver.

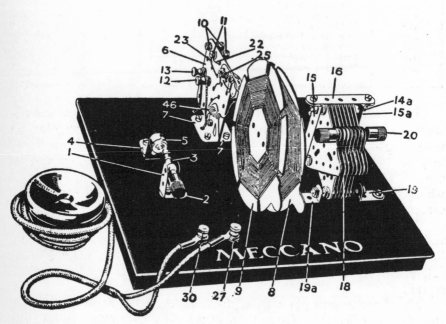

FIG. 13.—A Crystal Receiver made from Meccano Parts.

parts may complete their set by purchasing the other parts separately.

Meccano Part No.	Description	Quantity
5	Perforated strips 2½″	1
10	Flat brackets	1
12a	Angle brackets 1″ × 1″	1
12b	,, ,, 1″ × ½″	2
37a	Nuts	53
37b	Bolts $\frac{5}{16}$″	7
38	Washers	87
60	Double angle strips 2½″ × ½″	2
76	Triangular plates	15
81	Screwed rods 2″	4
102	Single bent strips	1
111	Bolts ¾″	4
111a	,, ½″	16
126	Trunnions	2
306	Terminals	8
F72	Fibre plates 2½″ × 2½″	1
403	Insulating triangular plates 2½″	14
404	Insulating handles	2
405	Brass washers $\frac{3}{32}$″	15
406	Insulated bell wire	3 feet
407	Inductance discs (hinged)	1 pair
409	Detector arm, complete	1
410	Crystal (in cup)	1
412	Mounting board	1

This receiver consists of three sections : (1) detector, (2) inductances, and (3) tuning condenser, and is suitable for the reception on wave-lengths of from approximately 300 to 500 metres. These limits may be increased if desired, however, by adding more inductance discs. These discs take the place of the tuning coil described above, whilst the condenser is an additional means of tuning by varying the capacity of the circuit.

The detector is made by securing a single bent strip (1, Fig. 13) and a flat bracket (2) to the mounting board ; this forms the bearing for the detector arm (3). To the upper end of a 1-in. angle bracket (4), bolted to the board shown, is bolted the cup (5) holding the crystal.

The detector-arm (3) is then placed between the faces of the bent strip (1), with which it forms a universal joint, thus allowing the arm to be moved, until the best position is found on the crystal for the fine contact wire, called the "cat-whisker."

To one corner of a 2½ in. by 2½ in. special fibre plate (6) are attached two trunnions (7), one on each side of the plate, as shown. At the upper corresponding corner of the same plate are attached the inductance discs (8 and 9) by hinges, so arranged that the discs may be brought together as closely as possible.   Two terminals (10 and 11) are connected in the two top holes of the outer corner of the plate (6), and a second pair of terminals (12 and 13) are connected lower down.

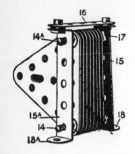

FIG. 14.—Fixed portion of Meccano Condenser.

The condenser includes the fixed and the movable portion.   First assemble the fixed portion (Fig. 14), by connecting eight $2\frac{1}{2}$-in. triangular plates together, at the lower end, by a 2-in. threaded rod (14).   These plates are spaced by inserting two nickel washers between each plate, and clamped at each end by a washer and a nut.   At the upper end a 2-in. threaded rod (14 a) is used.

Before threading the rod through the plates, two triangular fibre plates are placed between each pair.   They are spaced apart by a nickel and brass washer, so that the upper spacing is uniform with the lower, and clamped together in the same manner as the lower end.   It will be noticed that in these triangular fibre plates one of the corner holes is cut out to enable them to clear the washers on the rod (14), in order to make a better electrical contact.

The triangular plates may now be fastened in position between two $2\frac{1}{2}$ in. by $1\frac{1}{2}$ in. angle strips (15 and 15 a). A $2\frac{1}{2}$-in. strip (17) is bolted at the top, with a spacing-washer at each end, and extra nuts to centralize the plates.   The strips (15 and 15 a) are then secured to the board at 18 and 18 a by two No. 6 B.A. bolts, with an insulating fibre bush between each angle strip and the board.

FIG. 15.—Movable portion of Meccano Condenser.

The movable portion (Fig. 15) is composed of seven triangular plates threaded in a similar manner to those of the fixed portion.   They have two nickel spacing-washers at the top and bottom, but no triangular fibre plates are used.   This movable portion is then fitted into the apertures between the plates of the fixed portion, connected to the 1 in. by $\frac{1}{2}$ in. brackets (19 and 19a, Fig. 13), and lock-nutted on the outside of the same brackets.

The insulating handles (20) may now be screwed on ; these allow of the position of the movable portion being varied without causing the contact of the operator's fingers to interfere with signals received.

OPERATING THE RECEIVER

The wiring will be made clear by reference to Figs. 16 and 17.

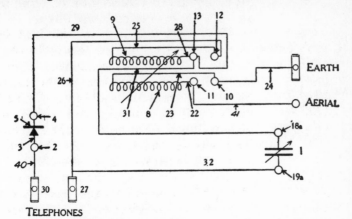

FIG. 16.—Wiring Diagram for Crystal Receiver made from Meccano.

2, Detector-arm terminal; 3, Detector arm; 4, Detector terminal; 10 and 11, Terminals for inductance disc 8 and connections; 12 and 13, Terminals for inductance disc 9 and connections; 8 and 9, Inductance discs; 18a and 19a, Condenser terminals; 22 and 23, Winding of inductance disc 8 connected to terminals 10 and 11; 24, Wire connecting terminal 10 to earth terminal; 26, Wire connecting terminal 12 to telephone terminal 27; 27 and 30, Telephone terminals; 28 and 25, Winding of inductance disc 9 connected to terminals 12 and 13; 29, Wire connecting terminal 13 to dector terminal 4; 31, Wire connecting condenser and inductance discs.

From the aerial terminal the wire 41 carries the oscillations to the terminal 11, and from here through one end (22) of the winding of the disc 8, through the winding to terminal 10, by the other end 23, and thence by the wire 24 to the earth terminal.

The impulses are induced from the disc 8 in the winding of the second disc 9, and carried through one end (25) of the wiring to terminal 12, and the wire 26 to the telephone terminal 27. The other end (28) of the disc 9 is connected to terminal 13, and wire 29 connects to the detector terminal 4, thence

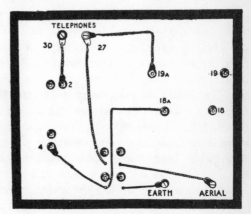

FIG. 17.—Underneath view of Mounting Board of Meccano Crystal Receiver.

through the detector-arm 3 and terminal 2 to the telephone terminal 30. Another wire (31) from terminal 13 also carries the impulses to the condenser, where it makes contact at 18 *a*, thence through the condenser to 19 *a*, and by wire 32 to the telephone terminal 27.

Having assembled the receiver and connected it to aerial and earth wires, the movable portion of the condenser should be placed in about the centre of its arc of movement, and the inductance discs brought close together. At the same time the detector-arm should be gently moved so that the " cat-whisker," or copper wire contact, selects the most sensitive point on the face of the crystal.

The " cat-whisker " should press only lightly on the crystal, the pressure being varied by the insulated handle of the detector-arm, which allows a very fine adjustment to be made. When the most sensitive point is reached, the discs or the condenser (or both) should be moved until the signals or telephony are heard at maximum strength.

Crystal sets are suitable for reception of telephony at distances up to about 15 to 20 miles. They will receive Morse signals up to and exceeding 100 miles. Sometimes these distances are exceeded, however, according to the conditions in which the receiver is situated. I know of one instance where a crystal receiver is receiving broadcast regularly at a distance of 33 miles from the Manchester Broadcasting Station. Even this distance has been exceeded ; and recently I heard of a case in which broadcast was received from the Cardiff Station at Dorchester, 60 miles distant. The same receiver receives time signals in Morse Code from Nauen (Germany) and Karlsborg (Sweden).

What You May Hear

Having erected your aerial, and connected the lead-in wire to the receiver, you are ready to listen-in. There is a wonderful experience in store for you, and you will spend many delightful hours listening to Morse and to telephony. If you live near the coast you will be certain to hear ships at sea communicating with land stations, and these latter replying. Most passenger ships are equipped with apparatus capable of transmitting up to 400 miles, whilst warships and large liners have more powerful installations, with transmitting ranges of 1,000 miles or over.

A knowledge of the Morse Code will enable you to intercept interesting messages and news items from ship to shore, and vice versa. You may, for instance, learn that some large liner is entering or leaving port, as the case may be, and you will be able to follow her progress from the successive messages she sends out. The course of the P. and O. boats and other ships may be similarly traced in the

English Channel by those who live in the south. A list of call signs, and a copy of Lloyd's Weekly Shipping List, will provide a vast amount of interesting information.

Often, too, you will be able to intercept telegrams sent by passengers on board ship to the shore. These messages cover all manner of things—from a request from some liner to a leading London hotel to reserve accommodation for American visitors on board, to insistent inquiries after baby's health from an anxious parent on a holiday voyage around the coast on a tramp steamer! Listening to Morse provides an endless interest, especially if you possess a long-range set, for then you will be able to hear French, Italian, Dutch, German, and Scandinavian land-stations chattering round our islands to their sea-going brothers.

As to the telephony that you will receive, little need be said. There are now continuous programmes from the broadcasting stations (enumerated on page 536) in this country, and in addition, there are stations on the Continent that are all within the range of more powerful apparatus than crystal sets. There are, in addition, amateurs in nearly all large towns who constantly send out good musical programmes and also speech tests, the reception of which is of great interest.

As an indoor hobby, Radio offers a vast amount of interest, and is of great educational value to those who make it their business to study the subject.

INDEX

THE END